Tulalip, From My Heart

TULALIP

From My Heart

AN AUTOBIOGRAPHICAL ACCOUNT
OF A RESERVATION COMMUNITY

Harriette Shelton Dover

Edited and Introduced by
Darleen Fitzpatrick

Foreword by
Wayne Williams

UNIVERSITY OF WASHINGTON PRESS
Seattle and London

Tulalip, From My Heart is published with the assistance of a grant from the NAOMI B. PASCAL EDITOR'S ENDOWMENT, supported through the generosity of Janet and John Creighton, Patti Knowles, Mary McLellan Williams, and other donors.

© 2013 by the University of Washington Press
First paperback edition 2015
Printed in the United States of America
Design by Thomas Eykemans
Composed in Minion, typeface designed by Robert Slimbach
19 18 17 16 15   5 4 3 2 1

UNIVERSITY OF WASHINGTON PRESS
www.washington.edu/uwpress

Unless otherwise noted, the illustrations in the book are from Harriette Dover's personal collection.

LIBRARY OF CONGRESS CATALOGING-IN-PUBLICATION DATA
Dover, Harriette Shelton, 1904–1991.
Tulalip, from my heart : an autobiographical account of a reservation community / Harriette Shelton Dover ; edited and introduced by Darleen Fitzpatrick ; with a foreword by Wayne Williams.
    pages cm.
Includes bibliographical references and index.
ISBN 978-0-295-99541-0 (pbk : alk. paper)
1. Dover, Harriette Shelton, 1904–1991. 2. Tulalip Indians—Kings and rulers—Biography. 3. Indian women—Washington (State)—Tulalip Indian Reservation—Biography. 4. Tulalip Indian School (Wash.)—History. 5. Tulalip Tribes of the Tulalip Reservation, Washington—History. 6. Tulalip Indian Reservation (Wash.)—History. 7. Tulalip Indian Reservation (Wash.) Social life and customs. I. Title.
E99.T87D68 2014   979.7'7100497940092—dc23   [B]   2013004569

To My Ancestors

They always spoke about the long, long time ago—a time so far, so far gone that we are looking at it through a mist or a fog. It is our time when we were on this earth. We have been here for a long, long time. We have always been here.

Contents

Foreword

Wayne Williams

GRANNY, my mother Harriette Dover, was fiercely proud of being Indian. She spoke of things driving her life. She always wanted to write a book about Tulalip but she was a procrastinator. Some years ago she met and became friends with Carol Harkins, who is a local social activist. One day my mother made the comment that she had always wanted to go to college and that her parents had encouraged her to do so. While attending Everett High School, after finishing Tulalip Indian Boarding School, she took all the required courses to qualify for college entrance. Carol responded, "You can go now!" My mother said she was too old (she was seventy-two years old). Carol said, "Oh no, there are older people now going to college." Next my mother objected that she couldn't afford to pay the costs and had no way of getting to Everett, where the local community college is located. Again Carol had the solution. She would seek funding from the tribe—which has a scholarship program for its members—and she would drive my mother to school every day. Finally, unable to find a valid excuse and after thinking about it, my mother said yes. Carol applied to the tribe for funding and in 1976 helped my mother enroll at Everett Community College.

My mother enjoyed her classes very much, especially anthropology taught by Darleen Fitzpatrick. The class dealing with the Northwest Coast Indians was most enjoyable, as it allowed my mother to offer comments about the class material, such as agreeing or disagreeing or talking about local customs, and so on. Rather than be annoyed by one of her students offering such comments, Darleen was pleased, as it added to the class.

As time went by, Darleen began to think about trying to save the information that my mother was offering. After pondering the matter, Darleen discussed it with my mother and they began a relationship that endured until my mother's death in 1991. In a sense it is still continuing today. After discussing the book with the University of Washington Press in Seattle, Darleen submitted the manuscript for review. After much disappointment, happiness, delay, and hard work, the material was revised and resubmitted and, lo and behold, the manuscript was accepted.

I cannot say enough about the tremendous amount of work that Darleen has expended in this effort. I and the readers will be eternally grateful for her unstinting courage and determination to see the project through to its conclusion. Thank you, Darleen.

Introduction

Darleen Fitzpatrick

FRIDAY afternoon. Driving west on Marine Drive N.E., the Washington highway that intersects the Tulalip Indian reservation, I remember Harriette Shelton Dover's comment, "Isn't that a classy address?" Soon after passing the turn to Totem Beach, where the tribal offices and the community house are, I turn right, away from a descending sun, at the unpaved driveway to the little blue house. Mrs. Dover is hard of hearing, but she eventually hears me knocking and opens the back door to let me in. Sometimes she says, "Oh, is it Friday already?" Or she says, teasingly, that she has not thought much about what to say next. Then she sits down on the couch in her living room, facing the highway beyond, and gives another brilliant narrative.

Once a week, from 1981 to 1983, we tape-recorded her narratives about her life as a Snohomish Indian and what she knew about Tulalip Reservation history. Our relationship was unusual since it was not the classic anthropologist-Native collaboration. I did not interview her. I was not doing a study of her or of Tulalip. She had a lifelong ambition to write a history of the Tulalip Indian Reservation, with her own life as a base, and I offered to help her.

Harriette Shelton Dover was a Snohomish elder from an eminent family. She was born on the Tulalip Reservation at Mission Beach, Tulalip Bay, on November 19, 1904. The Tulalip Reservation is near Marysville, Washington. It was named for a distinctive bay located in the midst of Snohomish tribal territory. Tulalip Tribes are organized as a political confederation that includes Snohomish, Skykomish, Snoqualmie, and other tribes who are successors to the tribes that signed the Treaty of Point Elliott in 1855 on the beach at Mukilteo near Everett. The other tribes include Sauk-Suiattle, Kikiallus, Skagit, Duwamish, Puyallup, and Stillaguamish—peoples who moved there as a result of marriage or because Tulalip was initially set aside as a reservation for all of the signatory tribes of the Treaty of Point Elliott. As a result, Mrs. Dover's autobiographical account and history of the Tulalip Reservation includes Snohomish tribal history and culture, since those traditions and beliefs are confounded with the Tulalip Tribes' history.

Her parents, William and Ruth Shelton, were descendants of important leaders.[1] They were from different tribes, but each was considered knowledgeable about the Snohomish and Tulalip (Shelton 1914, 1923; Maryott and Shelton 1938; Hilbert 1995). William Steshail, her father's uncle, was a signer of the treaty. Wheakadim, her paternal grandfather, was present at the signing as a teenager. Their eyewitness accounts, and those of other relatives and friends, were discussed during family dinners and gatherings through the years as both family and tribal history. Unfortunately, the accounts of Native people who witnessed the signing of the Treaty of Point Elliott have not been the subject of scholarly history.

Throughout her life, Mrs. Dover talked with elders from other reservations about their life experiences after the treaties were signed. Over the years, in what amounted to a lifelong research project, she collected documents and photographs pertinent to Tulalip history and did archival research. As she points out in her Prologue, her life spanned a long and important period in the history of the Tulalip Tribes and her own people regard her as an expert.

William Shelton, Harriette Dover's father, and Robert, her brother, were leaders who made a difference on the Tulalip Reservation. After their deaths, Mrs. Dover took their places in dealing with civic, political, and educational issues within the Tribes and with the public. She was elected to the Tulalip Tribes Board of Directors, their governing body, and served from 1938 to 1942, 1944 to 1946, and 1950 to 1951. She was the chair for one year in 1945 and was the first Indian woman in the state of Washington to be elected to that position. She served as a tribal judge in 1951 and followed her father in serving as a tribal broker between the Tulalip Tribes and the local non-Indian community. She served on the Marysville School Board, was a teacher's aide and a lecturer on American Indian cultures, and in her home hosted members of civic and church groups who met with her to discuss tribal issues.

---

1   Sehome, her mother's father, was a Klallam leader who signed both the Klallam and the Point Elliott treaties.

She was a member of the Seattle Historical Society, and she provided elder testimony for *United States v. Washington, Phase One* (1973), a salmon fishing rights case. Until 1980 she served as Democratic precinct chair in the Mission Beach area. She was well known in Democratic circles in Washington State, as well as by the public in the Marysville and Everett areas.

Mrs. Dover believed her life was typical of other tribal members and a measure of Tulalip Reservation history. Because they embody tribal or ethnic history, American Indian autobiographies have contributed to our national history for many years.[2] Mrs. Dover's story contributes to our knowledge of Northwest history because it recounts the social, political, and religious matters the tribes faced after they signed the treaties and were dispersed from their villages and confined to reservations. She pulls no punches. We have an opportunity to understand Indian people better when we know more about what happened to them from their point of view.[3]

In the Prologue, Mrs. Dover establishes an important link among legends, prophecy, and history, which is mentioned by other writers on American Indian cultures but which needs to be emphasized.[4] She cites a legend about the adventures of a culture hero, Letskaydim, in Tulalip Bay that establishes how long the Snohomish have lived in the area, provides a sense of time that is immemorial, and demonstrates that the Snohomish have an enduring loyalty to and first possession of places that others now also occupy. Value of the homeland and its various domains is often emphasized in American Indian historical narratives (e.g., Momaday 1969; Ortiz 1977; J. Martin 2000). We learn here what it means to have a sense of place.

The Prologue also sets the tone for the role that Snohomish, her native language, played in her life, her identity, and her cultural milieu. She learned to deal with her world through her language and culture. Here, and throughout the early chapters of her narrative, she uses Snohomish linguistic terms and concepts to explain and illustrate, to make a special point, or to teach us

---

2   See, for example, Winnemucca 1883; Krupat 1985, 1989, 1994; Krupat and Swann 1987, 2000; Brumble 1988; Ruoff 1990, 1994; Bataille and Sands 1994; Brumble and Krupat 1994; Miller 1990; Youst and Seaburg 2002; Schorcht 2003.

3   Mrs. Dover told me that she preferred to use the terms Indian or American Indian for the Native or indigenous people in the text.

4   See Tweddell 1953; Jacobs 1960; Spicer 1960; Stands In Timber and Liberty 1967; Momaday 1970; Hymes 1990; DeMailie 1993; and Wiget 1994.

about Native culture, since the entire area is "one great kin group" (Elmendorf 1960:49). She referred to her native language as "Snohomish" instead of using the term "Lushootseed" that is in use today; her mother, however, did refer to the Snohomish language as Lushootseed, or dxʷləšucid (Hilbert 1995). Snohomish is a dialect of the Lushootseed language that is spoken by tribes in the Puget Sound area, from the Nooksak River to the Nisqually River (Bates et al. 1994).

The first several chapters of her narrative cover the 1855 signing of the Treaty of Point Elliott by tribal leaders and government officials, the settlement upon the reservation after the treaty was ratified in 1859, efforts of tribal members to find work, some of the members' first experiences with white people, and childhood remembrances, especially of the grandmothers.

In her presentation of the treaty signing, Mrs. Dover tells us about the meetings the Snohomish held in their villages to discuss the signing, and about the speakers who supported the signing and others who opposed it. She describes the order in which the tribes sat on the beach at Mukilteo as they listened to the reading of the clauses of the treaty. Then, unlike Gibbs's account (1877), she explains that John Taylor, a Snohomish tribal member and a signer, translated the treaty from Chinook Jargon into his native language. Three other chiefs assisted him in translating the treaty for the people in their own languages (Duwamish et al. 1927; Snyder 1964; Hilbert 1995).

We learn what it was like for Snohomish and other tribal members to leave their villages on the mainland and on Hat, Camano, and Whidbey islands and settle around Tulalip Bay. Mrs. Dover develops a variety of themes pertinent to the physical and socioeconomic conditions they faced. There was not enough fresh water for such a large population to live around the bay. The wild foods available from fishing, hunting, and collecting in the smaller territory were not enough to sustain them. Their economy began to change. As a result of federal policy, they were not allowed to build the large cedar-plank dwellings that once served as their winter residences. They were not allowed to build large community or potlatch houses. As time went on, they could not practice their native religions or ceremonies because the federal government forbade them. They were expected to make a living as farmers.

Their first memories of white people provide insights into the feelings and impressions that were generated during the early days of contact and demonstrate just how vivid family stories can be. Grandfather Wheakadim, who witnessed the treaty signing as an eighteen year old, worked in Nisqually for the Hudson's Bay Company. He made a memorable trip to San Francisco to help deliver a herd of sheep. Mrs. Dover also tells us about her first impressions of white people, especially about their light-colored eyes. She wondered if they could see with them.

Mrs. Dover was an educated woman. The story of the dual educational institutions that were the heritage of Mrs. Dover's generation is fascinating material. She tells of grandmothers, parents, the Catholic fathers, and the government boarding school employees, and what it was like for a child to learn three religions and two languages. She spent ten months of each year and ten years of her life boarding at the Tulalip Indian School.

The Tulalip Indian School, as Mrs. Dover knew it, is the subject of her longest chapter (chapter 6). She mentions the school elsewhere in the text, too, because her experiences there had such a profound impact upon her. On a typical day, her discourse was laced with statements of regret and enmity about those years of her life. A scholarly literature on the federal boarding schools is developing.[5]

Her high school years occurred during the "flapper era" in America and during World War I. She wanted short hair. She wanted a silk dress and high heels. What did her parents, brother, and grandmothers want for her? She was sent to Everett High School, where she majored in science, instead of to Marysville, where her brother Robert had graduated. He wanted her to avoid the racial prejudices that he had experienced in Marysville. Today, Tulalip young people can choose to attend reservation elementary schools, such as Quilceda or Heritage, or the schools in Marysville, and there are meaningful youth groups, such as the Canoe Family and the Boys and Girls Club, that they can participate in.

Robert Shelton was an important influence in her life. He was for a time her eighth-grade teacher in the boarding school. She tells how he taught the students to be more aware of the world beyond the reservation and of what he and other Tulalip young men experienced when they were drafted into World War I (before federal legislation was passed in 1924 to allow American Indians to be citizens of the United States).

Robert and their father, William Shelton, founded the Tulalip Improvement Club in order to petition the federal government for rights they believed were granted in the treaty. At that time, according to Bureau of Indian Affairs

---

5   See, for example, Coleman 1964; Berkhofer 1965; Thompson 1979; McBeth 1982; Pratt 1992; Dietz 1993; Lomawaima 1994; Adams 1995; Childs 1997; Dinwoodie 2002; King 2008.

regulations, Indian people were not supposed to meet for political purposes. Certainly, a meeting to discuss treaty rights would not be regarded by the BIA as a commendable or even a legitimate undertaking. Mrs. Dover said her brother remarked, "How can they quarrel with us if we say we are meeting to improve ourselves?" They met. They discussed their gardens and orchards, their lost lands, unemployment, and health conditions. They expressed concern about the changes that were occurring in the traditional culture and in their relations with one another. Later, out of their efforts came an organization known as the Northwest Federation of Indians and the landmark (but unsuccessful) federal court case known as *Duwamish et al. v. United States of America* (1927), which sought the return of land and the implementation of fishing rights that the tribes believed were accorded them in the treaty.

Mrs. Dover tells us about the socioeconomic conditions that were her people's legacy as she and her contemporaries sought work. She does not say they sought jobs. Over the years, the socioeconomic conditions on the Tulalip Reservation have been desperate. They are better today because of improved services and sources of employment that the Tribes can now offer their members as a result of their own tribal health, bingo, casino, Quilceda Business Park, and other business operations. During the 1980s and 1990s, unemployment was at 43 percent and in 2010 it was in the teens, though it is still higher than non-Indian unemployment in the state of Washington, however.

As the narration takes us deeper into her life, Mrs. Dover reveals how her political consciousness and keen sense of injustice developed as she listened to the elders discuss the signing of the Treaty of Point Elliott. Then, during World War I, her point of view widened due to her brother's influence. Beginning early in the narrative, we are witness to a stunning presentation of race relations—from treaty times to the present—featuring the political, social, and spiritual legacies involved in finding work, fighting in the nation's wars, fishing rights, freedom of religion, building a tribal community house, the revival of the salmon ceremony, and other spiritual issues. For example, she reveals a fact unknown in the anthropological literature: that the Coast Salish—as the tribes in Puget Sound are known to linguists and anthropologists—believe in a deity. Their traditional religions are not based solely on the guardian or spirit-power complex. Spirituality is one legacy of the Tulalip Tribes. Mrs. Dover approaches these topics through the lens of how her grandparents, parents, and she herself saw their world. As a result, the cultural milieu in which she lived comes through clearly. It was through her native language and culture that she first learned to deal with her world. As an adult, she functioned very well in non-Indian settings. She had many lifelong friends who were white—especially from her high school years—but I think they remained partly alien to her. She had a special way of referring to "the white people" in a scolding tone of voice that could have been a bit unnerving to anyone who was not aware of the historical and social contexts of her remark. She clearly realized that the keys to dealing with white people were to dress as they did and be educated in their schools, but her ethnic identity was Snohomish Indian.

As we learn about Mrs. Dover's life, the personal dimension is pervasive. As a child she learned her tribe's language and culture at home, but learned another language and two additional religions in the traumatic setting of the boarding school. Her first marriage was a disappointment. Her second marriage was controversial. She raised two sons who were a generation apart. The deaths of her sister (from tuberculosis) as a teenager, her brother as a young man, her father, who was her best friend, and her mother as an elderly woman, all had a profound impact upon her. She took on political and civic responsibilities and fought the ever-present battle of race relations. We learn that she was an outspoken person who could be vituperative at times. Even though her narrative is tinged with wit and humor, it is occasionally ironic and bitter. She was warm, generous, and intelligent and as proud and firm as an executive who thrived on politics. She cared very much about young people and liked to be in their presence.

Editing the Dover Narrative

In the world of Harriette Shelton Dover, I was her former instructor, project assistant, and then editor. Somewhere in that mix we became friends. We began work on her manuscript on April 6, 1981, and taped her narratives until the spring of 1983. Then, before us were the review and editorial processes.

On the first day, I looked over what she had written thus far on her own, and we discussed a title and what she wanted the manuscript to include. We also discussed who her audience would be. She was aware that her audience was diverse; it included her own family, tribal members, the Indian and non-Indian public, and scholars. She felt that her background and experiences provided people in these groups with a unique opportunity, which they otherwise would not have, to learn about Tulalip history and Snohomish culture. Lastly, I assembled a table of contents with topical chapter headings that we aspired to use as an outline as she narrated the text. Her proposed title for the book was "Marching on to Victory." [6]

We decided she would narrate into a tape recorder because her health was poor at the time and because she had already successfully taped a life history narrative for Lawrence Ryggs's 1977 master's thesis. She was clearly comfortable working within a narrative medium. As we proceeded, she expressed at least three organizational principles: that the role of her native language was important in thought and expression, that the text should be organized by whatever topic was being discussed not by a chronological sequence of events, and that it was natural for her to speak in long, discursive sentences. As a result, we learn that the Snohomish oratorical style is to begin speaking about a topic, develop that topic wherever it carries us, and then return to the topic.

When we finished taping her material to her satisfaction, we worked on the photographs she had collected over the years. They were lying unsorted on a card table. I ran the tape recorder as we discussed them, and she added information, such as her grandmother's Indian name. She then selected the photographs she wanted to use in the text.

My initial role was as a facilitator—someone to run the tape recorder and help to organize the material. I should mention that I was familiar with the Tulalip Reservation; my study of the Indian Shaker religion began there. Martha Lamont, the Indian Shaker minister at the time, whom I interviewed extensively, as well as other elders, taught me that an interview should be a cordial, respectful visit. She said to me at the outset that if an interview was worth doing—that is, if my asking her questions about her religion was important—then I could remember what she said to me. She meant that there would be no note-taking. It turned out she was right. I could remember, eventually, as much as three hours of discussion. At the same time, I still hurried home to type it up.

As I listened to Mrs. Dover discuss Tulalip life stories, the annual rounds to collect the foods that sustained the people, and other areas of daily life on the reservation, the context she provided was helpful to me later when I did research and gave testimony for Tulalip Fisheries for *United States v. Washington, Phase Two*. In addition, over the years many students from

---

6   Mrs. Dover saw her life as a march toward victory, but because no one except she, Wayne, and I understood or liked the title, including tribal members, I took the present title from the first sentence of her Prologue.

Tulalip have taken my Everett Community College course on Northwest Coast Native cultures.

My role as editor developed gradually, after the narratives were typed up as transcripts and Mrs. Dover was not well enough to work on them. She did, however, work on the first one and made a few changes in her own handwriting. She said that we had done the narratives just in time. Her health was failing. She had fallen in the kitchen and broken her hip. When the manuscript was assembled in 1984, I read it back to her in a nursing home in Marysville, where she had become a resident, before I submitted it for review and publication.

When we received the text back from the review process, I was asked to make several changes. Paramount among the suggestions was to make the narrative chronological. I had feared this would happen. Editors of American Indian autobiographical texts have almost always been asked to remove repetition and to order the material chronologically; the only Native author who was not required to do so was the novelist N. Scott Momaday (Brumble 1988:11).

The structure that Mrs. Dover and I had agreed upon for the text was chronological in its overall sense, since she started with a Snohomish legend about prehistory then moved into treaty time, and so on, but the basic organization was not chronological; it was topical. For example, in chapter 2, she discusses how their way of life changed when they moved to Tulalip Bay to live and work, from 1859 to the early 1980s. Then, in chapter 3, she discusses the arrival of the Catholic fathers in the Northwest in about 1838.

Sarris, who published a biography about Mabel McKay, a Pomo basket weaver, points out that Native people view history topically, not chronologically (1993a:99). It is necessary for them to reach back in time as they proceed from topic to topic. They use the past to comment on present events and they use repetition to help their audience remember what they are saying. In other words, a chronological order happens within each topic of the narrative but it is not an organizing scheme for the entire work. The organizing principle is of interest in covering the details in each of the topics as they are discussed. As Mrs. Dover spoke about a particular topic, it seemed necessary on occasion to refer back to a previous time period in order to make a special point. The past is a touchstone, a point of reference, or a place of embarkation. Time forms a spiral as the narrator refers to the past and proceeds on, again refers to the past and proceeds on, as the topics under discussion are developed or elaborated upon.

After Mrs. Dover, her son Wayne Williams, and I discussed the reviewers' reports, she directed me to arrange her material chronologically because non-Indian readers would be better able to follow it. It did no significant harm to the text. However, chapters 7, 8, and 11 do not follow an explicitly chronological sequence, since doing so would disrupt the parallel layers of those chapters. These chapters cover Harriette Dover's last years in the boarding school, her high school years, and her brother's World War I experiences. In chapter 11, the last chapter, she narrates a vision/dream she experienced in her twenties, in which she received a song from a deceased paternal Skykomish great-grandmother that dovetails structurally with the legend she tells in the Prologue. Thus, chapter 11 retains the authentic order in which it was narrated.

Time is important in this text. The past, after all, speaks to who you are. Mrs. Dover refers to the legends about ancient times, and she tells us about the prophecy that warned the tribes that they would be invaded and changed by newcomers to the area. She wants us to know her people's history as they lived it, since events of the past participate in the lives of modern-day Tulalip peoples. Grandmothers are mentioned frequently because they are important sources of loving kindness and they are the perpetuators of tradition. When your life is guided by tradition, it is the elders' voices that tell you your history.

Mrs. Dover spoke much of the time in long, discursive sentences, in keeping with the oral tradition of her tribal background. When an oral text is in written form, as in a transcript, the first task is to divide the stream of speech into sentences. Decisions have to be made about where to place periods and other punctuation marks. I experimented with her to see if she liked long or short sentences and found, not surprisingly, that she greatly disliked short sentences. I imagine that the longer sentences are, again, an oratorical style and sound explanatory and gracious, whereas shorter sentences are blunt or abrupt and might sound demanding. By the same token, she preferred the passive voice in English to the active voice, and she made the latter a cultural issue since to her the active voice sounded like someone giving orders; it was too direct.

One of my goals for this text from the beginning has been to retain the voice of Harriette Dover. In other words, the text should sound like her talking to the people who knew her. Her narrations were warm but formal, not informal, conversations, and it did not seem appropriate to shorten or change the sentences or to polish the text to make it sound more literary or academic. Harriette Dover spoke grammatically, and she did not have an accent. Oratorical and written styles are not all that different, since both the voice and the hand belong to the author. Wiget (1994) affirms that a narrative style is a prose style. What seems like right or wrong may actually be an ethnocentric reaction to a text. Greg Sarris (1993a) advises us to "let the text speak for itself."

Krupat (1985), Brumble (1988), and others call for editors of oral histories or autobiographical texts narrated by Natives to explain how they edited the texts. I understand their concern, but since I did not interview Harriette Dover, my influence was indirect. She was not my subject. My role was more that of a copyeditor. I supplied all of the punctuation, gave titles to chapters and subject headings, added two sentences in the Prologue and chapter 1 (with Mrs. Dover's permission), added explanatory footnotes to help the diverse audiences, and drafted the maps. I also did library research in ethnohistory because she had her heart set on the University of Washington Press, an academic publisher, publishing her book, and I wanted to be sure that we were working well within that context.

There were, however, exceptions to my hands-off rule. She did not want to discuss her role in the revival of the Salmon Ceremony. It would have been a glaring omission for her not to discuss the revival of the ceremony since it was her idea to revive it. The people who met with her to plan the event, such as Morris and Bertha Dan, Bernie Gobin, and Stan and Joann Jones, would have been stunned. The revival of the Salmon Ceremony after a 150-year hiatus was a very important event in the history and culture of the Tulalip Tribes. It turned out that she had not wanted to discuss it initially because she did not want to appear to boast.

Secondly, as we were working, I asked her if she had experienced religious conflicts when she was exposed to Christianity in the boarding school. She realized, after she thought over the question, that she had had a plethora of religious conflicts, so she discussed them in chapter 8, along with the stellar advice her father gave her for how to deal with them. As a result of her thinking over her religious conflicts—such as being frightened by the Catholic priest and a high school science teacher and going to Protestant churches in high school—she decided to include a discussion of religious activity on the Tulalip Reservation in the last chapter of the book. She said less about the Smokehouse, or Syəwən religion, one of the traditional religions, because her family was not involved in it. The Syəwən religion is very popular today, especially among young people. She also discussed the Indian Shaker religion, which is an important religion in the Pacific Northwest.

I asked Mrs. Dover if she wanted to do a chapter on her father. She expressed enthusiastic interest in the idea, but it did not happen. I thought perhaps, since her father had been such a pervasive influence in her life, that she could not "telescope" him (one of her phrases) into a single chapter.

She was clear about which materials she wanted to include in the text and which she did not. She covered certain events more in Ryggs (1978)—such as a revenge killing, assassination attempts upon her father's life by other Indians, a story her father told about how they first learned about whiskey, her brother's marriage, and her brother's and father's deaths. She mentioned, but did not discuss, a dance group of Tulalip young people that she sponsored and led for several years. I understand that they performed at fairs and for other occasions in the area. Several people mentioned the group at her funeral; it was obviously very meaningful to them. I am sorry that I did not know about it. We can only speculate as to why she omitted it. She also did not discuss the Montessori preschool that she attended before the boarding school, which is still available to Tulalip youngsters.

The manuscript closes on an ironic and poignant note about time out of time. It is shaped around how Mrs. Dover, her grandparents, and her parents saw their world. It was my idea to close it that way since irony and poignancy characterize the text. The worlds of the three generations were similar, and yet they were different. There is a lot to regret. Their lives and their history bear a continuous thread of irony.

When Mrs. Dover came into my classroom at Everett Community College in 1976, little did I realize that we would develop a unique collaborative, professional relationship and then a friendship. As she took her seat in the front row, she announced to us that she had not been to school for fifty years. Then she settled into her chair, took out a notebook, and went about the business of being a student. I recall thinking, as I watched her, that some things must be difficult to forget.

I had known her for two years prior to her enrollment at the college because I had invited her to speak to students in my class on Northwest Coast Native cultures about Snohomish culture and to show us some of her family artifacts. Having her in class as a student made our relationship less formal.

She had enrolled at the college for several reasons. She wanted to be a role model for younger tribal members, who could now enroll at the local community college and be funded by the Bureau of Indian Affairs. This development had come about because of a change in the Relocation and Termination programs that specified that the federal government could no longer prevent local tribal members from seeking education and training at nearby colleges. She wanted to obtain more education in order to write a history of the Tulalip Reservation. She wanted to know what I was saying about Indians. As a result of those goals, she majored in anthropology and history and took three anthropology courses from me. Her remarks in class were plentiful and always informative. The students and I liked her very much. She enjoyed the courses and my liberal point of view, and she liked my study of the Indian Shaker religion. She received an associate of arts degree in 1978.

When she said she "wanted to know what you are saying about Indians," I experienced an emotion that was a mixture of curiosity and exhilaration. I accepted the challenge; it would be like having Einstein sit in on your Physics 101 course. It seemed only fair; after all, she was an elder. If I was wrong about something, it would be just as well that she tell me.

Let us preserve here her remarks to us in class about Snohomish culture and the Tulalip Reservation, as well as a remark she made to me when we were working on her manuscript. These remarks were about art, religion, traditional terms for new items or behaviors, the dignity of the high class, misgivings about people who had twins, and how her father convinced Dr. Buchanan to let the tribal members build a community house. Early in the quarter I asked her how Snohomish would say the word "art." I had asked Abner Johnson, a Tlingit carver and artist, the same question. Tribal societies usually do not have a separate word for art. It is often embedded in some other expression or institution in their system that speaks to what art means to them. She replied that the word X̱ala would be the best equivalent since it means "putting designs on a flat surface that mean something." The designs she referred to were spiritual or religious designs; therefore, art to the Snohomish is a form of writing, marking or decorating a surface with designs that communicate knowledge about spiritual matters. When whites came to the area, the Native people referred to their writing on papers and documents as "making designs on paper that mean something to them." The design on the sqʷədilič̌ boards, for example, represented intersecting paths that could resemble a cross, but it was not intended to be a cross in the Christian sense.

She said that when cars came into use, they were referred to as canoes, and the pistons going up and down were described as people dancing.

She explained to us that when she was young the Snohomish disapproved when parents had twins, since too much of anything was frowned upon. One should not drink a lot of water, eat a lot of food, sleep overly long, or have multiple births. Parents who had twins could be asked to leave the area and live elsewhere. I was reminded of her comment several years later when Snohomish twins, young men, took that same class from me.

Both boys and girls, especially the high class, or *siaʔb*, were expected to acquire a spirit power (*sqəlalitut*). Boys went through an intense pursuit that included rigorous physical exercise and going out alone at night to secluded places to bathe and meditate. The girls meditated at home or in a separate dwelling where they were secluded during their menstrual periods.

Families had certain places where they sent older children and teenagers to seek a *sqəlalitut*. The experience and the acquisition of a power, when a vision occurred, meant that a song, an instruction, and a gift for an occupation or some other life endeavor would be the outcome. The children ate very little during those times, drank some water, expended as much energy as they could, and were isolated. Older boys were sent out alone at night, which meant training that would accustom them to being alone in the dark. Training began when the children were three years old. As Mrs. Dover described the activity, we could see that, as imperative as this lesson was, it was also important to be kind to the youngster. After all, the Snohomish did not spank or strike children to punish them. A male relative, such as father, uncle, or grandfather, would take the child for a walk around the community house at night. For several nights the relative would walk with him and hold his hand. Then he would begin to walk behind the child, calling out to him frequently to show that he was still there and asking him to touch the community house periodically. As time went on, the relative walked farther and farther behind until the child was sent out to walk around the house alone. This process took several years.

Then boys were sent out at night to swim in secluded places and return with a small carving that an elder had left there earlier in the day. They were often sent out in storms, as her father was on Whidbey Island, for the benefit of the cold weather, and in his case, because his parents wanted him to see a killerwhale and Thunderbird power that he could encounter during a storm at a certain point of land. Harriette Dover said that, on occasion, her father paddled his canoe over to Lake Crescent from Whidbey Island, where he built a shelter and bathed and watched for the animals to come around with their babies. So, he probably visited the area in the spring.

She told us about when her father asked Dr. Buchanan, the agent for the reservation and the superintendent of the boarding school, for permission to build a community house where they could perform traditional dances. He said he wanted the community house so that the young people could see how terrible they used to live. Obviously, this was an effective exercise in reverse psychology because she said Buchanan was "happy over that idea" and permission was granted, since the message from the federal government had been eminently clear that they intended to change the Indian people completely. In chapter 6, Mrs. Dover discusses the building of the community house on the Tulalip Reservation, the first one since they signed the treaty, and the first Treaty Day celebration there.

One Friday afternoon when we were working on her history, she asked me if I noticed anything "funny" about the patient in Utah who had had a mechanical heart surgically implanted in his chest. I answered that I had noticed that his facial expression was blank, but then I had forgotten about it. She said, "In our belief, you can't do that—put a mechanical device into someone's body—since he then wouldn't be human. In our belief, the "mind" is the heart *and* the brain; it isn't just the brain." I am grateful to her for clarifying that, since my own cultural background suggests that mind and brain are synonymous and the heart is just a mechanical organ; although, of course, it is used to speak about feelings metaphorically. The Lushootseed Dictionary states that the "mind" is in the chest, but Mrs. Dover stressed the connection between the brain and the heart, between feelings and thoughts, to make it easy for us to see the metaphorical/symbolic ties being made among warmth or kindness, rational thought, feelings, and intuition.

The last time I saw Harriette Dover was on her birthday in 1990. I took her a card and a red azalea plant because red was her favorite color. I had to take my mother to an appointment, so I couldn't stay until Wayne came later before dinner. She decided to take a nap and asked me to tuck her in. I did not know I would not see her again. I did not know that she had breast cancer.

She died on February 5, 1991, and is buried in the cemetery at Mission Beach that overlooks Tulalip Bay, near where she was born. She was eighty-six years old. Local newspaper coverage revealed that her stature in life was also evident in her death. This autobiographical history of the Tulalip Indian Reservation community is one of her legacies.

On the afternoon that we finished taping her manuscript, she had explained to me that at her funeral a blanket would be draped over my arm and I would be given a basket that her aunt Elizabeth Shelton had woven. She pointed to the basket in her living room and said that it had a deliberate flaw, a sign of quality, on the rim. I appreciated her generous sentiment, her wish to thank me in a traditional way, even though the wish died with her.

On both days of her funeral, Friday and Saturday, it was very foggy. I enjoyed the fog. I had been impressed with her remarks about Mist— sqʷəšəb—a treaty signer who was named for the early misty days of the earth, which is a scientific fact, and so I found the fog uniquely comforting. Warm, misty rain has its own beauty, too. It felt as if the ancestors had come to get her and take her home. I wondered how I would get along without my author.

Acknowledgments

We appreciate the generosity of administrators and staff at Everett Community College who allowed us to use campus resources to accomplish this project. We thank anthropology students Candy Bennett and Marcella Gusman for their help; audiovisual employees Roslyn McDonald, Cheryl Cornwall, Polly Kelley, and Linda Weatherholt, who typed most of the transcripts; Lynn Mock, Ruth Torseth, and Virginia DeMouth, who did other typing; audiovisual specialist Jerry Tinker, who authorized his staff to do the transcribing for us; Jaan Smith in Word Processing and Mike Eason in the Photography Laboratory. Adminstrators and Board of Trustee members who expressed interest were Susan Carroll, Barry Curran, Robert Drewal, Dale Hensley, and Nancy Weiss.

Wayne Williams has been very supportive and is a good and patient listener. I look forward to the day when I can hand him a copy of his mother's book.

We thank Grace Goedel for the phonetic transcriptions. We appreciate Vi Hilbert for her vital translations and Dr. Loran Olsen for his photographs. Simon Ottenberg, Stan Jones, James Nason, Hank Gobin, and Wayne Ude deserve special thanks.

References Cited

Adams, David Wallace. *Education for Extinction: American Indians and the Boarding School Experience, 1875–1928*. Lawrence: University Press of Kansas, 1995.

Amoss, Pamela. "The Fish That God Gave Us: The First Salmon Ceremony Revised." *Arctic Anthropology* 24(1) (1987): 56–66.

Bancroft, H. H. *Native Races of the Pacific States*. San Francisco: A. L. Bancroft and Company, 1882a.

———. *The Northwest Coast*. San Francisco: A. L. Bancroft and Company, 1882b.

Basso, Keith. *Wisdom Sits in Places*. Albuquerque: University of New Mexico Press, 1996.

Bataille, Gretchen, and Kathleen M. Sands. "Women's Autobiography." In Andrew Wiget, *Dictionary of Native American Literature*. New York: Garland Publishing, 1994.

Bates, Dawn, Vi Hilbert, and Thom Hess. *Lushootseed Dictionary*. Seattle: University of Washington Press, 1994.

Berkhofer, Robert. *Salvation and the Savage: An Analysis of Protestant Missions and the American Indian Response, 1787 to 1862*. Knoxville: University of Kentucky Press, 1965.

Bierwert, Crisca. *Ways of the Lushootseed People*. Seattle: United Indians, 1980.

———. *Lushootseed Texts*. Lincoln: University of Nebraska Press, 1995.

———. *Brushed Cedar*. Tucson: University of Arizona Press, 1999.

Blackman, Margaret. *During My Time: Florence Edenshaw Davidson*. Seattle: University of Washington Press, 1982.

Brumble, David, and Arnold Krupat. "Autobiography." In *Dictionary of Native American Literature*, edited by Andrew Wiget. New York: Garland Publishing, 1994.

Carlson, Roy, ed. *Indian Art Traditions of the Northwest Coast*. Burnaby, B.C.: Archaeology Press, Simon Fraser University, 1982.

Childs, Brenda J. *Boarding School Seasons*. Lincoln: University of Nebraska Press, 1997.

Clark, Norman. *Milltown: A Social History of Everett, Washington*. Seattle: University of Washington Press, 1970.

Coleman, Michael C. *American Indian Children at School, 1850–1930*. Jackson: University Press of Mississippi, 1964.

Coste, Didiev. *Narrative as Communication*. Minneapolis: University of Minnesota Press, 1989.

Crampton, Gregory. "The Archives of the Duke Project in the American Indian Oral History Program." In *Indian-White Relations: A Persistent Paradox*, edited by Smith and Kvasnicka, 1981.

Crapanzano, Vincent. *Tuhami*. Chicago: University of Chicago Press, 1986.

DeLoria, Vine. *Singing for the Spirit*. Santa Fe, N.M.: Clear Light Publishers, 1999.

DeMailie, R. J. "These Have No Ears: Narrative and the Ethnohistory Method." *Ethnohistory* 40(4) (1993): 515–38.

Denzin, Norman. *Interpretive Biography*. Thousand Oaks, Calif: Sage Publications, 1989.

Dietz, Steven. *The Rememberer: Based on* As My Sun Now Sets *by Joyce Simmons Cheeka, as told to Werdna Phillips Finley*. Seattle: Rain City Press, 1993.

Dinwoodie, Phillip. *Reserve Memories*. Lincoln: University of Nebraska Press, 2002.

Dover, Harriette. "Memories of a Tulalip Girlhood." In *Vibrations*, Everett Community College, Washington, 1978.

Drucker, Phillip. *Northwest Coast Indian Cultures*. Menlo Park, Calif.: Chandler Publishing Company, 1960.

Elmendorf, William. *The Structure of Twana Culture*. Pullman: Washington State University Press, 1960.

Fitzpatrick, Darleen. "The 'Shake': The Indian Shaker Curing Ritual Among the Yakama." Master's thesis, University of Washington, 1968.

———. "A Gift from God: A Study of the Indian Shaker Religion in the Pacific Northwest." Manuscript. 1976.

———. *We Are Cowlitz: A Native American Ethnicity*. Lanham, Md.: University Press of America, 2004.

Gibbs, George. "Reports of Explorations and Surveys to Ascertain the Most Practical and Economical Route for a Railroad from the Mississippi River to the Pacific Ocean." Executive Document No. 91, House of Representatives, Second Session, 33rd Congress, Washington, D.C., 1854.

———. "Tribes of Western Washington and Northwest Oregon. Washington." *Contributions to North American Ethnology* 1 (1877): 157–241.

Gunther, Erna. *Ethnobotany of Western Washington*. Seattle: University of Washington Press, 1945.

Haeberlin, Herman, and Erna Gunther. "Mythology of Puget Sound." *Journal of American Folklore* 37 (1924): 371–438.

———. *Indians of Puget Sound*. Seattle: University of Washington Press, 1930.

Hess, Thom. *Dictionary of Puget Salish*. Seattle: University of Washington Press, 1976.

———. "Lushootseed Dialects," *Anthropological Linguistics* 19, no. 9 (1977): 403–19.

Hilbert, Viola. *Haboo: Native American Stories from Puget Sound*. Seattle: University of Washington Press, 1985.

Hopkins, Sarah Winnemucca. *Life Among the Paiutes: Their Wrongs, and Claim*. Boston: Printed for the author in 1883. Facsimile reprint. Bishop, Calif.: Chalfant Press, 1969.

Hymes, Dell. *In Vain I Tried to Tell You*. Berkeley: University of California Press, 1990.

Jacobs, Melville. *The Content and Style of an Oral Literature: Clackamas Chinook Myths and Tales*. Viking Fund Publications in Anthropology 26. New York: Viking Fund, 1960.

Josephy, Alvin M. *Indian Heritage of America*. New York: Knopf, 1968.

Kew, Michael. "Coast Salish Ceremonial Life: Status and Identity in a Modern Village." Ph.D. diss., University of Washington, 1969.

Krupat, Arnold. *For Those Who Came After: A Study of Native American Autobiography*. Berkeley: University of California Press, 1985.

———. *The Voice in the Margin: Native American Literature and the Canon*. Berkeley: University of California Press, 1989.

———. *Ethnocriticism: Ethnography, History, Literature and the Canon*. Berkeley: University of California Press, 1992.

———. *New Voices in Native American Literary Criticism*. Washington, D.C.: Smithsonian Institution Press, 1993.

———. *Native American Autobiography: An Anthology*. Madison: University of Wisconsin Press, 1994.

———. *The Turn to the Native: Studies in Criticism and Culture*. Lincoln: University of Nebraska Press, 1995.

———. *Red Matters: Native American Studies*. Philadelphia: University of Pennsylvania Press, 2002.

Krupat, Arnold, and Brian Swann. *I Tell You Now: Autobiographical Essays by Native American Writers*. Lincoln: University of Nebraska Press, 1987a.

———. *Recovering the Word: Essays on Native American Literature*. Berkeley: University of California Press, 1987b.

———. *Here First: Autobiographical Essays by Native American Writers*. New York: Modern Library, 2000.

Lowawaima, K. Tsianina. *They Called It Prairie Light: The Story of Chilocco Indian School*. Lincoln: University of Nebraska Press, 1994.

Martin, Calvin. "Ethnohistory: A Better Way to Write Indian History." *Western Historical Quarterly* 9 (Jan. 1978): 41–56.

———. *The American Indian and the Problem of History*. New York: Oxford University Press, 1988.

———. *In the Spirit of the Earth: Rethinking History and Time*. Baltimore, Md.: Johns Hopkins University Press, 1991.

———. *The Way of the Human Being*. New Haven: Yale University Press, 1998.

Martin, Joel. *The Land Looks After Us*. London: Oxford University Press, 2000.

McBeth, Sally. "The Primer and the Hoe." *Natural History Magazine*, August 1982.

Meeker, Ezra. *Pioneer Reminiscences of Puget Sound*. Seattle: Historical Society of Seattle, 1980; orig. pub. 1905.

Miller, Jay. *Mourning Dove: A Salishan Autobiography*. Lincoln: University of Nebraska Press, 1989.

Maryott, Teresa, and William Shelton. "Romance of the Snohomish as Told by William Shelton." Manuscript. 1938.

Momaday, Scott N. *House Made of Dawn*. New York: Harper and Row, 1956.

———. *On the Way to Rainy Mountain*. New York: Ballantine, 1970.

———. *The Names*. New York: Harper and Row, 1976.

Nabokov, Peter. *Indian Running: Native American History and Tradition*. Santa Fe, N.M.: Ancient City Press, 1988.

———. *A Forest of Time*. New York: Cambridge University Press, 2002.

Ortiz, Alfonso. "Some Concerns Central to the Writing of Indian History." *Indian Historian* (Winter 1977): 17–22.

Pojar, Jim, and Andy MacKinnon. 2004. Plants of the Pacific Northwest Coast. Rev. ed. Edmonton, AB: Lone Pine Publishing.

Pratt, Richard H. *Battlefield and Classroom: Four Decades with the American Indian*. New Haven, Conn.: Yale University Press, 1992.

Prucha, F. P. "Doing Indian History." In *Indian-White Relations: A Persistent Paradox*, edited by Smith and Kvasnicka, 1981.

———. *Indian-White Relations in the United States. A Bibliography of Works Published from 1975 to 1980*. Lincoln: University of Nebraska Press, 1982.

Ruoff, A. Lavonne Brown. *American Indian Literatures*. New York: Modern Language Association, 1980.

———. "Historical Emergence of Native American Writing." In Andrew Wiget, *Dictionary of Native American Literature*, 1993.

Ryggs, Lawrence. "The Continuation of Upper Class Snohomish Coast Salish Attitudes and Deportment as Seen through the Life History of a Snohomish Coast Salish Woman." Master's thesis, Western Washington University, 1978.

Sarris, Greg. *Keeping Slug Woman Alive*. Berkeley: University of California Press, 1993a.

———. *Mabel McKay*. Berkeley: University of California Press, 1993b.

Schorcht, B. *Storied Voices in Native American Texts*. New York and London: Routledge, 2003.

Shelton, William. "Indian Totem Legends of the Northwest Country by One of the Indians." Oklahoma Indian Agricultural School, Chilocco, 1914.

———. *The Story of the Totem Pole: Early Indian Legends*. Everett, Wash.: Kane and Marcus, 1923.

Shostak, Marjorie. *Nisa: The Life and Words of a !Kung Woman*. New York: Random House, 1983.

Silko, Leslie. *The Storyteller*. New York: Seaver Books, 1981.

Smith, James F., and Robert Kvasnicka. *Indian-White Relations: A Persistent Paradox*. Washington, D.C.: Howard University Press, 1984.

Smith, Marian. *The Puyallup and Nisqually*. New York: Columbia University Press, 1940.

Snyder, Sally. "Skagit Folklore and Its Existential Basis." Ph.D. diss., University of Washington, 1964.

Spicer, Edward. *A Short History of the Indians of the United States*. New York: Van Norstrand, 1960.

Stands In Timber, John, and Margot Liberty. *Cheyenne Memories*. New Haven, Conn.: Yale University Press, 1967.

Suttles, Wayne. "Post-Contact Culture Change Among the Lummi," *British Columbia Quarterly* 18 (1954): 29–102.

———. "Coast Salish Art: Productivity and Constraints." In *Indian Art Traditions of the Northwest Coast,* ed. Roy Carlson. Vancouver: UBC Press, 1975.

Suttles, Wayne, ed. *Northwest Coast*. Vol. 7 of *Handbook of North American Indians*. Washington, D.C.: Smithsonian Institution, 1994.

Tedlock, Dennis. *Finding the Center*. Lincoln: University of Nebraska Press, 1983.

———. *The Spoken Word and the Work of Interpretation*. Philadelphia: University of Pennsylvania Press, 1991.

Thompson, Thomas. *The Schooling of Native America*. Washington, D.C.: The American Association of Colleges for Teacher Education, 1979.

Tweddell, Colin. "A Historical and Ethnological Study of the Snohomish People. A Report Specifically Covering Their Aboriginal and Continued Existence and Their Effective Occupation of a Definable Territory." Indian Claims Commission Docket 125. Exhibit 10. Typescript, University of Washington Libraries, Seattle, 1953.

U.S. Court of Claims. *Duwamish et al. v. U.S. Court of Claims*. University of Washington Library, 1927.

Vizenor, Gerald. *People Named Chippewa: Narrative Histories*. Minneapolis: University of Minnesota Press, 1984.

———. *Narrative Chance*. Albuquerque: University of New Mexico Press, 1989.

———. *Manifest Manners: Postindian Warriors of Survivance*. Hanover, N.H.: Wesleyan University Press, 1994.

Wiget, Andrew, ed. *Dictionary of Native American Literature*. Garland Reference Library for the Humanities. New York: Garland Publishing, 1994.

Wike, Joyce. "Modern Spirit Dancing of Northern Puget Sound." M.A. thesis, University of Washington, 1901.

Youst, Lionel, and William Seaburg. *Coquelle Thompson, Athabaskan Witness. A Cultural Biography*. Norman: University of Oklahoma Press, 2002.

Phonological Key

Snohomish/Lushootseed terms are rendered phonetically in the text.

ʔ   glottal stop; like a catch in the back of the throat, such as *uh oh* in English. "Seattle" contains a glottal stop: Seaʔtle.

a   as in *father*, *say* or *at*

b   as in English

bʔ   *b* with a glottal stop

c   *ts* as in *mats*

č̓   glottalized *ch*; a popping sound

d   as in English

dᶻ   *ds* as in *lids*

ə   sound known as a "schwa"; the vowel in *cup*

g   as in English; soft *g*

gʷ   as in English

h   as in *happy*

i   as *ee* or *a* in *feet* or *fate*

I   as *i* in *bit* or *hit*

ʝ   as in *judge*

k   as in *kick*

k̓   with a popping sound, or *k* with a glottal stop

kʷ   as *qu* as in *quiz*

k̓ʷ   combines kʷ, with k̓ popping sound

l   as l in *live* not *feel*

l'   as in *feel*

ɬ   lateral *l* as in *lull*

x̌   *tl* as in *atlatl*

m   can be an alternative to English *b*

m̓   sounded with throat tension, as in *mussels*

n   can be an alternative to English *d*

p̓   as in *pop*

p̓   *p* with a glottal stop; has a popping sound

q   sounded farther back in the throat than *k*

q̓   glottalized *q*

qʷ   with pursed lips, as in *quick*

q̓ʷ   glottalized *qw*; has a popping sound

s   as in English

š   *s* as in *shut*

t   similar to English

t̓   glottalized *t,* has a popping sound

u   sounded as the double vowel in *boot* or *boat*

w   as in *work*

ẇ   sounded with a tense throat, as in *what*

xʷ   made with a blowing sound, as *wh* in *what* or *which*

x̌   a raspy *h*

x̌ʷ   a raspy *h*, as in *hate*

y   as in English

ẏ   sounded with throat tension, as in the slang term *yuck*

Adapted from Bates, Hess, and Hilbert, *Lushootseed Dictionary*
(Seattle: University of Washington Press, 1994).

Tulalip, From My Heart

Prologue: A Sense of Place

My name is Harriette Shelton Dover. I am going to talk about Tulalip: that is the name of this Indian reservation where I live. In my language, the Snohomish language, we have a word, *bečali?q^waad,* that means "to lay down the heart; to be at ease, at rest; not to worry." *Bečali?* means "to lay [something] down"; *q^waad* is "to leave it alone or drop it." That is what I am going to do here: *bečali?q^waad.* I am going to lay down my heart.

Tulalip is the name of the Indian reservation, and it is the name of the bay. Tulalip Bay. The name is mispronounced by so many people, but Tulalip is the nearest to the right pronunciation for the Snohomish Indian word *dx^wilap,* which means "the long bay; the bay shaped like a purse, long with a narrow opening; a bay going far inland because of its shape." Tulalip is a very ancient name, a prehistoric name; it is the name of a place, of a bay and, since 1855, the name of a reservation.

Tulalip was named in a legend by the Snohomish tribal ancestors in a time so long ago my grandparents referred to it as "a time of remembrance, covered by a drifting, deep fog or mist." Much has been written about Tulalip and its Indians by white people, but I believe this is the first history by a Tulalip Indian.

My grandparents and parents used to reminisce about the days when they were growing up, and they would remember what their grandparents said about their childhoods. This is how our people kept an account of their history from one generation to the next. They always spoke about the long, long time ago—a time so far, so far gone that we are looking at it through a mist or a fog and can't really see. What happened to our people?

We have our legends, which the Indians kept. We have a legend that was told about Tulalip Bay during prehistoric times. It indicates how long our people have occupied this area. This legend is about a prehistoric animal that we call *d'ɔg^wɔ,* a word that means "a fearful animal that comes from the deep water." It does not refer to any of the animals today, and since it was seen only once, we did not develop any other word to describe it. It was a fearful, mysterious animal.

Our people used to tell us about a young man, Lətsxkanəm, who belonged to our Snohomish tribe. One day he decided to walk from our village, which is at Hiboɫb, at Legion Park in Everett, a large village, to a smaller one at Spee-Bi-Dah [or Spibida]. Our people would stay at Spee-Bi-Dah in the summers, although there were some families who stayed there all year around. As the young man got to Tulalip Bay, to the south or Skayu Point, he was somewhat tired, and he did not want to walk all the way around the beach. So he thought he would swim to Totem Beach, which is just about where the Catholic church is now. So he came across, and just as he stood up, walking in the shallow water, walking up to the beach, he heard a fearful if not terrible noise behind him. He turned to look, and there was a terrible black animal, something he had never seen before. It was trying to get at him. So he started to run through the water and get on to the beach. He was terrified and running through the water—swimming and then running in shallow water—and he was so tired that he fell on the beach, but he was watching this terrible animal, dʼəgʷə. He said, "It was long, long like a whale, and on his back it had a lot of fins, not just one like whales have," and from what he could see, it seemed to have a big red mouth. It was thrashing in the water and trying to get at him, but it did not take long, even though it seemed like thousands of years to him, when the animal sank back into the water out of sight. The water seemed to be boiling when the animal was thrashing about, trying to reach him, just foaming. The water got quiet; that animal had sunk out of sight. The man was so tired and so terrified; he sat there for what seemed like a long time.

Then he continued to walk along the land to Spee-Bi-Dah. By the time he got there it was late, so the Indians did not do anything. They all came the next morning, and he came with them to show them where he saw this terrible, mysterious, great big animal. The Indians went out in canoes with their spears, feeling around in the deep water. They never saw anything and they did not hear anything. No one ever saw that kind of animal again. That was the last time our people talked about a terrible animal—bigger than a whale, with several fins along its back. When our people used to talk about it, they would say it was so long, long ago. It was a monster, a scary animal, they only saw once. If they saw it several times, they would have had a name for it. It took that young man several weeks to get over his fright.

Some people, the white people, say that we came here a little before they came. According to what our people say, we were here when there were some very mysterious animals that were still appearing in the water. I remember when I was a child, they used to tell us not to stay out in the bay, not to swim way out there and stay too long. "If you are going to swim in the bay, just swim the once and come back up on the beach." I heard about that animal only once. It did not frighten us, since we felt it was seen so long ago. Once in a while, we used to talk about it and wonder where it went.

Lətsxkanəm was the first Indian, our people (the Snohomish Tribe) said, who as a young man started the guardian spirit quest. The Indians were already doing that and fasting, but he went farther and he went out more days than anyone else up to that time. He had a vision of a longhouse, a community house like our people used to live in, that was deep in the water. Whales came to tell him that some of our forefathers are deep in the water, and that is where the tradition of the community house came from. The young man could see it in his vision: he walked way under the deep, deep water, and he saw a longhouse, a community house. The people there told him that all the house posts he saw had a simple carving on them of the mouths of whales, and they told him those were the different leaders—the *sqəlalitut*, or their guardian spirit. Lətsxkanəm was the man who had the vision of the longhouse, and that is when our people started to build their longhouses, and that was so long ago. The longhouse at Possession Point, where my father was born and lived, had the poles with the design of the mouths of whales carved and painted on them. The farmers tore the longhouse apart after the Indians moved away from there to the reservation. My father tells the legend about how to make a longhouse in his book *Indian Totem Legends*. He was the only man who saw something like a whale with fins all along its back. It was a time long ago, but it is in our traditions.

I am going to talk about what we call the Prophecy. I heard about it when I was a small child. My grandparents and their generation, their brothers and sisters, cousins, were talking about the Prophecy. They said in that time long ago, a medicine man in the Snohomish tribe who had X̌udab, what you call the power to heal, was out meditating. He was searching for his guardian spirit. He had been out in the woods, deep in the mountains, fasting for days and days out there. He came back after a few days and he told the people what he had heard. At almost the same time, my mother used to talk about a medicine man in her tribe, the Klallam tribe on the Strait of Juan de Fuca,[1] when he went out on his guardian spirit quest into the Olympic

---

1   The preferred spelling today is S'Klallam.

Mountains area. He had the same kind of vision as the man who belonged to the Snohomish tribe. The talk about their experiences went around to the other tribes. These men had heard that "there will come a man." Those were exactly the words they used. In the Snohomish language this would be expressed as *kluaxk̓ʷištobs*. In our language, *štobs* is "a man" and *kłu* means "it will" in the future tense, and *axk̓ʷi* means "to come." "There will come a man." There will come a man from far to the east, from the way the sun walks, which is from the east, coming over our mountains. As he walks over the mountains, his footsteps will sound like thunder and that noise, the thunder, will resound all over the country, all over the Puget Sound country. And our lives will change. There will come a dark night, and that dark night will last a long, long time. That man will bring a long, long night. So that was the Prophecy that I heard about the coming of the white people.

My parents were remembering the Prophecy again during the 1930s. My parents and their cousins used to get together for Sunday dinner. They would talk and reminisce about old times, the things that had happened to our people. Sometimes they talked about the treaty, the Point Elliott Treaty that was signed in 1855. Years later, after I read the treaty, I remembered what they said, over all those years, and what they said was just exactly about what happened at Point Elliott, that's Mukilteo, in 1855.

Treaty time, shall we say, was quite an upsetting time for the Indians, but nobody then had the time to think about it. My father said the white people were "just boiling in"; they came in waves of people across the continent. They "boiled over" into this part of western Washington. They were all over. It was quite an astonishing time, and I have often thought it was fortunate the Indians had reservations to go to even though these reservations were really too small. There was supposed to be land for all of the Indian men, but there was not enough for everyone.

I am going to talk, in this history, about the Indian people who came to live on the Tulalip Reservation. I learned about these things from our people, from my grandparents in particular, and through the events that happened in my lifetime. My life covers a long period of time. I never thought about it especially before, but it covers almost this whole century. The way things were for the Indians way back then was certainly different than it is today. Just like it is for all American people. My wish is to write down some of

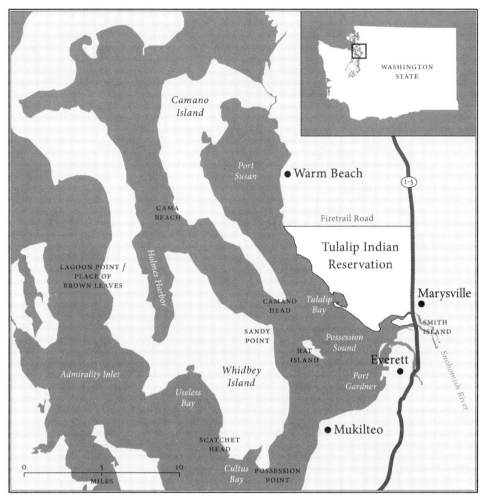

Part of Snohomish Indian Territory

the things I remember from my American Indian childhood on an Indian reservation in the Pacific Northwest.

My memories of Tulalip, where I was born in 1904, go back to 1908 or 1909. I remember the dates, I believe, because there was a World's Fair or Exposition in Seattle in 1909, called the Alaska-Yukon-Pacific Exposition, and my father was gone. He was at the Fair with the Puget Sound Indians' exhibits. I felt terribly alone and afraid, especially at night, with just my mother and me.

One of the things I certainly remember was my home. Home was a three-room house my father called a cottage. It was situated on what had been the old Tulalip Mission School grounds. Part of the old Mission School burned down, so the newer school, an Indian boarding school, was established across the bay; it was called the Tulalip Indian Boarding School. It was operated by the United States government, whereas the first school at Mission Beach was a Catholic Mission School. My father went there for two years when he was quite grown up—seventeen or eighteen years old. So he had a different kind of life than I had. I went to the Indian Boarding School.

Several vacant, large, old buildings remained of the Mission School, and we used to run and play in those empty, echoing rooms. When we became too noisy, my mother would appear and order us back outside. She said, "The buildings might collapse."

My mother was one of those people who ferociously cleaned up the house every day. And I always said that's why I don't bother with the house. If things fall on the floor, they can stay there; but my mother, at least twice a year, would scrub down the walls, and every week all of the floors and porches were scrubbed, and it seems like that's all I remember—tiptoeing around wet floors or helping mop up. That doesn't mean my mother was not a very loving person, because she was. But the people I remember as most loving were my grandmothers. I always called them the "dearest grandmothers." There were three of them who lived over past the vacant buildings,[2] where there was another building with four large rooms downstairs, a long wide veranda, and three bedrooms upstairs. It was not their home either. They were just living there. The house they lived in was once occupied by Father Chirouse, a priest who came to the area in 1857. Indians, in those days, just lived where they could. Usually they put up what were called "shacks": one or two rooms built of cedar shakes. My dearest grandmother lived in one of the bedrooms, and the two other elderly grandmothers lived in the other two rooms. They each cooked and ate and lived in one room. The veranda was used to hang bedding, laundry, and freshly washed sheep wool to dry.

Sheep wool was of tremendous importance to the dearest grandmothers and to all of us. It was carefully washed several times, worked over or "teased," carded, spun on native Indian spindles, and wound into large balls of soft wool ready to be knitted into socks and sweaters. I learned how to knit before I was six years old. I could help my dearest grandmother with only the straight knitting; the heels and toes came later, after much heartache caused by my mother's reprimands.

---

2 In the traditional kinship system, the sister of a grandmother is addressed and referred to as "grandmother." See Smith 1940.

My one remaining grandmother was my paternal grandmother. She was baptized by Father Chirouse with the name of Magdeline. She was a very pretty girl, so she received that name, which became Medline to us. But they didn't call her by that name. They called her zatskoliksə. The other grandmothers were Mrs. Mary Jake and Sally, who came from Suquamish.

I learned so much from my grandmothers and from grandmother Medline in particular. They loved me every time I saw them. I used to go running down there to their house every morning as soon as I could, and they would take me on their laps and hold me as they visited and talked, and I would fall asleep on a grandmother's lap. They wore velvet blouses and skirts, so that falling asleep on a grandmother's lap that had a velvet dress on and then waking again in her arms was the nicest feeling.

These people on the list I have here [see p. 15–16] came to our house and from them I learned about the early days of the reservations in this area.[3] These are some of the Indians I said I talked to during my lifetime. Some of them were Snoqualmie. They were very old. Some of these Indians were older than my grandparents. They were of different tribes, such as Snoqualmie and Lummi. They talk in English now. They would sometimes stay for several days and eat at our house, and they would walk over to the Agency to see about their problems, to talk with the agent or with the land clerk.

I remember my parents, these people, and my cousins and relatives would talk for several hours, and then they would get on to something else, like I do, and we would get back to it again. I would have a piece of paper and wait for them to get back to a topic, and then I would finally get to ask them: "What would the Indian names for March or April be?"—or whatever I was wanting to know, and then they would get to remembering what they did when they were children.

Speaking of the months of the year, someone I talked with one time heard the names of the Snohomish moons of the year. He didn't quite believe us that there are thirteen months in a year. He left to do some research; then he

---

3   Mrs. Dover is referring to a list of sources for her information about the early days of the reservation beyond her own immediate family. You could say that this was a life-long research project. Later she explains who these people are, most of whom were well known in their time.

came back and stayed for several hours, talking to my father and some other Indians. I remember he told my father, "There are thirteen months in a year. I didn't know." I guess a lot of people don't know. We just go by the twelve months in a year. We didn't name the days of the week like the white people do. The Indians had names for them after the priests came here. There was Sunday and the whole week.

I want to talk about the moons or the months in the Snohomish language. Our tribe, the Snohomish tribe, had names for the thirteen months of the year. Now, in the white man's calendar, you have twelve months, but with us we had the thirteen moons and there are thirteen months. They had names for all of them, and usually the name referred to what was available to eat at that time. Let's see, I have April. It's called *pəd waq̓waq̓waqus*; you should try that! It is the Moon of Frogs. I guess if you live in a city you never hear frogs. But in March and April they start croaking, you know, like a great big orchestra. My father used to tell us when we lived across there, across the road, just come out here and listen to my orchestra. Even if you were in the house you could hear them. There used to be millions of them along here, along this kind of a wet, damp area where this little crick runs, but they make those croaking noises for, I don't know, three or four weeks, I guess. Anyway, you know it's spring. These Indians called April the Month, or Moon, of Frogs. If you always lived in a city you never ever heard them, but you should.

Then, there is the Moon of Whistling Robins, *pəd x̌ʷwa'aac*. Robins have a certain kind of song in the spring; it is a whistle, the whistle of robins, and that is after March. The Month of Frogs and the Month of the Whistle of Robins is almost all together.

May is *pəd čaʔb*, the Moon of the Camas Roots or the time of digging camas bulbs. *čaʔb* is usually when our people went out to the prairies just south of Puyallup and Tacoma and on out to the prairies around Olympia, where they used to dig camas roots. And this is *pəd čaʔb*, the Month of Camas Roots.

June is *pəd təgʷa'd*, the Salmonberry Moon. *təgʷa'd* is salmonberries. If you never ate them, you have missed something. July is *pəd gʷədbix̌ʷ*, the Blackberry Moon. August is *pəd t'aqa*, the Salal Berry Moon. September is *pəd kʷəxʷic*, the Silver Salmon Moon. October is *pəd xʷičib*, the Challenging Calls of Deer and Elk. I will come back to that again. November is *pəd x̌ʷa'yʔ*, Dog Salmon Moon.

December is *pəd səxʷ šicəlwaʔs*, and that means Sheathe the Paddles. It's a real stormy month, and the people put their paddles up on the walls of the longhouse so that they were put into mats or something; that's why it says sheathe. It means to put something away. January is Hunger Moon, pəd x̌iqʼs, when people don't get enough to eat. February, pəd səxʷpupuhigʷəd, in our language is wind, really (breeze is something else), and means Month of Many Storms and Winds. March is pəd x̌ʷc̓abiƛ̓igʷəd, the Moon of Changing Weather. Then there is April, pəd waq̓waq̓us, the Moon of Frogs, where I started, and that is thirteen. ƛ̓əqʷqʷ.

I heard the challenging calls of the deer and elk on television. I think it was one of those documentaries on the elk, the Olympic elk, and that is where I heard it. You could hear them, a real loud call. My father said that was the male elk, and deer do that too. You know the Indians saw everything, heard everything, and so they used to hear those and that is really pretty loud because my father said it would echo through the trees and through the valleys. I thought it was quite a majestic thing. It is sort of a call of strength and power, and, of course, deer and elk will fight. Sometimes they lock horns and are locked for days and so that is what this challenging call of deer and elk is about. My father used to say, "Oh, you should hear that." They used to go out hunting and camp by Lake Stevens; that is a long time ago, the 1890s, and they would camp over night, and then they would hunt coming back—walking all the way. They say you hear that call at night and you really wake up and listen.

We didn't have days of the week like the white people do. Well, Indians had names for them after the priests came, when there was Sunday and the whole week, but I don't remember them now.

I would just happen to meet some of these people somewhere too, at a potlatch gathering, and then I would go around and sit down and talk with them. My grandparents and my parents said, "Talk and shake hands and greet the elderly people." They are alone because, for many of them, a lot of their family has died and they were almost alone. If they reminisce about their early growing up years, then you learn where they lived, what games they played, and what they heard; what was happening; what their parents talked about; what were the worries and the problems of the time.

I think in the American white man's civilization there is not much communication between the elderly people and the young or middle-aged. They seem to be quite separated. In my growing up years, my grandmother lived almost right next door.

While discussing the people on this list, I will tell which reservation they came from. Most likely the reason they came, as I said, was to go to the Agency Office and talk about some of their problems, which mostly seemed to involve land allotments on the reservations.[4] So many families died and left allotments where the nearest relatives were probably third or fourth cousins, so that land was divided up and given to distant cousins.

A lot of these people came to Tulalip, and they really came. Today, you can come all of the way from Bellingham down to Seattle in a matter of hours. Way back then, it would take them two or three days, because they traveled in a canoe and they just paddled. They were not really in a hurry like today, when you have to make time. Whole families would come—the uncles and their families. As they came along, they stopped to eat lunch and they camped at night.

Indians around here knew places where there was running water, fresh spring water. I remember my mother and my aunt Elizabeth Shelton, my father, and my grandparents would recall the places they had been so many times when they were growing up. They would remember where the running water was, the fresh running springs. As soon as the canoes touched the beach, the children were off and running. Any place you go today, you notice when the cars come to park, no matter where it is, if it is in a city, you will see the children hop out, and they are already on the sidewalk talking with one another. They are ready to go. The mother is hauling out the purses or clothes or coats. That was the way with the Indian children. As soon as the canoes touched the beach, the Indian children were off running up and down the beach. So when these people got together, they would remember the places where they had been and where they played.

My father used to remember that they would run on the drift logs. They would race to see who could run the farthest, all the way over to the Point [Skayu Point], and all the way back. He said they ran as hard as they could. The drift logs were not all the same size and they were not the same distance. If you fell off and into the sand, then so many points were taken off. Afterwards, my father, my mother, and the others said, "You can really get hurt running on drift logs like that."

Usually the girls didn't get to run around with the boys. We were supposed to be ladies. But Indian children played together and, usually, wherever they went, they could go either along the beaches or along the trails, and some grandparents or aunts and uncles walked along with them.

I remember my grandmother and her cousins. We used to go over there to Mission Beach and run up and down that beautiful beach. It was acres

---

4   Tulalip served as the federal agency in western Washington.

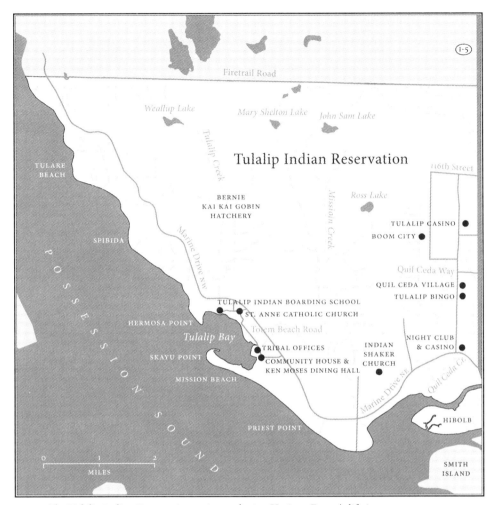

The Tulalip Indian Reservation as it was during Hariette Dover's lifetime

and acres of nice clean sandy beach. We could run up and down and make tracks—all kinds of designs—while we were running. We could be two, three, four blocks ahead of our grandparents. I would turn and look and see where my grandmother and the others were. They would be walking along and talking. I guess they remembered the times when they used to run up and down the beaches. She would be walking with her cane, talking and remembering.

My grandmother's sister was also my grandmother, so she was my other grandmother. Her husband and some of their cousins came from La Conner.[5] Some of their language is different from ours, but I understood them, since I heard them speak it so many times. They came to Tulalip from La Conner in canoes.

I will always remember when the canoes used to come into Tulalip Bay. When we were in Tulalip Indian School, if we had a chance, we used to watch the canoes come in. I don't think there is anything more beautiful than the canoes that we had—the Puget Sound canoes. However, any anthropologist I ever talked to about our canoes said the Puget Sound Indians copied their canoes from the Haida or northern style of canoe.[6] I always said I will challenge that statement. The heads of our canoes were different from the heads of the Haida canoes. Nobody would notice, except maybe us, but as soon as we see a canoe out there, we know right away if it is a Puget Sound canoe.

When my grandmother and my other grandmothers came, I waited for them down at the beach. I would call out to them and say, "Where are you folks going?" Of course, I was talking in Indian, in our Snohomish language. They would tell me where they were going, if they are coming to see my grandmother. A lot of people wouldn't bother to answer a child, just listen to them—or maybe you don't even listen. But that time my other grandmother came from La Conner and they were visiting and talking.

List of Sources and Commentary

William Shelton or Wheakadim, his Indian name. He was Snohomish from Tulalip. Ruth Shelton, Siest-nu, Klallam and Samish. Johnson Williams, Klallam. Emily B. Williams, Tsimshian. James Goudy, Puyallup. Jerry Meeker, Puyallup. Joe Swayell, Snohomish. Ellen Swayell, Snohomish. Elizabeth Shelton or Tsolitsa, Snohomish. Maggie Bagley, Snohomish. Charlie Shelton, Elder, Snohomish. Joe Sahlpud, Elder, Snohomish. Mrs. Joe Sahlpud, Duwamish. Bill Kanim, Snoqualmie. Mrs. Bill Kanim, Snoqualmie. Mr. and Mrs. Sam Wyakes, Snohomish. Jack Klatasby, Swinomish. Jenny John and John Long,[7] Snohomish. Magdelaine Wheakadim, Snohomish. Mary Moses, Snohomish. Peter Kwina, Lummi. Elder Chief Kwina, Lummi. Wil-

---

5   Refers to the area where the Skagit, Swinomish, and Kikiallus tribes live.
6   Philip Drucker, *Northwest Coast Indian Cultures* (Menlo Park, Calif.: Chandler Publishing Company, 1968), 28.
7   Husband and wife. This couple illustrates a Coast Salish custom whereby the wife and children take the husband's first name as their surname.

liam McCluskey, Lummi. John Hawk, Skokomish. Emily Hawk, Skokomish. James Tobin, Nisqually. Mrs. Tobin, Leschi, Nisqually.

I see the first person on the list is, of course, my father. He is of the Snohomish Tribe, which is also the name of the county and a city. He died in 1938.

My mother's name is Siastənu, Ruth Shelton, and she came from the Klallam Tribe which is the area from Port Townsend and Port Angeles to Clallam Bay. She was baptized with the name of Ruth.

Then I have my former mother-in-law and father-in-law. His name was Johnson Williams and he was a Klallam Indian. My former mother-in-law was Emily Brown. She was Tsimshian from southeastern Alaska, but they left there when she was a girl. Here were two different people who talked about the old days, from two different tribes.

Then I have James Goudy. He was one of my father's cousins. His mother came from Puyallup, and so he talked that language: Puyallup.

This next one is Jerry Meeker, who was also Puyallup, and then Joe Swayell. He was much older than my father. Joe Swayell was a small, small boy at the signing of the Medicine Creek Treaty on December 26, 1854. Of course, he just heard them talking. He couldn't see over the heads of people to where Governor [Isaac] Stevens was standing, but he could hear his voice. Our treaty, the Point Elliott Treaty, was signed just after the Medicine Creek Treaty, on January 22, 1855. When you drive to Olympia you go by Medicine Creek. The name of the creek is xʷidadəb, Healing Place of Helpful Spirits. In our language it refers to a medicine man, someone who has a xʷudab. He has a guardian spirit for healing, and he has *sqəlalitut* power too.

I have Ellen Swayell and Elizabeth Shelton or Tsolitsa. She was from this tribe, the Snohomish. She is one of the people who gave Professor Tweddell [1953] his information. Tsolitsa did not speak English, so when she answered I translated into English to Professor Tweddell. I already knew what these people, my mother and Elizabeth, talked about, since I heard it so many times in my growing-up years.

There is something interesting about Tsolitsa. All of my years that I was growing up, she was my *apus*. An *apus* is aunt. She was my aunt, but she was not the sister of my father or my mother. She was the first cousin of my father, but in our Indian relationship, she was just like a sister to my father. Her father, Tsolitsa's father, and my father's father, my grandfather, were brothers. Tsolitsa's father was older than my grandfather, but they grew up together way up the Snohomish River on the Skykomish River. They spent every year—spring and summer—on Whidbey Island with the other Indians, fishing and drying salmon and hunting and visiting. During my growing-up years, she was my *apus*. When my father died, she was called my *yəlab*. *Yəlab* is like a grandparent. They said no matter where I went, if I said "This is my *yəlab*," people would know that either my father or my mother had died even if they never saw me before.

I have Maggie Bagley. She was of the Snohomish Tribe.

I have Charlie Shelton. He was the elder. He was very old when I used to see him and hear him talk. He was from this tribe.

Joe Salpud or Salpuf lived on this reservation. He and his wife, Mrs. Joe Salpud, belonged to the Duwamish Tribe, Chief Seattle's tribe. I used to talk to them about Seattle and Chief Seattle. They knew him; they were related to him. These were the people who told me about Chief Seattle's younger brother. His name was Swiyayb.

I have here on this list Bill Kanim. Right now I can't remember his Indian name. Mr. and Mrs. Kanim were Snoqualmie Indians.

Then I have Sam Waykes and Mrs. Waykes. They are Snohomish.

And I have Jack Klatasby; he was from Swinomish, from La Conner, and John Long and Jenny John. They were from Swinomish.

Then I have my grandmother. She had been baptized with the name Magdeline Wheakadim. I have my other grandmother, Mary Moses.

Then, I have two people from the Lummi Tribe, Peter Kwina and the Elder Chief Kwina.[8] I used to hear them talk, and they used to talk to my mother in the Lummi language which I didn't understand, but they also talked in the Snohomish language. They would talk for hours and hours with my father in the evenings. They would go on and on. My mother would want to put me to bed. I would say, "No, no!" While I'd sit there on somebody's lap, I would keep collapsing—falling asleep—but I was listening to them talk.

Then I have Mr. and Mrs. James Tobin. They were from Nisqually. James Tobin's grandson is Bill Frank Jr.[9]

Bill Frank Jr. is a little older than my son Wayne, who is fifty-two. Bill

---

8   The Lummi Tribe is in Bellingham, Washington.

9   Fishing rights activist and executive director of the Northwest Indian Fisheries Commission.

Frank was arrested many times for fishing on the Nisqually River. He was the one who actually started the lawsuit that resulted in the *United States* v. *Washington* trial in 1973.

One time when they were arrested at a fish-in on the Nisqually River, I told Wayne, my older son, "I'm going down there just to be there." Wayne told me, "Don't go. There is liable to be trouble and you are liable to get hurt." But, I thought, I could bring potato salad. I could stop at some delicatessen and bring fried chicken and sandwiches, bread, butter, salt, pepper, coffee, and tea. We had big coffee pots; I was going take some of them. I got started late. We got a carload of some of our people, but we only got up to the gas station. They said there is no use going any further. The state patrol was all around the roads that led into the Nisqually Reservation. They told the occupants in any cars they found along the road to turn around and leave.

As Long as the Rivers Run is a film by Carol Burns that Darleen showed us at the college. It shows the "fish-in." Deputy sheriffs, who weighed about 280 pounds each, were shown clubbing those Indians. It's too bad the Indians didn't bring charges against them for that kind of roughness and cruelty. One of the last shots in the film shows them in the jail with the bars all around them. Indians were sitting on the cold floors with no chairs. They were thrown in there like a bunch of cattle. Some of the boys and girls were only twelve, fourteen years old. They spent all night and all day in jail with nothing to eat.

But, anyway, James Tobin and his wife are the grandparents of Bill Frank Jr. They were people I heard talking two or three times when I was little. When I was growing up, we were down there for two or three days at a time at the Tobins'. Of course, my father and they would talk and talk at meals and in the evening.

If it is in the evening meal, the Indians cooked so much food: a lot of baked salmon, a lot of roast beef, a lot of homemade bread, a lot of butter, a lot of coffee, tea — you name it. Many other people came; some were neighbors and relatives. There would be almost two dozen people sitting there and talking. Sometimes some of them were just listening.

Bill Frank's mother is Angeline. She is one of my father's cousins. Our Wayne used to get around to different places for meetings on tribal business. He met a lot of cousins, and Bill was one. That was interesting. Wayne would come back and I would tell him who were our cousins. We have cousins at Lummi; Cagey, Sam Cagey, is a big family there. There is another man at

Nisqually too.[10] Bill Frank's aunt and uncle, cousins, and then my mother had cousins. Wayne had them too in Neah Bay. Marcus Dennis. They are quite prominent in their councils.

About ten or twelve years ago, I was down to Nisqually to a wedding. I had a letter from Angeline, Mrs. Bill Frank Sr. One of her granddaughters was getting married, so she invited me to come with my family, but Wayne couldn't go. I met Iona Hawk; that was her maiden name. She was just a little bit older than me. I hadn't seen her for years. I was sitting by Angeline. The wedding was going to be outside on the lawn. It was a beautiful sunshiny day.

We were just talking. Then a woman came. There were several people who came from Pendleton, Oregon. They were relatives the other way. They were Angeline's relatives and therefore they were mine, too, but I had never seen them. Angeline said to that woman, she wanted to shake hands with me, and she said, "*dišdəkʷilit sidiša.*" How about that? *Dišdəkʷilitsidiša.* I had not heard those words spoken by anyone for so long. In their language, *kʷil* means "a relative." In the Snohomish language, it is spoken as *ssya'ʔyaʔ*. *Ssyaˀʔyaʔ* and *kʷil* in the Snohomish language are the same thing. Then, she said *sidiša.* In these languages, a word changes by just an addition to the front of the word. For instance, if I had been one of her men cousins, she would have said, "*tsidiša, dišdəkʷiltsidiša.*" Only I was one of her women cousins. She said *sidiša* and *tsidiša*, with a "ts" sound. Words for cousins and others are changed by a few sounds in the beginning of the word, just as in those two words, *sidiša* and *tsidiša*. If you are talking about a man or cousin or some little boy, you say *tiya.* That word is in my language: *tiya dibida*, "my son, my child." If it is my daughter, it is *siya'ʔyaʔdibida.* "My son," "my daughter," just by that difference: *tiya* and *siya.*[11]

Then I have William McCluskey. He was my mother's cousin. He is a Lummi Indian. He used to stay at our house if he had business at the Agency too.

I have Mr. and Mrs. John Hawk. Just plain Hawk and Emily. Emily Hawk was one of my father's cousins too. They are Skokomish[12] and Nisqually and Puyallup. Their language is similar to Snohomish, except some of the words are different.

---

10 From east of the Cascade Mountains.

11 Lushootseed is taught today" at Tulalip's Department of Cultural Resources.

12 From the Shelton and Hood Canal area.

1 / Treaty Time, 1855

THE first time Tulalip was mentioned in white history, you might say, was January 22, 1855, when these Indians, the Snohomish Tribe, the Duwamish (which was Chief Seattle's tribe), and all of the people from Seattle to the Canadian border signed a treaty at Mukilteo.

Tulalip is mentioned in the Point Elliott Treaty, in article 3, in which it describes the Tulalip area as the area that will be our reservation. But Tulalip, as you know, is really a very old name. It comes from a prehistoric time. It is also the name of our tribal organization, the Tulalip Tribe of Indians. When our people appeared in Judge [George] Boldt's court, when the *United States v. Washington* was being argued in 1973, our group was allowed to appear as the Tulalip Indians, but the Tulalip Reservation is composed of members of the Snohomish, Skagit, Stillaguamish, Snoqualmie, and a few other tribes.[1]

At treaty time, some of the Indians were having their usual gatherings, their potlatches, their meetings, and the leading chiefs got together to talk about what they were going to do and what the treaty would probably mean to them. The tribes were gathered at least ten days before the scheduled day of January 22, when they were to meet with Governor Isaac Stevens for the actual signing. They had meetings morning, noon, and night with the different tribes, and they talked about the treaty.

Tətaʔzad—Not Quite "Yes," Not Quite "No"

Our Snohomish Tribe has a word, *tətaʔzad,* which applies to treaty time and to a few other similar situations. Whenever my father listened to the radio, to President Roosevelt and a lot of the senators and candidates for offices, he

---

1   At this time, being Tulalip became an ethnic identity, whereas prior to this members would state the name of their tribe, and outsiders were required to remember to say Tulalip Tribes, not the Tulalip Tribe.

would say, *tətaʔzad*. "All they do is say 'not quite yes' and 'not quite no.' They behave like native pheasants." I guess you would have to be a hunter to know what he meant. When you are hunting for pheasant, the mother pheasant has her nest on the ground, but she hides it. When the hunter approaches, she leaves the nest and goes on the trail, or wherever, making him think she has a broken wing. She will fly from one side to another just as though she is terribly wounded with a broken wing, and she hopes the hunter will follow her away from her nest. Well, the Indian hunters never disturbed babies. They would probably shoot or kill the male. They would take care in certain times of the spring to see and make certain that they always ensured the cycle of life, forever, for every living thing. The Indians didn't kill birds or animals more than they needed. They just took what they needed and did not destroy or kill any more. This is the meaning of *tətaʔzad*. I could go around in big circles with the meaning of *tətaʔzad*.

By and large, candidates that we heard on television during the election are nice people. Politics is one thing. But *tətaʔzad* is when I would hear my mother talking to one of my nephews and she would tell him, "Do not prevaricate." Something has happened outside where children are playing and somebody is crying, or there is the sound of a crash, and a mother wonders what happened. Well, sometimes, they—the old people—are explaining something. They tell them, "*tətaʔzad*, don't make excuses. Don't say, 'I didn't see anything.'"

So, the Indians had this word that applied to many things. My parents applied it to politics, and, of course, it could apply to Indian politics, too. It applies to the time when our Indians signed the treaty.

Another word that applies here is *bəčad*, or "to lay something down." Another is *gʷaad*, "to leave it alone or drop it."

My grandfather Wheakadim, my father's father who they think was about eighteen years old when the treaty was signed, sat with his relatives in the council. My grandfather was there with his uncles, one of whom was Hixʷəčkaydəm, or Bonaparte, who said, "You sit with us and you listen and you watch." They told him to sit and listen to what the white man says. My grandmother remembered, too, when Governor Stevens got up to talk. They didn't understand him because he spoke in English, and they had to wait for the translation from Michael Simmons, but they watched him as he started to talk. They were listening to him even if they couldn't understand a word, and they said to each other, "It's a lie. He's lying." But they never moved. They sat courteously and listened to him, and all the time they knew he was lying. They said, "Whatever he is saying is not the truth." Anyway, if you read his speech—who knows what he said? The Indians didn't know what he said. I read what are supposed to be the minutes of the treaty discussions. His speech said, "You are my children. I will take care of you because you are my children." Of course, the Indians sat there and thought, "He is lying. Whatever he is saying, he is lying, ʔubadčəm."

The Indians sat in big half-circles in front of this great man from the white father in Washington, D.C. They heard him talking. He talked in English, and then what he said was translated into the Indian languages. The first interpreter was Michael Simmons. He was listed as the Indian agent and he spoke Chinook Jargon. He could understand what the Indians were asking for and so he talked. Governor Stevens talked just a short time, and then Michael Simmons explained in Chinook Jargon, a trade language, to the Snohomish, since they happened to be the nearest tribe to Mukilteo, and then all the way back on the beach the men from the other tribes were sitting. There were mostly men present, but the women came too. They sat in large half circles in front of Governor Stevens.

My grandparents said a table was there that, apparently, came on the sailing ship the *Decatur* with Stevens on that day. They and the older people I talked to said there were soldiers with the governor. They wore blue uniforms with gold buttons, but they didn't march off of the ship onto the beach. They walked and stood to the side of the governor—up in front. The soldiers stood on each side of him; then the others stood somewhat back from him. Of course, some of the Indians resented that because it was a show of power. It was harassment and intimidation since, as I said, the Indians had already talked about this. Michael Simmons had already talked to them about the treaty. The Indians were there ten days before they signed the treaty. They talked for hours and hours about what they were going to do.

Pre-Treaty Discussions

I want to talk about the person who was the ninth signer on the original copy of our treaty, Sqʷəšəb. My grandparents called him Sqʷəšəb, which means "mist," "fog," but on the treaty they called him Smoke. The name Sqʷəšəb is like the morning mist. Smoke is what the white man could think of.

On the days before January 22, he was the one who spoke the loudest. The Snohomish met back in their camps after they arrived. The minutes of the treaty say the Snohomish Tribe arrived the day before, on the twenty-first.

George Gibbs, who wrote the minutes, said the Snohomish and Snoqualmie are in now, so the Indians are all in. The Snohomish were there days before, but sometimes they went back to Whidbey Island, to Possession Point, where a large longhouse of the Snohomish Tribe was located, and they talked. Several tribes met, and they talked about what they were going to do about this treaty.

Sqᵂəšəb of the Snoqualmie Tribe jumped up and spoke (my parents and grandparents said) at a big council. He said, "Why should we sign anything? Don't sign anything. That piece of paper is the white man's piece of paper. Let the white man sign his paper; that is his paper. Let the white man sign it, because we don't know what it says. The white man will tell us what it says, but we don't know what it says. Don't sign anything. Let's kill them all. Why should we let them live? They are going to change everything. We don't have to listen to them."

If you look at a map of Washington State, you will see that the Snoqualmie River is also another river that rises in the Cascades, but it empties into the Skykomish, and then into the Snohomish River.[2] Sqᵂəšəb of the Snoqualmie is the one who articulated the thoughts of many of the Indians in his remarks, such as, "Why should we sign it?"

Another who spoke was my father's uncle, Tyee William. My great-uncle was one of those who said, "Why not sign the treaty? We are not going to be allowed to go home. You see what we have to go through every day. There are soldiers here, and they are here with their guns. They come here, get off of that ship and then stand around here with their guns. We have to sign that treaty—we should. We better sign it. Then we can all go home. Later on, perhaps, we can talk about this again. Maybe there will be a different white people we can talk to. There is no use trying to protest and create trouble. There is no choice. There is no choice." This is what Tyee William said. On the Treaty he is called Stishail. He was one of the young chiefs there, my father's uncle, his father's older brother. I have always been sorry I don't remember him, my father's eldest uncle. His thumbprint is on the original treaty. He wore a cross, on a black ribbon, around his neck that was given to him by Father Chirouse.

The chief they called Club Shelton—his Indian name was Tləbšiɫtəd—was my father's great uncle. My great-great-grandfather was Tləbšiɫtəd's brother.

---

2   This geography lesson is also political and social history that illustrates the relationship between these three groups.

He spoke, and he said, "Tell the white man they are welcome to live on this land as long as they want to. We will sign a paper where we will allow them to use our land and then they can just pay us so much for a year. Someday in the future we will talk about it again, but to sign something and make it final—that we will sell the land and we take the reservation—we should not do that."

Some of the other Indians talked and said that it would be better if we could do that, but one of the things Governor Stevens told them at the meetings was, "You will sign the treaty. The white father in Washington, D.C., wants this paper to be signed. He wants everything straight between the Indians and the white people." So the Indians themselves were not together. They were not of one mind.

"If we go to war . . ." Some of the older Indians said, "Yes, we can go to war and kill a lot of them. We could get some of the Indians to join us and, like Sqʷəšəb said, 'Kill them all.' Then in ten days there would be no white people's eyes to see the break of day. They would all be dead."

Many of the Indians answered and said, "We can do that, but where is our enemy?" "čiad tiyaʔatosʔ" Aʔtos is "enemy"; čiad is "where." "Where is our enemy? He is coming from the sea. Coming from the west in ships. Coming over the mountains. Coming from the north, from the King George men. Coming from the south. These people who are our enemies are all around us. We cannot fight an enemy like that. Our enemy has to be in front of us." Any enemy has to be in front of you, but if he is also at your back and at your right and at your left, then you are indeed surrounded. You would have to make the best of that kind of surrender. That is what these Indians did. They talked about it, and they knew we had lost. We had lost just about everything, but we will hope the white man means what he says when he comes with the treaty. We will talk about everything that we wish for, that we are asking for."

But many of them said, "Let's not sign the treaty. Why should we?" Tləbšiłtəd was one of them who said we should not sign anything. He was one of the people who left the treaty signing on January 22. He got up and announced that he was not going to stay and sign anything. He called on his people to leave, and he left. Two or three people left with him, but the majority of the Indians stayed there.

So, when we talk about the treaty, that is all it is, just a treaty that the Indians signed. No one knows or remembers how much trouble, how much worry they lived through, and how much discussion they had among themselves. When I think of them, I always feel lost. Personally, myself, I feel lost.

They had no attorneys to advise them or to talk with them. Their leader was Governor Stevens. He was supposed to be standing up for their rights. The one who was representing them, or talking for them, was Michael Simmons the Indian agent and the superintendent of the Territory. Many Indians said they thought if Michael Simmons was there, everything was all right. Those Indians could not read or write. They could not understand the English language. The sections of the treaty were explained in the beginning, first by Governor Stevens, who talked, and then by Michael Simmons, in Chinook Jargon.

Young people today wonder about the treaty. Wayne, my son, read the treaty when he was a sophomore in high school. He read it two or three times. When he came home from school in the afternoon he would read for two or three hours. Several days after he read our treaty, he came into our dining room, where I was drinking coffee, and said, "If they presented a thing like this to us today we would refuse to sign it." I said, "Anybody who could read would refuse to sign it. It is just nothing but a pile of words." He said, "Why does it say in our treaty that we should have a doctor, a nurse, a farmer, and a blacksmith? Why did they ask for a blacksmith?" You have to think about the time—the 1850s. If you read the history of the United States, you will find out that the blacksmiths had a lot to do with conquering the West.

Blacksmiths made the covered wagons. They made the wheels, and they put on the steel rims that covered the wagon wheels. Without the steel rims, the pioneers would have been a lot slower coming across the great continent. So the blacksmith made wheels or whatever people wanted. He made anything that a city or community or village wanted, such as fry pans. He could make kettles. Some of the early blacksmiths, during the Revolutionary War, were gunsmiths. They could make not only guns but revolvers. So the Indians asked for a blacksmith.

They asked for a doctor and a nurse because people were already dying of the white man's diseases. Smallpox had already swept this area about the time of the treaty. Whole families, whole tribes were absolutely wiped off the face of the earth. There was no doctor, and of course, the Indians had never seen smallpox before. The raging fever meant to them that they should take a cold bath, or they used the sweat bath and they were dead almost instantly. So that was one of the things that these Indians talked about. Some of the tribes who are listed on the treaty are now extinct.

The Signing

My grandfather said that hour after hour, paragraph after paragraph, the treaty was read in English, and since George Gibbs wrote it, he read it aloud. Then Michael Simmons translated it into Chinook Jargon. We had another Indian there. I don't remember his Indian name,[3] but his English name was John Taylor. He is also mentioned in the treaty.[4] He was the interpreter. He interpreted the treaty from the Chinook Jargon, since George Gibbs read it in English. Then it was translated, first of all into Snohomish because they were seated closest to Mukilteo to the side. Then the Lummis—they translated it into their language. Then it was translated into the languages of all of the other tribes—Skagit, Samish (their language is similar to ours, but Lummi is different), and so on. There were three interpreters who helped John Taylor: Pat Kanim, Chowitshoot, Goliah; these three . . . and Sdapəlq.[5] So, it took hours to translate it. After they heard each paragraph, the leaders said, "That is all right. That is what we asked for."

My grandmother didn't get to the council meeting. They didn't bring the girls to the Mukilteo council meeting. They just kept them at home. The men and the boys came if the families were there and camping around Mukilteo. A lot of the women went to the treaty, but most of them stayed at home with the children. Some tribes were very strict about women being there in a council, but some of the men told their wives to come and sit behind them. The women did not sit in the line of council. If they brought their son or daughter, the daughter sat behind too. They have been asked by their children and grandchildren, "What did you hear?"

As they came up to sign on January 22, 1855, the first one who signed was Isaac I. Stevens. It says on the treaty that he was governor and superintendent. Below him was Chief Seattle, the chief of the Duwamish and Suquamish tribes. Of course, you could almost tell where his territory was: the Duwamish River, Lake Washington, and what is now Seattle. He was the first Indian

---

3   Sah-ghu-ghlas (Maryott and Shelton 1938:162).
4   See Duwamish et al. 1927.
5   Quoting Ruth Shelton, Mrs. Dover's mother. The tribal affiliations are Snoqualmie, Lummi, Skagit, and Snohomish. Sdapəlq was Bonaparte Sr.

man who signed the treaty. He was one of the older men. He liked the white people because he was living at Seattle, near the Duwamish River, so that the people he met happened to be nice people.

The second Indian man who signed the treaty was Pat Kanim, chief of the Snoqualmie. The treaty said he is chief of the Snohomish, but some of the Snohomish very deeply resented that statement. He was not a chief of the Snohomish.

The third signer is Chowwitsut, chief of the Lummi. The Lummi are the Indians who have a reservation near Bellingham.

The fourth signer is called Goliah. He had an Indian name, but the secretary decided he wouldn't even try to write it. Then he asked him if he had an English name. He asked all of them, "Do you have another name, besides?" They said no, but many of them had been baptized because priests were here just before that time. But this man did say "Goliah," so it says Goliah in the treaty. He is a chief of the Skagit Tribe, which is the name of another river, the Skagit River.

The next one is xʷəltəb, which is how it is pronounced in our language. Here, in the treaty, he is called Kwalatum(b). He is another chief of the Skagit Tribe.

The next one is Sxotčsut, another one of the chiefs of the Snohomish Tribe.

I was always interested in this next one. On the treaty it says Sdapəlq, or Bonaparte. The white man called him Bonaparte. He was, it says here on the treaty, a subchief of the Snohomish, but he was one of the chiefs.

Then, of course, the next one is Sqʷəšəb, subchief of the Snoqualmie, and he is the one who said, "Let's kill them all."

Then, the next one after Sqʷəšəb is Siʔaləpəʔəd, or Seallapahan, who was also called "the Priest." He came from a smaller tribe, but he was also a devout Catholic, even by this time. If you should ever read the history of the Catholic Church here, this Seallapahan is part of that history.

The next one is Hixʷəčkaydəm [Heehuchkaydim], George Bonaparte. He is a subchief of the Snohomish. Just remember, George Bonaparte.

The next one is Sədaʔtalq. The treaty has his mark. His English name is Joseph Bonaparte. He is one of the chiefs of the Snohomish Tribe.

The Bonaparte Family

Now, there are two Bonaparte brothers. There is Hixʷəčkaydəm, George Bonaparte, and Sədaʔtalq, Joseph Bonaparte. The seventh name on the treaty is Sədaʔtalq; he was called just Bonaparte. On the treaty they are called Napoleons. He was the father, and those were his two sons, Joseph and George. I am very interested in them because this is a part of our unwritten history.

At treaty time the Indians were told that, in one year, they were to come down to Tulalip. They were to move to the Tulalip Reservation. The year would have been 1856. They did come, but there was nothing here — no agent — although there were three white men who had homes here and they had a mill. The Indians stayed for a month. Then, "since there is no Indian agent and no white people," they went back to their longhouses along the Snohomish River and over on Whidbey Island. It was too cold here at Tulalip because they came in November or December, after the fall fishing. Then the Indians were more upset.

My grandfather lived on Whidbey Island when a confrontation took place between the Bonapartes and another family that is mentioned here. I don't like to mention the name because they are a big family here on this reservation, and they are quite as belligerent as their great-grandfather. He, the leader of this family, blamed the Bonapartes, Sədaʔtalq, for the situation they were in. He was angry, and he said, "All right. What have you brought us to?" When I say these words, I hope you remember they did not speak English, but that is what the words meant. "What have you brought us to? You signed the paper. Where is our reservation? Where is some of the food they said they would bring? There are more and more white people running all over, going crazy, picking up all of the land. Just see where our people are. They are hungry over there on the Tulalip Reservation, and here we are.[6] There is no room on Tulalip for us. There is no agent, no white man over there to tell us what to do. We have drunken white men going by here in rowboats. They shoot at the Indians. There is no peace. There is nothing here anymore, and it is all your fault. It is what you did." The older man, Bonaparte, said, "We did the best we could. We had no choice. We had to sign it and hope the white man would live up to it."

They got into a big argument, and they threatened each other, and they

---

6 The tribal members weren't told the treaty had not yet been ratified by Congress.

met on a trail about halfway between Sandy Point and Useless Bay on Whid-bey Island. Most of the Indians who lived there were on the reservation, but some were still living at Sandy Point. A lot of Indians lived there before they went down to Tulalip. It was a lovely sandy beach. Then farther south from there on Whidbey Island is Useless Bay. That is the name of it, but the Indians had a different name. The longhouse was at Dəgʷasx̌, which was the Indian name for Useless Bay. It means "an inlet." My father and his group used to get upset with the white people calling it Useless Bay. I remember when I was little the beach was the greatest place to play. You could run, run, run on that beach.

Many of the Indians who lived at Sandy Point were on the reservation, but some were still there and they got into an argument. This is one time that I speak of on Whidbey Island. The younger Bonapartes had become addicted to whiskey. They were alcoholics. My grandmother used to tell about it when she was visiting us. They didn't talk about it all of the time. Long after my grandparents were dead, I asked my father and he repeated it again.

One leader said, "I am going to kill them. What they have brought us is—Well, where are we? We've got no reservation. We've got no place to go. Nobody to tell us anything."[7]

My grandfather was with the Bonapartes (I will call them Bonapartes). He was a young man. He wasn't married then, and he happened to be in the village with Napoleon. Napoleon's name was Sədaʔtalq. One of his sons had his name. On the treaty he is called Snatalq. In their argument, the Indians were divided into two groups. They were "broken up"—worried—over the argument between these two families, these two leaders.

The two brothers were very drunk. But they got ready for the confronta-tion because a runner came, an Indian runner, who said so-and-so "is coming after you and he has his group with him. They are going to kill you. They are going to meet you on the trail (between Dəgʷasx̌ and Sandy Point) right away." But these two brothers were so drunk. Their father talked to them and said, "I will go." One brother said, "No, we will go and meet them on the trail." They knew where they were to meet, because the Indians had names for places such as the bays, the points of land; whether they were called Sandy Beach, the Place of Brown Leaves, or whatever. The Indians knew where that was. So the brothers got ready.

---

7 Settlers were pressuring the native people to leave their villages so that they could claim homesteads.

They got their guns, muzzle-loaders, which will only fire once. Their wives cried and tried to hold them by the arms and begged them not to go. "Don't go. You can talk to them tomorrow when you are sober. You are not well. You can't talk to anybody now." They got ready and fixed their knives. Indian men carried knives—and I think a lot of the pioneers did too. They were double-bladed knives that were several inches long. My father said his folks told how terrible it sounded when they were getting ready: sharpening their knives and spears. Their wives still begged them not to go, but they went. They jerked their arms away from their wives and they left.

My grandfather [Wheakadim] said they had on calf-length moccasins and just a breechcloth. Indian men didn't wear the white man's trousers and shirts then. My grandfather's relatives said to him, "Take a gun." So he was one of those who went along. But he said when they met the other group, the leading man said, "I have come to kill you. You signed that paper, and we don't know what it said." The young men were trying to raise their guns, and that Indian pointed at him, and my grandfather said they both fired at the same time. The first brother, Joseph, tried to aim, but he was drunk and he was the one who got killed. The leading man killed him. Then, of course, the other brother fired, but that shot went far away. The other chief said, "All right, that's how I feel about you. I refused to sign the treaty. You signed it, and you are responsible for what is happening to us." He turned around and left because by then the old man, Bonaparte, the father, who went along with them, was trying to pick up his son, but he was already dead. The shot went right through his heart. They brought the body back to the longhouse. Then there was nothing but sadness, nothing but divided families. Other Indians said, "We will pay them back. They aren't going to get away with this."[8]

My father and the others said that it was too bad because those two younger men were just very nice, very kind people. They were helpful and kind to all people.

My mother saw Tləbšiłtəd when she came here in 1878, and she saw him just the one time at a meeting. She said he was a very austere man. He never smiled. He never said one word. My mother, coming from another tribe, went to the meeting with her cousins and they listened. When he did speak, he got up and he said, "You folks do what you want to do. I haven't anything

---

8   This incident at Scadget Head was reported in the *Pioneer Democrat*, September 18, 1857, page 2, column 3. According to the article, the mother, the two sons, and two other Indians were killed and several were wounded.

to say." I can't recall what they were talking about. I think it had to do with setting aside some of their land for a cemetery. He said, "I wash my hands of the whole thing. You folks do what you want to do. You're the ones that signed the treaty—not me." All of his life he was somebody who was just out there all by himself. He was my paternal grandmother's uncle. I don't think she liked him that well either; it seemed like she was a little afraid of him. As I said, he was an austere man.

My mother heard Tləbšiłtəd's younger brother, Steshail, and that was my great-grandfather's brother.

So when you read about the treaty, the white man is always so sure he brought us such a great thing. He brought us civilization. Actually, the people who signed this treaty were putting their lives on it because many Indians said, "I won't sign anything." No, they signed the treaty knowing one thing: It is not going to be any good, because that man was lying. Governor Stevens, the representative from the white father in Washington, D.C., was standing there lying to the Indians. The government didn't build a school, like they said they would—not for fifty years. There was no hospitalization for the Indians, no medical care. Medical care was just for the students in the boarding school.

Mission Beach at the turn of the twentieth century.

William Weallup and his wife cleaning salmon. Photograph by Norman Edson.

The Shelton family home at Mission Beach. Parents William and Ruth with children Harriette, Robert, Ruth, and William Alphonse.

William and Ruth with children William Alphonse, Ruth, and Thelma.

Grandmother Medline (Magdelene, or x̌adⁿk̓oliksə).
Photograph by Ferdinand Brady.

Tulalip leaders. Front row, from left: Charlie Hillaire and son Philander, Frank
LeClaire, Chief William Shelton, Bob Gwahadolch, Tommy Johnson, George Sneatlum. Back row, from left: William McLean, (name unknown), George Bob, Josie Celes-
tine, Charlie Sam, Alphonse Bob, John Brown.

Family members and other relatives picking hops. Martha Lamont (hand over face), Ruth, William, Robert Shelton, Magdelene Wheakadim, and Mary Moses.

A work party for the Priest Point cemetery.

2 / Settling on the Reservation

THE Indians came down to Tulalip after the fall fishing, in November or December, because they said it was already cold. The year was 1856, because the treaty was signed in 1855. They had been told to come one year later and they did, but there was nobody here from the government to meet them—no agent. No one came to tell them that the treaty was not yet ratified by Congress. The Treaty of Point Elliott was ratified on April 11, 1859.

Living Conditions

There was no housing and no water for the people who came, except for two creeks that were one half mile and another one mile away. Indian people were living at Spibida and Quilceda, and later at Priest Point, where Father Chirouse and another priest founded the Catholic Mission; that was how it came to be called Priest Point. But in Tulalip Bay there was not enough housing available for all of the Indians who came. If you were married with two babies, you would have to walk all of the way down here to this little creek and carry two buckets of water to do your washing. It is pretty hard to keep children clean, to keep yourself and your clothes clean. The reservations were like that—no housing and no water. The policy was to move Indian people onto the reservation and tell them to stay there.

By the fifth or sixth year after the Indians signed, they could certainly see the effects of the treaty. People were starving on the reservation. I think the starvation for the Indians was really worse in the Middle West, but for the Indians here it was bad enough because there were times the whites ordered these Indians not to leave the reservation.

During the Chief Joseph War in 1876–77, the Indians all over were ordered to stay on the reservation, nobody could leave. Some of the Indians would go over to Whidbey Island on their canoes to hunt or to dig clams. The revenue cutter, the United States launch, or whatever, by that time had steam engines; it would stop the Indians and tell them they had to go back to the reservation. "You can't go anyplace." My mother remembered that; she was older than my father. She remembered when she was a little girl that they were ordered to go back to Guemes Island. So, that was another time of great worry. My father was growing up on Whidbey Island where he was born, and he said every morning at daybreak all of the Indians there at Sandy Point and at Possession Point — what is now called Useless Bay, if you look at the map — would look and watch the day come. And my father and the others, my grandparents, would remember, what the Indians would say. "Where is he? Is he still all right?" Talking about Chief Joseph, because now and then white people would come by and say there is a big war. The army is chasing this man and his whole tribe. These Indians listened and tried to pray and hoped that Chief Joseph was all right. Every morning they watched the daybreak coming over the mountains. And I am telling you, young people, do that some time. Get up at three o'clock in the morning and watch the daybreak come. Even in a place like this you see the morning star, and it moves up really fast, but years back when I was growing up, my father would wake me up and over on Whidbey Island would want me and all of us young people to watch the day come, watch the day come over the Cascade Mountains. It is a very beautiful, majestic sight.

The Indian tribes I know about were people who bathed in the morning in cold water — in lakes, creeks, or certain rivers. The women would go to one place and the men to another. Western Washington is full of rivers and a lot of lakes, so everybody, as soon as they get up, can walk to the place where they are going to wash their faces and their teeth and take a bath. When the Indians moved onto the reservations, we read about how dirty, filthy the white people thought the Indians were. I would like to point out that the Indians, when they were put on reservations, were a displaced people, and not only displaced but they were dispossessed.

They moved to reservations from their old villages with just what they could carry. People here had longhouses that were scattered all over where they lived, and when they got on the reservation there was no housing, no readily accessible water. It was just a wilderness. But then Indians could get along — except for not having water. I thought it was no wonder they were considered dirty. If you had to walk two, three miles to carry a bucket of water when you wanted to bathe or cook or wash clothes, you can only do that two or three times a day.

When the Indians arrived in the bay, the women found it harder to walk half a mile or a mile to carry water. They had to carry water home in buckets, but usually the children and teenage boys and girls helped them. I remember when we were little we helped carry water. We carried smaller buckets of water to the house. If three or four people are going to take a bath, you have to carry a lot of water. If they were going to do laundry, they had to carry buckets and buckets of water. It is really hard to do laundry if you have to carry buckets of water.

I remember seeing people with tin tubs filled with water on an open fire, so that there would be a lot of water. When my grandmother and anyone washed clothes, it took all day. They had to carry the water, heat it, and wash the clothes on a washboard. They used big bars of yellow soap to wash the clothes. I used to help my grandmother and my mother hang up the clothes.

When I was in the boarding school, I saw Indians come down to the waterfront and get big buckets or cans, like milk cans and coal-oil cans, that they used to wash with soapy water and rinse and then fill the cans with water and carry them back home on the wagons.

You wouldn't think water would be a problem in western Washington because there seems to be water everywhere. The water here from Mission and Tulalip Creeks was fresh; it is running or moving water. I remember that the creek just over the hill from where we lived at Mission had clear running water. Sometimes when we had a lot of playmates, we went over there where the pipe was running for the horses and cows to drink from a trough. We used to go there in summer and play and put our faces in it. It was really cold, and we looked at each other and laughed, with water all of the way up to our heads—just soaking wet.

Here at Tulalip, you would think there was a lot of water, but not with 1,500 Indians camped out all around this bay. It was hard to keep clean and to keep children clean. Children are always into everything. They can find the nicest places to play, and they can sit right down in gravel or just dirt, even if part of it is a little bit of mud. It doesn't matter. If part of it is grass, they will play and get dirty. I think I am always trying to explain to people why we were considered dirty, and why we were considered stupid. Of course, the Indians eventually learned how to dig wells, and many of them have wells.

Shelter

The Indians who didn't live here at Tulalip Bay, near there or on the islands, moved down from their villages. Our Snohomish Tribe had their biggest longhouse at Possession Point on Whidbey Island. Several hundred Indians lived there together. We didn't live in tepees. The roof was open during the day. Some of the large, wide boards were lifted so the sun could shine in; or even if there was no sun and it was not raining, then they could open it anyway, so there was constant fresh air in a big longhouse. When they moved to the reservations, these Indians built their own homes, and it was easy for them because they already knew how. But they didn't have the ventilation of the big houses, and this contributed to the poor living conditions and the high incidence of deaths due to tuberculosis, as well as a poor diet later. Indian people were forbidden to build the traditional longhouses. They were supposed to drop all of their Indian ways.

Of course, the Indians took care of one another. They made speeches about staying together and helping one another. They had their own organizations, their own leaders. They lived together in extended families, living and sharing. The grandparents were the babysitters and took care of the children while the mothers and fathers cleared land. The Indians were such good workers. It took a while for the Indians to make enough money to buy the axes and saws to cut down the trees. You would need thousands of dollars to clear the land, let alone build a house. So they helped each other to build their little one-room shacks. They made their own shakes. Today, cedar shakes are very expensive. Way back then, Indians made them by the thousands. They cut down a cedar tree, sawed it, and then split the shakes, because they were, after all, natural woodsmen.

I have a picture of a man and his wife in front of one of those shacks. The Indian is an old man, and all of his children and grandchildren are gone. There are just these people left, and somebody helped them put the shack together. Somehow he was able to have money, and they bought a window. When I was growing up, those were the kind of houses I saw. They were either one or two rooms, and they were made of shakes.

Some of the women I saw were elderly, like I am now, and their family had died years before. They were all alone. In some of those pictures, you see elderly people sitting in front of their cabins made out of shakes. One of Edson's pictures shows an elderly lady or two in front of their mat house. The pictures are entitled "Indian Summer Camp." It is not a summer camp. It is their permanent home—although, a mat house can be warm because the mats are woven double and made of tall cattails that grow in wet places.

I have a cattail mat. You can see the way it is woven with a big wooden needle and sewn together with material from the cattail itself. An Indian woman would peel a thread off the very edge of each cattail. When it is dry, then they spin the thread on a spindle whorl. My mother also used to spin her wool yarn that way. They spun the cattail edging and made a strong twirled rope, like twine, and that is what they used to sew the matting together. Cattail mats were woven double in opposite directions: each cattail was laid over the other, like shingles are on a roof to make it watertight. They were windproof and almost, but not quite, watertight.

My parents had several large ones that were six feet wide and probably ten to fifteen feet long. They made them double and piled them high, and when you lay down on them, they were very soft.

Way of Life

Indians settled on reservations all over the United States. Indian reservations were much smaller than the areas the Indians had lived on. The Indians' way of life in the Northwest was a hunting and a food-gathering culture. It was not like the pioneers. They stayed in one place and planted their food, and the ones that planted, who were the farmers, raised enough food for many people. We didn't plant anything. We just harvested. Indians knew where to go for certain roots, berries, and all of the native foods. But when they moved to the reservations, then their hunting grounds were within the boundaries of the reservation and so starvation was a very great problem. Of course, to white people it didn't make any difference. They could see an Indian dying of starvation and they wouldn't know the difference.

I like the way Alvin Josephy put it. He tells what was happening to the Indians from 1860 to the new century in 1900.[1] In his book is a picture of a very old, old lady. Her hair looks about like mine, uncombed, and she is sitting on the ground, resting on one hand, on a little rug. I told some people, as we were looking at it, "This woman is dying of tuberculosis. I can tell. She is very, very weak." When the photographer got there, he probably said to bring her out here. "Tell her I will take her picture." She was inside a tent. So they brought her out. The other Indians who were there were not going to argue with a white man. He might have a revolver. So this poor lady was brought out and her picture was taken. You look at it and you will know one thing: Indians are dirty and stupid. They never combed their hair, because this woman's hair was tangled. She must have been lying for days and weeks, too

---

1   Alvin Josephy, *Indian Heritage of America* (New York: Knopf, 1968).

weak to get up. The Indians in that period, from the late 1850s, were starving there, and, as a matter fact, the Indians were starving on this reservation.

It was not complete starvation: hunger might be a better word, because our Puget Sound bays were rich, and the resources—salmon, trout, flounders, clams, mussels, and oysters—were all around us. We were certainly the richest people in the world, as far as food was concerned. In the woods there were deer and elk and, of course, smaller animals like rabbits. (If Indians ever ate rabbits, I never saw them. My folks never ate rabbit. There was so much food to eat; I don't think they would bother with such a small animal.) Deer and elk were plentiful here too, and they didn't have to go far to hunt. So that is part of our history.

But the Indians here were moved onto small reservations where there were no rivers. Each of the tribes in western Washington had a river. The Lummi fished the Nooksak River near the Canadian border. The Skagit River was south of there, where the Skagit Indians and some other tribes lived and fished. We had the Snohomish River, and the tribe affiliated with us—the Skykomish Tribe—they had the Skykomish River. The Snoqualmie Tribe had the Snoqualmie River.

Large areas were available for hunting, from the Cascade Mountains all of the way to Puget Sound—millions of acres of hunting and fishing lands. It was a shock for the Indians to move to a smaller area, even though this was part of their land too. We moved to a reservation where there were huge trees, and that was the richness of western Washington that was noted by Captain Vancouver of England who came here in 1792. He made a voyage around the Puget Sound, and he talked about the forests as a vast resource in western Washington.

We had the native food, but the timber has just about disappeared. They had to go from a way of life of abundance to a reservation where they had to start from scratch—just like the pioneers did. But there was a difference, a vast difference, between the Indians moving onto the reservation and the white pioneers. The area for hunting and gathering along this reservation is not enough to sustain 1,200 or 1,500 people. Our people went to the Cascade Mountains in late August for a certain kind of mountain berries and a certain kind of roots on the prairies. There weren't enough vegetables for several hundred people. Anyway, for the camas roots these Indians sometimes would go to Puyallup or Fort Lewis and dig baskets of camas roots. They would stay for a week and dig those. They didn't have money to buy food such as potatoes or rice. Just about every Indian woman made socks to sell, and that was how they made their money to buy food. They were not what you would call an agricultural people who stayed in one place and raised garden produce and hogs or chickens. Our hunting areas were on Whidbey Island and Camano Island. There were no clams to gather around here at Tulalip to supplement our diet as we would ordinarily. It was a bad time.

The Indians way back then couldn't go wherever they wanted. They were ordered to go back to their reservation and stay there. If the agent didn't tell them to stay there, they could go to other places to get native foods, such as the roots and bulbs the Indians used to eat for vegetables. Our people went out in their canoes to the islands, such as Whidbey Island and Camano Island, to hunt, and in the summer for fishing, drying of salmon, and digging clams. There were no clams here at Tulalip. If they couldn't go to those places, they would have no winter food. You could have pretty good food even if you didn't have a job. Besides fishing for fresh salmon or fresh trout, you could have roast duck, geese, or maybe pheasant. When my mother was living, she used to smoke-dry five hundred salmon every year. Then you work for several days filleting salmon. But, as I say, the reservation was too small to support 1,500 people in a hunting-and-gathering way of life. Indian reservations were never set aside as a good hunting ground or a good fishing ground.

The Indians used to smoke-dry salmon by the basketsful. I think a lot of pioneer families smoked bacon or hams, but for us, they were all dried salmon and they were all prepared the same way: filleted open and kept open by little sticks of cedar and then hung up in the smokehouses and dried and smoked evenly all around. They lasted us through the winter and spring, but they were also given to a number of elderly people. My mother would have baskets for them because the old people can't do that anymore, dry or fillet a lot of fish.

We used to dry the salmon eggs too. I remember eating salmon eggs. They stick to your teeth, so you have to chew very hard. My father used to tell me, "Just chew it good." Today white people use salmon eggs for fish bait. I'm not sure, but I don't think anybody eats it anymore. I was saying once, "Oh, you don't know what you are missing. If you want to feel better, just eat salmon eggs that have been baked in an oven." I remember some white people were talking about salmon eggs, and they wondered how we could eat fish heads and salmon eggs. I said, "You ought to try it if you want to look young when you are seventy-five years old. Just look at me. I ate a lot of it when I was growing up. I haven't had salmon eggs for a long, long time."

When the Indians moved onto the reservations, they lost their hunting and fishing grounds. Indian reservations were set aside so that Indians were pretty much out of the way. They were not farmers. Most of the land out here was too gravelly, anyway, to be suited for gardening—and so much of it was without water—but that is what the government wanted the Indians to do. So when the Indians moved here they were supposed to clear the land, which they did. In the 1914 Annual Report of the Commissioner of Indian Affairs, these Indians were ordered to farm. I remember when I was growing up, wherever we happened to go in the summertime, seeing Indians clearing land. They did nearly all of it by hand. They cleared the land not with dynamite or tractors; they didn't have those. They used fire. Some of them had teams of horses, so the big trees were cut down and they burned the stumps. Those stumps would burn for days and days; it seemed to me then that they were burning forever.

It takes a while to clear this kind of land, with its wilderness shrubs, wild roses, salmonberry bushes, and so many trees. Even if you planted apple trees, plums, or pears, they would take several years to grow and produce. Although Indians did learn the new ways. Many had orchards. Up to about ten to fifteen years ago, if you walked through the woods—back through this reservation—where there were a lot of alders, it was like a wilderness. There were apple trees in bloom. My mother and father knew whose allotment that was. There in the woods would be an apple tree with the prettiest apple blossoms. Or, once in a while, there would be pear trees blooming.

Indians left their allotments to go to the Puyallup Valley to pick hops in September or October. They talked to my father and asked him to come and look after their orchard, because all through the summer the bears would come and climb up the apple and pear trees and the branches would be torn and broken down from the trees. Bears killed a lot of the trees. They climb it, or they use it for their claws.

When I was little nearly all the Indians had chickens, so that they had a few eggs. However, if you moved to a place anywhere out here, you would have to go out and find work to buy food and that was usually in a mill or picking hops. The hop fields were owned by the pioneers; it was their way of having an income too.

I don't know why I should remember this, but my mother and all of them used to get together and go picking blackberries. My mother and her cousins, different friends, were way out there where there was a big patch of wild blackberries. My mother was busy picking, and she started to talk because she could hear, she was sure it was Mary Ann, her cousin, just on the other side of a big patch that went up several feet. So my mother was talking to her and she was moving along, and she wondered why Mary Ann didn't answer her because it sounded like a grunt. Well, she finally got around the bush and there was a black bear and it was picking berries off the same vines where my mother was picking, only on the other side. The bear was sitting up and reaching with its paws and the berries would fall in its lap and it would eat them. My mother said it was just as if somebody poured a bucket of cold water over her. Here was this bear and it was only four feet away and she had been talking to it for probably twenty minutes. She finally saw that she could move, so she turned around and started to run toward the road. Well, you really can't run through the brush. Her cousin said she wondered what happened to my mother. She had lost her old hat and her hair had got caught in all kinds of vines and small trees, and instead of her hair being braided it was all torn apart. She said, "What's the matter?" My mother could hardly speak. She said, "I thought I was talking to you." So, they had to come home because, you might say, my mother was really shook up. Talking to a bear. She said it finally dawned on her that Mary Ann doesn't grunt like that; Mary Ann always talks. She only took one step and looked. Oh, she was being pals with a bear!

Hunger and Starvation

Thousands of dollars were appropriated for this reservation. The Indians never found out what the money was used for. The Indians were hungry, and they were sick because of the scourge that went over the whole continent—sicknesses the white people brought, such as measles and tuberculosis. The Indians caught colds and other illnesses they never had before. Indians died by the hundreds of thousands from pneumonia. They never saw or had that before. Measles and a cold could turn into tuberculosis, and the Indians could not stand up to it. Nobody could. If you don't have much to eat, you won't have the strength to stand up to it. Indian health was broken. Hunger was an additional traumatic shock.

Now and then, some of us older Indians who can remember way back to 1909 talk about when there were outstanding Indian athletes of the world. American Indian athletes of our time made quite a big name for themselves. People saw their pictures in the newspapers and magazines, with articles about the various reservations they came from. They used to compete in the Olympics in Europe. They were good runners—in distance and in everything the Olympics had to offer. The Indians were winners. Of course, everybody thinks of Jim Thorpe, but there were a lot of other Indian athletes who were as good as he was, and maybe better.[2] Jim Thorpe was a full-blooded Indian. He was at the Olympic games as a long-distance runner, and, of course, he could run the 220 or half mile. A faster runner came from the Navajo desert country. His last name was Tewanima. Tewanima competed during the same period of time as Jim Thorpe.

Another Indian came from northern Wisconsin. His father and mother died when he was young. He didn't remember them, and he grew up with his grandmother. They were so poor. When he was around nine years old, the agent took him away from his grandmother and sent him to Haskell Institute to get an education. I forgot his name, but I will always remember he grew up with his grandmother, and he talked about going out to pick wild rice with her. He said they ate it a lot. It was ground or pounded into flour and made into all kinds of food. It was maybe ten years before he got back home again. He had to stay in the Indian school.

All over the United States, in all of those years, Indians were good athletes. You never hear much about Indian athletes. The Indians that have been available, in the last fifty years, are boys who grew up in Indian boarding schools. If they are in the Olympics, they don't make much of an impression. Or if they are on any football team, the famous ones, you never hear about them.

Starvation was occurring all over on the reservations all of those years. Indian children were kept in the boarding schools on a starvation diet that became apparent when Indian children were growing up. Today if you go to an Indian gathering, it is very noticeable that many of them are overweight. They are the ones who survived on macaroni, no cheese, just macaroni and rice or bread. They don't have the strength, or the staying power, to be football players or any kind of an athlete. Public schools, like Marysville, exhibit racial prejudice against the Indian boys. Some of them would turn out for football or basketball if they were allowed to play.

However, I am sure someone will remember Sonny Sixkiller. Sonny was an outstanding quarterback at the University of Washington. I would like to remind people that Sonny Sixkiller did not grow up on an Indian reservation. His father moved off of the reservation, and they lived in a town in Oregon. So Sonny Sixkiller grew up where his father could work. The majority of Indians had to stay on reservations.

---

2   See Peter Nabokov, *Indian Running* (Santa Barbara, Calif.: Capra, 1988).

All of the years since the white man has been here have been terrible years. Even the Indian agent talked about how tragically poor the Indians were. You would have to live that kind of life—to be hungry day after day—to understand. You can be hungry. The white man can be hungry today, and he can go out tomorrow and maybe find a job. Maybe he could find a job today. He could change things.

Now, the white people who came here chose where they wanted to go. They took up a homestead and built a small house. They could farm. They had the choice. My parents and we Indian children—we had no choice, none whatever. We didn't have freedom of choice for one hundred years or more. We had to stay on this reservation. No place to go. We were really prisoners of war.

My earliest memories are the funerals and deaths of our people. I have seen Indian people die from the time I could remember. I must have been four or five years old when I watched one of my playmates die. The Indian women would get together when a child was dying or someone was dying. There was no doctor or medication, so the Indians did the best they could. I remember going with my mother. I was told to sit still and I did. I could sit still by the hours and watch my playmates die. I didn't sit or stand there and stare at them. The Indian ladies knelt down and they said the whole rosary. Prayers went on and on. I sort of learned them when I was small, but I could sit still for a long, long time. Dying and death were all around when I was little and growing up. The death rate among the Indians was very, very high.

The summer my sister died, there were three or four teenagers who died. Some of them were our schoolmates. There was seldom a week that went by without at least two funerals—that is eight Indian deaths a month. The young women who survived grew up and got married—then they would have their first baby. Sometimes the mother died after her first baby was born, so that left behind a little orphan—a little girl or a little boy. Sometimes the husband and the child also died. So there was nobody left from the families. Whole families died—just disappeared from the face of the earth.

My father had one sister younger than he. My aunt had four children, and all of them died before they were four years old. She was married to a man from British Columbia. I don't think it made much difference where they lived, because part of the time she lived up on Vancouver Island. The deaths were caused by poor diet and poor living conditions.

Alvin Josephy speaks of the death rate of the American Indians. It was really a stunning, staggering death rate. There were no doctors, no medication, no care, nothing. All of the young Indian people that I saw die were at home, and, of course, way back then there was not much medication for the pain of tuberculosis. Tuberculosis is not a disease that people worry about today, but for years it was. Now we worry about cancer and diabetes—not only for Indians but for the entire population of the United States. Those two diseases seem to be incurable, unless the people discover it early enough for treatment. But the American Indian death rate continued to be high until well into the 1930s.

Tribal Lands: Allotment

In 1887, as a result of the Dawes Act, the Bureau of Indian Affairs in the Department of the Interior of the federal government began to allot land to individual Indians.[3] All of the reservations in the United States were divided up into allotments of 80 or 160 acres each. Married men, heads of households, received an allotment—that was their land and it was in their name, but it was held in trust by the United States government. When they allotted this reservation, it was divided into ninety-five allotments; that meant there were ninety-five men who were heads of families, and a few women who were widows who had families, and so the allotments were in their names.

If there were only ninety-five allotments, that meant several hundred Indian families were left without any land. Indian leaders went to the agent and told him that some Indians didn't have any land and, furthermore, that he had wanted them moved away from the bay. The agent had said in 1902 that no Indians were to be living around the bay. They had to move to their allotments, clear the land, and start farming. Quite a bit of this land is too rocky, as I said, to try and start farming it. Most of it wouldn't be farmland, but that policy went on for many years.

We were no longer allowed to live together around the bay. We had to move out to nowhere, where there was hardly any water or roads or houses until the Indians built them, and the result of that was to separate us from one another.

---

3   Also Article 7 of the Point Elliott treaty provided for the reservation lands to be surveyed into lots that would be assigned to individuals or families.

The parade of canoes for guests arriving for Treaty Day.
Photograph by Ferdinand Brady.

Girls in their uniforms attend Treaty Day. Juleen Studio.

The grandmothers. Photograph by J. A. Juleen Studio.

Boys in their uniforms attend Treaty Day. Juleen Studio.

The newly constructed community house, c. 1920. Photograph by J. A. Juleen Studio.

The interior of the community house. Note the design of whales' mouths on the posts at the far end of the room. Photograph by J. A. Juleen Studio.

William Steshail and his wife, Lucy. Photograph by Edmond Meany. University of Washington Libraries, Special Collections, no. NA 1216.

The Shelton home, after 1923. From left: Ruth, William, Coy grandchildren, Harriette.

William Shelton working in the sawmill. Photograph by Ferdinand Brady.

The little canoes race. Photograph by Ferdinand Brady.

3 / Finding Work in the Early Days

WHEN I was small most Indians had little or no income. White people feel that Indians received money every month from the government. They did not. Many Indians were migratory field workers. They could get work picking hops. In the Puyallup Valley there were hundreds of acres of land owned by the pioneers who raised hops. Apparently, hops was one of the early crops when western Washington was first settled in the 1840s and 1850s, so that was one of the few things that Indians had to do. There were no commercial berry fields, no bean fields, no fruit orchards—just hop fields. In later summer the Indians went to the Puyallup Valley, and they stayed there until the end of August and September, or maybe they would come home in October or November at the end of the harvest. Even children worked picking hops.

My parents and the older Indians I knew said picking hops was hard work. I have a picture of my father and mother and grandmothers working in the hop fields. Hops grow on tall posts in rows, like berries. When they are being picked, the foreman cuts down each tall post of hops, and then you pick off the little blossoms. They are soft. You have to pick very fast because if you are slow, the whole thing sinks down when you fill up your container and it packs down. They put the blossoms in boxes and baskets. They used to tell me, "You are pulling the blossoms off of the vines." They used to wrap their fingers in an old sheet or an old bandage to protect them.

Maybe I can describe it. It is not a clear picture. You would have to sort of get an idea of the long rows. Hops have a very pungent odor if you get close to them. Even within a few yards you can smell them. It is not a bad smell. It just smells like some kind of plant, but some people got sick when they picked hops. Then, for working all day long, perhaps, all you got was fifty cents. Of course, way back then, you knew you could buy fifty cents worth of flour, and it would last you a week and buy five or ten cents worth of salt and a little baking powder. Then you have flour, salt, baking powder, and if you already had some lard you could have some fried bread.[1] The amount of money they made was not enough. They probably made $100 a year. If you catch salmon or trout, or have roast ducks or roast geese or native pheasant, then you have something to eat.

There was little work anywhere. Nobody would hire an Indian. Why should they? The white people would not in the first place, so Indians went around living without a penny of income. That is how they started: no jobs, no income. We had a reservation. But it would take money to clear the land, to dynamite the stumps. You need thousands of dollars to buy fencing—which the Indians didn't have—let alone build a house. But if you read the life stories of the pioneer farmers who came to Washington Territory in the 1840s or 1850s, you'll know that one of those was Ezra Meeker, who wrote *Pioneer Reminiscences of Puget Sound*. He became well known and he was wealthy. I think you can still see Ezra Meeker's home in Puyallup.

Nobody could actually starve way back then, but hunger was a very real problem. Nearly all of the pioneers that landed here didn't have any money. By and large, they were misfits. They left the Midwest or the East Coast and probably had no jobs. They came across the country in wagon trains. Anyway, hops fields were initiated by the pioneers, and that is where the Indians made their money.

Hops were used to make beer; and breweries (and liquor) were one of the things that the white man brought. They were all over. There was one in Mukilteo. The first thing that was in Seattle—that became Seattle—was Yesler's Mill. Henry Yesler had a brewery, and right next door or near it, as part of the same building, was a hotel. In the hotel were a lot of prostitutes. So there was big business: a mill, prostitution, and a hotel.

Maybe a dozen Indian men in the whole of western Washington could find work in a mill. The first mill was in Port Gamble. In later years, at least up to the 1930s, logging and the mills were the big thing out here. Mills were how they made a living. You look around Marysville and Everett, there are still one or two mills, but before, Everett was ringed with mills. Now there is only Weyerhaeuser and Scott Paper, when before, there was Simpson and several others.

Some of the Indian men were able to find work in the logging camps, but the camps could take only so many. Some logging camps were initiated

---

1   Also known as fry bread; it is a yeast bread, deep fried in oil, invented by American Indians.

and operated by the Indians themselves. Of course, they were slower than the bigger companies, but it was one of the ways that Indian families had some income. But the prices would fluctuate. Sometimes cedar was three dollars a thousand feet. I think now cedar must be a hundred or a hundred and fifty dollars for a thousand feet. Way back then, three dollars a thousand feet was high, too.

By 1900 and 1910, these Indians were logging by hand. Living here at home then, the only work was hand logging. You could work with your family if you had two or three teams of horses. By that time, one or two Indian families had trucks, but they couldn't carry big logs on them or anything larger than fifteen feet. They were not working with the big logging companies. I used to see a lot of hand logging, producing what are called cedar shingle bolts, which are four feet long and any diameter. They are made into shingles. Many Indian men cut shingle bolts and sold them to a shingle mill. You could be flat broke one day, and if you worked hard for two, three days, by Friday or Saturday you could get a wagonload of shingle bolts to a mill in Marysville. Then you could have three or four dollars to buy supplies. But the living was really not that much, even for the pioneers.

However, the white people could change things. A man coming from back east with thirty-five cents in his pocket, and that is all he owned, could rent or even make a rowboat, and he could go anywhere along Puget Sound and cut down huge cedar or fir trees. Some cedar trees were on the average over 140 feet tall and 8 or 9 feet in diameter. Some were 14 or 15 feet in diameter. They cut down a cedar tree, cut off the limbs, and tied it to their rowboat and took it to a mill. They could make money just by helping themselves. It might take him a week to get to the mill, but he could get the money. But for the Indians, it was another situation. They couldn't just go out and develop logging operations on the reservation. They had to get permission from the Indian agent.

As I said, Yesler built the first mill here. The Dennys and Dr. Maynard gave him land in the middle of what became Seattle. He also built a hotel, or what passed then for a hotel. The upper floor was full of prostitutes, who were Indian girls. The pioneers talked about Yesler's Hotel, which was full of Indian women and girls. I'll bet I know how they got there. I'll tell about the experiences of my mother and father.

They grew up in the 1870s and 1880s. They were married in 1890. In the late 1860s they saw this kind of thing: My mother used to tell about when she and her family (an extended family since they were six or eight canoe loads of Indians) were traveling from Guemes Island, which is near Anacortes. Guemes is one of the beautiful islands where my mother's people had their longhouses, and that is where they lived.[2] It took several days of traveling by canoes to get from there to the Puyallup Valley. They would come along the Sound, and they camped at night and ate at noon. They stopped and ate lunch. Then they would go up the Puyallup River to where Ezra Meeker's hop fields were. Now, they didn't talk about this incident I am going to tell all of the time, week after week, month after month, but every once in a while, different Indians would remember an event of this kind.

On one of these trips my mother had a cousin traveling with them who was the same age, fifteen. They stopped for a noon lunch after they left Anacortes, built a fire near Port Ludlow, and made tea. They noticed a rowboat following them and her uncles. My mother's uncles said, "There are two white men and a woman following us, it seems." The rowboat stopped about a block down the beach from them, and the two men and the woman got out. They started walking down the beach toward the Indians, and my mother's uncles put my mother and her cousin in a tent. They had some Indian bread they were going to fry. They put my mother and her cousin under some blankets. They knew they were looking for Indian girls, because they had heard about it. My mother heard them approach. They said "Hello" or "How do you do?" And they talked about where they were going. The Indians didn't speak English. The white and Indian people talked to one another in Chinook Jargon, which is a trade language. One of the men had a bottle of whiskey. He poured it into a tin cup and handed it to the Indian men. They shook their heads and said no. The woman said, "Just taste it." They had learned to speak those words: "Taste it." The men said it wouldn't hurt. The white woman took the cup from the white man and handed it to an Indian man, and she said, "Just taste it. It won't hurt. It won't hurt you. Just taste it." The Indian men said no. They shook their heads no. So she took a drink, and the men, they took a drink and said, "See? It's good." Well, the Indians talked about it. They noticed every time the woman and the men drank they took a big breath, took a swallow, and said, "Aah." The Indians noticed and wondered why they had to breathe like that after they swallowed all of it. Anyway, they tried to give them the whiskey, and the Indians wouldn't take it. They kept drinking to show the Indians that it didn't hurt. They weren't drunk and they could

---

2   Her father was Sehome, a Klallam leader, who had moved to the Samish area to be with his wife's family.

handle it. But they kept looking around, and the woman walked around the camp. The Indian women were making bread. She was looking for girls, of course. The whites finally left, but they kept following them.

The woman must have known there were several girls with them. Many Indians were orphan children because families had died off, and there were thousands of Indians dying. First of all was the smallpox epidemic, and after that the measles went around and around. Whole families died. So there were girls, sometimes eleven or twelve years old, who lived with their aunts and uncles. They were very lonely. They were heartbroken young people because they had lost their mother, lost their father, lost sisters and brothers. When these white men with white women said, "Now come with me and I'll take you to Seattle. Tell the other Indians you'll find her in Seattle. I'll buy her some dresses and shoes. She can work for me." The Indian girls can't speak English, and, besides, they know what a dress is. Well, she has a dress but maybe just one, and it has patches. She washed it and put it back on while it was still damp. She is still crying and will go with a stranger. She will think, "This might be better." The uncles would say to her, "No, no wait." Those kind of people—white men and women—would take the girls, load them up on the rowboats, and leave. The Indian men and their families could paddle on down to Seattle and walk up and down the streets, trying to find the girls. They asked white people—white men, because the white women in town wouldn't talk to the Indians and crossed to the opposite side of the muddy street, away from the saloons. The Indians walked along there, and they asked people; they tried to tell them they were looking for two or three Indian girls. After a while, they found out they could go to a priest or a preacher and talk about the girls who had disappeared. So the houses of prostitution were filled with Indian girls.

When the history books are written by white pioneers of Seattle or their descendants, they speak of the prostitutes in Yesler's Hotel. There were prostitutes in Port Townsend, too. They were Indian girls, and they landed there not knowing what kind of life it was. If the Indian uncle tried to get in to get his niece back, they wouldn't let him. What house of prostitution wants an Indian man? He was told to go to the back door where the kitchen is. They would say, "You can't come in here," give him a big cussing and slam the door. So they never found the girls again. Of course, my father and mother said it's highly unlikely those girls lived very long. They had lived an outdoor life and were then locked in places like that, where they could probably go out once or twice a week with the madam of the house. So I have no doubt that there were lots and lots of Indian girls that were prostitutes. They were all very young, and they got into it not knowing what it was. Once they were there, they couldn't get out and go home. There were white women, white girls, who were prostitutes too. Very likely they got into it not knowing what it was either, when they were first picked up.

In our old customs, the old tradition, prostitution was unknown. A young woman going out was always told she had to be good, and I mean good. They tell you when you are going out, "Now, you be good." Nobody told you what "good" meant. You had an idea, but not quite. Just to be good. Those Indian girls didn't have a choice. Any woman or girl at home years ago, in the old tribal organization, who stepped from the narrow pathway where she was supposed to walk — if she stepped to one side, then it meant a man somewhere else out in the woods got a penalty, and that was death.

My father talked about the last family that did that here. The girl was young and married to a Klallam man from across the peninsula. She very deliberately came back and met the young man she loved. He came from her tribe. She kept coming home to visit, and finally her husband and her in-laws followed her here. They found out she was living with this young man she loved. Her aunts and mother told her, "You're doing wrong. You know you are. You shouldn't be coming home to visit." She said, "What am I doing?"

Her in-laws came and her husband came there. They knew they were in a place toward what is now Warm Beach where the girl and the young man she loved stayed in a camp away from the longhouse. The longhouse was at Spibida. There were several smaller longhouses there at Warm Beach, but she and the young man were in a camp away from there, farther north. Her people came too — her father and mother and her relatives — and tried to talk, but there was no use.

The husband killed his wife's lover. The lover was lying down with his head on the girl's lap. Before he could even get up, her husband's people had landed. She was madly in love, and here the canoes landed so quietly, and her husband and his people were already there. They took the young man and cut off his head. She was standing right there, and she was crying. I guess she was saying, "I'm sorry," but nobody was listening to her.

Her father and mother tried to talk. They killed them both. They cut out her father's heart and this young man's she was living with. They put her father's heart inside of her mouth, and, of course, that heart was large. They told us the heart of her father and of her lover were still warm, and there was a lot of blood. They tied up her hands and threw her into the canoe. They gave her her lover's heart to hold and took her. Nobody ever knew what happened to her. No one among the tribal members who were still alive was going to say, "Tell me what you are going to do with her." Nobody said anything.

I think it was told to us as a lesson. If I had a daughter, I would have told her. When we were young, that was a law. I think it is in one of the Ten Commandments: "Thou shalt not commit adultery." It was strictly enforced with the Snohomish Tribe and other tribes here.

I often wondered if those skeletons they found in Warm Beach could have been them.

There were problems, and in all of this, the Indians were trying to find their way. Most of the Indians did not speak English. As I said, they had a jargon or a trade language called Chinook Jargon,[3] which the Indians from different tribes developed so that they could speak to one another if they didn't know each other's language, and some of the white people learned to speak it when they came here. It was what linguists would call a pidgin language. Some of the pioneers in Seattle used to talk to me in Chinook. I was just out of high school, and they were always quite sarcastic that I didn't understand the Indian language because I didn't understand Chinook [Jargon]. In Chinook, *tillicum* is friend. *Klahowya* is a greeting, "hello," and so sometimes they would say to me, "Isn't it funny you're an Indian and you don't know your own language." I said, "That's not an Indian language. It is pidgin English." "What do you think *tumtum* means? Several of them thought that it meant "stomach," or if you are hungry. I said, "No, it means 'your heart' or 'your thoughts. *Mikə tumtum* is 'my thoughts,' or how I feel. But we, the women, did not learn Chinook Jargon, although I understood some of the words. We went to school. I speak the Snohomish Indian language, and my parents spoke several other Indian languages.

As the pioneers came along, they shot their guns at anything they saw, whether it was rabbits or any kind of bird. They shot them. If they saw Indians, they shot them, too. It was common when they saw one to shoot him. By the time they got out here to the coast, it was almost as though waves and waves of pioneers had to stop to take a breath, and they knew, vaguely, that they probably had reached the end. By the time they got out here, all they did was kill some Indians. They started to kind of slow their killing. Of course,

---

3   See dictionaries on Chinook Jargon by F. Long, J. Gill, and G. Gibbs. Recall that the treaties were negotiated and read in Chinook Jargon to the tribal members at the time of signing.

they killed each other in fighting brawls, because as the pioneers moved along, the first thing established in every settlement was a saloon. Liquor was the first thing they brought in and that would cause trouble, too. A lot of men can go in and drink and nothing happens; they are just relaxing. There is still another type who will go in and want to fight all of the way through.

The American Rifle Association doesn't want gun control. They say it is guaranteed in the Bill of Rights—I forget which amendment; it guarantees the right to bear arms. I am always saying that's not exactly what it means. It means a militia, and that means a group of men like an army. They bear arms to guard the village, the town, the people. I heard some of those men from the American Rifle Association. They were on the Dick Cavett Show some years ago. I always liked him.

There is a tragedy happening to the people in Lebanon—and we see pictures of mothers running with their babies; they are just clutching them. They are being bombarded by great big guns. Well, white people didn't have big terrific guns like that, but they had guns when they came over the United States, and there were Indian women running to escape just like in Lebanon. Sometimes it wasn't an army or a cavalry attack or anything like that; sometimes it would be just three or four drunken white men who came brawling into some Indian camp. Indian women and girls would have to go into the deep woods. They had shelters in the woods where they could stay and where there was usually some food put away. So the American Indians, quite a lot of them, have lived through that sort of terror. Certainly, the destruction isn't like what is going on in Lebanon, in Beirut, where that big city is, but it is being leveled by those big guns. And there are still men and women, and a lot of children, and they look so tired. Well, that kind of thing happened to a great many tribes all the way across this continent. It happens in many places.

Right now on the television news they have been talking about the atomic bomb that was dropped on Japan. There was a man from Japan who was talking; I guess he was a young man then, and he happened to be way out in the outskirts when the bombs were dropped, but he was talking about the awful destruction. Quite a lot of the Japanese have leukemia now. The Secretary of Health, years ago, said you can't prove it; nobody can prove such a thing. Sometimes government officials just go ahead, and to heck with the people.

Wayne, my older son, said that when he was in the army in the fifties, they came out of the desert after experiencing the deployment of an atomic weapon at ground zero in Nevada, and they marched back to their buses; he said that the first bomb was dropped from an airplane. The following week, it was in *Newsweek*, I remember; he called me long distance because he wouldn't be able to write for a couple of weeks, since they were going somewhere south of Desert Rock. I think they were something like ninety miles from Desert Rock in Nevada; it is an army base. They went on buses to wherever ground zero was. They were four or five miles from ground zero. He said they worried about the trenches that they were told to dig. The sergeants were running Geiger counters on them: they went up one side and down the other and around their heads. It was clicking pretty good. Wayne was going to say how is it, but the boy ahead of him said that, and the "sarge" said "Shut up and get on board." He said when they were in the trenches the hot sand blew over them; it seemed hot anyway. Well, sand wouldn't blow over everybody. I imagine that bomb . . . well, I don't know how it was. I don't think power is equal all of the way. There is always something that stops it; or if there are buildings or whatever. I wonder if that is why he has white hair and if that made it difficult for him to get a job since they always want younger people.

On the news they showed the people who were protesting the nuclear submarine as it came through the Strait of Juan de Fuca. There were all kinds of boats and rowboats strung all over the straits. I was saying, "What's the matter with them anyway?" That's fine. Everybody can get together and say we don't want a nuclear war, but to get that far out and endanger their lives and the lives of other people, skittering out there in the Strait in front of that big submarine—and all around were Coast Guard cutters. They have the right to do that, but not that kind of crazy protest. Like I said, they endangered their own lives and the lives of other people. The time for them to protest was when the submarine was first being built. If you saw the newsreel, that submarine came in almost like a bullet. It was really making knots, moving along. The protesters, with their launches and boats, could run circles around that submarine. I was wondering how that submarine was going to get through that mob, and just coming through at full speed that's the only way to come. I was thinking of my grandmother; she died in 1921. I was thinking about those protestors, and I was thinking what's the matter with those people anyway. There is a time and a place to protest. It should be done with a little more dignity, shall we say. A little more thought for the safety of themselves and others.

Then, I don't know why, but I remembered my grandmother, way back then I was running down the white people, and she said—she never ever spoke English, always in our language, so when I was talking with her, I always talked our language—"You must have pity on the white people." You know, I was just going to say something, but we never answered our elders, not ever. We just sat and listened, and we thanked them for what they said. I remember she said, "You must have pity on the white people. They really don't know, most of the time, what they are doing. Wherever they came from, they were a lost people." So, what they do here around this country, she was just speaking of our Puget Sound country, "for what they do that seems, you might say, crazy, you must forgive them. They don't know any better. Whatever manners they might have had have just been dropped or forgotten. You have to have pity on them. I was just thinking of her, and I was saying there is no answer to that. I could have hollered to high heaven. "Have pity on them? Grandmother, are you in your right mind?" I think that is why all of those little grandmothers seemed so placid. You'd think that nothing ever got through to them. Maybe. I used to think grandmother doesn't know what it is like to be a teenager. Well, she did. She said that times are different. Clothes are different. But nothing changes good manners. Kindness, courtesy never changes.

4 / First Memories of White People

ONE of the problems Indian men face is that the Indians have continuous unemployment. In the old days, an Indian man was a man. He was a hunter, a fisherman, a provider of food, and a protector. When white people came here, then Indians in various places had Indian wars. But eventually the Indians gave up. They moved onto reservations, where there was no work and nothing to do; a situation like that is very demoralizing for a man. He no longer feels as if he can do anything. He feels helpless. He feels as though he is not really a man. Nobody can change something like that; it is a big turnover of a people—the end of thousands of years of Indian culture and traditions. When any group of people is overrun by a greater number of people, they have no way of surviving. Then they lose much of what sustained them before in their culture. All of the tribes had their own ways, their own customs.

When the white people came, the Indians had to earn their own money to buy material—calico, usually—to make the women's dresses and men's shirts. They sewed their own dresses, men's shirts, and children's trousers.

In some instances they were able to go to Port Townsend, because Puget Sound Indians traveled in canoes. Port Townsend was the biggest town around here in the Puget Sound. The only other place they went was Victoria, British Columbia, and also Olympia, where there were a couple of saloons and a general store. As I said before, one of the few ways they could find work, where they could earn the white man's money so that they could buy material for clothes, was picking hops in the Puyallup Valley.

The Indians suffered because they had pressures from all sides. One of the biggest pressures was from the missionaries. Then there was the Indian agent. Another pressure was having white people live all around them. Hundreds of thousands of white people moved in in the 1830s, '40s, '50s, and '60s.

When the pioneers were moving across the United States, they had their own problems. If it wasn't wagons breaking down, or horses or mules dying, or Indian attacks, then, of course, they would have terrible sickness. They brought with them diseases the Indians never had before. I think that was the most amazing movement of people: the movement of white people from Europe across the Atlantic Ocean and then spilling all across the continent. You have to face the fact that a great number of them were misfits; they were uneducated. They left home when they were very young. Some of them claimed to be aristocrats where they came from, but they were not. Of course, that is my point of view. I used to meet some of them at the Seattle Historical Society meetings years ago. They were the men and women who were descendants of the first settlers in Seattle and in high society.

Once in a while, I used to talk at the Seattle Historical Society meetings about Angeline. In one of the photographs of her, she is shown sitting down, and she has a kerchief tied around her head. She was an elderly lady with a shawl on, and she held a cane. Her father was Chief Seattle. Chief Seattle was a friend of the Dennys, who were Seattle pioneers. Seattle told them, "I will move my tribe, the Duwamish, who own the river and all of Seattle, across the Sound to Suquamish—also part of our territory." But Angeline stayed behind. She got old—a very elderly lady, and poor—and those women at the Seattle Historical Society talked about how dirty she was.

She lived in a one-room shack down on the waterfront in Seattle. I usually didn't say anything, but one time I said, "You have to remember when you get old. I hope it doesn't happen to you, but probably it won't. Why? You have money. What did Angeline have? Nothing." She probably *was* dirty. Elderly people are very frail, and they don't have much strength. She would have to carry water in buckets and have a big fire and a big tub to hold a lot of water in order to bathe. Maybe she didn't have the strength to carry several buckets of water. She might have one bucket that she could fill and carry. There was no one to help her.

For several years now, Washington State and many other states have had programs where they have funding to take care of elderly people. Maybe they have poor health, so that they can't really take care of themselves—wash clothes, scrub floors, and wash windows. Maybe they can make a fire and make tea or have bread and tea to eat.

I understand the pioneers used to feed Angeline. She could walk up one of the streets and eat in a kitchen of Dr. Maynard or somebody else. But they talked about how dirty she was. I always have to find excuses. If you are elderly and have to carry buckets and buckets of water and heat the water with a fire, it's going to take a half a day or more to get a bath ready. By that time, you wouldn't be able to stand up anymore. Somehow she wanted to stay there, and here her father and all of the rest moved to Suquamish. I don't know why she stayed there.

The beginning of Indian and American relations, shall we say, was when the government decided the Indians had to be civilized and join the white people in the mainstream of civilization. In order to do that, they would have to drop their customs, their languages, and religion—no more of it. For several years, the Indians were a people who were dispossessed and discouraged. One of the things that surfaced was the Ghost Dance in the 1890s for the tribes in the Plains. It was not felt out here that much because there weren't as many white people out here in the 1890s. In the Middle West, the Indians were experiencing a death rate just like we were, and they were also mixed up like we were. They weren't supposed to be beating the drum or following Indian religion. But when the Ghost Dance came up, many Plains Indians joined it—even such leaders as Sitting Bull. Old, old people, old leaders—famous chiefs—they joined the Ghost Dance and, of course, they sang certain songs. They danced all night, and the leaders made their speeches.

Out here, we were supposed to be speaking only the English language. We were supposed to be part of the Catholic Church. When I grew up and got married, my father never set foot in the Catholic church again. He thought it was beautiful, but it didn't reach him, especially when the priest would tell the Indians, if you don't come to church, if you don't follow this, you are going to hell. My father lived through our teachings of the old times.

When I first remember seeing white people and hearing them speak, I was quite small. I must have been four or five years old—a time when you begin to remember things. At first, they are sort of like pictures moving along. The white people I saw in Marysville and in Everett all had light eyes, gray or blue. It bothered and worried me. I thought something was wrong with them. Their eyes looked so light, and I wondered if their eyes hurt them, or if they could see. It seemed they could see because they were talking with my father in the store with some other people. So I saw white people in Marysville when my father and mother went into town.

People here went into town on horses and wagons way back then. They went into town perhaps once or twice a month, because it was a long journey. It took about two and a half or three hours for us to go from here to Marysville. The road wasn't wide then. It was narrow and meandered so much it took a long time to go someplace.

As I say, seeing white people worried me. I don't know why I never asked my father about it, if that is what it was. I just worried about it. I thought perhaps their eyes hurt since their eyes looked so light.

Then, the speaking voices of the women—white women—were very noticeable in comparison to the softer tones of the voices of my grandmother and her generation and my mother and her generation. I can't tell so much with my generation, because we all went to the Indian boarding school where the teachers and the employees were white. They certainly had different colored eyes—some of them had light eyes and by that time many had darker eyes. It didn't bother me like it did when I was small.

My mother never ever went to any school. She grew up in a longhouse on Guemes Island. Father Simon, a Catholic priest, came there and baptized my mother when she was small, but she didn't remember him. She saw some white people when they traveled to the Puyallup Valley to pick hops. My mother, who had a quiet speaking voice, told about experiences they had with white people when they traveled, while she was growing up, that were really frightening. I told one story in chapter 3. In this chapter I want to tell another one.

They were traveling by canoe, in a group of several canoes, from Guemes Island to Neah Bay. They were invited to an Indian gathering, a potlatch, and they stopped to eat lunch near the Place with Brown Leaves.[1] Far across the bay were two white men. When my mother's family and her cousins were on the beach and spreading out their lunch, across the small bay all of a sudden the white men fired their rifles. The shots were landing around my mother and her group. Her uncles and the other men said, "Hurry up, hurry up! Everybody get behind the logs. Lie down in the sand." One of her uncles was the last one to come from the canoes. He called to tell them to keep still and keep out of sight, but my mother looked up just as he was running and jumping over the logs. She could see him. The shots caught him in the jaw and through the head and came out the other side behind his ear. He fell down. My mother's mother and some others crawled over to help him, to straighten him out because he was still breathing. He tried to say something, but he couldn't talk, and he died in a very short time. My grandmother went over to her cousin, brother in our relationship, but they told my mother to keep still and stay there. So my mother saw her uncle die. There were still some shots. After a while it quieted down, and the Indians crawled over to the uncle who was dead. My mother said she was heartbroken and terrified

---

1   Lagoon Point on Whidbey Island.

because they told her to keep still. They thought the white men were going to walk around or come in their rowboat and kill the rest of them. They didn't, and the shooting stopped. They spent the whole day, just before noon when this happened, and nobody had time to eat because they had just stopped for lunch. What really bothered them was having no water to drink, since it was still on the canoes, and nobody had time to unload it. There was no drinking water around there, and it was a very warm summer day.

My mother was always careful with water. When I was a young teenager, I emptied the water bucket for my mother. She kept a bucket of water by the kitchen sink. It was filled every evening with fresh water and all day long it was filled with water. I remember I asked her one time, "Why do we have this water here? Just turn on the faucet." She spoke to me in a very quiet voice and said to please sit down, and she told me what happened to them when her uncle was killed, and they spent a long, long day—terrified—and without water. Being without food was bad enough, but not having water was on the verge of being painful.

My father said it was dangerous, sometimes, for Indians to go out to the Sound. Of course, Indians here traveled in canoes. They would go quite a long way in their canoes. Sometimes they met white people, a majority of whom were not especially friendly, but they would call out and greet them in Chinook Jargon, like "Klahoya" or something, and keep going. My father told about another time he was traveling by canoe with relatives and two white men crossing the bay shot at them. It was the same thing that happened to my mother and her people about the year before.

My mother's older sister was baptized Julie. She married a white man who came here with some other young men from Illinois. They walked with a big convoy of covered wagons to San Francisco. They walked around there and looked at things and decided panning gold was not the way to go. It was just one mad mob there, so they got on a ship and came up to Puget Sound. They thought it sounded like what they wanted—farming land. His name was Daniel Barkhausen, a German name.

Dan told us about how they walked up this way, north, from California and somewhere in Oregon. Of course, this whole area then was called Oregon Territory. Later it was called Washington Territory. But he said one place where they were was flat land, with some open areas, and acres and acres of prairies. They were resting at noon when they saw some Indian women, at a distance, walking. Apparently, they were going home. They had big baskets on their backs. One young white man said, "Watch me hit one of those women."

He lifted his gun and, of course, at that time all of them just had the one shot. He fired, and they saw one of the Indian women fall. They heard the others crying. They lifted the woman, tried to move her, and they kept on where they were going. But Dan and his friends stared at that young man. "What have you done?" They said, "We better get out of here. When those women get back to their villages, we will be in big trouble." So they started walking fast. They were jogging along. The other young man thought it was kind of funny. Sure enough, they had not gone far when a group of Indian men on horseback came up to them. Dan said they didn't run. They said to each other, as the horsemen were coming toward them, "There is no use running. Horses can catch us. If we stand here, they will know that we haven't done anything." But the other young man kept on walking. He started to run, but the horsemen surrounded them and said something they couldn't understand. But Dan said they could understand that these men were asking who shot that woman. Dan said he made up his mind that he was not going to be torn apart, and he pointed at that other man. Both of them pointed at the young man. The Indians grabbed him, and they made a sign and made talk and told Dan and the other young man to keep going. They never knew what happened to their friend. They heard him screaming for a while as if he was in awful pain. Dan said they must have torn him apart.

My grandfather Wheakadim was fourteen or fifteen years old when he worked as a shepherd down at Nisqually House where Dr. Tolmie was employed with the Hudson's Bay Company. His father died when he was small. Some of the Indians went there and bought blankets, flour, sugar, and sold furs. When my grandfather decided to stay there, he met a lot of white people. He met a nice man who was his supervisor; he lived in a little cabin. One time they went all of the way to San Francisco to deliver a herd of sheep. They walked day after day, and they had two or three good shepherd dogs that kept the herd together.

Days and days they were moving. My grandfather was way out there, far away from the wagon where his supervisor was, and several other people were with two or three wagons. They traveled south of the Columbia River. He said it was a big river because they had to go on a barge; it took quite a while, a day and a half, to get the sheep across. When he found out he was that far away from home, he tried to tell his supervisor that he had to go home. His supervisor said, "You don't want to go home. You might as well go all of the way to San Francisco and enjoy it." He told his supervisor he was worried because his mother and sister were back in Nisqually. The next morning he was sick, and so his supervisor, being a kind man, told him to ride in the wagon, and he laid him on a pile of hay and sacks of feed for the horses. The supervisor brought him a bottle of clear liquid, poured some into a spoon, and told my grandfather, "You take this," and gave him a big tablespoon of it. Later on, my grandfather found out it was called castor oil. Of course, the supervisor told him what it was, but he felt so homesick and worried that he opened his mouth and swallowed it. It tasted bad and had the consistency of fish oil, and then he really got sick. He said he lay in that wagon for two or three days. His supervisor, though, was kind in bringing him up. There were hunters along. They would come in with deer, and his supervisor gave him broth and fried bread from his open fire. They had a good cook, but it took several days for my grandfather to get over the castor oil. And that was the only time he had castor oil. He said he would rather be dead, be sick and die, than take castor oil again.

It took them hour after hour to get their sheep across the Columbia River on barges. They paid the owner to get across. After they were into strange country, my grandfather was quite a distance from the cook wagon and the other wagon, and the others were on horseback. The shepherds walked along with the herd. The three dogs they had were intelligent. You could just whistle once, twice, and they knew which way to run or turn the sheep herd. By another kind of whistle, they knew sheep were straying or going in different directions. So my grandfather was far out, somewhere, going south.

He heard horses running, and when he stopped, he whistled to his dog and stopped the herd. By that time, he saw horses running at a distance and riding them were twenty-five Indian men. They were coming fast. My grandfather thought to himself, "This is where I die. They are not going to let me live." He said they came right up to him. I guess they saw that he was a youth, and two of the men called out in a loud voice and pulled up their horses to stop from a full running gallop. So here the horses were, right around my grandfather. The Indian who seemed to be the leading man talked to him in an Indian language. He made signs and asked. He could see that my grandfather was an Indian because he had long, black hair, and that my grandfather understood him. He asked him, "Where do you come from?" My grandfather got so scared that he just said, "I come from . . ." and made signs that he walked many sunsets and sunsets from a place where you have to travel by canoe. They said, "We understand. We have your words," and they talked together and then they all left. My grandfather said he was so frightened he could hardly stand up after they left because they had tomahawks and long Indian spears and a few of them had single-shot rifles. I guess they were part of the Modoc War.

Before they got to San Francisco, they came to the Sacramento River, and his friend and supervisor said, "This is where we go on." So they went on barges with all of their sheep, on down the river. Sometime after that, they got to San Francisco, and you wouldn't believe the noise.

His supervisor took him to a hotel. He didn't know what it was, but it was upstairs, and they walked on things that took them to the top floor. His friend opened the door and showed him his bed, and he said, "This is where you will stay." There was a bureau, because it had a mirror. For the first time, my grandfather saw himself. He had seen himself in lake water, but his friend stood him in front of the mirror and showed him. It was in the corner of the room. He could stand in the window and look down on the muddy, muddy street. He said there were a lot of men walking up and down that muddy street and teams of horses that were loaded down with goods. The men were screaming and cursing; he heard a lot of cursing for the very first time in his life. Indians could always learn swear words (or anybody can, even children) faster than other words. But my grandfather watched this mad mob all day long.

He said he finally got hungry and enough nerve to go out. His supervisor told him where to go. I think he took him downstairs and up the street. So he was able to push his way along. One place had swinging doors, and his supervisor told him, "You can't go in there." Those doors would fly open, and maybe two or more men would fly out of there, cursing and screaming. They landed in the mud of the street and were fighting. My grandfather was pretty frightened for a while, and then he found they went right by him. He thought they were going to kill him, but they didn't especially notice him. He found a place to eat. He had already been eating with a knife and a fork and a spoon.

His supervisor was gone that day. The second day he came back and gave my grandfather a handful of gold money. He told him to take care of it; it's money. But he said, "I'll take you to a store, and you can buy what you want for your mother and for anybody else." He took my grandfather to a couple of stores. He saw bolts of wool and velvet, and he made up his mind that he wanted to bring yards of black and blue velvet for his mother and his sister.

The Indians called velvet "dázał." Dázał is a fur of a very rare seal that didn't come into the Sound, but Snohomish Indians used to trade with Indians in Neah Bay for it. They had a lot of dázał pelts. They appeared in Neah Bay at certain seasons. They had a lot of beautiful black furs, dázał, and they made men's coats and vests and women's blouses with it. When the Indians first saw velvet, such as when my grandfather came back with several yards of velvet, he knew what it was; the Indians called it *dázał*, which was that kind of a rare fur.

As I said earlier, my grandmother used to wear blouses that were made of velvet, especially on Saturdays and Sundays. She would always put on either navy blue or black velvet blouses and skirts. All the Indian women that I saw back then wore velvet blouses and skirts for Sunday. Along about that time, the velvet, it seemed, began to disappear, because it seemed the priests and the agents—we were supposed to be getting civilized—didn't actively discourage velvet clothing but they didn't want us wearing it. My mother wore just calico all of the time except Saturday and Sunday; my grandmother used to wear calico, too. She always wore blue calico with tiny little figures in it.

My grandfather's supervisor-friend said, "You have to have thread." My grandfather used to help his mother with sewing leather shirts and vests, so he knew about needles. He got a pack or two because, he said, after that needles could get lost like nobody's business. Somehow they drop. His sister would be working and would lose a needle.

He came home with yards of black and blue velvet and thread and red ribbon that he thought was pretty. It was about an inch wide. He thought it would look nice on his sister to tie her hair because she had long braids.

His supervisor told him, "You can get your ship tomorrow and go back home." My grandfather had already made up his mind to go home, and he wondered how he could get back home. He thought he could walk, but thought he could also be in danger—some white people might shoot him. His friend got him on the ship. It turned out a cousin of his was on that ship, a boy just about his age, who had been a deck hand.

He had been in the city, too, for a month and had arrived with a load of lumber on a sailing ship. He worked unloading lumber in San Francisco. It was really booming—lumber, lumber, and lumber. His cousin also had yards of velvet and ribbon, thread, and needles. So my grandfather felt better. He thought, "Well, maybe I will get home."

The ship left San Francisco. It carried some other people—a white couple who appeared to be married. The women had such pretty dresses of velvet and hats with big feathers. At first, my grandfather and the passengers sometimes stood up on the top deck and looked at the land they were passing. There wasn't a single town. They couldn't see any houses for days, hour after hour, day after day.

He finally noticed a gambler on board the ship. He was dressed up fancy. He had a high silk hat and a shiny vest made of flowered taffeta. He came along on the deck, and my grandfather and his cousin were standing there just talking. His cousin was working on the deck, adjusting the sail. There were different sails on that ship. So my grandfather was standing on the railing, just talking to his cousin, who had already done what he was supposed to do. This man came along shouting at them. He hollered at my grandfather's cousin, giving him orders, but they had just turned their heads and were looking at him, trying to understand what he was yelling about, when the wind changed a little. The boom swung and hit the man as he was walking along the edge. The railing didn't extend all of the way to the edge of the ship, and he was knocked off of the ship. My grandfather said he could hardly stand the man. He was swearing at them. I guess he didn't want to see them standing there. He was probably telling them to get down below when he was swept off. My grandfather and his cousin bent their heads. Some people came along who were passengers, and they watched him fall overboard. My grandfather was terrified. He thought, "They are going to throw us overboard because it's our fault." But a few of the white people looked at my grandfather and smiled and said, "Well, he got what he deserved." He was a gambler and he earned a lot of money from several of them. They found out too late, but they should have known he was a professional gambler. Some of the men trailed a rope, but he passed it, switching around, and just missed it. The mate said, "Oh, let him go." Nobody wanted him back on board.

My grandfather said he was happy to come home, and then this happened. His friend-supervisor came up and told him, "It is not your fault. He had no business coming along there giving you folks orders, or telling you to stay downstairs. He was just a passenger kicking you folks around, and it was none of his business." My grandfather had some bad dreams about it afterward. He felt that even though his supervisor said it wasn't their fault, everybody should be careful swinging the booms.

After days and days and days of sailing, he finally caught up with his mother and the Snohomish Indians. They were still around the Puyallup Valley, not Nisqually. They must have left there, and I think they went there to pick hops. Somebody had a big field of hops. Some of the earliest pioneers planted hops, and the Indians would come and work and pick hops in the fall. And so my grandfather found his people. He said his mother already had her hair cut short because she thought he was dead. Indian women used to cut their hair like that when they were in mourning. They cut their long braids when somebody in their family died. His mother was in that camp with her hair all cut. She couldn't believe it when she saw him. Then, after she cried, she got kind of mad at him. She told him to go out and get to work. They all went out to pick hops.

My aunt, my mother's older sister, married a white man when she was almost sixteen years old. She had no choice because Indian girls didn't have a choice in marriage anyway. Her father let her go to a white man in what became Bellingham. He was an assistant to the superintendent of the mines there. It was an Indian marriage.[2] They didn't have a preacher. When my aunt became pregnant a couple of years later, he took another wife, and that second wife was her aunt. She was a year older, about seventeen or eighteen. So those two girls became the wives of this white man.

I asked my mother why did my grandfather allow his daughter and his sister to go to that white man and be the wives of this one man? Why? My mother said, "I think it was because he was worried about what would happen to them. It was a changing world all over, wherever the Indians went here on the Sound. Wherever they were used to going, there were white people. They were not exactly settled; they were camping or looking around, and there were quite a number of them who, shall we say, were brawling drunkards. Once in a while on Guemes Island, a few white men landed, looking around for homesteads. So my grandfather felt that his young daughter and his young sister should be someplace where they would be safe.

Here, then, were my aunt and her aunt married to this man whose last name was Fitzhugh. His first name was Edmund Clare. I have seen his picture. He was a very handsome man. He had a nice two-story house. My mother and father talked about what nice homes quite a lot of those white people built. My aunt and her aunt had a big kitchen, dining room, a big living room, and a couple of big rooms.

One time they were giggling around like girls do, and their husband came home. They hadn't noticed the time on the clock in the dining room because they were just talking. He came home, and they started stirring up a kitchen fire. My aunt and my mother and my grandmother all knew that meals were to be prepared on time. The same time every day. Have the food prepared

---

2   A ceremony in which gifts are exchanged between the parties at a dinner.

and hot. Don't take something from yesterday, warm it over, and say, "There you are." So my aunt and her aunt, here they were giggling around, doing housework, and their husband came home, and here they were just stirring up the fire. He came in and slapped them both. I suppose he had his own words, but he did slap them.

The next day, when he was coming home, my aunt said, "I'm going to kill him." He came in and he was mad at them, although they had the food almost ready. One of them brought him the dishes and set the place. He had nice things. He had dishes and a beautiful coffee pot that he wanted on the table in a certain place. He came in and sat down at the dining table.

I used to hear this story when I was growing up, when I was a teenager, and I remember it so well. I think Indians remember words and descriptions. My aunt picked up some stove wood and said, "I'm going to kill him." Her aunt was standing by the cook stove. "What are you going to do?" She said, "I'm going to kill him." She walked into the dining room and hit him on the head with the stove wood. My aunt was about my height. I'm five feet tall, so she was really small, but she was strong. She hit him on the head and he fell to the floor. Her aunt came to the door, and as he hit the floor, he moaned. They just stood there petrified. Her aunt said, "You killed him!" She said, "I don't care!" She went over and hit him again somewhere on his face or on his head. She didn't know where. She started to hit him on the side. Her aunt grabbed her and said, "Stop it!" She realized what she had done. He was dead. They ran into the kitchen, and their shawls were hanging on the back of the kitchen door. They grabbed their shawls and covered their heads and went out through the back door.

They said, "Let's go down and look and see if we have any uncles down by the campground." His house was near Bellingham—in the early, first Bellingham. They walked through the back of the house, through the woods, down to the outskirts of Bellingham (the southern portion—because they went across a point) and got to another bay where some of their uncles were. They said, "We are in trouble. We killed him." An uncle said, "Get in the canoe right away." So they got in the canoe, and their uncles and relatives covered them up with blankets and started paddling. Nobody said much of anything. They stayed covered up until they got back to Guemes Island.

My aunt told her relatives, "Nobody is going to make me go back. Nobody. I don't care what happens to me. I'm not going back. Nobody is going to slap me around." So they were hidden out.

My aunt had a son. They named him Mason Fitzhugh. He was taken away by Mr. Fitzhugh, his father, when he was small. Each of his wives had one child before they left him. He took the boy when he was two years old. He said, "I'm taking him to Olympia." He was taking him to a settlement because he didn't want him to be an Indian. He would learn English. He would not grow up to be like an Indian. My aunt never knew where he went or where he took him. She cried and begged and said, "Where did you go? Where did you take him?" Right after that, my aunt left him, but he already had the baby and he had already taken him away. She was only eighteen or nineteen years old.

Mr. Fitzhugh didn't die, but he left when my aunt beat him up. A sailing ship came into Bellingham. Some of my mother's cousins and uncles were standing around at the dock in Bellingham, and they saw Fitzhugh leave on the sailing ship. The girls really had beaten him up. He had a black eye; his jaw and face were swollen and black and blue, and somebody was walking with him. He was walking with pain. He walked with a terrible limp. He had a cane and his head was all wrapped up. He wore a high hat and a satin waistcoat. He seemed to be well-educated and must have come from a reasonably wealthy family because he could read and write.

Mason Fitzhugh, his son, later came to live in the San Juan Islands. What happened to him was just as traumatic as any novel you could read.

Mason didn't remember his mother. He grew up in Olympia, where he had a terrible time because he was half Indian. He was taken in by a doctor who kept him in his home. The man died. He and his wife didn't have any children, but there was Mason. His wife didn't like him. She never wanted him there in the first place. She used to chase him back into the kitchen, and she didn't buy him any shoes. He outgrew some shoes he had, and he didn't have any moccasins because he never, ever saw the Indians. In the winter times, he ran out and carried in kindling wood, and he didn't have any shoes, and it was so bitterly cold. He stayed in the kitchen, and they gave him food.

When he was fifteen or sixteen years old, he got a job on a sailing ship and went to Bellingham. He got off there and saw some Indians, and he went up to talk to them. The ship carried cargo for a store or a trading post there. Every day Indians went down there and watched as the freight was unloaded and sometimes they got a job, and they watched the people come and go. Here came this young boy. They saw him on the ship. They had thrown the lines that tie up the ship to the dock. Indians were sort of helping, and they figured he was an Indian. He said, "My name is Mason Fitzhugh and my mother is an Indian. I don't know who she is or where she is. She should be somewhere in this country." Some of them were related to my aunt, and they said, "Oh, we know who you are." So he got off of the ship and stayed with some relatives and he did find his mother. He stayed with his mother.

My great aunt had the most terrible life. First of all, she was married to Edmund Clare Fitzhugh, the one they beat up and left. I think they said he did come back to Whidbey Island, but he didn't stay long. He had a white wife. I read in a history of Whatcom County that he was killed in the Civil War.

My great aunt married another white man. You would think she had learned something, but I think once she was married to a white man, no Indian would have married her. His name was Phillips. He was the husband she shot and killed. I used to get so worked up when I heard about it, because it seemed she had such a terrible life. But she did have her older boy, Mason. Then she had a baby. She and Phillips had a farm.[3] They had what my mother called a "lime kill," and he had a partner.

He got mad at her about something, and he threatened her. "You just better watch out if you talk to that man, the partner. I'm going to kill you." When he went out of the kitchen, he stopped and told her again, "You just watch yourself, because I'm going to kill you." There was a rifle behind their kitchen door. She reached for the rifle. Her husband was already turning — ready to go back out to the field or the barn. Mason just came out of the barn where he had been working, and Phillips told her again. "Watch yourself. I will kill you and I will kill him. I will kill your son." My aunt reached behind the door, and she called to him. She didn't want to shoot him in the back. He turned around. She said, "I'm going to kill you," and she shot and killed him.

She was carrying a baby on her back. The authorities took her to jail in Port Townsend, which was an older town. She and her baby, Thomas Phillips, were put in jail to await trial. The Indians talked to a priest and told him that she has a small baby. He said he couldn't do anything. She did wrong.

My great aunt went on trial in Port Townsend. She told them she had so many threats from her husband it was kind of a hell on earth, you might say. She didn't have enough nerve to leave because, anyway, she couldn't go home. The judge let her go. He said she had been punished enough. She had already served three or four months in the jail.

Mason Fitzhugh came here once, all of the way from the San Juan Islands, to visit when I was a school girl, a teenager. He stayed at our house overnight.

---

3   Located in Port Susan.

He and my mother and father talked. He has a granddaughter on San Juan Island. She has a big farm out there—a homestead. He married someone who was half Indian too. There is a group of Indians who live on the San Juans who know they are half Indian. I'm not sure what tribe they belong to; I think they call themselves San Juan Indians.[4] I met some of them in Judge Boldt's court.[5]

Little bits of history like that tell you the Indians who married the white man had a bad time, but many of them were reasonably happy.

---

4   They are not federally acknowledged as a tribe.

5   She testified for *United States* v. *Washington, Phase One,* in 1972.

5 / Remember (What We Told You)

B Y 1855, the time of the treaty, there was a small Catholic school here in Tulalip Bay located at Priest Point.[1] There were other missionaries, but I think—by far—the Catholic priests came here first. When I say they came here first, I mean they came even before or just along with the white trappers. The pioneers came right after the trappers. So, these priests were moving across what became the United States, Canada, and Mexico long ago.

Father Pierre de Smet was a well-known priest in the Middle West. My father and others of his generation talked about him. They never saw him; they just heard about him. He traveled all over the Middle West—in the Dakotas, in Montana, and Idaho. I think he even touched on Washington Territory. He baptized little children and grown Indians who wanted to be baptized. He did a lot to pacify the Indians. Father de Smet would walk, walk, walk. I guess he went on horseback once in a while.

Father Eugene Chirouse and Father Paul Durieu were the first priests in this area. Chirouse was born in France. When he was fifteen years old, he read about the American Indians, and he told his grandmother he was going to dedicate his life to the church and that he would try and reach America. (He was an orphan but he had a grandmother.) He wanted to work with American Indians. Of course, they were all pleased over that idea.

Sometimes the religions just make me mad. But when I think of the dedication and the sacrifices of the priests and missionaries, I know their sacrifices were unbelievable. They walked across this country. They had to get across rivers; it snowed, it hailed, the wind blew, and there was the blistering hot sun.

Father Chirouse lived at the Mission at Priest Point. He wore a long, black garment to the ankles, with long sleeves. It was supposed to be made

---

1 In 1864 they moved to Mission Beach and opened the Mission of St. Anne, which burned in 1902.

of heavy, black woolen serge. He had left Montreal years before and his cassock was worn out. It had been patched and was all tattered. So some of the Indian women made him one from white, heavy cotton material that they got at the Nisqually trading post, which was an English trading post north of Olympia. An Indian lady made it just like the black one, but it was white. He wore it until he got a message that the bishop was coming from Portland to visit him in Olympia.

Olympia was where the roads ended, but it wasn't much of a place. Here he had a white cassock and nobody wears those but the Pope. His is supposed to be all black. He worried and worried. They started out for Olympia. Some Indians paddled the canoe for him. Some other Indians went along in another canoe. It was summer. They stopped to eat on the beach and make tea, or he would drink water. The Indians made their own kind of tea and had lunch. Then the Indians said, "We'll fix his robe."

They picked a lot of wild blackberries—real ripe ones—several bucketsful. They had a small tub, and they smashed them all up and put his robe in. They really soaked it up. They had started out early, so they were days ahead, and it was a good thing because they had to wait a whole day for his cassock to dry. When he put it on, he said it was black, pretty black.

They were getting close to Olympia. About a day or two days later a storm came up, and they had to round a point and they tipped over. There he was in the water. The Indians helped him to get to the shore. But the saltwater washed his robe—not white; it was sort of a light lavender or purple. Somebody in Rome can wear a cassock that color but not him. When he met the bishop, he explained it—and besides, he was still wet. But, you know, things like that happened to them. I was just thinking, "Oh, bless their hearts. They were so brave." Somebody else might say, "Oh, to hell with it. I'll just wear whatever the Indians have—a blanket."

My mother and father talked about one of the youngest nuns—the last—who came to Tulalip Indian School.[2] She came here in the 1860s. My brother remembered hearing about her. She was called Sister Leopoldine, which is the feminine of Leopold. The sisters had read about Father Chirouse and his mission. When she first got here, she was very young and she played baseball with the intermediate boys. She could bat a ball, even though it wasn't much of a ball, and run from base to base. The Sister Superior would see them out

---

2   In 1868 the Sisters of Charity, House of Providence, from Montreal, Canada, joined the Mission.

there on the playfield at recess time and come out there and tell her, "Sister Leopoldine, you stop that running around like that. You are showing your ankles." The young Indian students said, yes, you could see her ankles when she was running. She had black shoes and black stockings. Here she was running with those big heavy skirts, and she got into trouble over and over again. Sister Superior would come out there and tell her, "Now stop it! You can just walk around there real fast." She would say, "Yes, mother."

The school Fathers Chirouse and Durieu established on Tulalip Bay existed from about 1857 to 1902. It kept getting bigger. Father Chirouse received something like 5,000 dollars from the federal government about 1870. He was to educate the Indian children, but part of the Mission School burned down in 1902. There was a big building for the boys—the Boys Building; then there was a similar building for the girls, where they stayed, since it was a boarding school. Children stayed there eight months a year—probably less than that, because I think they went home in early summer for the late spring fishing.

My father went to the Mission School; he was already baptized, by a priest, with the name of William. He was about eighteen or nineteen years old when he arrived at the Mission School. He didn't tell his folks, who lived at Possession Point on Whidbey Island, that he was going. His parents and all of his uncles did not want him to go to school. They said, "If you go there, you are going to get sick and you are going to die." So many Indian children were dying. They died of measles, and if they caught a cold, it turned into pneumonia and that turned to tuberculosis. When the pioneers came, it seemed as though the Indians caught colds and other illnesses they never had before. They never had measles or pneumonia and so on.

He just left home one early morning and arrived there in a canoe. He met a cousin, brother, there who took him to the priest's office. The priest talked, and my father listened to him, but he didn't understand any of it. He said it seemed as if the priest was asking him something, so the cousin told him his name is William. The priest wrote something on a book and talked some more. His cousin told him the priest said, "You have to have another name. You can't have just one name." My father told my cousin, "You know, just William." The priest seemed to be listening and talking. My father had some older cousins who were there, and their name was Shelton, and so his cousin said something to the priest. The priest said, "Oh, that's his name: William Shelton." He wrote it down. So, standing in the priest's office, my father became William Shelton. If it had gone according to how the white people name their children—you take your father's last name—my father's last name should have been Wheakadim.

It was unusual that my father was named Wheakadim after his father. His name should have been William Wheakadim. But my father didn't want the priest to know what his name was. He stayed at the Mission School for two years until he got out in 1890. Then he met my mother and they got married.

In 1902 the Girls Building burned down, along with almost the entire school. I don't remember if they had an investigation about why and how it started. I think they discussed it. But some people saw one of the clerks who had been dismissed from the agency office walking around there about one or two o'clock in the morning. The fire started on one of the porches, a veranda, with a pile of burning oil-soaked rags as if somebody had rolled up the rags and poured a lot of coal oil on them and lit the pile. The fire just raged all through there. They got the girls and boys and all the employees out.

My father and mother lived where the agency used to be, across the bay from the Mission School, where a lot of Indians lived at that time. My father and the others got to the fire. They said they woke up because they heard a man shouting. They got up and went to the front porch and opened the door and stepped outside and listened. A man was riding on horseback, and he was going from here to the school and around the road and north and shouting that the school was burning, and they wanted everybody to come and help.

They had a bucket brigade. They got there just when the Girls Building was in flames. Some Indian men came, and they said, "All the children are out." The Sisters took care of even the little ones. They woke them up, but for some it was hard to wake them up and get them lined up. Then there are the little boys in their nightshirts, and they can hang on to each other and say, "All right, this is the way out." So they did get them all out, but they had no clothes to wear.

The word spread. Indian men brought in messengers and canoes, and they went to Everett. Everett was already a small town, and they asked at the Catholic Church for any kind of clothes for children. Some Indians even went to Seattle and Olympia, and so the word spread. Of course, pioneers were not that wealthy either. Clothes were hard to come by. A lot of them did their own spinning and weaving and made their own woolen cloth to make trousers or dresses and coats. They even spun yarn and knitted stockings and socks. They had to go all around to get clothing for the children.

My father said he and David Snapps, one of his cousins, got to the steeple of the church just as it was starting to burn. A couple of younger Indian men climbed up with a bucket of water. It is pretty hard to climb that far, and they couldn't climb up the steeple. By that time, the water in the bucket was half full, and to try and throw it up like that just didn't work. My father and they started removing the statuary—a large one of St. Sebastian and another smaller one of St. Joseph. By that time, the church was full of smoke and it burned down.

The Girls Building, the church, and some other buildings burned down, but the Boys Building was there when I was little, as I said, because we used to run in there and "clump up" the stairs. It would sway. We would be upstairs running around, and we would stop and look at it and it was swaying just a little bit. We would hear my mother's voice. She heard us and came running to tell us to come down from there. She said, "You can go on the first floor, but don't run around." But we went upstairs anyway and ran around and around together and watched it and listened to it creak.

When I was born in 1904, there was no school. Students who were big enough were taken to Chemawa Boarding School in Oregon. When I came along at school age, the school had been built again. The Indians cleared the land and burned the stumps. There was a Girls Building and a Boys Building, a classroom building, and a number of other buildings for the homes of the employees. They had a club building. It was a two-story building, with about six or eight rooms where the single employees stayed. Then there was a kitchen and a dining room where they ate.

Dearest Grandmothers: Manners and Religious Training

If the white people ever think about it, they probably think we arrived at the boarding school like a bunch of wild animals. White people think we are absolutely savage. We were savages or, shall we say, barbarians, but we still emphasized what we believed to be good manners. I remember one of them was how I should eat. How I should chew my food. You never chew your food with your mouth open. Never, never. You take small bites of food. We were taught how to sit and how to walk and how to enter and leave a room. As a matter of fact, all of us were taught before we were of school age how to say "please," how to eat at the table, and, in the old days, the really old-time Indians never allowed children to eat at the table with the older people. All of the children ate separately. They gave them a piece of smoked salmon, a slice of bread, and then they ate around their mother. They were not allowed to talk. They were not allowed to stand up and run around. They must sit there. They could talk to each other or to their mother, but there was no loud talking. The Indian children were already quiet. When we played, then, we were noisy, shall we say, but when we went into a room, any room, classroom, dining room, then we were supposed to sit down and keep still.

The Indian children always played together. Usually wherever they went, they could go around the beaches or they would go along trails, and some grandparents always went with them or aunts and uncles went walking along with them. I remember my grandmothers and all of their cousins used to go to Mission Beach when I was little and we would run up and down that beautiful beach, and that was acres and acres of nice clean beach. And we could run up and down and make tracks, you know; we could make all kinds of designs. We could be two, three, four blocks ahead of our grandparents, and I would always turn around and look and see where my grandmother and them were. They'd be walking along and talking. I guess they were reminiscing about the times when they used to run up and down the beaches. Walking with their canes, talking.

I remember I have talked before, so many times, about when I used to run down to my grandmothers all the time. She lived about a block away. In that big house there were two other elderly ladies that lived there. In the next room was Sədulitsə, Mrs. Mary Jake, and she was about the same age as my grandmother. In the other room was a much older woman, and she came from Suquamish. The agency called her Sally. I can't remember her Indian name. But I remember when I learned how to read; every morning I would run down to see my grandma. My mother would be calling me, but I would go flying out the door, and maybe my mother would just want to start unbraiding my hair. All of us had long braided hair. All I would do is slap some water on my face and just run my wet hands over my hair. I'd give my face a big slap with a towel and then I would run out the door. One time I told my mother, "I'm going to eat breakfast with my grandmother." Well, my mother would keep calling me, you know, "Come back, come back." She didn't want me running down there starving to death and eating. My grandmother would probably feel nobody fed me.

My paternal grandmother was the one who tried so hard to make me into a fine Indian lady. My mother's mother I don't remember. I don't remember one thing about her and she lived with us too, or near us. I often wondered what they would think if they heard me getting mad and swearing. I will always remember going to my grandmother's house every morning. My paternal grandmother was the only grandmother I remember. I was very close to her, I spent a lot of time with her. I think that was the way of life with our Indian people way back then, for generations, for hundreds of years, the grandmothers had a lot to do, in fact almost everything, with raising their grandchildren. They always seemed to have a big interest in us young children, because I used to meet other older women about the same age as my grandmother and sometimes they would tell me the same things that would help me in my lifetime that my grandmother told me.

As soon as I ate breakfast, I went hopping down there. I knocked at the door and opened the door and walked in. My grandmother would be knitting socks, and I used to help her. That caused a lot of tears. I mean, my mother always got upset because I never learned that fast about heels and toes on knitted socks. But my grandmother said to just do it over and over.

Then one day I knocked at my grandmother's door that special time. I guess I was about five years old because it was before I went to Tulalip Indian School. I knocked at the door and I opened the door and I went "clumping in." There was a hallway there and I got to the open doorway and she was sitting in her little home there, and she was always knitting socks. The heavy woolen socks that the Indian women made, and they sold them to the stores in Seattle, Port Townsend, Olympia—all of the first towns. Of course, Seattle way back then was probably just a saloon and Yesler's Mill and probably Yesler's Saloon, too. Then, Olympia was mostly saloons and a store. Port Townsend was a bigger place. But I went hopping down to my grandma's, knocked at the door and went "clumping in," as I said. When I sat down there was always a little box, with a big cushion on it, beside her. So I flopped down and I was yakking away, telling her something, and she said, "It is time that you learned how to walk into a room, and into any place, like a real fine Indian lady. You know how you go, "oh, oh, what did I do now." My mind is going around, and I know I am not supposed to go "clumping" into a room like that. So, she told me—she never ever raised her voice—in a quiet speaking voice, she said. "You will go back out the door and you will knock, and when you hear my voice telling you to come in, you will come in, and you will not slam the door, and when you walk into a room you will take shorter steps and don't have your feet and your shoes fighting with the floor. Lift your feet, take shorter steps, and when you sit down here by me, sit with your knees together, and you will remember that as long as you live. Go back outside. Knock at the door, and when you hear my voice, come in. Please walk with short steps, and please don't lift your knees too high. When you sit down, you will sit here with your knees together, and you will remember that as long as you live. You will always sit with your knees together."

I walked back out and shut the door. I remember I looked at the doorknob for a while, and I thought maybe I had better go back home. As soon as I thought that, I knew my father and mother would hear about what my grandmother tried to teach me. Everybody would be disappointed that I ran away from something I was supposed to do. So I knocked at the door. I could hear my grandmother's voice. I walked in, in short steps. I never had the nerve, until about five years later, to ask her how was I going to walk without lifting my knees. I never, ever asked. If they told you to do something, you did it. I will always remember that business of sitting like a lady with my knees together. Now that I am much older, I always notice how every woman sits.

The other thing I learned that same summer was also from my grandmother, my real grandmother's sister, Sədulistə. Two sisters came from La Conner to visit my grandmother at her house. They came with their husbands. Whenever they, my grandmothers, came in the summer, they would stay for perhaps two weeks and then go back home, and then they never saw each other again for the year. Those grandmothers came in canoes, paddling. They were all older people like my grandmother. I used to sit and listen to them talk for two or three hours at a time. If I fell asleep, they would put me on their laps and wake me up again.

When I talk about my parents, my grandmothers, they all talked in our Indian language, the Snohomish Indian language, and I also talked in the Indian language like them. As I was growing up, I spoke two languages. I talked in Indian—Snohomish—more than in English. My father worked at the agency, where he had to talk English. When he came home, he talked English to my mother, and that is how I learned to talk English to some extent. Otherwise, we talked in our Snohomish Indian language. So when I was talking with my grandmothers, that is the language we spoke.

Another lesson I learned, that I never forgot, was with my grandmother's sister, Sədulitsə, but she was also my grandmother. My other grandmother and her husband and some cousins who came from La Conner were visiting my grandmother. My other grandmother was married to a man from La Conner, he was Swinomish. Some parts of their language were different from ours, but I understood them perfectly. I heard it so many times. They came from La Conner, and they came in canoes, naturally. When the other grandmothers would come, I was always down at the beach waiting for them, and I would call out to them, "Where are you folks going?" I was talking in

Indian you know, and they would always tell me they were going to see my grandmother. Some people wouldn't bother to answer a child, you know, or maybe you don't even listen to them babbling.

There were other men and women who came with my other grandmother, Sədulistə, so there would be a room full of my grandmothers' relatives and they would be talking. They would talk for hours and hours, remembering when they were children, or they would talk about what they heard or knew about the time of the treaty in 1855. The treaty was something that was important to us. I never realized it then, but I heard those words so many times—the treaty. But that was what my grandmothers and their husbands would talk about. Some of them were small children at the signing of the treaty, and they didn't really know what it was, but they knew that it was treaty time. My grandmother didn't go to the council meeting.

Anyway, that time when Sədulistə came from La Conner, we were all visiting and talking. They would talk hour after hour where my grandmother lived. They had been talking, reminiscing, for two or three hours. There would be quite a number of them. I turned my head to look at every one of them who spoke and as they moved about the room, because we were going to have tea or coffee or lunch. I was sitting on a little box on a big cushion and when someone spoke, I turned my head. Sədulistə put me on her lap and said to me, "You must never turn your head like that if people are talking in a room. You must not turn your head at any place where there are groups of people, where there is a council meeting. Do not turn your head that rapidly. If you are going to look at people or different persons, you turn your head slowly. You must not be turning your face so fast and in so many directions. People are going to talk about you. Different women from different tribes will talk about how you throw your face around, so you remember, don't ever turn your head like that just so rapidly from person to person. You can turn your head more slowly without throwing your face around. A fine Indian lady turns her head very slowly and looks. If you turn your head like that your earrings are swinging all over, and a lot of strangers—there will be hundreds of people in a longhouse—will watch how you walk and how you turn your head. They will talk about how low class you are, how stupid you are. We have to be careful. You don't want people to think that you are low class, or that you are stupid, or that you are silly, crazy." At that age, four or five years old, I already had earrings. They pierced my ears. I barely remember anything about having my earlobes pierced.

Believe me, I remembered what she said. I tried. I tried to follow what she said. I was about five or six years old, since it seemed to be quite a while before

I went to the boarding school. It seemed as though all of the grandparents, different relatives, all had an interest in us younger people. By the time I was fourteen, I wondered when they were going to stop picking on me. I felt that they were picking on me all the time. However, after I got older, I certainly appreciated them. By that time, most of them were gone. The grandmothers were always anxious to tell us how to be.

I remember thinking years afterwards, "Who cares? Nobody is going to notice how I turn my head." But way back then, all through our travel life—hundreds, thousands of years ago—grandparents, and grandmothers in particular, had a lot to do with how children were raised. They are the ones who emphasized manners, the manners the Indians believed in.

Another thing that happened to me had to do with one of our legends. We have legends that tell of the baby who was born. He was called the Sky or Star Child. His name was Duk^wibəł our Spirit Creator.[3] Our legends are a little different for the different tribes. In our legends, he became a good hunter. He had a little vest, a little coat, that was made of many colors of feathers. In my father's booklet, "Legends of the Totem Pole," the legend is called "The Little Man with the Coat of Many Colors." These legends are old, old, old. They come from a time my parents said was in our history hundreds of years ago. A time that is like in the morning: if you look over toward the mountains or over the water toward Whidbey and Hat islands, there is a mist that drifts and takes maybe an hour or so before the sun shines through. That is what those Indians used to say. It is like a time that was behind a curtain, a fog, a mist. It is our time when we were on this earth. We have been here a long, long time. We have always been here.

I was the youngest in my family. My sister Ruth was a year and a half older than me. I loved her dearly, but now and then I would forget and I would say, "Me first, I'm first. I'm closest to my mother. Me first." I would take a step in front of my sister. One time my grandmother was there, and my mother was making doughnuts. My mother was a marvelous cook and a good housekeeper. She let us put sugar on the doughnuts she made. My grandmother was there knitting Indian socks. I said, "Me first. I choose this. I want the biggest doughnut with the most sugar on it." We had to sit down and eat. We were not allowed to run around like chickens. When we got through, I was talking to my grandmother.

---

3 Duk^wibəł was not a deity. He was born from the union of an Indian woman and a star (see Haeberlin 1924).

She said, "Let me tell you a story." It was about two sisters. The younger one was selfish: always saying, "this is mine," "me first," "mine, mine," "me first." One evening they were sleeping outside. They could see the whole wide sky. They were looking at the stars. The younger sister said, "I choose the red star; that is the prettiest. It's mine. You can have the blue one." Her sister said, "All right, mine is the blue star." They watched those stars twinkling. When they fell asleep, the Great Spirit came, and he lifted them up into the high sky. He said, "Now, each one of you will meet the red star and the blue star." The red star was a young man with very sore red eyes, and the blue star was handsome and beautiful. My grandmother said, "You must remember not to grab at everything, not to say, "me first," "this is mine," "me first." You are going to have a husband with red sore eyes."

When she told me that legend, it made more of an impression on me than saying over and over, "Now you stop it, stop it." It's a long story, and it is very pretty and romantic, but it is shortened to teach the girls not to be "grabby" and selfish and say, "Me first!"

Can you imagine what a nice society it was? All Indians. And each one not pushing and not grabbing; no one is laughing out loud or in a loud voice. Nobody is squealing; no girls are squealing. How quiet, helpful, really helpful to each other they were. They shared everything. When everybody shares, it gets to be a very loving, quiet place. Of course, that is not to say that we were good all of the time. You can't be. There were bound to be mistakes.

Religion

I have talked with some of the girls I went to school with, in my age group, and many of them never heard about where the longhouse came from or about the mysterious animal Lətsxkanəm saw in Puget Sound. Most of the girls I went to school with were all very strong Catholics.

When I think about those times, when I was small, I remember how strong the teachings of the Catholic Church were. How fearful, I thought. I was terrified of the priest. I never ever wanted to see the priest, but I went to church because my mother went every Sunday. I remember being in church a lot of the time during those days.

When I was real small the priest lived here. The priest I used to see was Father Gard. He didn't speak English very well. I guess he came from France. I remember he used to always point at me with his cane, and I died ten thousand deaths. I was always hanging on my mother's skirts. I would try and hide from him. Every time he saw me, he would ask who I was. I thought he couldn't remember, but that was all he could think of to say to a child. "Who is that, and what is your name?" But he would talk with my father and mother. Friendly talk.

One year—it must have been Christmas—because I could hear the choir singing in St. Anne's Church—my mother and the Indians were lined up. All of us carried candles, and while the choir sang, we moved toward the altar and over to the side to the statue of the Virgin Mary. The Indians brought special candles that were made of beeswax, and they were used on the altar of the Catholic Church.

I think that is interesting. My father and mother wanted me to know about our Indian history, our legends, and at the same time they wanted me in the boarding school. I talked with my grandmothers in our own language. When you are little, from the time you are a tiny baby, you are learning your parents' language, and I was learning from my grandmother. Most of the time my parents talked in our own language, although they spoke English, too. But my grandmother did not speak English. So here I was, really, learning two languages simultaneously. Then I had to learn the Catholic religion, all of its prayers—the ordinary mass of the Catholic Church. I was learning a lot of things. On Sunday in the boarding school, we spent the evening listening to Dr. Buchanan[4] read verses from the King James version of the Bible.

I wonder if anybody ever had that many religions? I was hearing my grandparents. They wanted me to know the legends and everything about their time and the ways and traditions because they tried so hard to make me into a fine Indian lady. There were some white people who thought it was a great, wonderful gift for us when they came with civilization and Christianity. I have always felt differently. A lot of Indians felt differently. A lot of our Indian life involved our customs where we wouldn't care about things like the Indians of today. Way back then, people were together.

We learned two religions. When you are little, you are learning a religion from your folks or the pastor or the priest. At the boarding school—in the morning and most of the time—we were Catholics, and in the evening on Sunday we were Protestants. Now a psychiatrist or knowledgeable people among the white people talk about a young person in trouble. They talk about how they had a mixed-up childhood. I think if anybody had a mixed-up

---

4 Buchanan was the agency superintendent, physician, and head of the boarding school.

childhood, we did—two religions, two different gods, and two different traditions, shall we say. Although they emphasized nearly the same principles: you must always tell the truth; you must be honest to yourself and to everyone. I remember I used to wonder, "How could I be honest with myself?" But I didn't ask—not my grandmother and not my mother.

My paternal grandmother spent so much time with me every day before I went to the boarding school and during the summer months when I was home. I would run down to her place. As I said, she only lived a couple of blocks away, but I could run that far for a little while. For hundreds of years grandmothers had a lot to do with raising their grandchildren. They always showed an interest in us young children. I used to meet other older women about the same age as my grandmother, and sometimes they told me the same things that my grandmother told me, things that would help me in my lifetime. For instance, I don't know how many told me about keeping my hair combed and clean. Of course, my parents emphasized that too. Hair always shows when it is clean, shining, and looks alive. But if it gets somewhat dirty, then it loses its shine. So it just seems to me the older women talked a lot about their personal appearance. All of the women I ever saw washed their hands first, before they handled food.

They had so many things to say about everything, such as being physically clean. They emphasized that over and over. I was to wash my hands and wash my arms and wash under every fingernail before handling food. I used to see the Indian women doing that, and I never thought about it until some years ago that that was always what they did. As I said, there was not any running water, so hands and arms had to be washed in a basin right outside the back door. That was a really strict rule from my grandmothers and they emphasized that so many times: washing my hands and washing under the fingernails. It seemed the grandmothers always talked about personal appearance. I was to bathe every morning. Get up early. How I was to wash my hair every few days, shampoo my hair at least every week. My grandmother showed me a plant that grew in a damp place near where we lived.[5] It had a nice fragrance to it, quite a penetrating fragrance. I was to take the leaves and little branches of it and braid it into my hair after every shampoo, and it would make my hair smell good. It was supposed to be done all of the time.

I remember after I got older, I was going to ask her, "What am I going to do in Tulalip School," since there would be no plants to use for my hair. I

---

5   Miner's lettuce or *Claytonia sibirica L.* or *stol'tū·xked* (Gunther 1945: 29).

don't think I quite realized how much my grandmother meant to me until some time after she was gone. She was my only grandmother by the time I was twelve years old. It broke me up when she died. All of the long years since she died, in 1921, I have missed her just as much. I spent so much time with her. It seems to me, I spent more time with her than I did with my mother.

One of the things I remember so well, that seemed to help me when I was in the Indian boarding school, was when I was five or six years old. My grandmother and I were walking home. It was a summer evening. She had been visiting cousins a couple of miles away. I always held her hand when we walked any place. When we arrived at the fork in the road where we lived, she said it was time for me to tell the spirits of the earth who I was. I didn't ask her what she meant exactly. The other grandmother was visiting, too, so there were two grandmothers.

My grandmother stood in the middle of the intersection, and she had me walk in the four directions: east, north, south, west. When I walked in each direction, she stood in the middle of what would seem to be the intersection and watched me and told me to walk slowly—very slowly. When I got to where she wanted me to be, I was told to raise my arms and look out over the trees and the sky and tell my name. Of course, we were speaking in Indian. I spoke out loud because I started when she told me to, and then she said to speak louder—"Louder so that the earth and its spirits can hear you." I called out in a loud voice, looking out over the trees, up in the sky, and I told them my name—my Indian name [Hialth]. I called out and said my name, and then I had to tell the spirits of the earth who my mother was and give her name, give my father's name and give the names of my grandparents so that the earth would know me, recognize me, and help me to grow up and to grow old.

I will always remember the first time I called out my name to the first direction. I must have expected an answer because I looked up in the sky and on the trees, but nobody answered. She told me to walk back to her, and so in that way I walked four directions, and each time I called out loud and told the earth who I was—my name, my parents' names, and my grandparents' names. That made a deep impression on me.

Now that I think about it, I didn't tell my mother or my father about walking in the four directions and identifying myself to the earth. Of course, they must have known about it, and I do know that my father did that for my son Wayne. But William, my younger son, didn't have that done for him. It made an impression on me; I used to think about it when I was in school. I used to get so homesick. We all did, because none of us went home for ten months out of the year. I used to call out, when I had to, to Dukʷibəł.

Dukʷibəł was the creator of our world, our people. The tribes around here have legends about Dukʷibəł . My father and mother used to tell a legend about our languages: why there are so many smaller tribes here in Puget Sound country. Dukʷibəł, the Creator, came from far to the east, and as he walked toward the west, he created the land and the people, and in his hand he carried a handful of languages. As he created each group of people, he gave them a language. When he arrived here, and he created this Puget Sound country, he stopped at the edge of the big water, and he turned around and looked at what he had made, and he said that he had created enough land and enough people. This was the most beautiful land that he had made, and this was the end. As he looked over this beautiful Puget Sound country, he still had a handful of languages left. So he took those languages and threw them, broadcast the languages here in western Washington, because he didn't want to create more land or people. So the many languages that were broadcast over this western Washington area is why we have so many tribes and more languages. Over toward the east of this country, the languages were different and the tribes were bigger.

My grandmother followed the Indian way, but she knew how to pray with a rosary even though she didn't go to church. Somebody would have to take her. She couldn't see very well, and now that I think about it, I think my mother ignored her. I better not say it quite that strongly since she was her mother-in-law. My grandmother came almost every day to our house and sat in the afternoon and talked a little bit. My mother would be ironing or doing something. When my grandmother left, I walked with her, holding her hand.

As we walked, I learned to notice how everything appeared, because my father talked about how the sky looked too. They noticed how the sky looked and how the sunrise looked and what kind of clouds were in the sky: Were they big overcast dark clouds, or were they puffy clouds moving across the sky? Were they moving fast, or were they just moving? Sometimes my grandmother and I walked over toward Mission Beach to have our lunch. She couldn't see anymore, but I held her hand, and she would ask me the color of the sky. Are the clouds white, puffy, like wool? How does the water look? Sometimes the bay looked a very deep blue, and I think they would have called it a cobalt blue. You don't see it like that anymore. Sometimes the water looked green. So I told her. I told her how the mountains looked. She liked to know how Mount Rainier looked—if there were puffs of clouds near the top of the mountain. The Indians used to be able to tell by the puffs of clouds that were on Mount Rainier what the weather would be.

Once in a while, people ask me about the weather. I say, "I don't know." I don't know if it is going to rain, or if it is going to be a cold winter or what. Somebody said to me they thought Indians knew all about the weather. I said. "I didn't." I didn't grow up at home. I grew up in an Indian boarding school. So I couldn't tell about the weather.

My grandmother used to say, "Don't be discouraged. kʷikʷatsqʷaligud. Don't ever be discouraged." She didn't really know much of anything about school. I guess she used to see the Mission School once in a while, and she learned about classroom work when my father went there to school.

I was told you are to live your life according to Dukʷibəł's teachings. If you do all your life what is right, then Dukʷibəł will look upon you. If you do something wrong, or continue in the wrong, he will turn his face away from you—what they call xʷohʼosəd. He will turn his face and will look upon you with his face turned away, but he has his eye on you. If he looks at you like that, then you will have bad luck, and he no longer looks upon you. He never said that is the only way to go. Live the life that is right in everything. But for the Spirit Creator to turn his face away from me was almost like condemning me. Things would happen to me that didn't happen before. It seemed I heard that a number of times, and my father repeated it: "Whatever you do that is good and kind to other people will be returned to you. Whatever you do that is bad, mean, or cruel to other people will also return. Somebody will do mean, cruel things to you—perhaps not now, tomorrow, or next year, but it will surely come." This is a teaching. It made an impression on my father and mother when they were little. It was not repeated every day. It was told to me by my grandmother at one time, and then my father said it twice in his lifetime. Perhaps the third time I heard it, I was grown up and married, and he was just remembering and repeating things. My grandmother and my father and my mother were very special when I was five or six years old.

My grandmother said that when I called out to the spirits of the earth, it was so that the spirits of the earth would know me and always be sympathetic and helpful to me. If I did all of the teachings and followed all that Dukʷibəł said, he would look upon me, and he would always be sympathetic and helpful to me. My father and grandmother emphasized how Dukʷibəł would turn his face away from me, and he would look at me with his eyes slightly averted. This look would be in the form of a cross.

I Remember My Grandmothers

I used to hear my grandmother and the others talk about Semiahmoo Bay, Lummi Bay, and Victoria and Sxlahad, or San Juan Island, where a village of that name was located. The word means "an enclosure," from later times when they saw a fence or a stockade around the village. Some of the Indian tribes stopped there in their canoes. So, they were just being prepared or careful about who was going to be coming through the gates. So that is the name of San Juan Island; it was called Sxlahad.

Chuckanut, the highway that goes to Bellingham along the waterfront, would certainly surprise my grandmother. She would be actually astounded at the number of cars, and how fast they go, and maybe she would be afraid. She was one of the first ones who told me when I was twelve years or so old, "Forgive the white people. They don't know anything." I didn't laugh way back then at anything she said to me. I was sitting on a box, on a big pillow, by where she was sitting knitting socks to sell. I sat there, and she told me legends, or I asked her about when she was a girl, and she remembered things to tell me. One day I said some white people stopped at our place, and I was running down the white people. We didn't see that many white people when I was little. The only white people were at the boarding school. They were employees. Otherwise, there were no white people out here. The nearest were in Marysville.

My grandmother never, ever spoke English. She always spoke in our language. When I talked with her I always talked our language. She said you must have pity on the white people. I was just going to say something, but we never answered our elders, not ever; you were to just sit and listen and thank them for what they said. She said you must have pity on the white people. They really don't know, most of the time, what they are doing. Wherever they came from, they were a lost people. So what they do around here, around this country—she was just speaking of our Puget Sound country—what they do seems, you might say, crazy. You must forgive them. They don't know any better. Whatever manners they might have had have just been dropped or forgotten. You have to have pity on them.

I was just thinking of her, and I was thinking, there is no way to answer her. I could have hollered to high heaven. "Have pity on them? Grandmother, are you in your right mind?" I think that's why all of those little grandmothers seemed so placid. You'd think that nothing ever really got through to them. I used to think, oh, grandmother, she doesn't know what it is like to be a teenager. Well, she did. She said times are different. Clothes are different, perhaps, but nothing changes—good manners, kindness, courtesy never changes.

She was saying, *ʔošəbdxʷ*, meaning "have pity." Have pity on the white people. They don't know any better. They run around—*saxʷsaxʷəbid*, which means "running and jumping all over the country." "You find them all over. They seem like they don't know where they are going, or what they want. But they are going fast." They used to come around in rowboats, walking on the beaches and looking at the timber, rivers, lands, and everything. She said, "It is as though they were a lost people—wherever they come from." She didn't know where they came from. They just came from far, far away across a big body of water. She told me, "You must forgive them. They don't know any better. It seems like wherever they were born, they don't stay there. It just seems as though they are a lost people, and they are not too certain what they are looking for, or where they are going; they are going fast. You have to forgive them. They don't know any better."

I thought it was kind of funny years after she was dead and gone. I thought, "Grandmother, what do you mean: 'be good to them'? They are a bunch of brawling, drunken people. People who call me names. Tell me to get out of there. And you want me to be kind to them?"

Of course, my mother was like that, and my father was too. He said, "You have to overlook a lot of things. Your best friends are going to be white, you remember. A few will be your friends and will stick by you through thick and thin. Maybe some of your relatives have helped so far, but not as it gets to be too much for them."

I forgot all about that until about two or three years ago, and that is when I thought: Oh, grandmother, you don't know what you are saying." She didn't run into many white people in her later years when she came here to live. She didn't go into town. Everything she had my mother and other relatives bought for her. The pitiful poverty of those elderly ladies like my grandmother is another thing. My father worked at the Agency, and he bought all of her groceries. Every month he went to see what she wanted: flour, salt, lard, baking powder, and meat. My mother baked bread for her and cooked roast beef. When I think of them, I think how brave they were. If I was in a situation like that, where my husband had died, most of my children had died, my grandchildren had died, and I was all alone, and the roof over my head was a poor one because it was just one room, I don't think I could take it.

My mother bought the calico for her dresses when they became worn. The calico material was usually blue and had a design made up of tiny flowers. The dresses had wide skirts and a fitted blouse my mother called a "basque": it buttoned all the way up to the neck. The sleeves were two or three inches above the wrist and showed their bracelets. Almost all of the older Indian ladies had Indian jewelry made from hammered silver coins. My grandmother wore the black velvet blouses and skirts for Sunday. The velvet blouses and skirts were somewhat discouraged because we were supposed to be getting civilized.

I remember my grandmother would have her sisters and brothers-in-law come from La Conner. They came in their canoes and brought their friends and slept all over or in some of the vacant buildings around Mission Beach. They cooked and ate in grandmother's little place. They came to visit, and they stayed for maybe two or three weeks. In a way, that was interesting. I knew Indians who went visiting and stayed a week, two weeks, or maybe two years, or all of the rest of their lives. They are welcome in a place where their brother, sister, or cousin is living, or even cousins-in-law. There was plenty of food: deer, native pheasant, clams, different kinds of fish. Food was not a problem; although, it would be now.

Elderly little women knitted heavy woolen socks. Somehow, somebody got them to town or to Everett or all of the way to Port Townsend. Western Washington logging, timber, and mill workers wore those woolen socks that the Indians made. So there was usually a place to sell hand-knitted Indian socks. Those women worked almost day and night. They drank coffee and ate a piece of bread in the morning, and then they started knitting. They fixed something to eat for lunch and kept on knitting and knitting. No matter where they went, if they were walking along, they knitted.

Some of the Indian women had spinning wheels that were made by Indian men. You would think Indian men way back then wouldn't know how to make one. But they saw the spinning wheels someplace and noticed how they were made; then they carved the wheels and put them together. I have seen the handmade ones. My aunt, my father's sister, had a homemade spinning wheel.

I used to help my grandmother, too, in preparing the wool. Teasing the wool, doing like this, is called *cədʼx̌əlqid*; this is the beginning in the preparation of the wool. The wool has already been washed, so you fluff it up. Then after it is washed, it is dried, and the thorns or dried leaves will fall out of it. Then the pile of fluffy wool is carded. It is made into pieces one and one-half to two inches in diameter and fourteen inches long in a skein. The pieces are then put onto the spinning wheel to be spun into yarn.

My aunt spun wool that way. She put the small piece on the end, and she had her foot going, and that spinning wheel was turning, and she turned her fingers and spun the wool on it. I thought it looked easy. I asked if I could try it. She said, "Oh, of course." She talked Indian, "Just go ahead." She told me something about how to do it. "Be sure to turn it as it goes and feed it in." I couldn't do that and move my foot and turn the treadle and do as she said with my hands. The thing spun around and broke right off. So I stopped it, and the wheel was flopping around. She said, "You didn't turn your fingers. Turn your fingers so that it spins through your fingers. Don't hold it that tight. Let it turn in your fingers." So she patched it up and let me try it again. I broke the yarn again, and she said, "You will have to do it a little more often."

My grandmother used an Indian spindle and so did my mother. I thought, "That looks easy: you spin it on your knee with one hand and with the other turn your fingers with the wool that is spinning." My mother and grandmother said, "Move your fingers. Don't hold it so tight." Anyway, I broke the wool again.

I have one of those spindle whorls that my mother spun white wool on. She said she got it too tight. She couldn't see very well then. She must have been 100 years old. I have tried that too, and I flopped it onto the floor. I thought at first, "Oh, that's easy." I was showing some white people who wanted to know how in the world you use it. It went spinning off of my lap and went around in a big circle. I said, "Oh dear. Oh, well, now you know." My father used to say, "Don't go rushing into something you really don't know about. You think it looks easy. Don't go rushing. You are liable to end up looking like you didn't know anything to begin with."

So, that was how I ended up. I had a hard time with that Indian spindle.[6] I don't think I could do that now—not anymore.

Childhood Pastimes

Every Indian girl had to know how to sew. By the time I was six years old, I could sew. I also knew how to knit. I went to a Montessori school then. When I was seven years old, I went to the Tulalip Indian School. I have a dress my sister made for her doll. You should see how fine the stitching is. We sat on the floor, on a couple of cushions, or sometimes we sat on small toy chairs when we sewed. The chairs were made for little ones to sit on. We had to sew.

I knew how to cut out a dress with a yoke. My sister cut it out so that it

---

6   The spindle is an important decorative item in Coast Salish art; see Suttles 1975.

would fit, and she made the little pants. My mother let us have scraps of cloth to sew on. Sometimes we made little quilts for our dolls—not very fancy ones. Every Indian girl knew how to sew and could also do straight knitting. (I still have my doll with the kidskin body. It had dark brown hair that I used to comb.) We sat and sewed almost every day, and my mother looked at our stitches and would usually ask us to "make them smaller."

My paternal grandmother looked at what we were sewing when she came to visit. When Indian women came to visit, even those who were my mother's age looked at what we were sewing. My mother and her mother learned how to sew with the white man's needles. Before that, they didn't have little needles like the white man's steel needles. So when they got the white man's steel needles, they said you have to make small stitches and make them even. Don't have big sloppy stitches. People will look at your clothes or your moccasins and if they have big sloppy stitches, nobody will marry you. They will know you are lazy and good for nothing. I don't know how many times I heard that during all of the years I was growing up: "You had better learn how to do this."

The only thing I never learned was how to cook. I mean, anybody can peel potatoes and boil them. One of my cousins asked me one time why I didn't know anything about cooking. I really wasn't home that much. My mother didn't want us fussing around in the kitchen. I would be in the kitchen with my mother when it was time to prepare food for some meal. I was the one wringing my fingers and saying, "What shall I do? What to do?" My mother would say, "You can do this or that." One time my father said, "Don't stand around and say 'what shall I do now?' Watch your mother and the other women as they prepare food and then you will know what to do." Well, I didn't learn. After I went to the boarding school, I was home only two months during the year. You would think I would learn, but I didn't. I wasn't interested in cooking. After my sister died, my mother never insisted that I cook or that I do anything.

My sister and I cooked peeled potatoes. We put lard in a frying pan and poured peeled potatoes for fried potatoes. My sister knew how to cook, but when we were home my mother didn't want us to disturb her kitchen. When she had bread rising we stayed out of there. When my mother made donuts, once in a while we asked to help. Indians didn't have that much, to be wasting grease or oil for donuts, but they were good. She let us cut our initials in the grease, and it kind of changed shape. Then when I got in school, there weren't any donuts or cake or sugar.

As I said before, my mother spent her childhood at a longhouse on Guemes Island, where the Samish Tribe had their main village. She had a pet cat. I guess they got it for her when it was a kitten. When I was little, I remember seeing quite a number of Indian women carrying their pet cats in their arms. They carried it along in the canoe. If they were living on Whidbey Island, they took their cats, and after a year the men would say, "Are you taking that cat along or something?" The Indian women didn't especially listen to those men. They were just talking. I had a pet cat. I remember my father said, "Don't hold it too close to your face." I was running all over, carrying my "child." He was wrapped up in a shawl.

My mother and her cousin were about the same age. When they were children together on Guemes Island, they both had kittens the family got from Victoria. My mother called her cat her grandson. We used to laugh when I was growing up that my mother, when she was a little girl, played that she was a little old grandmother and that she had a grandson. Her uncles built little mat houses exactly like the grown-up mat houses that were used when they went out to the islands for fishing, clamming, and drying salmon and clams. Their mat house was just big enough for them, so that they could put a blanket and a cushion in it and they could sleep there. I think they used to have hard tack to eat in there too. They didn't have anything then like cookies. Their mother let them take an old frying pan and maybe a pot to carry water in.

My mother remembered one time her cat disappeared. She had picked up what she thought was her grandson in an empty roll of cloth. The cat was gone. So she and her cousin came out of their little mat house, looking around. A couple of her uncles were walking by. They said to my mother, "If you are looking for your grandson, he is running way down the beach that way." My mother and her cousin felt kind of embarrassed. They didn't know that any of the grown-ups knew—that they had a grandson. So they ran all over the beach, trying to catch the grandson. Her uncles came and helped catch her grandson. Her mother said, "Let the cat run around. You can't hold him wrapped up like that all day."

When my father was little, his uncles made him a little canoe just big enough for him. He said he didn't know what happened to it, but it was an absolutely beautiful tiny canoe that he played in. Somebody helped him build a rowboat too. He said in the early days when the white people first started coming here, the Indians wondered what kind of people would travel backwards in a boat? Why would they travel in the direction they couldn't see? He remembered rowing around in his rowboat, making his own oars, and trying to figure out why the oars didn't slip when the white people rowed their boats. So he used to paddle around in a small rowboat and a small canoe. Sometimes his cousin got on, and they all sank.

My father talked about how he and his cousins dove when they were swimming around and walked along the bottom. Way back then, the water was clear blue. They carried big rocks with them in order to stay down. Then they met each other under the water and talked to each other, but they didn't stay down long. They had to drop the rocks. They had to come to the top, and then they laughed and laughed. They talked to each other under the water. He said they looked different to each other. Their eyes looked funny. When they talked, big bubbles came out. Paddling to the top, they laughed and laughed and told each other how funny they looked.

My father and his cousins played hunters chasing deer. My father said he was always the deer. He used to complain and say, "I don't want to be the deer this time. I want to be the hunter." His cousins looked at him and said, "No, you be the deer. We will let you be the hunter next time." So he had to run through the woods, and they were chasing him. They were all bigger than him, and they could catch him when he got back on the beach. He tried to run through the water. They caught him and rolled him over and tickled him and made him laugh. But he said he got scared of them when he was running through the woods. He yelled and yelled in the circle when they were talking about what they were going to play. Somebody said, "Let us be hunters. William can be the deer." He protested, and they said, "You can be the hunter next time," but next time never came.

We weren't supposed to play Indian games. My mother and her cousins played with wooden dolls that their uncles carved. They weren't very big. My mother said they were less than a foot long. They were just wonderful. Years later they saw china dolls that came from the white stores in the cities and towns. I still have my kidskin doll. It was one of the last dolls my parents got me for Christmas. My sister cut out the pants and the little dress. We both had the same kind of dolls; my mother would buy two so nobody would get into an argument. My mother would let us have scraps of cloth to sew the outfits. The doll had real, dark brown hair that I used to comb, although I didn't comb it much because it wasn't meant to be combed. But we would sit and sew almost every day, and my mother would come and look at the stitches, and she would say, "You can make them look smaller." My paternal grandmother, and every Indian woman who came, would want to look at our sewing. Sometimes we were trying to make little quilts for our dolls, but they were not very fancy quilts; every Indian woman knew how to sew.

Once in a while, I look at dolls at the stores at Christmastime, and a great number of them are blond, blue-eyed dolls. You see black dolls, too. But Indian dolls are always the same. They make them wrapped up in blankets. Years and years ago, I first saw them. I don't think those type of dolls have changed very much.

When we were little, there were times when we didn't have the china dolls. I accidentally dropped mine when I was running to my grandmother's house and it landed on a rock, all broken up. I cried and cried. But my mother and grandmother made dolls for me out of rags. They just rolled up a piece of sheet—something that was sort of tan or a yellow color. All they did was tie part of his head, then another tie or another small roll and put it between, and that is the two arms. Then it is tied at the waist, so the arms won't fall off. I thought they were just grand. I carried those rag dolls around. My mother would go over to my grandmother's house—I called her aunt then[7]—she lived about two blocks away. I showed her my doll. Sometimes it seems like little children can be very happy with something very simple. Who would be satisfied with a rag doll made like that? I thought they were just grand. Sometimes my mother crocheted or knitted little bonnets or a sweater for the doll—for the little rag doll.

The Indian boys had a bigger area to play in than the Indian girls. We had to stay very close to our mother or our grandmother. We were not allowed to go walking way out somewhere into the woods to look for wild roses or whatever. We had to stay close by.

One of the pleasures we had when spring came was to walk with some of our friends around the lilac bushes. We'd put our arms around one another's shoulders and go walking around the playground at the boarding school. The lilacs filled an area more than a block long, but they were planted close together, and there were places where you could squeeze through. They had been there for years.

My mother had lilacs just like the ones that were at the school, and their fragrance was very pronounced. You could smell them a long way off. If my mother had any spare dollars, she bought a plant. She bought some Persian lilacs one time. They were a darker purple. But those beautiful things didn't

---

7   This woman would be a sister or a cousin of her father or her mother, not her paternal grandmother.

have the fragrance that the old-fashioned ones had. They had double blossoms in big clusters.

We used to play a game in the boarding school called Auntie-I-Over. (I was asked to speak to a fourth or fifth grade class in Everett several years ago. Another woman came to talk at the same time. They asked if it would be all right if both of us came. I said it would be grand. I never saw her before. She was born in Norway or Sweden, and she said they played Auntie-I-Over, too.) We made a round, handmade ball of old rags. My sister and some of her friends stood on the other side of the woodshed or a house. Some of the homes were small, shall we say; they were almost shacks. They had just an outside wall, no inner wall and no ceiling.

If I had the ball, I would shout loudly — "Auntie-I Over" — and throw the ball over the roof. I could imagine what it did to the roofs. Then it would roll off of the roof. My sister and her friends would catch it, and then we moved to the other end. Maybe we were at the front door of a woodshed. Then I went running over to the other end; the friend on the other side did that, too. You could just tell about where he was, or any of us were, by where our voices came from. We would catch the ball. You run clear to the other end, and here comes the ball right over, and you have to run and run to try to catch it before it falls on the ground. I will always remember my sister and her friends and us running over to the other end and throwing it, and it's not where they think it's coming from, and they would miss it. You could hear them saying, "Ohh!" They would say, "You are not supposed to do that! You have to stay in the same place after that." "Auntie-I-Over" is hollered. But sometimes we hollered that out, and we ran — ran to a different place and threw the ball.

We made our own ball out of strips of cloth that were wound round and round. (The lady from Europe said they made theirs, too.)

We had homemade bats. We could bat the cloth balls half a dozen times; then it went flat. You couldn't play with it anymore. We had to unroll our ball and ask somebody to roll it up again and make a new ball.

Now, when you go to stores there are all kinds of rubber balls of every size: soccer balls, basketballs, and footballs. Here it was a problem keeping a ball. Sometimes if we played baseball, somebody would bat the ball clear into the brush. Maybe we were running around the bases, and we were hollering. "Lost ball, lost ball. You have to go back to home plate. You can't run!" You can't make a home run on a lost ball. We tried to settle it. It's the law. They didn't have football in the boarding school, but they did have baseball and basketball.

We used to go over to Mission Beach. On the high bank, way up, are some black roots.[8] They have bulbs on them that taste like raw peanuts. We were always eating them. We liked to climb up that sand and dirt hill and slide down. My grandmother and her younger sisters were there one time with my father when he was about three years old. They spread a blanket on the beach—the tide was way out—and they told him, "You stay here." So his mother, the next sister, Mary (Martha Lamont's mother), the next one was Mary Josephine (Henry Gobin's grandmother), and Jenny (the youngest sister) were there together. The only one that was married then was my grandmother. They were about seventeen years old.

One of my aunts said my father hollered and hollered—standing up on the blanket—and hollered at them. "Let's go home." Of course, he is talking in Indian. "Let's go home. Šəlus will get you!" Well, Šəlus was Father Chirouse. When he was little, they used to scare him by saying, "You have to keep quiet. Don't leave this blanket, or Šəlus will come after you." He was terrified of Šəlus. "If you don't keep quiet, the Šəlus will come after you." So, he would keep quiet. He was afraid of Šəlus. He finally caught a glimpse of Father Chirouse—but the priest at the school when my father came there in 1888 was Father Simon.

I remember my grandmother had another sister come from La Conner; her name was Jenny. She remembered my father hollering and trying to scare them that Father Chirouse will get them. My father said he remembered they would laugh, and here he was all by himself, scared, looking around, and they were pulling up those roots, filling up their aprons and baskets to take them home and wash them and eat them. My father said his mother and the others would laugh and laugh and giggle and giggle, and he would sit there and get so tired. He would try to scare them. "Father Šəlus will come and get you! Prayer will get you."

T'aywəł is prayer. Isn't that interesting, we had a word for prayer? T'aywəł.

Somebody was telling me that Tommy Gobin and his family are very religious people. In Adam's church,[9] Tommy gets up and preaches, talks about the sinfulness of the Indians who never knew Christ and about people who are not saved. They didn't know anything about God or prayer or anything. I was saying it is interesting that all tribes have a name for prayer. In our

---

8   Beach peas or *Lathyrus japonicus*; see Pojar and MacKinnon 2004, and Kruckeberg 1991.

9   Adam Williams, pastor of the Church of God.

tribe prayer is *t'aywəł*. It means "to ask," almost in the way of pleading, but "to ask for information" is *tk^wwk^wq^w*. "To tell news," like our newspaper, is *siəʔdsəb*. "To ask for information" is *tk^wwk^wq^w*. *T'aywəł* is only "to plead to Duk^wibəł," to an almighty spirit for guidance or for courage. For instance, my father would be hollering at his mother that prayer will get you. He knew about prayer, but he thought the prayer he had never seen was in church. He had never been in the Catholic Church. He was terrified of the priest, of Chirouse, and he was terrified of Chirouse's prayers. So that *t'aywəł* came from our own beliefs; they called that Father Chirouse's "prayer" that's *t'aywəł* He would holler at his mother and his aunts, "Prayer will get you folks! Stop your laughing! Let us go home! I am hungry! I need a drink of water!" They would come back and bring him water. There was a spring there. They would bring him a tin cup of water.

He remembered that once in a while, and he said, "No wonder they never came. They didn't get scared of prayer. They hollered, 'You are okay.' 'Don't worry.' 'Quiet now.' 'Everything is all right.'" Now that I think about it, I really shouldn't have been confused—that my grandmother would tell me to remember all of the legends and all of the traditions she told me and her sisters told me and all of the Indians told me, or the ones whom I met.

Every Indian woman I met, way back then when I was little, would always greet the little children. Every little child was greeted by a grandmother, any grandmother, even if they never saw them before. All of those older grandmothers—not just my real grandmother, but the same generation as my grandmother—would greet me. They would put their hands on my head and say the nicest loving words to me. They would say, "Oh, *k̓^woy[əʔ]*." It is almost like saying "oh, precious, precious." They would all put their hands on my head and brush my hair. My hair was always parted down the middle and braided tightly into two braids. They would always do like that with my hair. They would smooth my hair, and then they would hold their hand on each side of my face and kiss me on the forehead—every one of them that I met. The very elderly men would put one hand on my head and say, "Oh, *k̓^woy[əʔ]*, and that one word in our language—Snohomish, Skagit, Snoqualmie, Puyallup or Duwamish—is *k̓^woy[əʔ]*. You say that to a young girl, your daughter or your granddaughter.

My mother and father called me *k̓^woy[əʔ]* in our Snohomish language. S.k̓^wuyi is "mother" with an "s" sound in the beginning, but that is not quite what they called the little girls. It is *k̓oy*, which means "precious little mother" or "daughter." The Indians seemed to feel every little girl was going to be an important mother of the tribe. Her children would be additions to the tribe, and how she raised them was going to be important. So you have to treat her like a little lady. Let her know she is important, and the same way for the boys. Every little Indian child had his or her own blessing.

I haven't thought of that for fifty or sixty years. They would put their hands on each side of my fat face and say, "Oh, k̓oy, oh, k̓oy." A couple of years ago, some of us were remembering. Ethel Sam said, "Remember when we used to meet the elderly grandmothers and grandfathers? They would always put their hands on our heads and say such precious, loving things to each of us, even if they never saw us before."

My father was the one who told me, in a specific way, in powerful, slowly spoken words, "You always remember that you are an Indian. You are an Indian girl. You will always remember." I never, ever asked, and what is more, I know I am an Indian girl. But how do I do this? I am supposed to . . . If time passes, I am here or there, and I know I am an Indian.

My father was the one who made it clear about pride, about being proud. "You must always be proud that you are an Indian. You remember. You be proud." Being proud can mean different things. You can be proud and be really mean. That is not the kind of pride to have. It has to be with the knowledge that you have humble pride—that, I think, is the closest you can come to describing what kind of pride I was supposed to have.

I remember thinking when they would repeat it every once in a while, "You must always be proud you are an Indian. That is something very special. Don't throw your face around, or stick out your little finger and pick up your food or cup, or have your little finger sticking up." I remember thinking, "Oh, dear, I wonder what they mean by 'humble pride.' How can I be proud and still be proud and humble?" Those two things are totally different. If I asked, I don't know what they would have said. Furthermore, I know better than to be asking. Somehow, you learn.

6 / The Tulalip Indian Boarding School

I N school we tried to follow what our grandparents said. When I arrived at the Indian boarding school in 1912, I was seven years old. It seemed so cold, and we were always running, running, hurry, hurry, hurry. Compared to my home, it was a traumatic shock. I don't think anyone stopped to think how hard it was for us Indian children to be taken to an Indian school and suddenly have to get up at 5:30 in the morning. At home I woke up around seven or nine o'clock in the morning, and I could always eat. My mother would fix something.

My mother did the laundry for the agent. When I was really small, I used to follow her around, tell her I was hungry, and she would finish her washing or whatever she was doing. Then she would take me to the kitchen and fix me homemade bread and butter. The Indian women made homemade yeast bread. Every week my mother made loaves and loaves of wonderful homemade bread.

The boarding school was a dreadful monotony: getting up early, and our shoes and stockings were left downstairs in the basement playrooms. We took off our shoes and stockings in the basement playrooms at night, and we marched up two stairways to go to bed. In case we tried to run away, we were separated from our shoes. I consider that like a life in a penitentiary. If a bell rang, I ran. The discipline was to civilize us.

It was a terrifying time to arrive at the boarding school. I never saw my mother, but I saw my father every other day or so. He worked there at the agency and he was there every day, but sometimes I didn't see him. I was so very homesick. I used to cry. I wanted to go home. My sister was already in the school. She was almost two years older than me, but she used to talk to me and tell me not to cry. She said you will get used to it here and you will have some fun. I never could see why I would have fun, but I eventually did. They had a very short time for us to play in the evening.

The little girls stayed in dormitories C and D. That is where I used to sleep. When I first got to the school, I was in dormitory D, where the little girls were, and then when I got bigger—a teenager who was fourteen or fifteen years old—I was naturally with the big girls. The big girls' companies were A and B. I never got to be tall enough for Company A, even though that was my ambition.

As soon as we got up in the morning, we made our beds. Believe me, the sheets had to be absolutely straight and stiff. You talk about how you can bounce a quarter off of the sheets in the Army. Well, ours were like that, and I mean they were absolutely straight and stiff. Each one of us had two Army blankets. They were wool, but thinner—not what you would consider wool today from a department store. They were Army blankets. The two blankets and top sheet were folded a certain way over the foot of the bed, so that the sheets were all showing. They had to be absolutely smooth and straight. Pillows were straight up and down.

I wonder where they got the pillows? The pillows and the mattresses were filled with straw. They were actually pretty good, I guess. But all of us had single beds. They were narrow steel beds. Each one of us slept separately.

When we got up in the morning, it was so bitterly cold. I remember my teeth chattering and everybody's teeth chattering.

We had a clothing room. On one side were the cupboards. Actually, they were just boxes. All of them were numbered, and every week that is where my clean socks and everything came back from the laundry. Everything was folded up and put in there by some of the girls.

We wore uniforms. The girls' uniforms were made of wool serge. Blue wool serge is the heaviest, scratchiest material that was ever invented on the earth. In the spring and summer, when we were marching into the church and then sitting in the church, sometimes it would get too warm. The dresses had long sleeves and a high, tight neck. My skin itched, and it was most uncomfortable. All of those ten years that I was there we had navy blue uniforms, and they were all made alike. They were made in the sewing room and made to fit each one of us. Sometimes they were trimmed with white braid and maybe the next year with black braid, but it was still navy blue serge.

We wore one workday dress every day, and then we had one school dress that was usually made of navy blue material that had little figures with tiny leaves or tiny flowers. We didn't wear heavy serge to the classroom; it was for Sunday. We had school dresses, and they were made alike too. We had a small crossbar gingham dress for everyday. The small girls had red with tiny flowers in a flocked design, and the big girls had navy blue with small white flowers. They had high collars and long sleeves, but they weren't hot and scratchy like the blue serge.

The boys' uniforms were navy blue, with a high choker collar and gold buttons, and they had to be buttoned tight. Their school clothes were brown corduroy pants and blue work shirts.

After we washed up, dressed, combed and braided our hair, we lined up and put on our coats, and we were outside by six o'clock in the morning. We did exercises like the Army does for half an hour. We did deep knee bends and every kind of jumping exercise you could think of that was exactly like the Army does today. We were hungry and cold. Even in winter we were out there exercising, and we were freezing. The ground was frozen; it was all frosty white. We jogged around the quadrangle on the sidewalks, company by company, and all of us kept in step because we had officers, and the matron was out there on the porch where she could see us. She shrieked at us about keeping in step, and believe me, we learned how to keep in step. We were better than any army you ever saw.

Once in a while, I see the Army on the news. Their exercises, their running, is what we did when we were little children. It was really a military school. You might say it wouldn't hurt anybody. I don't think it would hurt anybody, but there wasn't enough for us to eat. We were hungry there.

Then at 7 A.M., we all marched into the dining room for breakfast. We marched everywhere. We all marched in, company by company, from the tallest to the shortest. We lined up around the tables. The tables held twelve boys or twelve girls. The girls sat separately from the boys, where we ate across the room. On each end of the tables sat a bigger girl or a bigger boy and a platter of bread.

I have to say something about the bread. We had the nicest bread. It was homemade; baked right there by the assistant baker. She had the big girls working in the bakery. Loaves and loaves of the best-tasting bread were baked every day. Now and then I say that the bread must have helped us survive, because otherwise the food was inadequate.

Actually, we were almost starving. I am quite sure people who hear me say that would say, "Oh, now, you know when you are little, you get hungry and think you are starving." But in that school, the food was never, ever enough. We ate roast beef and potatoes, and it tasted really nice. We even ate roast beef and potatoes on Thanksgiving and Christmas. Sometimes the potatoes would last until January, February, and then the potatoes wouldn't be anymore. So we just had meat and bread. Of course, there were never any vegetables and there was never enough milk. The pride of the Indian agent was the dairy herd, but the milk that those cows gave for over two hundred children was never enough. I usually got, maybe, a fourth of a cup of milk. There was never any fruit. On Thanksgiving and Christmas each one of us would get an apple. But once in a while, since the school had orchards, we would have one slice of apple pie on Sundays. I don't know what happened, but there would be years when we would have less to eat.

In later years, it was actually written in government reports that the food given to the Indian children in the boarding schools was, as I said, inadequate.

One year we didn't have any towels. Everyone had their own towels hanging in the lavatory by number. I remember my number; it was thirty-three. My towel, my dresses, my stockings, my shoes, my uniforms all had my number on them. They were sewn inside.

It seems to me I ought to go to paradise for all of that suffering. The discipline and the schedule were the killing thing.[1] There wasn't even enough time to go to the bathroom. It never varied from one year to the next. All of those years I was there, I knew exactly what I was going to do one year or two years later, and where I would be at a certain time. I would be either in the kitchen, the sewing room, or the laundry.

It was quite a traumatic shock for the little Indian children to be brought to an Indian boarding school and no one, outside of our parents, worrying about us. Nobody seemed to worry that we did have a big shock to go from home, where it is warm and where you hear your mother's voice all the time. You go to a boarding school like that and you never see your mother anymore.

I saw my father, really, more often than I saw my mother. He worked at the Indian Agency.[2] He operated the mill where they made lumber. I guess you might say it was rough lumber, but it seemed it was always needed for the barns, the dairy barn, or repairing fences all over where they had the school cows.

They had a school herd of cows, about sixteen cows, that the schoolboys milked every morning and every afternoon too, I think. But, really, they gave so little milk because the milk was never enough for two hundred children. I would get maybe a fourth of a cup of milk or sometimes none at all. It all depended upon how hungry someone else was.

---

1   See Dr. Buchanan's boarding school schedule in the Appendix.
2   He was also responsible for the grounds and transporting the superintendent and visitors to and from Everett in the agency launch.

Work Details

When I first got there, I was seven years old, and we went to school for half a day, from 1 P.M. to 4:30 P.M. We worked in the morning from 7 A.M. to 11:30 A.M. We worked in different areas that were called "details." The details were assigned by age and grade. They had a kitchen detail where the bigger girls worked, a laundry where some of the others worked, and then a sewing room.

When I first arrived at the school, I worked in the dining room. We cleared the tables. Somebody washed the dishes. We wiped the dishes and we set the table. Then, along about that time, we sat there for two hours or more and peeled potatoes. Every day we peeled about five or six buckets of potatoes—that is the way they came. They brought in a bucket, and we peeled and peeled potatoes.

Mrs. Andrews tried to make a good worker out of me. The doctor and my father wanted me to be outdoors. I used to have to mop the porches: the porch at the dining hall, the porch at the Girls Building, the porch at the agency office. That used to just irk me because I would have to walk down there with a bucket of soapy water—not real hot. Then I'd have a broom and a mop. I'm going down there, and I always met a lot of people, and I've got brooms, and they're hitting my head. I used to feel real embarrassed. You know, I felt very low class.[3] I'd mop very hard. Mop it with soapy water. Then I'd go over it again with plain water, and that made her—Mrs. Andrews—just howl and howl. She said, "You tell that Harriette Shelton to get back here and mop this porch; this is terrible. Look at this." They'd look at it. And they didn't know what was the matter with it. It looked clean and okay. She was always saying that. "You tell that Harriette Shelton to get back here. Harriette Shelton, you just get down to the office and you mop that again. You ought to be ashamed of yourself. Doctor is very mad over that porch." So I would go down there. I don't see how I lived through that, you know. I think the only reason I lived was because I was so mad at her all the time. She was bound and determined to show me she was going to make a good girl out of me, and I was a good girl. I wasn't bad. She just wanted all of us to jump as soon as she said something. We moved, and I mean fast. She said if the bell rang, then you line up and I mean right now. If you were in the bathroom and you had to go, you let that go and you lined up. I thought that was like torture

---

3   Mrs. Dover is referring to the Snohomish (Coast Salish) class system; see Suttles 1951.

when you were in the bathroom and you wanted to go and you couldn't go. If you look at the schedule [see Appendix], you would see there was no time for recreation and no time to go to the bathroom. It was half hour by half hour by half hour from five o'clock in the morning to nine o'clock at night when everybody was in bed. Some girls just folded up and died.

When I was twelve or fourteen years old, I worked in the laundry, and that was a killer. I worked in the front building, the club building. Those washers were big, like five to six feet wide and five feet high, and they turned back and forth, and they swished the clothes in a big barrel. They had a mangle that ironed the clothes. It rolled continually when they turned it on. That used to scare me when I first worked there. They told us to be careful.

We had to shake the wet sheets and fold them just so. When you ironed them, you put the wide edge first and it goes through, and you have to hold it so that it goes in reasonably straight. Then the pillowcases—you put the other end in first, not the edge. It was hot. You have to be careful. If your hand got caught, you couldn't pull it out again. It just goes on. Those things were hot. One of the girls, she was the same age as my sister—Violet Firgrade—her hand got caught in that mangle, and oh, lands! It was terrible. Violet's hand was mashed, and it looked just awful because her fingers were turned. You would think Dr. Buchanan would try to fix it. Her hand was scarred up. She didn't seem to mind it. She tried to use it, but she couldn't hold anything. That used to scare me. I'd be just terrified. That was hard work.

We would get there at seven in the morning. It was bitterly cold in December, January. The laundress would build up the fire where we ironed. There were three of us; we ironed all of the boys' shirts, the girls' dresses, and the girls' aprons. The sheets and the pillowcases were put through the mangle.

I put some pillowcases in the mangle. I found that awful hard, to stand there all day. After the first day, I could hardly lift my arms. It was hot and steamy in there. No wonder the children died of tuberculosis; that place was dusty. If you opened the doors, it was bitterly cold, and then the wind would blow on you and you were sweating. That was really something. We worked like grown people.

Working in the laundry was a killer. It was the hardest of the work in school. We ironed from 7 A.M. to 11:30 A.M. with heavy, old-fashioned irons, set irons, for the whole school—130 girls' dresses and the blue shirts for the boys. It took us several days to iron them. We stood there for four hours, ironing. In spring and summer it is pretty hot to be ironing that long, but by July it is hot and suffocating. There was a special woodstove that was about five feet high, especially made, so that the irons can stand right on it, and the fire had to be very hot so that the irons are hot enough. There were several rows around the stove where you can set your irons so that they would get hot. You just take another iron and go on. You go back and put it there and take another one. I didn't think I was going to survive standing there, ironing. That's a job.

We worked by age and by grade. When I was twelve years old, I worked in the laundry for five months, and then the next five months I worked in the sewing room again. Then the next year I did what they called "housework" in the Girls Building.

I worked in the sewing room, too, when I was small. We sat there and darned stockings and socks by the millions. Those stockings and socks had such big holes. I already knew how to sew because my mother taught us, and I liked it. We also sewed patches, rips, and tears in the dresses and shirts of the girls and boys. But we could sit down and relax too. They had chairs for us little girls. The chairs had the legs cut off so that they were low to the floor, so it was comfortable.

But I never especially learned how to cook. My sister and I used to make things like cake or something, and we peeled potatoes to help my mother, but cooking—that just upsets me. Some women wondered how I could grow up like that and never really cook. So I always have to tell a big long story that I wasn't at home. I was in that Indian boarding school from the time I was seven years old.

When I had the housework detail, we started upstairs in the dormitory. We had certain brooms—they were wide and long—and then we went over the whole dormitory with dust mops. We ran over all of the 130 beds with dust cloths and dusted everything—even the windowsills. That is why I don't do anything. The dust can pile up in my house and it doesn't bother me. I don't dust. But when we were at home, even our mother had us dust the house.

When I was fourteen years old, I was on the dining room detail again. I was the bigger girl, so I washed all of the dishes for 200 to 230 boys and girls. Today I always say I am not washing dishes. Those dishes can stand there and pile up, and if I really need them then I will wash one. I washed dishes for 230 boys and girls, twice a day. I washed them in the morning and at noon. If I went to school in the afternoon, then I didn't do them at noon but I washed them at supper, and I had to sweep the big dining room. There were little girls to help. They set and cleared the tables, but you have to watch what they are doing. I used to get so tired of washing those dishes.

We washed them in a big washtub. They didn't have dishwashers. I think in later years they got automatic dishwashers, but way back then we washed the dishes by hand. I used to get so tired—that is an awful lot of dishes—of leaning over that hot tub of water. It would go on and on. We had to change the water several times, because with that many dishes the water gets cold. Working in the dining room wasn't really hard; it just went on and on and on. I washed dishes twice a day, but at noon I didn't wash dishes because I had to go to school in the afternoon. As soon as the meal was finished, we all went downstairs and got dressed in our school clothes. Then we spent four hours in a classroom.

We used yellow bars of soap; that is a strong soap and it burns your skin. Knives, forks, spoons were all poured into one washtub where I was washing them. We learned to take two enamel plates and just stir them around. Otherwise, it took several hours. But it took longer to wash the forks because we had to scrub them. But with that many children to help, we had ways of shortening the work. When I got the dishes done, then I helped the smaller girls set the tables for the next meal and swept the floors.

I don't know how I lived through that, now that I think about it. When I got through, about four o'clock, I went downstairs so that I could wash my hands and face and comb my hair again—braid it and tie it up with ribbons. They were long, long days. Many of my cousins and my sister just folded up and died from lack of food, the continual cold, and the long days, long hours.

Religious Training

You would think that Sundays were something nice, but I always found Sunday in that school was a big worry for me, and if it was a big worry for me, then it must have been for others. We went to church, and the priest came, shall we say, from the old school. He was strict. I remember when I was first in school, when I was little, I often fell asleep in church. I used to be terrified because if the priest saw me he might slap me around. He used to slap the boys, but he didn't slap any of the girls.

The whole day of Sunday was never a day of rest. It was as bad as or worse than the week days. I remember we were always so tired and so hungry. We got up early at 5 or 5:30 A.M. We were all Catholics, so on one Sunday of each month we fasted; we didn't have breakfast or supper the night before if we were going to confession and communion. They were such poor meals we never really had enough, so we were really starving. We went to church.

The priest came on the mail boat at 11:30. So then we had mass from 11:30 to 12:30. So then we had our first meal at one o'clock, and that wasn't much food. We had to go through the morning and afternoon, from the night before, on the evening meal and that wasn't much. We had to go all of that time with nothing to eat. I used to get so hungry I could hardly walk.

Father O'Donnell slapped the small boys around when he asked them questions about catechism. They were too frightened to talk, and he would slap them hard. It just about knocked them down, and then they would cry. Then he would slap them on the other side and tell them to stop crying. Here the poor, tiny things were trying to choke off their crying, their sobbing, and the rest of us were so terrified we could hardly breathe.

He was always mad and always shouting. We saw him all day on Sunday. He actually yelled at us and talked to us about being sinners, and how we were going to hell. When I was small, I was afraid to fall asleep because I thought if I went to sleep I would go to hell, and I could see the burning flames—great big flames and nothing but fire.

After Mass in the morning, we marched back to the Girls Building. We changed from our uniforms of blue serge into our everyday clothes—denim overalls and blue shirts for the boys and calico dresses for us girls—and had our noon dinner. We called it dinner. Then right after that, at one o'clock, we changed back into our school clothes—and our school clothes were different from our Sunday clothes. Sunday had navy blue serge for the girls and that is so scratchy and so hot. Our dresses had long sleeves and high collars. In church, the livelong day, those things just itched and burned. Our school clothes had long sleeves and high collars too, but they weren't as bad as the wool serge.

We marched down to the school assembly hall. We would be from one o'clock to four o'clock sitting down in the assembly hall of our school building. And that is all of the boys and all of the girls, all 230 of us or more. The Girls Building and the Boys Building and then the classroom building were all about five blocks away. It was an attractive campus. It had green lawns, sidewalks, and no flowers, really, but they did have lilac bushes that bloomed in the late spring.

Then from 1 to 4 in the afternoon, we studied the catechism of the Catholic Church, and that was terrifying. The teacher was the priest, and he was just meaner than mean. He was always mad. He slapped the small boys around and asked them questions. We had catechism in our school clothes. And then that mean, just really cruel, priest—if the little boys didn't know the answer to some of the questions in the catechism, some of them were too terrified to talk. But, oh, lands, he would slap them so hard and just about knock them down and then they would cry and then he would slap them on the other side to stop them crying.

Father O'Donnell was the priest the livelong ten years I spent there. I was in that school for ten months of every year and then home for two months and back again. So ten months every year for ten years, and every Sunday I had to put up with him.

I want to emphasize I did not enjoy Sunday except for one thing: my mother came to visit every Sunday afternoon. When she came, she visited in the playroom with some of the other parents who were waiting for us to come back from the school where we were in catechism. Her visits saved my life. She used to bring cornbread. She made it in big pans and wrapped it in a clean dishcloth. Then she brought Hershey's chocolates and apples. If she brought two dozen apples, then we gave all of them away. I gave two apples to my friends, and then sometimes some of our relatives came. They hated me, and I hated them, but they got the apples and some of the candy too. I used to get so mad, but I didn't say anything. I wanted my mother to know I was kindhearted; at the same time, I was wishing they were dead.

I always said I think if I had a choice of feeding somebody I would give them cornbread; that is a really nourishing thing. I am always saying to my boys, "You know, if you look at all of the black athletes, they have the most beautiful teeth." And, of course, they came from across the sea and apparently they were already tall people. It's incredible, their strength, they play football—tall and they are strong. They grew up on cornbread and corn porridge, corn meal mush. In England they always say they feed the cornmeal to the horses. Oh, it was some Englishman, an aristocrat, who said, we feed that cornmeal to our horses, but in America they eat cornmeal porridge. An American had a response to that; he said, "Where in the world can you find better horses and better men." Best horses in England, and they feed them corn. Best men in the world in America; they feed them cornmeal. That Englishman didn't have much to say to that. But, anyway, cornmeal bread—I just loved it.

After catechism, we marched back up to the Boys Building and the Girls Building, and then there was a skimpy Sunday supper. We had a half a cup of cocoa and a small piece of coffee cake. It must have had one cup of sugar in it for more than 200 boys and girls, because you couldn't taste the sugar. But I am quite sure somebody would say, "Well, it isn't good for you to have sugar." We rarely had sugar through the whole ten months. The coffee cake was a treat, but it was small. It was probably about two inches square, but it was really good. It had brown sugar on the loaves when it was baked. It was a treat because we never, ever had sugar on the table. Sugar was put in the oat meal mush, but you couldn't really taste it. They probably put a cup of sugar for the 230 children, so you couldn't really taste the sugar. The cook was a good cook, given what she had to work with.

On Sunday evening, small girls could play from six to eight o'clock, when we went to bed. By the time I was thirteen or fourteen years old, I was in Company B. I was a big girl, and on Sunday evening we put on our blue serge uniforms that we wore to church. We marched down to the assembly hall again, and we sat in chairs from 7 to 9:30 P.M. We sat in chairs all Sunday afternoon and evening. Two hours in the evening may not seem very long, but it gets pretty paralyzing. Believe me, those chairs got harder and harder until it was hard for us to stand up and walk. We were kind of paralyzed because we had to sit so still.

All of the bigger boys and bigger girls in A and B Company attended Sunday evening chapel, which was totally different from the Catholic Mass on Sunday morning. Chapel was nothing like the Catholic Mass or the afternoon catechism lessons. Chapel was Protestant. At the evening chapel, two girls and two of the boys read verses from the Bible—not the Catholic Bible, the King James Protestant Bible. The girls' matron (I think she was Episcopalian) and the boys' disciplinarian picked out the two boys and two girls who read the Bible verses. So the evening chapel was all Protestant. I did enjoy the Bible verses because the agent talked for an hour about what the verses meant, and he insisted that we sit absolutely still. The prayer we said was the Prayer of St. Chrysostom, which was a beautiful prayer. I have never seen it anyplace else. It probably belonged to the Catholic Church. It went: "I would be true, for there are those who trust me. I would be brave, for there is much to dare." That is all I remember. But it was a really nice prayer.

Dr. Charles M. Buchanan, our superintendent of the school, was also the Indian agent.[4] The employees were Protestant, so they went down to Sunday evening chapel. The superintendent-agent wanted everybody there except the little girls and boys. Sometimes I enjoyed Sunday evening chapel because the Indian agent was the most interesting man. He was a strict disciplinarian.

---

4   He came to Tulalip as a physician in 1894 and served as physician and agent from 1901 to 1920.

Actually, the man could be cruel. He could beat up the boys, give them the biggest strapping—actually, a flogging. He used to walk by the Girls Building and throw handfuls of nickels over the playground, where there was a basketball court. He would throw those nickels, and we scrambled all over. Some of us got five or six nickels and some didn't get any.

Dr. Buchanan was also a physician. He was a very well educated man, which was kind of rare, because we very seldom got educated people in the Indian Service. They worked in the Indian schools, most of them just two years through high school, teaching us. He was born in Alexandria, Virginia. He came from a wealthy family. He graduated from the University of Virginia. While in college, he also studied music and languages; he knew Latin and he was an accomplished musician.

He also talked to us in chapel and played the piano and the organ for us on Sunday evenings. He played compositions for us by famous composers like Mendelssohn, Mozart, Beethoven, and several other famous composers. When he would play compositions from those marvelous people, he showed us each composer's picture and told us where he was born and about his childhood and the kind of life he led. Then he played pieces by each of them and told us the differences between Beethoven and Mozart. For example, some of the music seems like falling water—really delicate running notes. Beethoven was a heavy, more dramatic-sounding music. I truly enjoyed all of it; it was something worth living for the livelong week. You could just sit there. But, then, you had to sit so still and our clothes were always so stiff. But that was Sunday evening chapel, and we had to sit there from 7 to 9 P.M., and for the livelong day we had been going since 5:30 in the morning. So by ten minutes to 9, we were marching back to the Girls Building and the Boys Building.

I think we lived for and enjoyed the music. We also used to sing hymns on Sunday evening that he liked. We sang things like "Onward Christian Soldiers," and "I Heard the Voice of Jesus Say," "Come Thou Almighty King." In the Catholic Church, we sang something totally different. We sang through the whole Mass, the elevation of the Communion and the Processional. It is a wonder I can remember it—that's a long time ago.

Back at home, now that was totally different, too. Now and then there were some drumbeats on the Indian drum, but not very loudly. My father was very careful. It was against the regulations for Indians to sing their songs or to talk the Indian language. I mean, it was also against the regulations for the Indian children at the school to talk in their Indian languages.

Then at Dr. Buchanan's Sunday evening prayer, we said the Lord's Prayer, the Hail Mary, and the Prayer of St. Chrysostom. Now, I enjoyed that and it was interesting. We listened and read out of the Protestant Bible, and in the morning we had been suffering through catechism. You would think that I would be very knowledgeable and deeply religious. When I was at the boarding school, I said, "Believe me, when I get out of school I am never, never going to church again. I am never going to look at any Bible—never." But, of course, after I left school, I forgot what I said.

Then we marched up to bed—upstairs to the dormitory. We could take off our uniforms and wash our teeth. They had some kind of a gargle we gargled with. So we'd say all of our prayers again: the Lord's Prayer, the Hail Mary, and the Prayer of Saint Chrysostom. The beds were so cold. There were radiators there and there was supposed to be heating, but there was never enough when you needed it, the ten years I was there. They had huge furnaces in the basement, in the furnace room, of every building. The watchman was supposed to keep the fires going. He threw in four-foot pieces of wood, but he would fall asleep somewhere and the fires would go out. When we got up in the morning, it would be so bitterly cold. I remember my teeth chattering and everybody's teeth chattering. Get up and run, run, run. Afterwards we washed our teeth, washed our faces and combed our hair, and all of us had long hair. We combed it and braided it and tied it with ribbon.

But that routine never changed, from one miserable year to another, the ten years I spent in the Tulalip Indian School. On the Sunday closest to Thanksgiving, we had to go to communion. One Sunday of every month was for confession and communion in the Catholic Church. That was quite a punishment because when Christmas Day came, we still had to get up at 5:30 A.M. We couldn't eat because we were fasting before going to communion; we were not supposed to eat or drink water, and so we didn't have any breakfast. During all of those hours we had nothing to eat. I used to get so hungry I could hardly walk. Of course, we didn't sit around and moan about it. We played and ran around. By 1 P.M. we came back from the Catholic Mass, changed into our everyday clothes, and then, finally, had something to eat.

Discipline

When we first went to school, nobody cared that we only talked our own Indian languages. They didn't have bilingual programs or ESL [English as a Second Language] like they do now. Recently, on the television news and in the Seattle papers, they were talking about people from Vietnam and Thailand who came here. Several thousand dollars are budgeted to teach them English. Well, no money was appropriated for the language programs, and some of the teachers were saying, "That is terrible. There has to be more money to teach them." They said to us, "All right, you speak English," and we did. If you are around people who speak one language, you will sort of learn it. When we got to school, we were surrounded by over a hundred girls who were all speaking English. Then you learn. If they say, "Come here," you know what they mean.

I was given a whipping for speaking our own language in school when I was nine years old. It sounded worse than if I had killed forty people. Every time I think about it, it makes me mad: to have other people babied around and me beat up. I wasn't very big when I was nine years old.

Two or three of us were talking "Indian" [Snohomish] downstairs in the playroom in the Girls Building. Somebody probably told on us. It was against the regulations for any of the students to speak their Indian languages. Agnes, one of the girls I was with, didn't speak our language. The other girl was Sarah. Agnes was just listening to us. But the matron strapped all three of us. The girls' matron came downstairs from her office. You could hear her voice two miles away. She was screaming, and she had the strap.

Everybody was terrified of that strap. It was made out of a horse and buggy harness. It was used on the children. In later years, we read that that kind of strap was used on convicts in penitentiaries, and it was made illegal because it cut the skin and made it bleed; it was really thick. It was made of three layers of pliant leather, about two inches wide, and put together with little rivets. So it had holes in it and a long handle, so that when she hit you with it you really felt it. It could make your skin bleed after several hits. It jarred your teeth and your head and your whole body. Some of the boys got a flogging with the strap and almost died.

The matron strapped us from the back of our necks all of the way to our ankles for talking in our own language, and I mean she laid it on. The strap wrapped around my whole body. She was a tall woman, big and strong. She swung her arms way out, and she made that strap sing around my neck, and she nearly knocked me out. She could hardly breathe she was so mad. I went sailing across the hall and my head crashed into the wall. I am surprised I didn't faint. I wasn't expecting something like that. She said to me, "You get back here." I did, but I couldn't see very well, since the blow had had an awful jarring effect on the back of my neck. It made my head flip back. She laid the strap down on us—all of the way, close together—from the back of our necks to our ankles. I remember I thought to myself, "I hope I live to see the day when you burn in hell."

I had a dream about Mrs. Andrews last week.

Believe me, we never talked "Indian" at the school again. Some of our people, such as those who were my sons Wayne's or William's age and some of the girls, were kind of shocked and disturbed over the fact that they never heard our language. They said their mother never spoke the language or their father or their grandmothers, and so they said they didn't know a single word of their Indian language. I gave a talk somewhere to a group, and I explained the reason why we seldom spoke Indian: it was beaten out of us. We were severely punished, and some of the boys and girls got worse punishment than I did.

I should mention, first of all, that we Indian children were not slapped or pushed or spanked at home. I was never ever slapped or pushed or spanked by my mother or my father or my grandmother. All I ever heard were soft speaking voices. My grandmother had a soft voice, and my mother did, too. But once in a while, my mother could shout if she had to call out loud and clear when we were playing outside away from the house—then she would call out. Otherwise, my mother didn't raise her voice. As I say, we were never slapped, never pushed, never spanked, never whipped.

My mother punished me for laughing out loud. Let's talk a little bit about punishment. American Indians are a loving people, and they put up with a lot of little mistakes by children. I like to stress that the American Indians are not as mean as you might think. But I was going to speak of the punishment given out to children when they made a mistake.

I was told a number of times not to laugh out loud, not to open my mouth and shout. Shouting and loud laughter by Indian women and girls were absolutely unacceptable. When I think back about my mother, my grandmother, and mothers of those generations, I never ever heard them laugh out loud. They smiled a lot. When they laughed, they chuckled very softly. But I am speaking of the time when I was about nine years old; I laughed out loud. It was summer, and I was playing with my sister and some of the neighbor children. It must have been really loud, because my mother came to the door and called to my sister and we went right home.

Their rule was, if your parents or grandparents or someone older is speaking to you, you are to stand on both feet and face that person who is giving instructions or reprimanding you. You don't stand on one foot or stand way out there and say something like, "What, I can't hear you." You must go right back to your mother or whoever is calling you. You face them, hold your arms down, and tell them you are sorry. I was told when I was four or five years old not to laugh out loud, but at that time, when I was eight or nine years old, I forgot. I laughed out loud.

I think somebody was chasing me, or we were playing a game. My mother called us and we went right in, and she told me and my sister, "You know you are not to laugh like that—not ever. You never throw your head back or open your mouth and laugh like a horse. Never. You can laugh, but it has to be a soft laughter."

I had to stay inside that day, and I had to learn how to sew on my mother's Singer sewing machine. I had not sewn on it before. My mother cut out an apron for me to sew. It was different from the aprons you think of today. It was the kind of apron that is made like a dress: it buttoned in the back, and it had long sleeves and cuffs and a high neck with a collar. And so I had to work on it.

It seemed as if I cried gallons and gallons of tears and that the day lasted a million years. It was such a nice sunshiny day outside. My sister was not allowed to sit in there with me. She had to go outside and stay outside. So there I was sewing on that machine, and it kept going backwards. I started it, and then the thread would break. So I would try and fix the thread. I usually did it wrong, and it seemed as if it took me ten million years to learn which way to put the thread on the machine. My mother would come in and fix the thread, and I sewed some more. After I was sewing for a few hours, I began to enjoy it. The machine didn't go backwards as many times, and I sewed the apron together.

It was blue-and-white-checked gingham. My mother saved the miserable-looking thing, and I found it again about fifteen or twenty years ago. I thought I saved it but I can't find it anymore. The sewing is crooked on the seams. I was supposed to make French seams. I will always remember the sleeves. They had a lot of gathers, and I put the wrong sleeve on the wrong side, and so the sleeves were hanging backwards. I had to rip it all out. Then I sewed it again, and I had the wrong sleeve on the wrong side or the right sleeve on the wrong side, but I worked and worked on it. Believe me, I never laughed out loud again. I used to really laugh and play, but not that much.

When I saw them punishing the boys and girls in the school, I am not surprised I have heart trouble. I know a lot of people have heart trouble who didn't go to Tulalip School. The punishment that the boys and girls received was too severe. When some boys couldn't take the strict regimentation anymore, and the hunger that we lived through, they ran away from the school and tried to go home. Usually they were caught around Mount Vernon because they were walking, and they were brought back to the school.

Dr. Buchanan shaved their heads, caned them, and made them wear girls' dresses. They weren't locked up. They had to go to work and go to school just like the rest of us, and so we saw them hour after hour. It used to jar me, and I am quite sure it did the rest. Those were our classmates, and they were in big trouble. When they got out of school or got back to the building from work at 5 o'clock, they were fed bread and water for two weeks, in an isolation room. I saw the bread and water that was taken in to them.

The children who ran away from school got more punishment than anyone else. They had to march at seven o'clock to sick call. Actually, anyone who either got hurt or sick told the matron or the disciplinarian, and they wrote your name down on the sick call list and you lined up. The girls came first, and then the boys came in about half an hour later. But the matron would push at their shoulders and say, "You're not sick; you're just lazy."

At the end of sick call, Dr. Buchanan took the runaways to another room. They took off all of their clothes and were made to lie over a stool, and then he would strap them. He was a big strong man. You could hear them calling and crying because they would roll off of the stool. The strap burns—it hurts. He strapped them all over their bodies, and he followed them all over the floor because they rolled over, and he hit them on their heads or wherever he could hit them.

I used to see the boys in their dresses coming from the hospital at recess time. We were in the classrooms by eight o'clock, and by ten o'clock they would be walking back from the hospital to the Boys Building. Believe me, they could hardly walk. They took little short steps. It broke me up—and the other boys and girls too—because it took those boys two or three hours to get back up to the building. They could hardly walk. They were almost dead, really. That's a long, long road to being civilized.

It was a shock to see our classmates with their heads shaved. They looked so different. Of course, all of them had a lot of beautiful black hair. The nature of the punishment was out of this world. Other times, the teacher took a stick and beat them, or had them hold out their hands and rapped their knuckles. I enjoyed the classrooms, and I imagine the other students did too, but the memory of the whole thing is nothing but worry and sheer terror. I was terror-stricken every time I went back there the first of September. Then I could go home in July.

Joe Hillaire from Lummi told about when he first came to the Tulalip Indian School. When he arrived at the boarding school, he noticed a pond and waterfalls nearby. At home he got up early, dressed, and bathed somewhere. On the first morning at the boarding school, he went running down to the pond to bathe. He had a bar of soap, and he was having a great time in the cold water when Dr. Buchanan came upon him. Dr. Buchanan got up early in the morning and walked all over, very quietly, through the whole school grounds—just looking at everything. Well, he was walking around early in the morning before everyone was up, and here was Joe Hillaire bathing down at the waterfalls. I don't know how, but my father got there too. The pond was near where the totem pole used to be, but that was long before the totem pole was put there. Joe said his teeth were chattering and he was getting cold standing there. Dr. Buchanan jerked him around by the hair, and that was the first morning he had been away from his home. His father and grandfather told him, "You remember to bathe every day. Don't forget. Get up early in the morning and bathe." So he did. He was only ten years old.

My father came along. He was on horseback. He said he asked, "What is the matter?" He didn't expect to see anybody around there, and here was Joe Hillaire shivering and his teeth were chattering. Dr. Buchanan said, "He is taking a bath down here in the waterfall. He is not supposed to be around here. He is supposed to be on the playground or in the Boys Building. He isn't supposed to leave there." He was going to take Joe down to the hospital and beat him with a switch. My father said he talked to the doctor and explained this is what Joe was taught at home. "He wants to be clean and take a bath. He didn't know where to go in the Boys Building. He saw this place the day before when he came, and so he came down here. His father and his grandfather told him, 'You remember, you bathe every day.' So that's what he did." Joe said, "Mr. Shelton saved my life. I would've gotten a big, big switching."

Every time I think about it, it makes me mad: being severely punished for something that you were taught to do at home, such as taking a bath early in the morning. Joe Hillaire told us how much he appreciated my father. When he came to the school, they cut his hair short, so he was already upset, and then after that evening, he was going to be punished the next morning for taking a bath. He always felt my father had saved his life.

Long years afterward, when I was in high school, I told my parents about being beaten with the strap. Of course, my mother thought the word "hell" was inexcusable; you can't say "hell." However, I did, and I was not very big. Of course, my father couldn't say anything. I didn't tell him when it happened. I saw my mother every Sunday afternoon and my father about two or three times a week. He worked at the Indian agency. Sometimes I saw him working around the school campus, and I waved at him and he waved back. I didn't tell my parents what went on at the school, about the food, about anything, about the harassment, the punishment, until I went to high school. I don't know why.

Years later my brother talked about it too. He heard about it after he left the school. I heard him talking about it to my father and several other Indians. They said they should bring charges against the superintendent of the school for inhumane treatment.

Being civilized is a long, long road. Once in a great while, when I have been in Seattle or some other city, I have seen Indian men and women. They are usually under the influence of liquor—shall we say, plain drunk. When I see them I try to share two or three dollars I might have. I tell them to go and eat. My husband said, "You know good and well they are not going to eat—not with that money." I said, "Just let them use it the way they want." You still see them once in a while, and you know good and well they grew up on a reservation in some Indian school where they were hungry much of the time. They probably got a whipping once in a while. The ones who are alcoholic grew up in Indian boarding schools. Today, this reservation takes boys and girls who have been in trouble to Oregon to Chemawa Boarding School; so, in some ways, you can tell the boarding schools were reform schools too.

I have met white people who said they were whipped, too. Their fathers took them to the woodshed and gave them a whipping. I said there is a difference between being spanked or whipped by your father or mother and a flogging with a strap by somebody else. It is different. Believe me, if an Indian strapped a white child like that, the whole city would kill him. When the children told their parents, the parents came in to talk to the agent and protest the food and the treatment of the children. The agent laughed and said, "Do they look like they are starving? They are getting taller. They are putting on weight." We were all growing.

All of those years I was growing up were the years when the Indians all over the United States were dying off. The death rate of the American Indian was very high. Even about ten years ago, I had white people come here to see our Indian collection. Once in a while, one of them would ask why the Indians are always dying of tuberculosis. Why is it that they are sick quite a bit? You wouldn't have the strength to withstand measles or the common cold. You would get very sick.

Discipline Continued

When I first got to Tulalip Indian School, breakfast was often oatmeal mush. I ate it because I was hungry. It was six o'clock in the morning. We were having breakfast. All of the smaller children ate it, but it wasn't much. It was in a bowl, and it was probably about four tablespoons with about two tablespoons of milk on it and very little sugar. But there were little white worms in it. I looked at it when I was small, but I was too hungry so I just ate it up. Anyway, the matron went around to all of the tables and ordered everyone to eat it. If you didn't eat it, then you had to stay there, and if you stayed there, then you got a good "lickin.'" So you had better eat it.

But the first time I had breakfast there, it really turned my stomach. When we were marching out, I was "hanging on," my teeth were clenched, and I was shaking, trembling, because my stomach was so upset. We went marching out, from the tallest to the shortest, and here we were, the little girls, at the end. I just got through the double doors of the dining room, opposite the doors where the boys came in, and I vomited. It went "splat" over the waxed hallway, the shiny floor. I was so sick I didn't care. The matron was standing there, and she was watching us marching out, and she said, "Lift your feet. Lift up your feet and stop talking. Stop that whispering. Keep your head up." But, anyway, I vomited right there—just sicker than sick.

She got so mad, and I thought she might kill me, but I didn't care. She didn't dare slap me. She used to slap some of the girls who got sick like I did. She said, "You are not sick; you are just lazy," and she slapped them.

I knelt down, and I leaned my head against the wall. I thought, "I don't care if they kill me. I can't get up anymore." My knees were shaking and I was sick to my stomach. I was retching. I heard her tell a girl to go and get a bucket of water and a mop and clean up the floor. I never found out who cleaned up that awful mess. She told me to go to the hospital and line up for sick call. Sick call for the boys and girls was at 7 o'clock. That's when we came out of breakfast. From 5:30 to 6 we were getting up. From 6 to 6:30 we were outside doing our exercises. Then we marched in to breakfast. Well, with the meals we had, we could eat in five or ten minutes; there wasn't much of it. So by 7 o'clock we were back out of the dining room, and sick call lined up. We had to tell the matron if we were sick, had a cold, or got burned in the kitchen—burned a hand or wrist or an arm or got hurt, skinned a knee. She put my name down on the sick call list, so then I had to go down. I put on my coat and went marching down to the hospital. There was another small building there they called a hospital. The doctor asked what was wrong with me. I told him I vomited. He told the nurse to give me something to drink.

The hospital had about twelve beds: six beds for the girls and six for the boys. I thought the nurse gave me a glass of lemonade. It was in one of those "faddish" looking large drinking glasses. I gave it a fast glance and took a big swallow and found it was Epson salts; that is the worst tasting stuff. I took it away from my mouth, and some of it spilled and went on my lap. The nurse said, "You drink it." The doctor said, "Make her drink all of it." Nobody in my opinion could ever drink a big glass of water, but this was a big glass of Epson salts. She grabbed my head and my hair, and then she put the glass up to my mouth. She said, "You drink that." She poured it into my mouth. So I did drink some of it, but I had to stop and breathe. I was upset, and so I turned my head. The Epson salts spilled down my face, my chin, went on to my dress, my coat and my hair. She pushed the glass on my mouth, my teeth. She held onto my braided hair and tipped my head back when I turned away and so the Epson salts landed on my hair, my face, my clothes. I drank most of it. But I started to retch, almost vomiting. She said, "Better take her and put her to bed." I was taken to the ward.

She took me to the bathroom first. I barely got there and was vomiting some more, and I kept vomiting. She took me into the ward and gave me a nightgown that tied in the back. I had a fever. I was sweating, and I really got sick. I was there for two weeks.

I tried to get up and walk the next day. I fell down. The nurse came and said, "You get up and walk to the bathroom." I got up, but I was shaking. I fell right down. I couldn't stand up, and she got mad, but she didn't slap me. She shook me a little bit, and she put me back in bed. She got one of the girls who helped in the hospital and told me to use the bedpan. So for the first time in my life I used a bedpan, and that was quite an experience. But, anyway, so much for the lemonade that was Epson salts.

If we went down to the hospital, no matter what happened, we got Epson salts to drink. If you had a broken arm, you got a big glass of Epson salts. But I was so sick that time, they let me go home for a month.

We had cornmeal mush for breakfast too, which I liked, but it had a different kind of worm in it.

I remember when I was little, the cook in the kitchen made cookies. We had two cookies for each child at Christmas and Sunday evenings and one third of a cup of cocoa. Hundreds of these cookies were put down in the basement. I don't know what happened, maybe the girls didn't cover them, but mice got into them, because quite a lot of the cookies had mice dirt on them. They were put on our plates. The matron came along and said, "You eat that now. Don't leave it." Well, some of the girls tasted it, and they said it was bad. So I tasted it. But I was scared because I thought she might slap me. So I have said I know what mice dirt tastes like; it is gritty, and, well, it has a taste of its own. I told one of the doctors in Marysville. He said I have heard that before, and I am surprised the Indians still have stomachs left or even parts of their intestines, considering what they were fed.

For two whole years we lived on bread and gravy. The gravy had bits of meat in it. Bread and gravy for breakfast, two slices of bread for each boy and girl, and that was put at your place. Two slices of bread and about three or four tablespoons of gravy for breakfast, and the same thing for noon lunch and the same thing—bread and gravy—for supper.

Going to Tulalip Indian School, I remember this little detail. All of us students underwent a physical examination. We all, girls separate from boys, lined up army fashion, with the tallest first, and we marched, and I mean marched—one, two, three, four, left, right—down to the hospital. There, as each of us, 115 or more girls, entered the door into the hospital hallway, one nurse would order us to unbutton and then take off the tops of our clothes. We slipped the tops of our dresses, underskirts, and underwear off to the waist. This always made me feel so cold and forlorn. And for many years, the doctor would listen to my puny chest—millions of years it seemed—fix on me a fierce blue eye and ask me if I was scared. I would whisper back, "No doctor," while my poor little heart and soul died ten thousand deaths with fright.

Classes

I was in the Tulalip boarding school for ten years, from 1912 to 1922, and in those ten years I went through six grades. Another interesting thing that happened to me at this Indian reservation school was that I skipped the second grade, and I skipped the seventh grade. Skipping the second grade was a big mistake. But I have to tell you what happened.

I went through the first grade. I really loved the first-grade teacher. While I was in the first grade, our teacher taught us how to dance. I wasn't allowed to go to the dances. The school had a dance once a month on a certain Saturday night. It was only for the A and B companies—the bigger girls. C and D companies didn't see anything.

We learned how to dance in the classroom. I remember she taught us how to do the minuet. Imagine what we looked like! The sewing room made wigs out of white cotton. I remember the girls made them pretty fancy, in rolls, like Martha Washington and those people. They were even able to make a roll of cotton so it curled down our backs. Can you imagine, with our dark skin? We had long white dresses that we made in the sewing room out of white crossbar muslin. So we had long white dresses and white wigs, and so did the boys. We had green kerchiefs that tied around our shoulders. They were a medium green with little pink flowers. They made two puffs that went around our waists. We must have looked super! I heard the matron say, "I wonder how those children learned to dance that way?" I guess Dr. Buchanan was astounded. He talked about it for months afterward.

You should have seen us dance. We danced the minuet across the lawn and counted the steps, "one-and-two." Maybe we looked all right because we could do it together. We knew how to do things together. Our teacher played a record on a Victrola. We had real music to dance to. I just happened to hear the matron talking with some others. They talked about us as if we were not there. She said, "How in the world did those children learn how to dance like that? It was really lovely." Dr. Buchanan was very impressed because he saw the minuet danced when he was growing up in Virginia.

Then I was supposed to be in the second grade, and I must have started, but after about a week or two weeks I got sick and I was sent down to the school hospital. I stayed there for two weeks. My mother came to see me every afternoon. When I got well, I went back to school, and I went into the second-grade room.

A different teacher was there, and somebody was sitting at my desk. I was standing there. I didn't know where to sit. I was terrified. The teacher asked me my name. I told her. She came over and put her hand on my shoulder. She said, "I don't think you were in here last year." I said, "Yes, ma'am. I was." The first grade was in there in the morning, and in the afternoon the second grade was there. I was in that room the year before, but I didn't get to tell her that I was in the first grade. She said, "I don't think you are supposed to be in this room. I think you are supposed to be in the third grade." She took me out of the room and down the hall and knocked on the third-grade door. She went in and told the teacher. It seemed as if the whole roomful of students turned around to look at me. I was too terrified to tell her again that I was supposed to be in the second grade, that I had been sick for two weeks. So I was put in the third grade and I skipped the second grade.

Maybe you think I didn't work. There were multiplication tables I didn't have in the second grade, but then I hadn't been in the second grade. Then we learned how to write with a pen and ink, and that was different from the pens you have today. You have to dip your pen into an inkwell and then you write. We had to write with a pen and ink in all of the language classes and all of the arithmetic classes. If you made a mistake, you couldn't erase it. Oh, me! I don't know how I lived through it. I was too terrified to tell them, "I am not supposed to be in here, damn it." I stayed, and I got through that miserable year.

Language, strange as it may seem, was not too bad for me. We learned to speak English quickly and easily. Even after we were there only a few days, we learned to say several words in English. My parents and grandparents said to pay attention to words, what you read in books. You read it, word by word, and learn it. My father said, "Learn the white man's language and learn it good. You must learn how to use those words and speak their language as good as the best-educated people because their language can also be used rather commonly." He used to mention that the Indians didn't have swear words like the white man does. Spelling was easy. In geography we had to learn the countries and the people who lived there.

Then I went into the fourth grade. I was in the fourth grade for three years. I skipped the second grade, went into the third, and then into the fourth. Almost at the end of the fourth year, the doctor said I should go with my father to Seattle and have my tonsils out.

I suffered. They just used the local anesthetic. He was busy talking with my father. He had what seemed like a long needle. I didn't really look, but he stuck it in each tonsil and pushed the handle down. I was swallowing all of the dope, and it was going down and burning into my stomach. I tried to tell him, but he kept the needle down there. I couldn't shut my mouth. I was still trying, and he was not paying any attention. So I swallowed most of the Novocain—that is what they used to deaden the tonsils when they cut them out. He used long-handled surgery scissors. I could feel every cut he made.

Every time I think about all of it, I think, "Poor, poor me." I can laugh about it now, but I couldn't eat anything for two or three days. Your throat is so sore you can hardly say "yes" or "no." You just have to keep your head still. You can't turn it.

So I got my tonsils out, and I didn't finish the fourth grade. I was out for about three weeks, and they had their finals. When I came back, I took one examination, I think. It was in language. If the teachers had thought about it and if I had been more aggressive, I could have talked to the teacher and asked if I could take some of the examinations by myself. I could have done them. But I didn't take the fourth-grade examinations. So when I went back the following year, I was in the fourth grade again. I went through the entire thing, and I almost knew it by heart. I went through the same book and the same arithmetic lessons. But that year I went home again because my sister got sick.

My Sister Died

My sister was named Ruth, after my mother. My mother was baptized, as I said earlier, when she was just a girl, but the priest was not Father Chirouse; I think it was somebody called Father Simon. So my sister was named Ruth, and she was about a year and a half older than me. She caught a cold in February and it turned into pleurisy and pneumonia.

I saw her in the morning. She was sick. She had her coat all buttoned up and she was hunched over. It was raining outside. We were jogging—the boys and girls—on the big quadrangle. It was raining a fine, cold rain, and our heads were dripping wet. We would come in from outside with our hair dripping wet. We gave up wearing warm hats because you have to take it off and hang it with your coat on a numbered hook in the hallway and it would fall on the floor and people would trample on it. Some of the boys and girls had knitted tams or warm knitted hats like you see today, with the pom pom on top. Our hair was long, and we wore it braided and tied up with ribbons. The water dripped off of our eyelashes. We looked at one another and laughed because we looked so funny. We were little. The rain dripped off of our noses. But for those who had colds, like my sister, then they would get worse. We went back into the building for breakfast, and usually by then the heat was on in the radiator, and it would get very hot. The windows were closed, and by the time we got into the classrooms, they were hot.

When I first got there, I was thankful it was hot in the room, but after you are in there for a while, half an hour or so, it becomes suffocating. Most of us were too frightened of the teachers to ask if the windows could be opened. Some of the teachers in some of the grades would open the windows, but there was a long row of windows. Some of the teachers were very nice, and they would open the windows that were not right next to the children where they were sitting at their desks. Some of the teachers didn't care. If they did open the windows, they opened them too wide and the cold wind blew in on us. If your hair is wet and then you are sweating and the cold wind blows in on you; then you get really sick. I got over my colds. I made up my mind. "I am not going to die. I am not going to give up. I am going to live. When I get out of here, I am going to come back and kill that matron who strapped me."

I didn't see my sister for a month. I finally saw her at the hospital, but I was up at the Girls Building, so I just waved at her. If it was a sunshiny day, she was out on the hospital veranda in her bathrobe and wrapped up in a blanket. I was too terrified to ask if I could go and see her. By March or April, the doctor at the agency told my father she should go home. So my sister went home. I felt real lonely and deserted. Then I found out that I could go home. I came home the first part of April. When the agent let me go home, then I knew my sister was very sick. But when I got home, she was still able to walk around. My father and mother told me that my sister was dying. My father had taken her to a doctor in Everett. In fact, the agency doctor had told him he had better take her to a certain doctor in Everett, and that doctor specialized in lung diseases. He was the one who told my father that she had tuberculosis. And so I was allowed to go home because my sister was becoming steadily weaker, and so I finally got home in the first part of April. So I used to spend a lot of time with my sister all day and part of the evening, and she just got weaker and thinner.

We had a three-room house. Our living room was a big room, but in the kitchen the windows were only about a foot from the floor. My father made the window into a doorway, and he built a room big enough for a bed and a heating stove, a wood stove, a table, and two or three chairs. Way back then, we didn't have overstuffed furniture. We had a Morris chair. It had a velvet cushion and cushions on the bottom and the back. The velvet had big flowers on it. It was a pretty chair, wrapped in blankets—that is where my sister used to sit.

When I got home before the end of March or the first of April, she could still get up and walk, so we walked slowly down the trail and we would almost get to our grandmother's house. But she would get tired, and we had to start walking back. The room where she had her bed was all open. My father put a wire screen around it, and outside they had canvas, and he fixed it so they could roll it up with ropes so that she could see all around. Apple trees and plum trees were close to the house, so we could smell the blossoms in my sister's room. When the canvas was rolled up in the morning, the entire place was surrounded with blossoms. The birds came back, and we listened to them. My sister identified a lot of them. Of course, my grandmother came and visited, and she had names for the different birds.

I spent a lot of time with my sister—all day and part of the evening, and she got weaker and thinner. My mother tried to do everything that the doctor said: give her meat broth, give her eggnog. My mother made eggnog every morning or halfway between breakfast and one o'clock and gave us eggnog. I stayed well, but my sister got weaker and weaker. That was one of the tragedies we lived through. I watched my sister get weaker. By the end of May, she couldn't get up out of bed anymore. She just lay in bed, so I sat with her all day and read something to her from the fourth-grade reader or the sixth-grade reader.

Her dying went on for three weeks. The last two weeks were a dreadful nightmare. It took me thirty years to get over it. I cried in the night. I cried throughout the day. I had bad dreams where I screamed at night, and my father and mother got up and sat on my bed and held my hand, and my mother slept with me.

My sister suffered terrible pain for days. I can only say to die of tuberculosis is a dreadful, painful death. I don't think many people see that kind of death anymore. I think there is medication to help the pain, and there are things the doctors can do now. There was no doctor then for my sister. I used to kneel down by her bed and hold her hand when she was suffering such pain, and she always had such a high fever. She would pull at my hand. The suffering she went through came at every hour or two hours. It lasted, maybe, an hour. It seemed the pain wracked her whole body, not only her chest, but also her stomach. She cried out. She just screamed.

My father was home all of the time then. The last week or two my father and mother held her. They tried different ways of holding her. My father took her in his arms and tried to change her position a little bit and see if it would help. She was so weak she couldn't sit up anymore. I put cold compresses on her forehead and little things she wanted to have done. Her dying was a big cross for us to bear. She died on May 24. It is a little better now; after all, this was 1917, but that stayed with me for years.

It was the same evening my brother graduated from Marysville High School. He went to the Indian schools out here, and then he went to Marysville High School for three years. My parents didn't attend his graduation. When my brother Robert left early that evening, he went on horseback all of the six miles to Marysville and went through the exercises. He said he would hurry home.

As I said before, I saw other deaths when I was smaller. One of our cousins, Marguerite Jules, died two weeks after my sister. My sister was fifteen years old, and I think Marguerite was sixteen or almost seventeen. After my sister's funeral, we used to walk up this road to the Jules's house around ten o'clock in the morning and stay with the father and mother and their daughter. Marguerite was in bed, of course, but when we got there we piled pillows around her, and she could talk. It seemed to make her feel better when people came to visit. In between the pain, she talked with us. She was just like my sister.

My sister crocheted lace edging for her pillowcase and bureau runners. When I was seven or eight years old, my sister taught me to crochet, so I fiddled around with crocheting when I was sitting with her. But Marguerite Jules did the same thing; she crocheted in between the awful pains. Every time she had the spasms of pain, then, one of the mothers took the crochet hook and the ball of thread and put them on the table.

Another Indian girl and two Indian boys died that same summer my sister and Marguerite died, and they all died within about two months of each other. All of them were teenagers. In just two months, five young people died: my sister, Marguerite Jules, Cecelia Weeks and her cousin Edwin Weeks, and Edwin Hillaire. Edwin Weeks was seventeen or eighteen years old.

Some of the boys and girls who were brought to the boarding school were already not well. You could see they were not well. They were very pale and thin and they kept getting thinner. After a while, they couldn't get out of bed, and then they were sent home. Their parents were notified, and the parents would come by boat—by mail boat or train—and take their child home. The following September when we got back to school, we would meet every group that came in by boat or launch from the reservations. The Swinomish would come in one day or one evening and the Lummis would come in a couple of days later. We would get up in the morning and go all around to see who came. We were all happy to see each other, but I used to ask about someone, did so-and-so come? No. She died. Or after school started, I would remember some of the boys and I would ask, and they would say, no, he died. The death rate among the Indians way back then was very high.

Babies died of other diseases, such as spinal meningitis.[5] Sometimes there would be Indians living in tents down by the beach, in some of the fields or meadows, and we would go to visit, or go every afternoon. I would hold those

---

5   Buchanan stated in his archival record that the Indians of Puget Sound and the Yuman tribe in Arizona had the highest infant mortality in the United States among Native peoples.

babies. Mostly they were dying of spinal meningitis, you know, where their eyes move back and forth. They were sort of unconscious and they moaned with the awful pain. I held so many babies who died of that disease. It is a lingering, horrible death. The babies are practically in a coma the last two weeks or so, but they seem to come out of it, and then they cry and cry and cry. They are just gasping because they are so weak, and the pain must be so terrible. They can't eat. The mothers try and nurse them, since they were still being breast-fed. They were hungry and so they tried to nurse, but they were gasping and crying.

Sometimes it was measles; quite a lot it was measles. There was no doctor for all of those deaths. Of course, you might say no doctor would be able to cure tuberculosis anyway.

As I say, my sister's death lived with me for years and years. I have said I hated the white people with an undying hatred. The white people brought diseases such as measles, tuberculosis, smallpox, and trachoma. Tuberculosis was rampant on every Indian reservation across the entire continent. Indians died by the thousands. All over, on every reservation, Indians had eye infections. It was called trachoma. Nearly all of them advanced to almost total blindness. For the ones that survived all of that, diseases and things, I wonder what they ever had to eat. If they were elderly like me, even though they had canoes and things, they wouldn't be able to paddle across to the islands to dig clams and certainly not go to other places for camas roots and things like that, and then they didn't have any money to buy food and there was no medical aid, no doctor, no nothing.

My sister's dying was a big cross for us to bear. Speaking of watching someone dying, or holding their hand while they are dying, I saw other deaths when I was smaller than that. I remember some of my playmates died when we were four or five years old. I barely remember. But I remember sitting . . . the Indian women would always get together when there was a child dying or someone dying, there was never any doctor, never any medication, so Indians did the best they could. I remember going with my mother, and I was always told to sit still and I always did. I could sit, it seemed like, by the hour; just sit absolutely still and watch my playmates die. I mean I didn't sit there or stand there and stare at them. The Indian women used to kneel down, and they would say the rosary; the prayers would go on and on. I sort of learned them when I was real small. But I could sit real still for a long time. So dying and death were all around when I was little and growing up. The death rate among Indians was very, very high.

I stayed home all of the time my sister was sick and dying. The superintendent-agent didn't make me go back to Tulalip Indian School after my sister died. My father took me to a doctor in Everett. I was all they had then. I was the youngest, and my brother was gone in the army. I was thirteen years old and thin because I came out of Tulalip School. The only reason I lived was my sister dying, because then I got to come home.

I had swollen glands in my neck and under my left arm. We went to the doctor in Everett. He gave me iron drops—five to ten drops in a glass of water. It tasted bad and made my teeth turn black. They wouldn't give you iron drops like that anymore. But way back then, that is what the doctor said I should take to build up my blood and help my swollen glands. I talked to one of the doctors in Marysville about it recently, and he said he never saw anyone with swollen glands. I said we all had them. There must have been forty or fifty boys and girls with swollen glands. It was a miracle if they lived. I had another doctor who said they must have been tubercular glands. I said I wouldn't know, but just about every Indian child I knew had swollen glands. The doctor I talked to said people get tubercular glands in some of the backward places where there is an inadequate diet.

It took me almost two years to get well. My mother had cows, so there was always fresh milk and cream. She made eggnog. She had chickens so that the eggs were fresh. I always said, "Put a lot of sugar in the eggnog." I never got enough sugar in Tulalip School. I had an eggnog every day. After a while, I didn't appreciate it as much. It gets tiresome every day, but I did get better. My glands stayed swollen, because about a year later the doctor in Everett said, "You should have them lanced."

I went to Providence Hospital in Everett. I was in surgery from 9 A.M. to almost 1 P.M. because the doctor said the gland on the right side of my neck was grown around my vocal cords, and then I had a big one under my left arm. Another Indian girl had a gland on her neck down to her chin, and she and I both went through surgery.

The agent's wife came to see me. My neck was bandaged up, but I guess my ears were showing. She brought me a novel. It was one of the first ones I ever had that was a hardback, called *The Strawberry Handkerchief*. Of course, it had a lot of love and stuff, which was just great, but they had put iodine all over my neck where the surgery was and it must have gone along my right ear. She came in and said, "What's the matter with your ear?" Well, I couldn't see my ear. I was sitting in bed and just getting over the surgery. I hadn't started to walk yet. I said, "I don't know." Anyway, I was afraid of her.

She leaned over. She had gloves on and a small hat. No woman ever walked on the street without a hat and a veil in those days. It was tight on her face, so when she talked the veil went over her lips. She took my ear and she was looking at it. I am remembering a particular thing, because that is what we were always living through—with some white people saying, "What is the matter with this?" or "What is that?" or "Isn't that funny?" She said, "Your ear is almost black." I said, "Maybe it's because I am an Indian. She said, "Oh!" I guess it finally dawned on her she had this Indian by the ear, because she let go of my ear and said, "Well, I hope you get better and I hope you enjoy the book," and she left. I said, "Thank you." I appreciated the book, so I got into it, but now I don't remember who wrote it.

I read those kinds of stories in *Redbook* way back then. The girls' matron and the other women employees got *Redbook* magazine, *Cosmopolitan*, and *Ladies' Home Journal* and put them in the girls' reading room. When I wasn't old enough to go in the girls' reading room, somebody brought me a magazine, and there I was all "humped up" down in the dining room or in the dark playroom, reading it. Later, I used to sneak in there and steal them. I would hear her voice—the matron. She would be calling me from upstairs, and I would run. I would tiptoe and put my magazine in the clothing room. The matron was always, shall we say, calling for me. She knew I was reading somewhere in the basement playroom. I read *Little Women* by Louisa May Alcott. I enjoyed it. I read *Little Men*, too. I discovered Kathleen Morris's romantic novels. Anyway, I was far away from scrubbing porches or sweeping the room. I was way off in my imagination while the matron was bawling me out. One of my good friends, a cousin from La Conner, said, "Harriette, why don't you do the work and get it done?" I did. It's all done. I guess the matron didn't believe it, and then I had to do it all over again. It seems like that's all I did for a long time: scrub the porches, scrub along the stairways.

Classes Continued

When I was in the sixth grade, something happened. I skipped the seventh grade and went into the eighth grade, so then I had to work hard again. I had to pick up things that I missed in the seventh grade in spelling and arithmetic. But by the time I got into the seventh grade, I was doing well in classes. The teachers had talked about it. Classes were getting easier. I could do everything, so they thought I could skip the seventh grade. Anyway, I had spent three years going through the fourth grade.

Then, our eighth grade teacher resigned during the first week we went to school. We were wondering what was going to happen when we got to the schoolroom. We looked, and somebody said there's a new teacher. We got into the room. We all came in staring. Who is the new teacher? It was my brother Robert!

As you know, he finished high school, and I thought he did pretty well too. A number of students who go to high school have a father or mother or older brother or sister who can help them with algebra, geometry, and so on. He didn't have anybody to help him. We only had oil lamps then, and I remember seeing him sit at the small living room table. I had my elbows on the table, and I watched for a long time when he was doing algebra. The following year it was geometry, and he had taken up studying German.

At first when he returned from being drafted into World War I, he worked in an office as a typist and a clerk. Robert was fourteen years older than me. There were four brothers and sisters in between, but most of them I didn't see because they died when they were babies from the epidemics that swept the Indian reservations: measles and complications, pneumonia, tuberculosis. He went to the Tulalip Indian School, but at the time they had different employees such as cooks and teachers who were friendly with the boys and girls. There was an employee who could play band instruments. He taught a lot of the Indian boys how to play.

My brother studied trombone and cornet and the French horn. He could play all of those instruments, but the one he liked the best was the trombone. When I was home for a vacation—if he happened to be home, not working or in between like the weekend—he practiced and practiced the trombone. I sat and listened to him play "Tromeroy." I forget who wrote it, but it was beautiful. Another one is in the German language: "Forsaken" or "Verlassen." I heard my brother playing all of those beautiful things. He was very musical, but it didn't seem like I was.

When Dr. Buchanan first heard my brother play, he wrote a letter to John Philip Sousa. He had a band in Washington, D.C., and it was very prestigious. Dr. Buchanan wrote to him that there was an Indian boy here who could play extremely well, and would he listen to him? John Philip Sousa wrote back, eventually, and he said we do not allow Indians or Blacks into our organization; this is all "American." So I had already heard about things like that by the time I got to high school.

The agent wanted my brother to go to the Hampton Institute in Virginia.

My father said he is not going any place away from here. So he went to Marysville High School.

If I ever thought it would be easy to have my brother for a teacher—it wasn't. I used to get so frightened. As he called on each one of us, we had to stand up in the aisle and answer the question. Usually it went on and on. Sometimes I didn't answer and made believe I wasn't there because I was too scared to stand up. He "blasted me" right up to the sky. He said, "All right now, stand up and speak up." He shouted, "Speak up! Don't mumble to yourself. The whole class is interested. They want to hear." I almost dropped dead, but I got over it. I guess I got used to standing up and speaking. It was a neat way. My father did that to me when I learned how to read. He made me stand up. I was in the second grade. He borrowed a reader from school, and I had to read to him every evening. Of course, he didn't say, "Don't mumble. Speak up."

I think the students who had Robert for a teacher thought he brought to us what the outside world was like. All we knew was a very limited life on the reservation. It was just us—just Indians. I learned a lot from my brother, my grandmother, my father. My mother was all for the Catholic religion. I had to learn a lot of the prayers and how to say the rosary. And I was learning two languages.

My brother had a nice personality, and he was a good public speaker. He married a white girl; that upset the whole family and created quite a turmoil, but she was a wonderful person. All along the way, I met people who taught me things. She taught us how to drink tea from a teacup and how to make sandwiches so they were small and looked appetizing. She worked in the boarding school too.

I remember some years ago, several white women said to me, no wonder I had nice manners—I grew up in an Indian boarding school. I didn't have time to say, "Oh my god, what are you saying?" All I remember is line up, right face, left face, squad right, squad left, company halt, forward march—march to the dining room, march to the classroom, march out of the classroom. March, march all of the time.

The boarding school didn't have anything to do with Indians who became leaders, such as Sub Williams, myself, and others—Indian leaders like Carol Wilbur, Tandy Wilbur from La Conner, and Cyrus James from here. Clara James and her husband were both in Tulalip Indian School, but they were quite a bit older than me. James Norbert. Clara married his brother, but now that I think about it, Norbert stayed in Lummi. His daughter Florence

McKinley is very prominent in the Lummi Tribe. She is one of my cousins. La Conner is the only reservation where we didn't have a lot of cousins, but that seemed to be because of the rivalry. I am related to Morris Dan and Robert Joe. Isadore Tom is from Lummi. The boarding school had nothing to do with the development of any of these people as leaders. They taught us how to say "please" and "thank you," but anything else that I might have learned came from my grandmother, and that was the same with the Indian leaders.

There is one good thing I will say about that school and that is they had good classroom teachers. We really must have had good teachers for them to come and teach children who knew two languages, and we were just learning English, but some could speak the English language very well. They did really well. When I went back to school, things came back to me, in English, that I had had in the Tulalip school. I must have had it in high school, too.

When I went to Everett Community College, things came back to me that I had learned in Tulalip Indian School, just general things that they teach you in English classes. The classroom teachers in the boarding schools made my life and the lives of the other children bearable because the classroom was enjoyable. Those teachers were absolutely wonderful. They were the ones that made my life worth living. Oh, they truly did. It was nice to go into their classrooms because they were never upset or worried about anything. It was a nice experience to walk into a classroom and have the teacher speak to us in a nice speaking voice, not giving a lot of loud orders. Those teachers never seemed to be upset or worried. They just seemed to repeat, but I don't think they had to repeat that much.

I never had a teacher who beat up the children. Some of the older grades had teachers who were always beating up the children, and they usually were the boys. Usually, the boys answered back, and the teachers ran after them or grabbed them by the hair and jerked them out of their desks where they were sitting and slapped them hard. In some of the grades, we had two grades, so I saw that done. All of them refused to cry out, but they did there because then the teacher would take a stick and really beat them. She would have them hold out their hands and beat the tops of their knuckles.

Even though I enjoyed the classroom, and I imagine the other students did, too, the memory of the school is nothing but worry and fear—terror. I was always terror-stricken. I'd get back there the first of September; then I could go home July the second, and in all of those years I didn't tell my father or my mother what it was really like at the boarding school.

Treaty Day

In this period from 1908 to 1910, 1912, my father was trying to get permission to build a hall or a longhouse for the Indians so that they could gather. First, he asked the agent if he could have a building where the Indians could gather and have Indian dancing and singing so that the young Indians could hear things they had never heard. It was quite a radical thing for my father to be asking because it was absolutely forbidden for drums to be beaten, and Indian singing was against the agent's rules. However, there were places on Whidbey Island, Hat Island, and Camano Island where Indians could gather, where they could have their own drums beating and remember the old times.

My father and a lot of the older Indians said they felt lost. I think the people who came from across the Atlantic Ocean or even the Pacific—even today or twenty years ago or sixty years ago—no matter where they came from: Germany, Norway, France, Spain—they still remember their own language. If you are alone with people who are speaking one language, you will learn it faster than if you are sitting in a classroom learning it out of a book and not speaking it. Many Indians no longer speak their own language, because those of us who were in school had to speak English. I mentioned before what an awful thrashing I got for speaking Indian.

I used to hear my father saying, "It's too bad, because the Indian songs and the drumbeats are going to be forgotten." Once in a while, my father would beat the drum in the evening and sing some of the chants, but not very often because if someone heard us they would report it.

He talked to a lot of the Indians first, then he went to the agent. There is a picture of a number of the Indians and my father; they were the group my father talked with; they were men from here. Of course, their wives were always there at their little meetings, and the women talked too. Men listened politely because there were some tribes where women were not allowed to even be in council meeting, but out here I always thought maybe it was because the weather was milder; it doesn't get that hot in the summer or that cold in the winter. In the Middle West and other places like it, the weather is bitterly cold. They have deep, deep snow and blistering hot summers.

My father went to the agent and said, "We would like to begin again. We would like to have a day where we could all gather together—the older Indians—and have them sing the old songs and beat the drum. Could we do that?" Dr. Buchanan, who was the superintendent of the agency and also the boarding school, told my father, "No, you can't. That is against the Department of Interior regulations, which say no drum beating and no Indian dancing." Indians on other reservations were sent to jail for doing any of the Indian ceremonies. They were tried in the tribal court and charged with disturbing the peace and beating their drums and singing the old chants. They often served thirty days in jail, with bread and water three times a day. Dr. Buchanan liked my father. He and my father were nearly the same age. He told my father to write to the commissioner of Indian Affairs and ask for permission.

My father also asked to build a longhouse. He called it a potlatch house: a place where the Indians could gather and have a dinner. The agent said, "I want you to write the commissioner of Indian Affairs. Write the letter yourself. Don't ask someone to write it for you. Tell him what you just told me. You want the younger Indians in school to see and hear the old chants and see some of the old ceremonial Indian dancing." My father said, "I will do that if you give me the address." So the agent wrote down the name of the commissioner, Cato Sells. "If you write to him, you had better write to the secretary of the Interior and ask him too." So my father got the name of the secretary of the Interior and his address.

My father's command of English was poor, shall we say, but I remember him writing in the evening, because I happened to be home. My mother told me to keep still. "Don't be jumping around." Sometimes I played with my kitten. I sat still too. My father sat at the round table in the middle of the living room. He had a big frown on his face while he was writing. He wrote the letter with an indelible pencil.

I found a copy of his letter in some of his old papers about twenty-five years ago. It was a very long letter, a very touching one. He misspelled some words, and didn't really know how to use periods or commas, and so the periods are scattered over every sentence, about three or four, and it may not be the end of the sentence but there is a period. Some of the younger people here, young men who were on the board of directors, said, "It's too bad you can't find the letters because we think they are important. We would like to see them. What did he say, and how did he say it?"

I used to hear my father talking to my mother about having a Treaty Day and building a longhouse. He went to La Conner to talk to the Indians there about it. In those days, you had to go on horseback from here to Marysville to get to the train. He must have written to somebody on the reservation because he got off of the train in Mount Vernon, and a number of his relatives were there. They had horses, so they went on horseback from Mount

Vernon to La Conner. He talked with them and told them what he had in mind. Of course, they all made short speeches that they would help and be glad to, too. He went to Lummi and talked to them and, of course, they were happy over it.

I remember my father's table piled up with all of the papers and letters from the superintendent, the commissioner, and the Interior Department when he was trying to get permission to build a longhouse. He told us the agent said a letter came from the secretary of the Interior and for him to tell the Indians they can have a Treaty Day for one day and one evening. They are not to dance all night or until daylight. They will have to go home and take care of their livestock. They did have horses, sheep, and cows.

We read about it ten or fifteen years ago, and it sounded like such an unusual order. For instance, that it would not be tolerated for them to neglect their livestock. The Treaty Day "business" got off all right. Dr. Buchanan selected January 22 as the day for us to gather to commemorate the signing of the treaty at Mukilteo in 1855. That is why they called it Treaty Day.

Treaty days were held in 1911, 1912, and 1913 in the Tulalip Indian School. I was in the school then, and so we got to go into the dining hall and see the singing and dancing. For the first time in my life and in the lives of all of us school children, we heard so many drums and so many Indians singing and various kinds of dances that these Indians had—spirit dances. I was deeply touched. I think all of us children were. It seemed as if we recognized the drumbeats and the singing even though we had not heard them before. It just seemed to answer a need for me. It was rather satisfying and, of course, the dancing and the singing went on almost all day.

On the first day of Treaty Day, the dances were held through the day. In later years, in the longhouse, they were usually done at night. I remember several hundred Indians singing. Each one stood up. We couldn't see some of them because the dining room was so filled with people, but we could hear their voices. They cried when they got up to speak. They told that they were very, very small when they were at the treaty. Some of them said they had been there, but they really just heard about it because they were too little to remember. Of course, they spoke the Indian language, and they told where they were when they got their *sqəlalitut*. We call the guardian spirit *sqəlalitut*. They were only boys, anywhere from twelve to fourteen years old, when they were sent out to seek their spirit power, and they did the same thing that my father did—fasting and going out to the forest, the Sound, Deception Pass, and staying there overnight, and in the day sitting quietly in meditation. Each one of these Indians told where they found the *sqəlalitut*. They didn't just walk out into the wilderness or the forest and stay overnight a day or so. There had to be preparation. They fasted. They were allowed to drink water and sit in little shelters in different parts of the forest in quiet meditation. Eventually, after five, six, seven, or ten days of fasting, they had a vision, which we call *sqʷədilič*. It means that they heard the vision: usually some kind of an animal spoke to an Indian in our own language and sang its own guardian spirit song. So all of the Indians sang and danced that day all that long time ago. All of them had different songs and different dances from one another, as they still do today.

By 1914 we had the longhouse down here at Mission Beach. I was still in the boarding school. We saw the canoes come in to Tulalip Bay because most of the Indians came by canoe. They were real Indian canoes, and they were just loaded with Indians. The women had on bright colored shawls and bright kerchiefs on their heads. There must have been seven or eight canoes that came in from La Conner in one day. We were let out of class at 11:30, and we were lined up to go marching back to the building, boys and girls, and here came the canoes around the point. We said, "What is that?" We heard the drumbeats, and then here they came. I remember saying, "I will remember that forever." They had about eight canoes tied together, so that all of them were standing up. They were beating their drums and keeping time as those canoes came in very slowly. The teachers let us stand out there and watch them come in. The drumbeats were coming in over the water, and the canoes were coming around the point, coming in very slowly, and as if all the canoes were dancing. The heads of our canoes look like some kind of mysterious animal. The canoes went past our school, and they came in down there where they were camping. There were hundreds of people there who hadn't seen each other for a long, long time.

We dressed up in our Sunday uniforms. They were blue, wool serge dresses, and they were scratchy. It was January, and it was cold, so we wore rubbers when we marched to the longhouse from the school. I think it was about three-quarters of a mile. The seamstresses and the group in the sewing room used to make our clothes. We had gray wool capes that year; they had hoods sewed on. The hoods were lined with red plaid and came to a point on the top. I thought they were pretty. We appreciated the warmth, but it was funny to have a hood with a peak. I heard the seamstresses talking about how nice we looked—all fifty or sixty of us, marching with those little peaks bouncing up and down.

They brought our lunch from the school to the longhouse in a horse-drawn wagon in big clothes baskets. Lunch was thick slices of homemade bread, made right at the school with thick slices of roast beef on each sandwich. They were almost scary, the slices were so thick. Now that I think about it, the bread was real good. Then, wrapped up separately in newspapers, was a slice of peach pie for each of us. They were made of dried peaches soaked overnight and were very delicious. I was working in the kitchen one time when we had to do down into the basement to get buckets of dried peaches for pies. Then we brought them upstairs into the pantry and put them in pans of water so that they soaked through the night, and the pies were baked the next day. Oh, that pie! Sometimes now I wish I had some. I don't know why, but it seemed to be really sweet. The school never ever had sugar—not on the tables.

When we went to the longhouse, it was the first time for all of us to see one and see how big it was, with the fires burning in the center. It was the first time I ever saw the *sqǝlalitut*. I remember somewhere along the side they had their *sqʷǝdiličˇ* boards and their poles that move. Each one was held by a young man. I saw a woman sing that kind of a *sqǝlalitut*. The poles are long; they almost reach to the big logs that cross the longhouse roof. These had red Indian paint and shredded cedar bark that was tied on like a scarf or a red ribbon.

My mother went down to the longhouse. She usually didn't go to meetings because she wasn't from this tribe. She worked with several of the women for two, three days, cooking and baking. They baked cakes and pies at night. Many of them peeled apples for apple pies. They donated whatever quarters they had to buy sugar. I don't think they had to buy apples because the school had apple trees. The dishwashing went on all day and much of the night.

My father saved the 1914 program of Treaty Day. The first speaker was Dr. Buchanan. Then my father and quite a number of Indians from Lummi, La Conner, and Tulalip spoke. They traced some of the history of what Treaty Day is. I remember my father saying that it is not exactly a celebration; it is a commemoration, because the Indians were not having a good time when they met to discuss and sign the treaty.

The longhouse was the first and only building that these Indians had during the reservation times where they could meet together. Before that was built, it was forbidden for the Indians to meet, that is, to get together. All over Puget Sound, it seems, the Indian agency told the Indians, "You cannot have meetings." A lot of these Indians at Treaty Day were quite along in years when

I saw them in 1911, 1912, 1913. They cried when they got up to speak. They said that they were very, very small when they were at the treaty grounds. Some of them said that they had been there, but later they heard what went on because they were too little to remember. That really was something. I know my father talked about it. I heard him talking to my mother.

It is interesting that the chiefs who signed the treaties were so interested in having the young Indians learn to read and write. I remember hearing them when I was small. They said, "Pay attention to words. We will never be able to catch up. We don't know anything about what the white man thinks or plans unless we know his language—unless we can read it. All of those marks—designs they called them—they make on paper mean something to them."

When they started the celebration at night, somebody started to sing and others beat the drums. When I was there in 1914, I thought it sounded kind of familiar, but not that familiar. I had not heard it that often. Three or four dancers went around the longhouse like a flash. They had red paint on their faces and scarves tied over their heads. They ran around very fast and then went out the door. The drums started again; then almost immediately the dancers went around a third time to a rapid drumbeat. They came a fourth time. The drums were beating slower, and here they jumped right over the fire. The fires were six feet across. We were keeping time and watching. It was my brother and his friends who were jumping across the fire! My father was so astounded. He wondered who they were. Their faces were painted. I guess they saw it when they were children, because things had changed by the time I came along. My father and some of the other Indians said they were really full of the spirit. That's quite a bit of a jump over a six-foot fire. They went clear over to the other side and landed on their feet with the drumbeat and just kept on going.

That was in January. I wasn't in the longhouse again until summertime. My mother went to the meetings on Saturday or Sunday afternoon, because the Indians were getting together and talking about putting on a fair. They were also clearing a big wooded area to put in an athletic field. They played baseball there. It was a racetrack too. When the tribe had their Indian Fair, a number of Indians came from Lummi, La Conner, and Nisqually, with their racehorses. Indians just loved betting on horse racing.

We revived Treaty Day here in 1960. They rebuilt the longhouse we have now. Wayne, my son, was involved in it. Several Indians got up to speak. Some of them came from British Columbia. They still remembered my father when they were just children. They spoke of Chief William Shelton. They remembered it was my father who got permission to build the first longhouse because he talked to them, and they put in the money. They collected the money to buy nails. My father cut the lumber at the mill where he worked.

Treaty Day on January 22 is usually observed in Tulalip or La Conner and sometimes on the Lummi Reservation. It is a commemoration—not a celebration—as my father and the others said, for a time of worry and a time of great change. When white people first arrived here, they came rapidly and in great numbers. They spread around here in western Washington, and it upset the Indians. They didn't get upset like you think a neighborhood would. They got together and talked about the changes that were taking place all around, and how they would stay together and give each other courage. They made speeches about staying together and taking care of each other.

Dr. Buchanan Dies

Dr. Buchanan died in 1920, when I was still in the boarding school. His death was a stunning experience for us. He was mean; in some ways, he was too mean. But, in other ways, he was a nice man to know. I mean, we didn't know him; we just saw him. But he would stop and talk with us around the playgrounds. Then, I heard him on Sunday evenings when we were at evening chapel.

He was cremated, and I think his remains were sent back to Virginia where he was born. The Indians collected money, and they had a bronze plaque put on a large rock about five feet in diameter near the superintendent's house. Some of them gave twenty-five cents, fifty cents, or a dollar. The plaque gives his name, where he was born, where he died, and his birthday.

When we learned he died, we were all lined up and waiting in the hallway to march into the dining room at school. A telephone call came, and the matron came out and told us that Dr. Buchanan had died. He was somebody who was important in our lives, and I was terrified of him. My father was quite broken up. He was the same age as Dr. Buchanan. When they first met in 1894, when Dr. Buchanan first arrived here, they were both young. My father was already working at the agency then. Once in a while, they got into a quarrel. Dr. Buchanan didn't apologize always, but he told my father, "Well, William, let's forget it." My father worked for Walter F. Dickens, too.

Graduation

When I finished school at Tulalip, they had a graduation exercise for us that lasted several days. One day they had a "field day": this was where they have a hundred-yard dash, relay races, obstacle races—things like that. We saw the boys go around or through barrels, swings, and things in an obstacle race. Then, another day they had a water festival. We went down to the waterfront. We were allowed to stand on the wharf and watch the small canoe races, with just one paddler, the larger canoes with two paddlers, and the big war canoe races that had eleven paddlers in each one. The races lasted all day. We had a picnic lunch outside. We had to stay together, but that was fun. We sat on the grass, and they passed out our lunch from a big laundry basket. I always thought that was the grandest lunch. The Indian girls who cooked in the kitchen were good cooks. We'd have big thick slabs of roast beef and thick slices of their homemade bread. We never ever had butter, but, gee, that was good. We would always have a pie. They made the pies there. I remember those pies would always be flattened out because they were piled up in the basket for a hundred and fifteen girls, so those on the bottom would be pretty well mashed up. They usually had peach pies that were made out of dried peaches. We scraped the mashed up pie off of the newspapers with our spoon and saved every little lick. The third day in the evening we had the last assembly down in the school assembly hall.

The entire school marched in and sat there: 230 boys and girls, and probably 20 or more employees. The farmer and his wife came, the carpenter and his wife and family, the superintendent and his family, the assistant, the chief clerk, and two or three clerks, plus all the teachers and their families.

I think I said before that I had surprisingly good teachers during those years, and for them to come out to a small place like this—an agency and a boarding school—when there were places like Chemawa, where instead of 230 students like us they would have 600 or 800 who came from Washington, Oregon, and Idaho. I think they had a school down at Riverside, California. It was big, too, and those were still different tribes. They had those Indian schools scattered all over the United States.

My mother bought white organdy because they said we should have white dresses for graduation. My mother bought a white petticoat. I told her, "I want a lot of lace on it." I don't know what there was about my mother, but she was bound and determined that I should wear plain cotton. Even if I crocheted narrow lace and put it on my petticoat, she said I shouldn't have it.

I don't know why; I thought about it this morning, when I was getting dressed. I used to ask my mother if I could have lace on my petticoats. Usually, the lace on my petticoats at home was white. When I was small, petticoats were white. They were made out of flour sacks with crocheting on them and an inch or an inch and a half of lace on the bottom and around the neck and armholes. I asked for real lace from town. I don't know how old I was. It was after my sister died. I must have been about thirteen or fourteen. My mother said, "Why is it that you are always asking for something you can't have?" But I wanted a petticoat with lace. At Tulalip Indian School we wore petticoats that must have been part wool. They were a hideous gray, and they had gray and black stripes. The stripes were an inch wide. They made bloomers for the little girls because they are warm in winter and another thing that was good about them was that they had elastic in the waist. They were nice, but in May or June they are hot.

My mother bought me a tatting shuttle. It was white ivory and about two inches long. You can tat with it. I used to make yards and yards of lace with it, but there was nothing to put it on. If I heard the matron's voice, I used to stick the tatting shuttle in my bloomers. Then I am real innocent standing around when she would say, "What are you doing? Get out of here." Sometimes she would let me tell her, I just came from the dining room. I just got through wiping dishes for 230 kids. Well, we didn't use the word kids. My mother always said, "Don't say 'kids.'" I think they said that in school too. They told us "Don't call children kids. Kids are goat's children."

The church said you shouldn't wear such things as lace on your clothes just to feel good about it. It is a sin. I was always in sin; wishing for lace on my clothes. The few times I had narrow lace, crocheted lace on my petticoat, it would last for two or three years, and then you would have to take it off a worn petticoat and put it on the next one.

Some students who lived in Lummi and other areas and their parents were too poor to provide organdy; then the school sewing room furnished them with white crossbar muslin dresses.

In the graduation program, they had kindergarteners on the stage sing, and then the first graders, second and third, and then there was us. I couldn't believe we were getting out of there. It was a really happy time. My mother allowed me to have a petticoat with some lace on it, but not much. I had white slippers—my mother thought that was a sin—and white stockings. I don't think my mother would have broken down and bought me all of those things except my father said I should have them.

High School Plans

It was a nice summer, but in August I was worried. My brother said I should not go to Marysville High School. My farther didn't want me to go there either. I would have to go six miles on horseback or by horse and buggy from way out here. They certainly couldn't let me go alone. Somebody had to go with me every morning and come back in the dark in winter. We didn't have a car. The mail came at noon all of the way from Everett. There were a few cars, but in certain places this road was almost impassable. It took two and half to three hours to go to town and the road meandered all over. The Indians were always working on the road. They hauled gravel with a horse and a wagon, but it seemed to disappear in some places, and there would be water all along the muddy road. Anyway, my brother said I should not go to Marysville. It was too . . . "hidebound." They don't like Indians.

Some of my classmates didn't go to school. They just went back home. We were quite along in years. I wasted so much time in the boarding school. I was seventeen years old when I graduated from there in 1921. When I started high school, I was eighteen years old. Some classmates got married within a year or so. They had their children. Two or three girls went to Haskell Institute, a big, big boarding school in Kansas. They were able to finish high school there and then went to work at other Indian schools and agencies. They worked in the laundry or the sewing rooms of different schools.

Some of my classmates started high school in Marysville, such as Abra-ham Fryberg and Noble, as we called him, or Cyrus James. Cy was just remembering that a couple of years ago. Cy said they went to the Marysville school in the morning and found out which classroom to go to, but nobody told them what to do at the end of the hour. They were supposed to move on to the next class. So they sat in the first classroom all day long. The teacher never spoke to them, not one word, nor anybody else. They just walked by them. They listened and tried to write down what the teacher in the first class said. The next day they were back there, and after that they never went back. Nobody talked to them, not a single teacher, and not a single student told them what they should do. So those three or four students who tried to go to Marysville High School just dropped out after the third day.

One of our Indian young men, George Jones, went from here to Hampton Institute in Virginia. He said it was all Negro with a few Indians and they were all Indian young men. There were no girls. All George did was fight—they didn't get along. George just walked out of there one day. He was walking around New York City having a great time. His folks used to send him money so he saved it, and he was going to come home. He went to Detroit where he met another young Indian. His name was Joseph Dunbar. Well, they took Joseph from here the same time they took George Jones to Virginia, and they put him to work in a carriage factory. Nobody helped Joseph or any of those Indians. They just traveled to big cities, and they had to make their own way. Apparently, Joseph had a hard time finding a place to stay, and because of the high room rent, he didn't have much to eat. George and Joseph had written to each other so they were able to locate one another, so George went to Detroit, and he said, "Let's go home." Joseph was already sick, he was already thin. I remember seeing him. He would be walking home from Marysville. My father would stop and pick him up and talk to him. He was just so thin and so pale. He lived two or three months after he came home. He died of tuberculosis. But George made out all right. He was in a different place. It didn't work because young Indians got to places where they needed counseling, or needed somebody to see to it that they received their treatment.

I was the only one who went to Everett High School.

I went to Everett High School because my brother said that is where I should go. Some friends told my father to put an advertisement in the *Everett Herald* and ask for a family who would take an Indian girl who was going to go to high school. An attorney friend of my father's helped him to look at the answers. They chose a woman who lived just two blocks from the high school. She lived all alone in a duplex. She was a widow. Her five-room apartment was upstairs. So I moved there.

Her name was Mrs. Zanga. She and I got along fine. A nice couple lived downstairs. The husband was a policeman in Everett. I heard later that some women told Mrs. Zanga they thought she would have a terrible time with an Indian girl who probably did not speak English and was probably the dirtiest or the biggest drunk ever, and they said, "Oh, my lands, you are asking for big trouble!"

Mrs. Zanga's husband had died years before. He was born in Italy. She was born in North Dakota. She was Scandinavian. I asked her once how they got along, because once in a while she said her husband was "flighty." He would get mad over things, and she had to put him in his place. Anyway, that part was interesting.

I thought she would help me with my classes because going from an Indian boarding school to a high school in Everett was quite a jolt for me. Mrs. Zanga was Baptist—not a Catholic. All of the churches are the same to me. They are different in the way they have their rituals or services, but they all believe in the Christian religion. It was quite a jolt for me because during the years I was growing up all of us Indians were Catholics. As I say, I thought the lady I was boarding with would be able to help me. She only went to the fourth grade! Way out there in North Dakota, there is not that much schooling. But she was a wonderful person. She went to church, and she believed in Christianity, all the best of it, and she was a most marvelous cook. I think I weighed something like eighty-six pounds when I started living there, and by the time I was in school and eating her food, her cooking, I had gone up to something like eighty-eight pounds.

Students at the Indian boarding school. Photograph by Ferdinand Brady.

Mary Jane (Lummi) and Harriette Dover (Snohomish), when they entered the boarding school in 1910.

Dr. Buchanan and his family.

The barn where the boarding school boys worked. Photograph by Ferdinand Brady.

The laundry where the children worked. Photograph by Ferdinand Brady.

Harriette Shelton in her
graduation dress, 1922.

24

William Shelton, with the children in the boarding school, c. 1912.
Photograph by Ferdinand Brady; courtesy Museum of History and Industry.

William and son Robert on the Tulalip Indian School baseball team.
Courtesy Museum of History and Industry.

Robert Shelton and his wife, Arvella.

William Shelton carving the Everett totem pole. Juleen Studio.

7 / Treaty Rights
Are Like a Drumbeat

THE war in Europe had been going on since, I think, 1914. The United States declared war in April 1917. Then World War I finally hit the whole United States. My brother had to register for the U.S. Army in April. All of the Indian boys of that age group, from twenty-one to twenty-eight years old, had to sign up. We were all worried, really sick with worry, over my sister because she was dying. When she died at the end of May, as I said before, she died the same night my brother graduated from high school in Marysville. Then he was called up by the draft board and he left home.

The first World War was something we read about in the newspaper. Incidentally, newspapers came here one or two days late. Today you can get your paper the same day it is printed, but way back then, the mail for Tulalip came from Seattle and Everett on the mail boat. People came on the mail boat, too—anybody who had business to do at the Indian agency. The mail boat arrived here at 11 o'clock, 11:15, or 11:30 A.M. Every time the mail boat came, you heard a whistle. Today mail is delivered by the mail carrier from Marysville.

Robert and his cousin Clarence Shelton were called up together, and they both left on the same day to report to Fort Lewis. That was another big worry. There could not have been very many Indians to call up because the death rate had been so high. If I remember correctly, we had eight of the Indian boys from this reservation who served in the U.S. Army. They were in Fort Lewis for three months or ninety days. They had rifle and bayonet practice.

When my brother got several days' leave to come home, then we sat around and listened to him telling how to use or swing a gun with a bayonet on it. I felt as if I knew how, because he was telling us. Way back then, the Indian described everything he saw. We had a different language, since my brother talked in English, but he saw everything too.

They had the bayonet practice over and over. They had a Frenchman, a soldier, who taught them. He had been severely wounded, and we could guess that he had an artificial leg. I remember Robert said, "You certainly have to see to it that the enemy doesn't get to you first. The first thing you try to hit is just below the ribs, because if you do like that, but turn it, you are liable to have that bayonet in a rib; so that is why you jab and turn and pull. Try for here; try and jerk it down, because if you just try and cut a big vein—and then you also have your breathing tubes on each side." So, hour after hour, the grandparents, cousins—everybody—are listening to him. Then, of course, there was the awful worry that American soldiers were going to be sent to France.

My brother told about how they got an awful cussing when they first got there. But it was easy for him and his cousin to be in the Army because they had already been in an Indian boarding school. They knew exactly how to march. They knew which were "squads right," "squads left," "forward march," and "come to a halt." In Tulalip Indian School they knew how to do the right-hand salute by your numbers: "one," and you had better have that little elbow out right at the end of your eyeball. You had better have your eyes front, chins up, chests out, stomachs in, and that is what they had to do in the Army. So it was easy. They already knew how, but for the others it was tough. They had to get up at five o'clock in the morning and run around out there in the cold, doing all kinds of exercises.

At the end of the three months, then, we knew maybe my brother would be going. But the strangest thing happened to him. One night they loaded the regiment on the train. The officers were counting the men as they got on. My brother said they were loaded down with their cans of food. Way back then, canned food was absolutely the lousiest food you could have. I think in World War II the cans of food the soldiers had were bad enough, but World War I was worse.

My brother was at the very end of the regiment. He was one of the shortest ones. He wasn't more than five feet eight inches tall. Some of the young men were six feet tall, and they got on first. At least, that is the way the companies were lined up: from the tallest to the shortest. In the Army everything is hurry up and wait. It was dark. They were giving them a big cussing, and the whole group of taller soldiers went over to France. They took my brother and the others back to the barracks. Here they were up all night; then they had to get up again at 5 A.M. and start running around—exercising—again. They hardly got to sleep. He went from there to a spruce camp.

When they signed up originally, they had to put down their occupation. A lot of those young men had no job. My brother put down "lumberjack," since he worked in a logging camp. I have a picture of him; it was made like a postcard. He was in Hoquiam, Washington. He said he was camped seventy or eighty miles from Hoquiam in a spruce camp in a large forest, and he was with a logging company. So my brother and his cousin spent the rest of the war there.

I have often said spruce was used in the frames of airplanes. There weren't that many airplanes in World War I. Five hundred American soldiers were paid one dollar a day, plus their food, and they worked there for two years, until 1919. Wages were cheap. They should have earned more than one dollar a day, but that was Army pay, and the logging company got cheap labor. They wouldn't have received much more than that if they were paid regular wages. They took out huge trees—three to four feet in diameter—and the company made plenty of money.

Elson James was a soldier who didn't come back from Europe. Our other boys did. Some of them went to France. Elson, who was the same age as my brother, fought the Germans all of the way across France. He was in the battle of Argonne. He marched across Belgium, Holland, and then to Germany when they signed the treaty. They quit just as the American and English soldiers got to the border of Germany. The English, French, and Americans kept on marching in, because Elson didn't get to Berlin. The Spanish influenza was just beginning.

Influenza went around the world. It was fantastic the way people died. People in the cities and towns in the United States had to wear surgical masks on the street so they would not catch Spanish influenza. Now it is just called the flu. Way back then, people got ferociously sick. You could catch a cold and by evening you would have a raging fever and by midnight be delirious with a high fever. It seemed as though there was nothing that would help. People died all over. They died on the streets. Elson went all the way through in every battle and every bullet missed him. Then, just as they were getting into Germany, he caught the flu. A lot of soldiers did. He died in some strange city with a strange name, and it was something like two years later that they brought him home in a casket.

The Indian soldiers who were in World War I—in fact, in World War II, too—were outstanding soldiers. They were good in scouting—that is what Elson did. A lot of Indians in World War I could crawl out of the trenches in the night across what they called "no-man's land." Of course, they carried hand grenades and their bayonets in their mouths. It was pretty close; what they call hand-to-hand fighting. Sometimes, if you were crawling along with a rifle, you could hit a rock and the enemy could hear you. The Germans, or both sides, sent up a very bright light, a light-gun that shoots up a light that stayed up in the sky for quite a while. It was a bright light, and it shone all over a big, big area, because then it shone all over the whole battlefield.

Elson James's lieutenant wrote a letter to Elson's mother. Of course, she couldn't read or write, so the agent read it for her: about what a good soldier, what a good scout he was. It said he was an especially good combat soldier.

Three others from here were in the back of the German lines. Elson was the only soldier from here that didn't come back. There were six or seven from here. All of them got to France, but the war ended before some of them got all of the way up there to Germany. One of our Indians was in the Engineers. He said, "We built railroad tracks all over that France." I don't think they knew what they were doing. They worked early and late. In World War I, they used the railroads a lot because they didn't have trucks and jeeps like they had in World War II. He said he built enough railroad tracks to go around the world ten thousand times! Every once in a while there were some German airplanes that went over them, but nothing like in World War II. But every time they went by, they would have to run for the brush or the trees and fall flat, and if you landed in a ditch with water in it, that was tough. You had to keep working even if you were covered with mud.

When the Indian soldiers came back home, they had been to many places—England, France, Germany—and then even if they didn't get overseas, they still had been to California, Kansas, Virginia—wherever the training camps were. So they got to see and meet hundreds and thousands of white people. They saw different parts of the world and met many people. Indians went to France and met French people; and after a lot of loud talking and waving warms, they finally understood that these American soldiers were American Indians. Many of the French came and looked and stood around and watched the soldiers. They were all over in cocktail lounges, in fraternal organizations and clubs, so Indians met a lot of different people in those places.

Some of the boys went to other places to work when they came home: maybe to a mill in Everett or over on the Olympic Peninsula in some of the logging camps. There wasn't much opportunity for Indians to find work. The only places were logging camps or mills, but most of the mills wouldn't hire Indians—even up to the 1950s. Some of the employment personnel in some of the mills in Everett would not hire an Indian if they had a choice. If there were several Indians and several whites, they took the whites, because they said the Indians were unreliable. They were good workers, and they worked every day and they learned fast, but when it came time for the fishing season in June, they said, "I have to go home." The personnel directors said, "If they are going fishing for two or three months, they can just stay away. We're not going to keep those jobs open for them."

The 1920s all over the United States were still a time of high employment. Wages went up in the logging camps and mills—shingle mills, lumber mills. Some Indians were working in a logging camp in Monroe or on the Olympic Peninsula. They were making eight or ten dollars a day, which was a lot of money compared to what they got before World War I, which was a dollar and a half. After the 1920s, wages went up to twelve or fifteen dollars a day for an eight-hour day. That was really making money. Today, in some professions, you can make that much in one hour.

When my brother and the other Indian men came home from World War I to the Tulalip Reservation in 1919, there was a big change. They spoke up when they came home. They said we should talk about more land for the Indians. Many of them were landless and homeless. They said, "This reservation is too small." They wanted their own land in addition to their fathers' allotments, and they wanted medical care for our Indian people. The reservations were not big enough for all of the young men who were growing up. The money that was appropriated for Indian welfare was not reaching the Indians. I remember in 1934, 1936, Indians would always know in July or September that there was money in the agency, since the agent and his personnel would start going to town and all around in brand new cars. The Indians used to say there goes some of our money. There were brand new cars for the agent, the doctor, and the forester. The money was all supposed to be for the benefit of the Indians. Some of the minutes of those meetings are lost.

I think that is what happened to many Indian men in World War II as well. The young men were not going to put up with the agent giving orders. If the agent or the priest wants you in church every Sunday, you'd better be there. They almost had a life-and-death hold over every Indian. Everybody was supposed to be speaking English, although great numbers of our Indian people never learned English. Their viewpoint changed as a result of traveling in the different states and then across to France, from the perspective of the reservation to an Army camp. For the first time, they read the treaty our people signed at Mukilteo in 1855. My brother read it, and I read it. Of course, I was only fourteen or fifteen years old. I was interested, but it didn't "tear me up." They talked about the treaty and about the needs and problems of our Indian people, especially since many were still homeless.

For years and years, since I was small, I heard my parents and other Indians talking about the things that were happening to them. Indians came to our house every Sunday. They were cousins of my father, relatives of mine, and friends. My mother cooked a big meal, and then they stayed and talked to my father all afternoon. We would often have fourteen or fifteen people for dinner. It seemed all I did on Sunday was wash dishes.

I remember several times waking up in the night and hearing somebody talking or several people talking and some woman crying. The first few times I heard that, I thought it was my mother, so I got up and I went to my bedroom door and listened. It's not my mother; it's some stranger. Somebody from our reservation. Somebody in their family had whiskey or something to drink, and there was a big upset. My father would get up and get dressed, and my mother would go with him, and they took the woman home. She usually had one or two children with her. My father would get to where they were living and find the man and talk with him and square it away.

Different Indians came and stayed at our house and in the evening talked in our Indian language. I sat there and listened to their troubles and problems. In 1910 or 1911, I remember one Indian man, Walter Hathaway, who was a cousin to my father. He came from the upper Skykomish River, where he worked and lived in a small town. I think he lived in Index, in a logging camp. His wife died years and years before, and he never married again. He had one daughter who was in the boarding school for a while. She was not very well and she left and never came back.

He was wondering what happened to his allotment. He received a letter from the agent, Walter Dickens, telling him he had money in the office from a land sale. The agent was, shall we say, wheeling and dealing with the mills in town and the land sales here. Mr. Hathaway was surprised, since he had not signed anything. He was talking with my father when he came in from work. He said, "I wonder how I happened to sell a forty-acre piece of land with a beautiful sandy beach?" I don't know what it is called now. Tulare is another allotment. Tulare Beach. All of the allotments have big, white settlements—people who have lived there for years now. They bought land lots on the beaches, and so they have very lovely homes. They have lovely homes on Tulare and Spibida and one or two other beaches in that area. That was a long time ago. I was a little girl. It was in 1911 or 1910, because I barely remember the evening when Mr. Hathaway said he received a letter that his land had been sold.

He said, "I didn't give the agent permission to sell the land." The agent said, "Oh yes, you did, because your name is on here." Nearly all the Indians then couldn't read or write. They had put their thumbprints where they were told on documents, but in many cases, they didn't know that meant they were selling their land. Some of them didn't receive any money from their land and never knew the land was sold.

One of my early memories is of Walter Hathaway wondering how he got the money for land he didn't agree to sell, and it was located on such a beautiful, beautiful beach. Around Tulalip Bay it is muddy. Further out in some places, the beaches have gravel, but there is very little sand on them.

When my father was old enough to be a leader, by 1913, he talked to the Indians and asked them why they couldn't have the reservation logged.[1] The Indians had some meetings, and they thought that was a good idea. A lot of the Indians were doing hand logging. Today they call it "gypo logging."

For several years, there was a company, the Everett Logging Company, that was logging trees on this reservation. They were taking out prize, prime cedar and fir trees, the biggest trees, which were commonly nine feet in diameter. The Indian owners of the allotments where those logs came from never received the money for that timber. There were big trees here—big, big timber—and that was one of the reasons the Indians picked out this area for their reservation. The land here was not really fit for agriculture, except for the growing of raspberries.

Roland Hartley owned the Everett Logging Company. He was also governor of the state for a couple of terms. During this time, off and on, my father and some of the other Indians were having trouble with the agent over the logs that were being taken off of this reservation. The Hartley family owned the mills, and thousands of dollars of prime cedar and fir logs were going out from the bay here to the Everett mills. The Indian owners of the allotments, where the logs came from, were not receiving payment for the timber. My father and a delegation of Indians went to the agent because of the timber Everett Logging was taking out. They were thieves, really, and the Indian owners were not getting credit. I guess it is all right to mention the awful

---

1   He wanted the Indians to do the logging themselves and thus earn a living from the sales, instead of letting companies come in and profit from reservation properties.

thieving of Hartley's company since it was documented in Norman Clark's book *Milltown*. He tells about the logging of the Tulalip Reservation and the losses suffered by the Indians. (Sherry Smith mentioned that part, too, in her thesis when she graduated.[2]) Nearly all of the loss was on Indian land sales here. When they got through logging here, the Hartley family could retire. They made thousands and thousands of dollars just from the timber on this reservation, and it was all stolen from Indian land.

The Indians here complained for several years about the logs that were being hauled down to the railroad and off of this reservation. There was a railroad that went through this reservation. They had a dock just beyond the Catholic church. The logs were brought there—just splashed into the water—and then a boat company took rafts and rafts of logs to the Hartley mills. The Indians complained to the agent, Walter F. Dickens, who came here after Buchanan, that a lot of logs were not marked. Now, any person who is logging will mark their logs on the end with their own mark, so that when the logs are taken to a mill they will know who owned them, who brought them in, and who gets paid. Thousands of dollars worth of our timber went out of here like that, and quite a lot of it went to the Indian agents. Tulalip Indians were robbed of timber by the thousands of dollars by the logging company owned by Roland Hartley.

Mr. Hartley kept the money, or he also shared it with the Indian agent. The Indians would go in—four or six Indians—and talk to Walter Dickens. He would say, "All right, all right, I'll find out. You don't have to come back. I'll just let you know." The Indians waited perhaps a month, and then they went back. He said, "All right, all right, I'll just let you know." So for months, years, all of those thousands of dollars just went out.

I remember when I was a little girl at home, any Indians that came here from any reservation would come here to see the agent at the agency office because it took care of several Indian reservations. If those Indians had a complaint or something to talk about they came here and way back then the Indians came on trains or on the mail boat from Seattle or Everett. I remember different Indians coming and staying at our house, and in the evening they would all talk in our Indian language, or their tribe's language, and so I would sit there and listen and I would hear lots of things—their troubles, their problems.

For the first time, many Indian families who had allotments had money

2   She was also known as Sherry Guydelkon.

from the timber sales, and then their allotments were logged off. We had a lot of cedar trees on this reservation up to 1950. Some of the Indian families had $20,000 to $30,000 coming to them from the timber sales. Of course, the money was paid into the agency office. The agent and the chief clerk handled it. The Indians would go in the first of every month—that is, the ones whose allotments were logged, since they thought there was money there. So they got their checks for maybe $100 or $150. Some of the Indians asked for $200, but the agent wouldn't let them have it. He said they would just squander it.

If they were like me, I would squander it too. By the middle of the month, I am almost flat broke. I always want to go somewhere to eat. I took a Human Relations course at Everett Community College from Dr. Palmer. One time he had us write down what we liked to do best. We handed in our papers, and the next day he handed them back. He said, "To eat, Mrs. Dover?" I said in my paper I like (1) to eat, (2) to eat lots of food, (3) to have lots of really nice food prepared by someone else, (4) more food. I grew up in an Indian boarding school. I starved for ten months out of the year, for ten long years, from 1912 to 1922. Hungry, hungry, hungry.

Along about this time, an Indian woman came from Lummi. She was pregnant and had a sick child at the boarding school. She and her husband were staying at the school in one of the bedrooms in the club house. She was going to have the baby, so her husband walked down to the hospital to see the agency doctor. Of course, he got kind of upset. They had twelve hospital beds: six in the women's ward and six in the men's ward. The doctor wouldn't put her in the hospital, and he told her to go someplace else. "We don't have facilities for maternal care of any kind." He loaded them into a car. He brought them in the woods up here with another family. It was after midnight, and the family was sound asleep. She just barely got into the house. She didn't even get to a bedroom before the baby was born.

Another case was a brother and sister who were in their seventies or eighties. They lived across the creek. They were a widow and a widower. They had been married long years before, and their families had all died. There was nobody here to take care of them, so they moved down here to be near my father and my mother. The elderly woman cut her hand with an ax. She was splitting wood, which is what everybody did way back then. She cut her hand badly. The tendons on her first two fingers were cut, and the wound was open. She and her brother walked a mile and a half to the hospital. It was 8 A.M. The doctor had already seen the school boys and girls who came down for medical care at the hospital. The nurse came out. They were sitting on benches in the hall, and she asked what was the matter. She said, "You should not be here." So the brother said, "She cut her hand." His sister had her hand wrapped up in a clean dishtowel. We used big flour sacks for towels that were washed until they were nice and white. She had it wrapped with a couple of those, and she wrapped it some more, but the blood went through her skirts and was going past her feet out into the hallway. The nurse said, "You can't stay here. You'll probably have to go home. Just go home and wrap it up." The brother tried to tell her it was bleeding badly; it should be wrapped better. The nurse was "yakking away," telling them to go home and get out of there. She saw the blood and said, "What is that?" And then she went back and told the doctor.

She told the doctor the first time around, "A couple is out there—an Indian woman with her hand cut by an ax." The doctor said, "Oh, tell them to go home. A cut isn't anything." When the nurse saw the blood and went back to the doctor and told him the woman needed attention, the doctor finally did see her.

Those two people came to the house and told my father about it. The Indian woman was trembling. She had an awful shock. My father gave her an aspirin. My father and mother didn't take aspirin, although they had it because I sometimes used it. Anyway, my father took them home and made a fire in their cook stove. It was just a one- or two-room shack. My father often heard about experiences like that one, but my brother got roaring mad when he heard about it. They called a meeting.

Calling a meeting was done very carefully way back then. Indians were discouraged from having a gathering of any kind. The agency didn't trust meetings of all of the people. We had the Tulalip Improvement Club by then, by 1912, but they weren't involved in claims against the government until later. There had been wars all across the United States, and they didn't want Indians around the agency here. Anyway, my father and the others talked it over. They went to Everett and got an attorney. Way back then, attorneys didn't know anything about Indian law. But they felt that kind of treatment—to anyone—was just not acceptable. So it was in the newspaper, because my father talked to the editor, somebody he knew in Everett, and it created a big upset. My brother belonged to the American Legion in Everett. He talked to them, and their organization expressed their sympathy and their interest in helping the Indians. He wrote to James Wickersham, the Washington State representative in Congress then. Usually Congressmen didn't know anything about Indians, and they couldn't care less. But Mr. Wickersham was somebody who actually got involved in Indian troubles, such as when he helped the members of the Indian Shaker Church.

The Tulalip Improvement Club

The first tribal organization here was the Tulalip Improvement Club that was started during the years 1912 to 1914. My brother and father said to call it the Tulalip Improvement Club, since how can they quarrel with us for meeting if we say we are trying to improve ourselves? My father said if we say "improvement" that ought to mean something. The club helped the Indians to get together in the earlier years. The Indians never got together, really, except for the Improvement Club, because for quite a lot of them, they would have to hitch up their horses or come in their cars on real bad roads down here to a meeting. As I said, the agent told us we could not meet together. It was not permitted. The man who was called the farmer, at the agency, would come to their meetings. He stayed at the school all of the time. But he came and talked and listened to them several times. Otherwise, the Indians went ahead with their own Improvement Club. Sometimes the meetings were not well attended because the club was not doing much, so there was not as much enthusiasm. They put on the Indian fairs from 1915 until after World War I in 1918. Then no more fairs were held.

The Tulalip Improvement Club put on the fairs, but they used to meet through the year and they talked about our roads and our cemeteries. The Indians took care of the roads from the agency to Marysville. If they needed gravel, then they picked out certain people to haul the gravel, and that was done with horse and wagon. It was real slow work. The road from the agency to Marysville has been considerably straightened. All of those turns have been changed and the road made straighter. The Indians used to work every year on that road to widen it and to bring in more gravel. Some families who worked on the road camped out in tents. It was enjoyable to them because they were together again. They paid the man who had the workhorses and wagon to haul the gravel. They collected the money to pay him. Some families might give a dollar and others twenty-five cents.

The Indians took care of the graveyards, too. The only time my father could go was on Sunday since he worked twelve to fourteen hours in the sawmill at the agency. One time I went with him to work in the cemetery. I found the list of Indians who donated the money to put a fence around the cemetery.

Indian Fairs

When they had their Indian fairs from 1913 to 1918, my father was the president of the Tulalip Improvement Club. The Indians here got together. They had the nicest gardens. They had their potatoes, carrots, parsnips, rutabagas, cabbages, and so on, all lined up on display, and the women came with their baking—bread, pies, and cakes—and then dressmaking, and quilt making, and all of the handcrafts were displayed. We have a few pictures of some sections of the fair that show some of the quilts in black and white. There was no color film way back then.

A lot of the people who came were merchants who had stores in Marysville and Everett. My brother and my father went from store to store in Marysville, and since most of the owners knew my father, they donated prizes for the fair. Sometimes they were pretty dishes for the women for best bread making, best dress, or best quilt. The prizes were on display and it was a nice, exciting time. The merchants from Everett came with their families and there was a picnic all day long. It was called the "merchant's picnic." They came on the boat because it was easier. There would always be rivalry. They had foot races, baseball games, and sometimes canoe races—the racing canoes and the war canoes. Sometimes they invited the Lummi Indians; the Swinomish and the British Columbia tribes came in their racing canoes. That was a big, exciting time.

My mother and my sister-in-law said later they hardly ever saw my father and my brother during that time. They were strangers. They left early in the morning and ran home at noon to grab something to eat and ran right back out, and they were still eating when they were leaving the house. At the fairs you could see that a lot of the Indians were good workers. I don't know how the Indian and white communities would get along now, but the Indians in Seattle, who are from different tribes, put on a salmon bake by the American Indian Women's Service League at Alki Point, and a lot of people come to it.

The club met at least four times through the year, not only to put together fairs but to get together if there was a funeral in any family. Indians always get together for a funeral and collect money and donate food, since there would be many Indians gathered together, and they had to provide three or four meals a day for several days.

People like my brother spoke English all of the time. The older Indians could understand most of it, but they spoke in our own language at the Improvement Club. Later, the younger people just talked English. They stood up and talked about what was needed or made a report on what they were doing. They talked about their gardens and about their orchards. Some of them took turns at the gate at the fair and charged each wagon an entrance fee—or people coming in cars, later on.

Now and then I used to hear the older people say, "Now we're like white people. We talk in their language." The pressure wasn't that bad in the late 1920s and 1930s about being civilized, but it seemed to me that when I was in the boarding school and just a little later that business of being Christianized and civilized was just a terrific pressure. It was a big pressure on the Indians, especially the Indian children.

They talked about our roads. The Indians took care of the roads from the agency to Marysville and the cemetery. Working on the road was enjoyable because they could be together again. The Indians were separated on their allotments by several miles, and the roads were practically nonexistent, so they walked over muddy trails. Some had horses and farm wagons, but to go very far with a farm wagon was really something because the roads were in bad condition. They went over stumps and logs. My father and the Indians got together, and they worked about three days each in the summertime on the roads. If the Indians needed gravel, then they picked out certain people to haul gravel, and all of that was done years ago with a horse and wagon. It was slow work. The road from the agency to Marysville has been straightened considerably and widened. Of course, women worked there, too. Women and children helped by cutting the wild roses and other brush.

It looked like it was a lot of fun because there were children there. I asked my mother, "Why can't we go and camp out halfway between here and Marysville?" with the families who did. They camped out in tents, and the children could play. They didn't get paid. They collected money and paid the man who hauled the gravel. Some of the Indians were very poor. If they gave, it was a dollar from each family. Elderly widows might give fifty cents. As they widened the road, the brush had to be piled up, and they burned it after it was piled there for several weeks, when it was dry. Prisoners also did quite a lot of the roadwork.

Today the Indians still take care of the graveyards. They come and volunteer. If the tribe hires two or three men, then they are paid the going wage. I have a list of the Indians who donated money for the fence that is around Tulalip cemetery. I remember hearing them talk about the cost, and where they should put the entrance—a small gate for people who are walking in. There was a big gate for the horses and the wagons to go in. My father worked at the cemetery on Sundays because he worked at the agency twelve to fourteen hours a day during the week. So the only time he had to go to the cemetery was on Sundays.

The club meetings were stopped during the war years. There were no meetings except for talking together outside the church after Mass on Sunday. Sometimes the men met for half an hour outside the church, even if it was frosty. They stood around and talked. A few times I saw them talking with my father somewhere. They gathered around his horse and wagon. The women usually went to the wagons and sat there waiting because the men were talking. That was the only place they were able to meet.

After World War I, when my brother and the others came home, they knew how to write, so they started keeping minutes of the meetings of the Tulalip Improvement Club. Once in a while, the assistant superintendent from the agency, Mr. Walters, attended. Later on, the Indians went on with their own meetings and nobody from the agency came. I think they must have had somebody to tell them what was discussed, since during all of those years it seemed the Indians were watched all of the time.

The Indians who came to the meetings were the Snohomish and Snoqualmie tribal members. The two tribes were polarized, but they tried to come together. The Snoqualmie all sat together. Now that I remember, I used to be scared of some of them. There really wasn't anything to be afraid of; they had their children and grandchildren with them. But Snoqualmie have a reputation for fierceness. The Snoqualmie stayed together. There was rivalry. My family were Snohomish, not Snoqualmie. But at first when they met, they were still together. Snoqualmie and Snohomish and Skagit and all the Indians that were on the reservation met together. Sometimes the Snoqualmie met in Carnation, so the Snohomish started meeting here. Then they would talk about their gardens, their orchards.

The Tulalip group wanted to talk with the whole group of Indians, not just the people on the reservation, and said we ought to invite all of our tribe to the meetings and let them know we are meeting and we are talking about trying to get better medical care, better hospitalization, and more land. There are too many landless and homeless Indians. Some of our cousins lived on Whidbey Island. Another cousin worked up here in a big logging camp. So when they went home on the weekend, they told their brothers and sisters. So the organization got bigger and bigger. The Snohomish tribal members decided to write letters so people knew to come to the first meetings. We had a cousin who lived in Port Townsend. They left their address, and my brother wrote to them. The Snohomish organization grew.

Treaty Rights

When the fairs were revived again after the war, then the Indians were starting to talk about their claims against the government. Eventually my father
would have noticed the problems of our people, but it was really my brother
who started the claims against the government. In 1923, I started high school.
In 1924, the Club, my father, and my brother invited people here. We met
with a government attorney, Mr. Stormont. We took the testimony of some
of the elderly people who came to our house so that they could bring the
fraudulent land sales and other matters such as fishing rights to the federal
government. My brother and I helped them to type a lot of the testimony
and the minutes since we could understand their language. Later, the Boldt
Decision came pretty much out of what those elderly Indians said or testified
to Mr. Stormont. My brother and father made a big difference from 1923 to
1926, because the Indians were supposed to receive medical care from the
agency doctor. It says so in the treaty—but the doctors refused to treat them.
The Indians talked about their treaty rights when nobody else paid attention
to the Indian. Treaty rights are almost like a drumbeat—treaty rights.

My brother and my father got the older Indians together, talking to them.
I have two pictures of our parents' home. Out in the yard, fifteen or twenty
of the older, older Indians in my grandmother's generation were gathered in
a meeting. I really don't know how my brother accomplished that—getting
those people together. An attorney, Mr. Stormont (I don't remember his first
name), came from Washington, D.C.; he had a secretary with him who took
down every word. He asked questions of the Indians. My father or somebody
interpreted, because none of those Indians spoke English, and most of them
could not understand all English words. They could probably understand
"yes" or "no," like my grandmother could. It took hours, several days, for
them to take their statements. Each person who testified told where they
were born—such as on Squaxin Island, where their father and mother were
visiting, out on the Pacific Ocean, or on one of the rivers south of Aberdeen.

One of the people who testified was a cousin of my mother; his last name
was Edwards. He was a frail, elderly man, but he had been at the treaty signing
in Mukilteo, January 22, 1855, when he was a teenager, like my grandfather
Wheakadim. He said they brought presents for the Indians. The presents that
he received were one fishhook and one yard of narrow red ribbon. That was
the big payment he received for giving up his share of the land—from the
Canadian border and from the islands, all of the way to the Cascades and

all of the way south of Seattle—giving up millions and millions of acres of land. His share was one fishhook and one yard of red ribbon. Those were the kinds of presents the Indians received. Others received, maybe, mirrors and beads. You read it in the history of or recorded minutes in treaties such as in the Middle West—Colorado or somewhere—where big, big tribes would receive maybe a couple of yards of red ribbon or a looking glass. The Indians had never seen mirrors.

I have a string of beads that were given to the Indians at Tulalip about four or five years after the treaty. They were Hudson's Bay trade beads. They are a pretty bead. They were brought by the English Hudson's Bay traders. They are two shades of blue Venetian glass. They are good glass. They are not cheap. It is Venetian glass that came from Italy. The English brought tons of them to Alaska and all along here, but I don't think any farther south than the Columbia River. Hudson's Bay trade beads are a part of the Northwest now. You read in the history where they got glass beads. They were the first of the trade beads. A short time after that, another kind of bead came from China. They were called a "cranberry bead" (but they are not really red)—handblown—because they are perfectly round and none is exactly the same. The glass beads came from China; they were distributed by the Hudson's Bay traders or any trader. They are also heavier than the others.

We went to federal court for more money and more land, for the land we gave up. The reservations in this area were not big enough, even if they received allotments, and many Indians were left landless and homeless because they didn't receive allotments. We wanted more land, but it didn't have to be eighty acres. We had an attorney from Seattle, Arthur Griffin, a kindhearted man. We had to collect money to pay the fees. We had dinners, and people gave what they could. Some of the old, old people just gave a dime or twenty-five cents. Some of those who were working gave one dollar or five dollars. They collected money time and time again. Our attorney had to appear in the Circuit Court of Appeals in San Francisco. The judges there ruled against us. They said there was no more land to add or to allot. I don't know what else they said now, but we didn't have a case.

We appealed to the U.S. Supreme Court, so Mr. Griffin went before that court. They gave him and a couple of attorneys for several other tribes fifteen minutes to present the case. We lost that one. The Supreme Court upheld the Circuit Court's judgment. The attorney sent me the decision; I think it is in my son Wayne's house, but it is twenty-five years since I looked at it. The way it ended up we owed the government money—thousands of dollars—

because they had provided meals and room and board for the Indian children in the boarding schools here. They counted up every penny they had spent on every child for, whatever it was, thirty years. So they charged us room and board for the Indian boys and girls in the Indian boarding school here. Nobody brought up about the worms in the oatmeal. We used to have corn meal mush, too. I used to like that, but that had a different kind of worm in it. The attorneys wrote letters to the agent and the commissioner of Indian Affairs in Washington, D.C. They never even answered.

Then, in 1927, they held the last Indian fair—like the ones before World War I.

Fishing Rights

When I was little, these Indians used to fish all over, not just on the reservation. They could fish around Whidbey Island and fish on the beach with a net. But, gradually, as the years went by, Washington State Fisheries began to order the Indians all over the Sound, in western Washington, and also up the Columbia River to stay on the reservation to fish.

I talked with one of the girls, Eileen Williams, who attended Everett Community College when I did. She came from the Colville Reservation. She said her father fished on the Columbia River close to the Canadian border, where the river is still rather small. But then the river gets around and makes the big turn and it touches Oregon and then it is a big, big river. When she was little, her grandfather had his net beside the river where they fished for hundreds and thousands of years. The Washington State Fisheries people would come along and tell them to get out of there. "Get out. Get out. You're not supposed to be here." If they didn't move, if they tried to say, "We've always been fishing here," well, then, those men would just move in and grab that net and just cut it up with a big knife—just shredding it. Of course, those Indians were as poor as any Indians around here. You have to buy twine to patch the net. Twine that will last in salt water or in fresh water is more costly. Time and time again, for her grandfather and her father, too, and all the Indians she knew, the Washington State Fisheries people would cut up their nets. So then some of them did give up, but some of them would keep trying.

The Bureau of Indian Affairs in the Department of the Interior, secretary of the Interior, has charge of the Indian Bureau, but nobody cared what was happening to the Indians' fishing rights, which were guaranteed by the U.S. government representatives when the Indians signed the treaty. The representatives said those things that are written in the treaty will stand as long as the sun shines, rises in the east, and as long as the rivers run from the mountains to the sea, as long as the grass grows green. These words and promises hold true; they will be carried out. Of course, that is a whole lot of words. The Indians were being arrested.

In 1912, 1913, and 1914 the Indians were arrested by the Washington State Fisheries or game wardens, and they were tried in court and sentenced to thirty, sixty, or ninety days in jail. Long ago most of them couldn't speak English very well. Certainly, most of them couldn't afford an attorney. So when they appeared in court, the game warden or the fisheries man read where he found him, what he was doing, where he was fishing. The judge talked and sentenced the Indian to jail. Indians were in jail in Bellingham, Mount Vernon, Seattle, Olympia. The rights of the Indians were practically extinguished by Washington State until the Indian tribes got together again.

They had meetings with their leaders—meeting after meeting. They decided before the time of the Boldt Decision something should be done. We had the Tulalip tribal meeting minutes, which my brother and I started taking from 1924 to 1926. When I testified in Judge Boldt's court, one of the things the tribal attorney asked me was if I could remember the years 1924, 1925, and 1926. The attorney has the book of the minutes of some of our tribal meetings. A lot of it is my typing and my brother's, so I guess it was in his office after the Boldt case. I was telling Wayne we ought to ask for that again since it used to be in our house. He showed it to the attorney and he said, "Oh, gosh, this is just what we need." Well, Louis Bell died; I don't know how long ago, several months ago. His son or his two sons, the Bells, now have the attorney's office. I should remind Wayne again to try and get that back. It belongs to our tribe, the Snohomish Tribe; it is probably lost for good. We worked on that project for more than thirty years.

In 1927, I was with my brother and father. Several tribes here in western Washington brought a suit against Washington State that went on for months and months.[3] When the case was heard in the Supreme Court of the United States, they upheld the Supreme Court of Washington State. The Washington

---

3   The case is known as *Duwamish et al. 1927*. The judges would not accept Native testimony or hand-drawn maps of tribal territories. The issues in the case were not resolved until the Indian Claims Commission cases in the 1950s and *United States v. Washington*, 1973, also known as the Boldt Decision.

State court said the Indians had no rights. They had no business fishing off of reservations. The Indians started over again. There were no attorneys the Indians were able to hire. We collected money. Some Indians, again, were only able to give fifty cents or twenty-five cents. Some attorneys worked for something like five, ten, fifteen years on fishing cases and ended up with a decision that wasn't quite yes and wasn't quite no. Our fishing case should never have been tried in a superior court. It should have been tried in a federal court as in the *United States v. Washington* [1973].

Freedom of Religion

My father helped with the churches that were established on this reservation. Of course, the first one was Catholic. But along about this same time period, I heard Indian people in our house speaking with my father in the Indian language about an Indian man whose name was John Slocum. He had started a group of people known as the Indian Shakers. They told him, "Our people are in big trouble." They have been tried by the Indian court, and they were locked up in a couple of cells in a jail in the old mill or sentenced to work because they had joined the Indian Shaker Church. My father never saw them because he was working there on the campus at the boarding school, and he didn't hear about the trial or the arrests until after they were in and locked up. Some Indians came and told him, "Some of your cousins are locked up down there." My father went down there, and he was talking to them and they were telling him what they were doing.

They said my father ought to go there and see those Indians working on the road. They have women working—not only the men. My father was at work. He left the sawmill and went and got on his horse. Several miles toward Marysville, he found Indians working on the road, and there were women, and, of course, they had their children with them who were helping too. He stopped to talk to them and said, "What happened?" They said, "We were in court, and we were sentenced to thirty days of hard labor for joining and 'working' in the Indian Shaker Church."

My father thought he'd better go and attend a Shaker meeting. They were held at Ambrose Bagley's home. It was big enough, so that lots of Indians could meet there. They told my father, "This is where we have been meeting and this is what we believe in. We take care of our own people." They had just had a funeral. The Shakers got together and paid for the casket and the whole funeral. These Indians used to do that anyway. When I was growing up, they took care of everything: the caskets and the over box. Of course, they always had big dinners.

Anyway, my father talked to them. He had women cousins there. One of them was Mrs. Bagley, Mary English. They told my father they were joining this new church. They told him about John Slocum and some of the other Indians who had established this new religion. They met every week on Saturday and Sunday. They all wore long white robes on Sunday, and they had white scarves in their hands. They all shook hands with everybody who was in the church group. They extend their brotherly love, what Christ taught, we are brothers and sisters, all together. My father went to one of their meetings, and he saw what they were doing.

My father talked to Dr. Buchanan, and he told him that it is not right to arrest people or to punish them for something they believe in. My father was an intelligent Indian. He only went to the second grade, and he didn't remember the First Amendment to the Constitution of the United States that guarantees freedom of speech and freedom of religion. He didn't know about it. But somebody told my father that everybody is supposed to have their choice of religion. Dr. Buchanan told him, "William, you don't know what you are talking about." He used to be able to talk to Dr. Buchanan. My father told him, "You are making a big mistake to punish them and try to break it up, because you will not be able to break up that church. It is already very firmly established, and, furthermore, I think it answers the need of the Indians like no other church has ever done."

Dr. Buchanan saw my father a day or so later, and he said, "Well, William, you win. We better leave them alone." But the Shakers took a lot of punishment.[4]

Lots of other Indians belonged to the Catholic Church and many of them did not talk to the Shakers, either. The Catholic priests said that what the Shakers do is of the devil. It somewhat divided the Indians again. But, of course, for my father and mother, nothing divided us. The Shaker Church members endured months and years of punishment. It was almost like being ostracized by some, but not all, Indians.

My father helped them to collect money when they built the first Shaker church on this reservation, and, of course, the money collected later was

---

4   According to Buchanan's correspondence in the Federal Archives in Seattle, he continued to prosecute the Shakers even above the objections of Cato Sells the Commissioner of Indian Affairs and Congressman James Wickersham.

donated. Indians were actually good carpenters. They had already worked with wood or timber or lumber. They were, in their own way, master craftsmen with their Indian tools. They had lived in longhouses so they knew how to put a building together.

By the time I was in high school, I went with my father to the Shaker church, but he was not a Shaker member. We stayed there from 7 or 8 P.M. until 1 o'clock in the morning. It really appealed to Indians who didn't go to the Catholic Church.[5] The Catholic Church was the dominant church in western Washington among Indian people. There were Protestant missionaries by Hood Canal and Olympia, my father said. The Shakers met regularly, and they all extended friendship and brotherhood to each other, which was something that had been pretty well lost. The Indians lived so far apart that they didn't see one another for a month or two or three months at a time. You would think they would see each other every week.

My father talked to a number of the Shakers because he wanted to know how they got involved in the Shaker religion. Of course, he heard about John Slocum, and then I heard the Shakers tell my father about John Slocum.[6] He was an Indian who started the Shaker faith. He came from Squaxin Island and Nisqually. It seemed to me he was under a lot of pressure. I used to hear the Indians who came to our house, who were coming to the agency to see about their land or something, and then they would stay at our house because there was no way for them to get back to Marysville or Everett because they would have to go on the mail boat. There were no cars, and the road from here to Marysville wasn't much of a road. So everybody went by the mail boat or they went by canoe.

I listened to them talking in the evening after supper, telling my father and mother things that they know (if they came from around Shelton or Olympia, it's the same language but it has different words). So they would tell about John Slocum. I heard that name so many times, but I never ever saw him. As I remember, they said he got sick and was dying. He said he would come back again. The Indians said he did die. They had him in a coffin, and they had a big funeral. Indians always have so many speeches at their funerals. Speakers from families of many tribes came. At the funerals, they all speak and express their sympathy. Sometimes they trace the his-

---

5   Many new "joiners" in the early days of Indian Shakerism were former Catholics.

6   See Erna Gunther 1949 and Homer Barnett 1954.

tory of the bereaved family: where they came from; who the grandfolks or great-grandfolks were; what tribe they came from. They give a kind of family history—anyway, speeches and speeches. Some women said John Slocum was breathing. They helped him out of the coffin, and he was able, as the Indians call it, to be himself again. He told what he had seen and what he had heard. God talked to him and explained to him how he was to talk to the people and teach them what they would do to build their own churches. I was just coming out of Tulalip Indian School, in about 1920, when I used to see them. I was about nineteen or twenty years old.

I remember going to the Catholic church on Christmas, right here with my mother, and there would be a lot of Indians. They would come by horse and wagon and quite a lot of them just walked. I remember going to midnight Mass when I was real small. I don't know how we got there. We must have come on a buggy. I remember it was kind of dark in the church, but it seemed as though there were hundreds and thousands of candles that we lit in that church. It was just beautiful. Up on that high, high ceiling was a structure in the shape of a cross that was just covered with candles, and all around the walls, and there were candles all over the altar. We lined up during a certain part of the Mass because I remember my mother gave me a candle and they lit it, and all these Indians are lined up with the priest standing there and the choir singing. The woman ahead of me had a shawl on and she was holding a candle. I was holding a candle. My mother had me by the wrist and she was saying, "Now hold it up. Don't let it shake." Well, they were quite tall candles. They were special candles that were allowed on the altar. I remember going up in the procession, holding the candle, and, oh, my, they have a lot of candles. There is genuflection you have to do in front of the altar and then you go to the side where there is a statue of the Virgin Mary.

So there I was on Christmas in a procession, holding a candle, and yet back home every day there was my grandmother, and she didn't speak English. I think I said that before. She had been baptized with the name Magdalene, but she never went to church, and I guess my grandfather didn't go to church either. He said, "It's wonderful, but it's not for me."

My father was not born on the reservation. He was born on Whidbey Island. That is where my grandfolks stayed. They had a chance to work in a logging camp, so they were able to earn money. That was the only thing the Indians could do and that was logging. There were heavy stands of timber all around. That was almost second nature to them to chop and saw down trees. By that time, they were sawing down dozens of cedar trees. In the old days, the Indians didn't cut down like that; they just cut down one tree for a canoe or enough trees to make a longhouse.

8 / Public School and Marriage, 1922 to 1926

I WAS terrified when I started high school. My brother picked out my classes. He wanted me to take the science curriculum—the hardest course in the school. I had to have a foreign language and English. I said, "I don't want to take those courses. Just let me have the general studies program, and I can take cooking and sewing." But my brother picked out my program. He and my father wanted me to go to the University of Washington when I graduated. You might think I learned to cook when I stayed with Mrs. Zanga, but all I did was study.

My brother said, "You move fast going from class to class. Don't dabble along, because there isn't much time between classes. As soon as you hear the bell, gather up your papers and pencils and books and move out of the classroom and go on to the next one. If you have time, then you can go to your locker and get your next class book. If you don't have time, then you better carry two or three books and have them ready so that you don't have to be running. You can't run in the hallways."

My first classes were Algebra I, English I, Spanish I, and General Science I. When I looked at the algebra book, I wondered, what in the world are they talking about? Furthermore, what am I doing here? The teacher explained, and I listened with all of my being. My brother and my father said, "You listen to every word the teacher says. Everything she says is important, especially when she first starts talking at the beginning of class. All of the way through, be sure you hear what the teacher says." Of course, my father, my grandmother, everyone said the same thing: the teacher is not talking just for fun. My brother Robert was the one who prepared me. He was fourteen years older than me, and there were four brothers and sisters in between. Most of them I never saw; they died when they were babies because of the epidemics that swept the Indian reservations, such as measles and the common cold and pneumonia and tuberculosis. The teacher explained, and I listened with all of my being. What is she saying? It wasn't too clear, but, vaguely, I got it.

When I got home that evening, I brought my algebra book. I looked at it because my brother said, "Now read it. If you don't understand what your teacher said, then read it again. If you don't understand what your teacher said, then read what it says at the beginning of the lesson. Read and read it again. Read again, sentence by sentence; and as you read each sentence, look over the book and think what it says. Know in your own mind what it says." So, that is what I did. I suffered with algebra until I got it. About the second evening, a terrible bright light broke, and I could see what they were doing—X and Y and everything.

All mathematics just "breaks me up." I counted on my fingers in school. I never really learned the time tables. The teachers emphasized how very important it is and how much easier it is to learn them. I looked at those numbers and I thought, "Oh, dear, do I have to learn that?" So instead, I walked around and talked with my friends. I remember now that seven times seven is forty-nine; that is easy. The algebra came easily.

Halfway through the semester we had to identify fifty songbirds and other birds in western Washington in order to get a grade. I spent every weekend with my father. He knew a lot about birds, but he knew the names in the Snohomish language. I had a book from the library. You couldn't say "barn swallow," for instance. We had to tell the color of its back and wings, color of the throat, and other things. It was kind of nice, in a way, sitting out there by the trees— listening. When you hear a different song, you walk around very slowly and ask, "Who is that?"

I don't see how I made it through Everett High School. I still have my report cards. My father and my brother said listen to every word the teacher says. Everything she says is important, especially when she or he first starts talking in the beginning of the class and all of the way through. See what they say. On my report card I got an A in Algebra, a B in Spanish, and an A in English. I thought, oh, this is going to be easy. Well, not easy, but I could work with it.

I got on the honor roll. Spanish was easy. I could talk Spanish as well as the teacher. Then, by the end of the semester, I was almost flunking algebra because of fractions. I got all mixed up. I could add up piles of fractions on both sides of the line, and for a while I could do it and get an A or a B, and then for a while I got nothing but an F. I used to tell my children, "You know things get like that—just don't give up. Sometimes you are going to wonder if you are ever going to come out of that deep, black mud you are in." My teachers were just wonderful all of the way through high school. They made us study. It seems to me in the last few years, in some high schools, students are just "dawdling." They don't especially learn. They aren't doing any book study.

I was the only Indian in Everett High School. Nobody, not one single student, boy or girl, through those four years ever said anything to me about being an Indian. In the beginning of the school year, there was an article in *The Kodiak*, the high school newspaper. I mentioned that my father carved the totem pole downtown. But I wasn't singled out for friendships. Friendships came about, and I was part of a very nice group.

There was an English teacher in the school who first taught in an Indian school somewhere but not in Washington State. She said she enjoyed the Indian children so much. It was a landmark in her life because the Indian children were all so courteous and they had such good manners. When they played, they were more active. When they spoke in classes, they used good English and it was a joy to teach them.

We had a reunion about two years ago. My son William took me. It was our fifty-fifth or fifty-sixth. I said to them, "Let's not count them anymore." I recognized a lot of my former classmates and, of course, they recognized me with my white hair. They called to me from across the room. We had a dinner at the Holiday Inn south of Everett. Nobody was going to throw me out this time.

Now and then I think of my brother and how bound and determined he was for me to take English, algebra, geometry, and history. He said, "You don't have to take cooking. You learn that here at home." But in my junior year, I took a sewing class because I thought, why can't I have a little restful time? I struggled through geometry, struggled through Spanish III and IV and all of that English, all the way through four years of English.

I remember telling some students that I already knew how to speak English, and I wondered why I had to take this class. We had to parse sentences. I used to pull my hair. I said, "Who cares whether they are adverbial clauses or whatever." The second or third year, we spent a semester on English poets and another semester on American poets. We had to learn three or four lines of certain poems. The teacher would say, "This is the part that is important. You will hear it again." In Longfellow (the teacher ought to hear me), I think it is the one called "Evangeline": "This is the forest primeval, the murmuring pines and the hemlock." The teacher would stop reading and talk. You could hear, and you could see, the murmuring of the pines and hemlock. An English poet wrote "Sunset and Evening Star": "And one clear call for me, and may there be no moaning of the bar when I put out to sea." I think it is called "Crossing the Bar." And then there was the one that Whittier wrote about the barefoot boy: "Blessings on thee, little man. / Barefoot boy with cheek of tan, / and thy merry whistled tunes, / and thy ragged pantaloons."

Believe me, we learned them. I used to know several of them. I could stand up and recite. I remember my brother saying, "It won't hurt you. It will help to improve your mind, expand your mind so that you should be able to have a wider point of view. It is going to be vitally necessary. Things are going to change for the American Indian, and we are not going to be isolated on the reservations anymore."

I struggled through the entire thing. My brother moved to Everett, so I didn't see him on weekends. There wasn't anybody for me to talk to about what I was going through, but I got through two years of Spanish, algebra, and geometry. When I was a junior, I took physics and chemistry. I wasn't any good in physics. I got a C all the way through. I used to "howl around" and say, "Why in the world do we have to listen to my brother? He said for me to take chemistry. Why? Here I am measuring water, acids. Some of them smoke."

At the end of the year, the class was talking about the "unknowns." We had ten or twelve unknown compounds or chemicals to analyze and identify. You put the unknowns in a test tube with a little bit of water and shake it up, and see if it is soluble in water. Then you go through a hydrochloric acid test. I used to wonder, what insane maniac dreamed up all of this? I thought about the unknowns. I bet I won't find any of them. I went through all except one, all twelve. It was kind of a blue-green crystal that looks like salt. It was cobalt. I got that just once, and I got the others in the book that look like salt. The teacher said, "Do not taste it." I thought it looked like salt. I tasted it and it was salty. It was potassium chloride. Most of them we had never seen before.

The teacher was gone for a while. We had a young lady substitute. She was a senior, an A student. The teacher had a little black notebook that he kept in his desk, filed away somewhere, so that he could tell what unknowns each one of us had. When we got our unknowns, I went to tell her that I had potassium chloride, or maybe it was sodium chloride. It was something simple. She looked in the book and said, "No, it wasn't." I said, "It wasn't?" and she turned and walked away. I went through the whole miserable thing about three times, and I came out with the same thing. Each time you do it over, you go from A to B, and if you miss B, you get a grade of C. She said it was wrong. The next day or so she was gone and the teacher was back, so I went up to talk to him. I said, "I can't get anything else but potassium chloride." He looked in the book and said, "That is what it is." I said, "That is what I told her." He said, "You told who?" I said, "I told your substitute." He said, "Oh, I'll talk to her." Well, I got a C or a B on that one anyway. I got worked up over that, too, way back then.

Haircut

I wanted my hair cut, but my mother said no. My mother said, "Absolutely not. Don't ask. Just don't ask." The style then was short hair. It was called "Marcel." I thought about it for two weeks, and I thought I know what I am going to do. I asked her one time, summertime, if I could have my hair cut in the Marcel style. She said, "What do I have to tell you? Now, don't ask. Indian women and girls don't have short hair." I walked out and went to the garage and talked to my father. I said, "Could I have my hair cut?" He stopped whatever he was doing and he looked at me. "What does your mother say?" "She said it would be all right." He said, "All right. You get ready and I'll take you into town. Where would they do that?" I said, "In the beauty parlor." He said, "All right. Get ready. We'll go." I ran in the house and I got my coat and purse, and I told my mother that my father said I could have my hair cut. "We're going into town." He came into the kitchen to get his other hat and my mother was standing there. She got real mad, and she said in English, "My goodness!" She was swearing like anything.

I imagine what happened to me, in having my hair cut short, was probably what happened to many girls, even white girls. It seemed as though many people of the older generation were shook up over short hair and short skirts. The music changed, too, to something like jazz. It seemed as though the younger generation was not really going to heaven.

I will always remember the reaction of my aunts and uncles to my hair being cut. The one I remember so well, and it bothered me somewhat, was Uncle Joe. He was my father's uncle. He was older than my father, and, furthermore, I could not really explain anything to him. When he came through the door, I was usually in the kitchen helping my mother. He would stop and look at my hair from side to side. The whole family was coming in with him, and everybody stopped and looked to see what he was looking at.

He was looking at my short hair, and he would always say the same thing. "Oh, dudah," and the longer that "oh" goes, the worse it is. "Ohh, dudah. Her husband must have died." Then he would go on into the other room, and his wife or somebody would laugh. His wife said the same thing, "Oh, leave her alone. It looks nice." So there I am with short hair. It's Marcelled, and I thought it looked super. But he always said the same thing. I didn't even have a steady boyfriend. So there I am—a homely little person out there, and that is all he said loudly every week. "Oh, dudah. She must have lost her husband." It seemed like he did that for months and months until he got used to it.

The older people were upset. Indian girls were cutting their hair. The only time Indian women cut their hair then was if their husband, son, or daughter—or somebody in their family—died. It was a sign of deep mourning. I don't know why, but there always have to be trials and tribulations for people growing up, and that was one of them. Nobody said (it should have been my father who said), "You should follow the Indian way and keep your long hair." If anybody had said anything, it would have been Uncle Joe. But he didn't say, "It's too bad to accept the white man's short hair." Now that I think about it, that is one of the things that jarred him, too. I was following the white man's fashions and that was not our way—to have short hair for girls and women. As my mother said, "Indian women don't wear short hair. They never cut their hair. The only time it is cut is when they are in deep mourning." If my father had said no, I would not have had my hair cut short, except he was usually in favor of anything that I wanted. I never used him like I could have—now that I think about it.

I asked him for high heels along about that time too. My grandmother and several of them came to the house. He told me to walk across the room. I did. Of course, I had been taught to take small steps. You don't take long steps as if you are plowing a field. I hadn't thought of that for so long. I had to walk across the room several times for my brother and the others to see how I walked with high heels. They rocked a little. Maybe they were exaggerating a little. Anybody could walk in high heels.

My father was such a marvelous person, and he had a fantastic life. He had a real Indian life—as real as it could be at that time. They wouldn't be able to live that way now. There are just too many people around. Way back then, his uncles were right on him like a bunch of bees. They were always giving him advice, and all of it was important. One of the things I think of now that my father found so helpful was one of the last things his uncle told him: "It's all very fine to have a temper, but you have to learn how to handle it. You can get into big, big trouble if you don't control your temper." Some people can get really violent. Today you read about people who shoot other people because they get so mad and frustrated. My father told me several times that his uncle said, "You have to control your temper, or it is going to control you, and it can damage your life, and it can almost ruin it." It is all very fine to have a temper, but there is a time and place to use it, and one of the times to use it is to learn how to live your life. There is usually so much frustration and disappointment to live through.

My father and I were good friends—real good friends. Whatever I did might have seemed kind of crazy to my mother. She never used the word "crazy," but it would almost sound like it. My father was more understanding of boys and girls. He said, "It is natural to do things that seem outlandish or crazy. It seems like it to our people or to your relatives. The young people learn. You could tell them things, but sometimes they have to learn it themselves."

He used to play the fiddle for dances, especially square dances for Indians, and even white people who happened to be around would go to dances. They had square dances and waltzes and schottisches that began in the evening and would last until six or seven o'clock the following morning. My mother let me go a few times with my father and my brother. My father played the fiddle all night. They stopped about midnight to have an entire dinner: roast beef, chicken, boiled potatoes and carrots, homemade bread and butter. People brought their children, even little children, and they fell asleep, but everybody took care of them.

I didn't go to dances when I was a teenager because my mother wouldn't let me go—but my brother did. My father told me one day why he didn't go to church much. He used to play for the dances. The priest, who had this parish at the time, was very mad at my father. He said he was the leader of the devil. He said, "Don't you know you are the leader of the devil when you play all night like that, and that is why people don't come to church the next day?" My father never forgot that remark. He used to say the same thing that my grandmother said in our own language:

> Whatever you do that is good and kind will come back to you. Somebody will do you a kindness, and you will be a bigger and better person. Whatever you do that is wrong or mean, it will come back to you. It will be bigger and worse than what you did. If it doesn't return today or tomorrow, or the next year, it will return as surely as the night follows the day. If

you don't pay for it, for whatever you've done, your children will pay, and whatever happens to them will be bigger and worse.

I always thought that part was more frightening than anything I ever heard at church. I don't want anything to happen to my children or grandchildren. My father was an outstanding Indian leader. He had been taught all of the things, the qualities, the Indians required of their leaders, and that was certainly the business of being honest.

When I was growing up, I used to wonder, why do they get into such a ruckus, because they were always emphasizing honesty. But I didn't say anything. You were not supposed to say anything. If your father or parent or grandparent is talking to you and telling you something or giving you advice, you take it kindly and courteously. I have heard some young people—Indian and white—get so mad over their parents and grandparents giving them advice or telling them what to do. I have heard them say, "My parents raised their own children, and all I want them to do is leave me alone and let me raise my own children." But that is not the way I was taught. I listened to my parents and grandparents.

For example, I remember when I got through high school and I was engaged to be married. It seems as though that news spread around, because in June or July some woman and her husband came to our house. I didn't remember ever seeing her, but they were the same age as my parents. But I will always remember her giving me advice and saying, "Remember one thing. Don't ever feed your husband warmed-over food. You cook a good, warm, and entire meal. He is working every day, and it is especially necessary that he have warm food that is just freshly cooked and you lay it on the table when he gets home." Of course, she talked about not allowing your husband to go around with messy shirts. "See to it that the laundry is done regularly, every week."

I didn't say anything. Mother thanked her, and I said thank you too for talking to me. Afterwards, I was asking my mother, "It seems like Indian people keep reminding me to take good care of my husband and everything. What about me? Who is going to take care of me?" My mother said, "Oh, just never mind. You just do what you are supposed to be doing."

Several of us who were about the same age would get together and once in a while we talked about how our people, our parents and grandparents, preached. It seemed like they never ever stopped what we thought was preaching. Now that I think about it, all of it might not seem important, but it does make a difference in your life, your daily life. The young Indians of today feel as though they were terribly picked on if somebody tells them, "I wouldn't do that if I were you." I guess young people have thought that ever since the beginning of time, that older people talk and give advice and preach. I think it was important. When I think of my grandmothers, my mother, and all of them, I am always impressed with one thing and that is their courage way back then. Actually, the Indians would be hungry. The reservations were never really set aside as a good hunting ground or a good fishing ground. Indian reservations were just set aside so that the Indians were pretty much out of the way.

Religious Conflicts

My mother was a very devout Catholic, and in school we had to follow it, too. My father, as I said, didn't go to church. I didn't really notice because by the time I was seven years old I was in the boarding school, so I wasn't home. By the time I got into high school, then I was home on the weekends. If my mother asked my father to go to church, it was on Christmas or Easter. Otherwise, she didn't say anything to him about church. She only reminded him.

My father's parents probably went to church once in every five years. My grandfather didn't accept the Catholic Church that much. He told my father to follow it when he came to the Catholic school. "You follow this religion, but remember the things that we told you. Remember the things we taught you." It bothered my father. It bothered me some years ago, and I know my older boy went through trying to reconcile two different cultures, shall we say.

My grandmother only talked the Indian language. In the school they spoke nothing but English, and the teachers were all white people. They told us the order was, you can't speak the Indian language. I don't know if it is really sadness—when you are trying to put those things together, you feel sadness, since you are trying to believe the Indian is important. It's mine, but I have to take the white man's language. I have to take his religion, and I have to reconcile it with what my grandmother said. I realize that there are white people who are kind, but there are others who want to send us off somewhere.

I'd like to have a velvet blouse and skirt because that is what my grandma used to wear, in black or navy blue, especially when she went to church. They also used to make skirts out of material that looked like wool for everyday; they were green. I saw a lot of green dresses or skirts. But I never ever saw green velvet. But I saw black velvet and blue—navy blue. I never ever saw red. When I was wishing for a velvet dress, my mother always said it was a sin to wish for anything. She said, "If you haven't got it, don't wish for it. That is a sin." I used to get so really worried about my sinning. I used to really worry about hell because I knew that was where I was going. I think, generally, everybody way back then in the Catholic Church was under a lot of rules, and you followed them. Maybe other churches were like that, too. You go to church and you sit there, and if it's cold, ice cold, that's too bad, you sit there. Or even if you are hungry and starving to death, and the priest keeps talking, preaching about something, you sit there.

I think it took me some time, because when I was in high school it all seemed so worrisome. Religion bothered me. For the first time, I went to a Protestant church and found they have beautiful services too. The pastor didn't seem sinful to me. I thought he was wonderful, warm, and more understanding than the priest. But it took me several years to get myself to the point where I was rolling along. You feel it is a time of sadness. You could have a lot of fun and laugh and go to a dance, but then there were times, quiet times, when you have to think it all over again. After a while, you begin to think somebody told you something that wasn't true.

High school was, then, the time when I think I had a religious conflict. Generally, way back then, I think anybody in the Catholic Church was under quite a lot of rules. The priest keeps talking, and I'm not listening. I'm falling asleep and my feet are freezing off. I used to really worry about hell because I knew that was where I was going.

In high school I had general science the first semester and then the second semester I had zoology, which began, really, with the beginning—amoeba, those little things that you could see in a drop of water. Then, of course, it tells about the beginning of life. You could see in that little drop of water those little "weirdees" that are going around in it, and then they divide up and you get more and more. I had come from home on the reservation, and all I had heard all of those years is that I have to be in the Catholic church and never, never set foot in any Protestant church because that is, absolutely, a sin. You are not to go into any Protestant church; those churches are pagan churches. So, when I got to high school there were the lessons; I had zoology, general science also—about flying birds of all sizes and everything, different kinds of fish, all the way to whales, and all of it was not what you would call in depth. It was just mentioned, kind of explained.

I did go to church with the woman I was boarding with, and she went to the Baptist church. I don't know how I happened to be there on a Sunday, from eleven to twelve, but they sang a lot of songs that we sang in the Indian boarding school. I think I mentioned before, at home my mother was a very devout Catholic, and my father never ever said anything about church; he just never went. It wasn't until I was in high school, because I think I was talking about some of my classes, that my father started to talk about his boyhood and what they taught him. Then I really wanted to hear him talk about everything he remembered, everything he did.

At the same time, I am saying the big, long rosary, and I have to remember all of it. By the time you get through something like that you pretty much know the ritual of the Mass. I used to try and stay awake. The thing that would wake me up was the ringing of the altar bells, which ring at something called the elevation of the Holy Host. I remember they used to tell us you are not supposed to stare at the Host; it is big, beautiful and shiny almost like the sun's rays, almost like a goblet, really, I can't quite recall because we weren't supposed to watch, but now and then I would watch, because I was almost falling asleep.

In high school we were studying about the very beginning of life as it was explained in general science and in zoology. My botany teacher made just a casual remark one day; he was just walking from one blackboard to another and he was saying, "Religion is just a ploy to keep the people subdued, so they don't complain about any hunger or any of the things that happen to them." I remember I thought about that one, too. I don't know why it hurt so much. It seemed as though it hurt in my heart, too. I could feel it in my chest and, of course, in my mind. I'm supposed to be doing algebra, geometry, physics, chemistry—the courses I had when I was a senior. I had to do a lot of homework. Suffer, suffer, suffer. And then I am worrying about religion. I'm going to the Baptist church. I like it. I like all of that singing; like I say, we sang those same hymns. I went to the Methodist church, too, to some kind of a revival. You know, I was just so frightened of that revival because it was a traveling preacher. I don't remember which church it was, but it was very big. I was there for the evening service. I think he had the services all day. The big wonderful pipe organ was really just booming. Even if it is playing softly there are some very low notes that you can almost feel with your feet. You know, I just got so terrified because I was in the wrong place and I was going to hell again for sure.

I was in the wrong church. What about the Catholic church? I was not supposed to be in a Protestant church, that is a pagan church, but their songs or hymns are what we sang in Sunday chapel. But in the boarding school it was not altogether Catholic. It was part of the Protestant church; that is why we sang "Come All, Christian Soldiers" and "Come, Thy Almighty King." I think the "Come, Thy Almighty King" is the Italian national hymn, or it used to be, and I thought it was so pretty.

I used to stay awake and just pace the floor—tiptoeing along—because I am really torn up about religion. I could almost see the flames of hell for me, doubting the Catholic Church. I thought how all of those years somebody was not quite telling the truth, and how do I know that this Baptist church is the one way, because the preacher said the Baptist is the true church because Jesus was a Baptist. Christ Jesus was a Baptist because he was baptized by John the Baptist, and so that is the true church.

I talked to my mother and, of course, she said, "Just say three Our Fathers and three Hail Marys. Then go in your room and get down on your knees and pray." Well, I do that. I wear out my knees.

I went out to see my father where he was working in the garage, or what became the garage, and I got up enough nerve to tell him I'm really worried and I'm mixed up. He doesn't answer right away. He thinks about it and listens to me. So, then, he told me about part of his boyhood, and what his uncles taught him. He said, "Don't worry about all of that. When you stand on this earth, you stand on grass, or the earth that is the creation of a great creator, a great mysterious creator. You are not lost. And you see all of these trees, everything that grows; you could see the birds, hear them sing. All of that is part of that great mystery, a great power. His creation is for you to see, to enjoy, and be part of. You can walk on the earth; you can live on it. You can maybe chop down one tree, but you don't destroy it."

I think definitely by that time there was a lot of logging all over and, really, that was an income for a lot of people: the lumber mills, the logging companies operations all over.

Anyway, I had a nice talk with my father. It was not long, but it made me feel as though I had come home. So I used to do what my mother said—get down on my knees and pray.

Religion, the churches I had gone to, and studying any kind of science—like the beginning of mankind, where you read and discover that the first people who appeared to resemble human beings were in East Africa (by that time I was going to the community college, where I took anthropology classes)—things like that didn't bother me because of what my father said. He said about the white man's god: he said it always was and it will always be. Well, that is the way with Dukʷibəł, the Indian creator, Changer. He was always there from the beginning of time. He was always there. You don't have to worry about any of it; it has just been going on—change and time—time is nothing to a great mystery or a great mysterious creator. He always was and he will always be. Time is nothing. A million years, a billion years of mankind changing, that is only a blink of an eye to him. So, when it says he created Adam, just like that, that is what he did because time is not in God's life. Time is what people count from days, nights, sunrise, sunset, middle of the day; and now we have clocks. It is time for you to go! We are slaves to time. People are slaves to time. You know you can get up and look at the time and say I have ten minutes to get down to the school building in about seven minutes so I can take another drink of coffee.

When I was on the board of directors all those long years ago, one morning I went running out, said goodbye to my mother, had my jacket on and went running out and jumped into my car. I had my father's old car and I backed out of our driveway and I was shifting and turning the wheel and I noticed my dress. I thought, I don't remember putting on a black dress, and then I felt it again and it was satin; it wasn't soft silk and it wasn't rayon. I picked up the hem and it had a little narrow row of lace, and so I sat there and I was feeling it and I was saying which black dress is this. I don't remember a black dress with black lace around the edge. I sat there and I felt it and there was little narrow lace all of the way around. Then, it dawned on me I didn't put on my dress. I just grabbed my coat, and I put it on and I ran through the dining room and the kitchen—my mother was sitting in the kitchen drinking coffee—so, I said, "goodbye, I have to go now," and I tore out the door and it slammed. It usually slammed open so she got up and closed it. Then I came running back in. Oh, I drove my car back in the driveway. Put on the brakes. Open the door. Get out. Shut the door. Then run around the car and run to the porch and jump through there and I ran through the kitchen and I said I forgot something. I never told my mother because she would get mad. She would say, "You have to think about everything. I keep telling you. Remember everything. Remember." So I said I forgot something. So I went running through the kitchen back to my room and grabbed my dress.

I had some papers I had to have at the agency where I was going. So I had those papers—I laid them on the bed—and put on my dress and I roared out again. I don't want to explain anything to my mother. She would bless me down good. I ran out and jumped into the car and then I remembered those important papers. Somebody had to sign them and I had to get them back to the agency. So I put on the brake again and turned off the motor, climbed out of the car, ran through the kitchen. My mother was still sitting there. She would always say *oʔhaydəb*.

High school was the time when I had a religious conflict. My grandmother was my dearest friend when I was small. Any time I had any kind of trouble with my mother, I ran down a couple of blocks to where my grandmother lived and I could crawl up on her lap. She held me and after a while would say, "What is it this time? What did you do?" Then I told her, and she always said, "Your mother is somebody who loves you, and you have to mind her." After I talked with her, I went back home. If my mother knew I was running down to my grandmother to tell her my problems, maybe I would have been in trouble some more and maybe not. She died in 1921.

It seems as if there was a conflict all of the way through, only I didn't know it. That kind of conflict is pretty hard on a young person. While I was growing up, there was my dearest grandmother and her teachings, all of which could be put alongside the white people's beliefs. She and her sister were the ones who told me not to turn my head too fast and to always sit with my knees together. All of those older people had something to say to me. They talked to other young people, too, but I listened and I thanked them for talking to me.

At school I had to go to the Catholic church every Sunday. Being in a boarding school for ten months out of a year was frightening. I was terrified of the priest, terrified of the agent, teachers, and everybody. Now that I think about it, I don't know how I lived through it. The only happy times I remember when I was growing up were when I was home from boarding school.

For power, the Indian had what they call *sqəlalitut*, or guardian spirit, you might say. I believe the Indians had something that answered their needs that could be used today: your own guardian spirit. My father used to say one of the reasons these Indians of Puget Sound or western Washington had to search for the guardian spirit during the teenage years is because it gave the young people a goal, an ideal to work for. As I was saying, I had quite a time for years trying to put those things together. During high school I went to several Protestant churches. I finally told myself that what I had was just as good—better—and it answered my needs. I believe my grandparents and the older Indians had something remarkable in their practice of fasting and meditation.

What we call a "search" in our language is *alatsut*: "to look or to search for the guardian spirit." I believe in it, but when I started school I thought not, because the priest said all those things are of the devil. That is what they told my father when he went to the Catholic Mission School—those things Indians do are of the devil. I think the members of the Catholic Church felt that way about the Shakers. They are not Catholics; therefore, they are doing something of the devil. Quite a lot of Indians never accepted the Shaker religion or even set foot in the Shaker church, like my father and mother did. In years past, when my father and mother got older, both of them went back to their old Indian culture—the belief in the guardian spirit.

They didn't, in fact, talk about their creator, who also has another name but I have forgotten what it is.[1] My father in his group always called it Dukʷibəł, the Creator, but long before I believe I heard a different word for Dukʷibəł.

Of course, my mother's language was totally different; it was Klallam. She used to tell me what their word was for their creator. I heard my mother talking once with someone who spoke her Klallam language. I can't recall who that was. I was small; it was before I went to school. She said their word for their creator was Ngslemen: "Nobody knows." Some years later, when I was in high school, I asked her: "Was it a man, a spirit?" She said, "No. Nobody told me, but they told us children never mention that word. It is a great, great spirit—qʷiqʷi qʷaʔtə is not to be mentioned in any conversation. It is only mentioned when you are in meditation and you are all alone." She didn't say what that was because I asked. "Is it a man, a spirit, a woman? Is it something you see or feel? Is it a spirit like fog or mist?" She said, "Nobody knows. Nobody ever said."

I thought it was interesting that the Mormon Church has something similar to the Indian belief. I wonder what it is about them? I have heard something that was written in their book. I want to know. All I ever heard about the Mormons was in high school, where I heard about and saw other churches. But my father said the white people are down on the Mormon Church. They are absolutely too far out. Years ago, what my mother said about the Spirit—that nobody is allowed to talk about it—I think is in the Mormon Church. My father met with a couple of Mormon men who came and visited a couple of times. I thought, I don't think I am supposed to talk to them because the priest said all of those churches are out. They are misguided.

---

1   *x̌ax̌a*. See Ruth Shelton in Hilbert (1995); Snyder, appendix (1964); Bates, Hess, Hilbert (1996).

Some of the young people—now and then you hear them marching up and down the streets—are misguided too. They are searching for something and they don't know what.

Now you know how I felt—like a lost, lost person—and for a while I thought I was going to burn in hell for having such thoughts as wondering, what does that kind of church teach? Then I tried to find out and I went. I went to church with Mrs. Zanga. She belonged to the Baptist Church. I thought, I am going to burn in hell. It is a pagan church. Here the pastor was a marvelous speaker. Someone there asked me if I was a Christian. I didn't know what to say, so I said, "Yes, ma'am. I was baptized in the Catholic Church." I don't think she was impressed. When I was growing up, this is what I had to believe, but if you have some doubts that you are committing some sin, you wonder.

Graduation

When we graduated, I made my own dress. The class advisor talked to us and told us what we could do. We talked with one another and said what we would like to have. Some of the girls said they wanted taffeta for their dresses; it is stiffer. Others said, "No, let us have crepe." I like crepe. After some debate, we decided to have crepe de chine.

My mother took me into town. She didn't do any preaching that time. She let me pick out the material. In Tulalip Indian School, remember, I had plain, stiff white petticoats, plain gingham dresses, stiff navy blue uniforms. When I asked for a lace petticoat or lace around the neck of my dress, she would get mad and tell me that is a sin. It didn't bother me when I was ten years old. When I was fourteen years old, I kept asking. By the time I was fifteen, I asked for a silk dress. It was 1919 and the end of World War I, and the women's fashions were changing. By the time I got into high school, it was called part of the Roaring Twenties, but we didn't know about it.

When I was a junior, my mother allowed me to buy a navy blue silk taffeta dress, and I was in seventh heaven. During the Roaring Twenties, the blossom skirt came out and fit like a basque, kind of tight. The sleeves came just below the elbow. My mother wouldn't put in short sleeves. It was a sin to wear short, short sleeves. It was interesting that she would get so worked up—and it was not all of the time, just when I wanted lace on my clothes. But it was a sin. My father was always in favor of everything. "If she wants lace, get her some lace."

Marriage

People should know too that I had trouble like other people. My first marriage didn't turn out too great. All I remember about it is crying and being unhappy. He was always asking me, "What have you been doing?" "Where have you been?" I was alone. I didn't have anybody in Seattle. I never even went to church. He said he loved me. He was twenty-six or twenty-eight years old. His folks thought he would never get married.

I met him at a dance at the Knights of Columbus in Seattle. There were a group of Indians who got together and put on a real American dance. It was mostly Indians who came. He had not been there before either. He was always working and never had time to go. I was almost out of high school. I don't know why I thought I had to get married. It seemed like everybody was getting married. Why in the world is it, you grow up and you think about getting married? So I met him in a dance hall. In a way, that always sounded funny to me—not "funny," really—a girl in a dance hall, but what kind of a girl would be in a dance hall? My father and mother took me that one time. A lot of Indians came from all over western Washington to those dances.

I'll call him Frank. His name was Francis.[2] I remember my mother saying, "You don't know him. You don't know what kind of person he is." I thought she was being just like she always was: you better not do this, don't do that. So when she said I didn't know him, I said, "Oh, yes. I was introduced to him by somebody who knew me and so I figured I knew him too."

I got married in the First Presbyterian church in Seattle. When I came back home, Francis and his parents invited me to come and visit them. They were living in Sequim. So I went to visit them on the ferry he worked on. He said, "We are going to get married tomorrow." He was afraid if I went home, I might meet someone else. I was already wearing his ring. I said, "How can I change my mind?" I listened to him. The ferry landed about four or five o'clock in the morning. By nine or ten A.M. we were married.

There was just his cousin for a witness, and the other witness was a white girl who worked in the church. I was honest, but I can say here I don't know how I could have been so dumb. Nobody else would go ahead and get married like that, because I wanted my folks and my brother and sister-in-law there.

---

2   His full name was Francis Williams. He was a member of the Klallam Tribe, and his mother was Tsimshian, one of the coastal tribes in Canada. Mrs. Dover's mother was also Klallam and Samish.

He said it would be too hard to stand up in a church with a big wedding. I listened. As I said, I don't know how I could have been so dumb. But that is the way I grew up in the Indian boarding school—somebody told me to do something and I did it. I felt like I had to do it.

When I came back home, my mother and father came to pick me up at the ferry. I was already married. I told them, of course. She told me, "Don't you ever change your mind. You are always changing your mind. You are married and you are going to stay married." My father chuckled, and he said, "Your mother still thinks she is the boss. You have another boss now." If my mother hadn't ordered me to stay there, I would have come home.

My sister-in-law had a shower for me, and I got a tablecloth, pots and pans, and a lot of things. I listened. If anybody asked me, I would have come home after a month of marriage because I was all alone in an apartment. He was gone all day, or he would go back to work. He worked with the Washington ferry system in Seattle. He left at 7 P.M., and I didn't see him again until 6 P.M. the next evening.

I went to the public library on Fourth Avenue in Seattle. I spent a lot of time there, and that is when I read Bancroft. It was a big book. I read a lot. When I was in Tulalip Indian School, I was always getting into trouble for reading.

I got so homesick I went home. The time he worked changed. If he worked from midnight to 6 A.M., the following two weeks or so he worked from 6 P.M. to midnight, and it rotated. Some of the time he stayed aboard the boat, and then I went down and met the boat. There were several women who met those boats when their husbands got off their watches. I went down on the dock every evening. Some of those women had been meeting the boats there for fifteen years or so. It was an old thing for them. But, anyway, it got to the point where he would shake me up and wonder what I was doing all day.

Later on I said, "What could I be doing? I don't have any money!" That was really interesting. I was starving hungry much of the time. Money was something he thought I didn't need. He paid for a nice apartment on Queen Anne Hill. I used to get on the streetcar to see where he was, and after a while I just walked. I walked those long, long blocks because I didn't have any money. He was making good money, too, for that time—from 1920 to early 1930. Most of his money went to his mother. He bought a new car, so I could drive from home to go down and meet his ferry. One of the things he said to me was, "I bought you a car." It was in his name, but I drove it when he wasn't home.

Now that I am along in years, I understand he was under pressure—working long hours on a ferry, with constant noise and vibrations above the engine room. When you lie down in your bunk, it vibrates—and you wonder how they took it. One of my nieces is a very attractive girl, and I know her husband kept her up at night wondering what she was doing. She wasn't doing anything. He was just jealous.

I found out he had a very bad temper. He didn't trust me. I met someone I went to the boarding school with. She was living in Seattle too, but it seemed as though she was what my husband called a "streetwalker." I didn't know about it at the time because she had an apartment in town and she worked as a waitress in a small café. Francis thought she was somebody bad. I met her now and then when I was walking down to the dock. I talked to her, and he got mad. "You know, if you are going to talk to people, streetwalkers, then that is what you are." I never saw them before. I didn't know what they were. They didn't have them out here in Marysville or on the reservation. It was all new for me to live in a big city.

9 / Political and Social Conditions

W HEN the decision came down from the Supreme Court in 1928, that was when my older boy was born, so the decision was kind of secondary to my new baby.[1] I listened to my brother discuss the case because then some of the other Indian tribes started to be aware of and talk about the promises that were in the treaties that were never kept. Through the years things just got worse.

About this time my brother Robert had a radio show. The city of Snohomish, Washington State, and the Snohomish Pioneers helped him. He was a member of the Snohomish Pioneers. They put on an hour radio program on KFBL in Everett. Wayne was just a baby then, so I never got to go. I went once. They did a drama about a tugboat that exploded and sank around here. All of the pioneers were screaming. I listened to them, and that is all I remember.

My brother wrote the dialogue for another radio play about the first courthouse trial. He took it from the history of Snohomish County. It was on every week for several months, and it was a big thing for the county people, since so many of the early settlers from Everett, Stanwood, and Seattle were still living. My father played the fiddle on the program. You could hear people dancing. It was recreation for the settlers.

Robert had a program on the Treaty of Point Elliott. Some of the employees from the boarding school and some of the chiefs had speaking parts. They talked about how much the Indians discussed the treaty before they met with Governor Stevens. I used to hear about the treaty so much when I was little. The Indians were not together on the treaty. It always seemed as though the Indians were clapping their hands and so happy over the whole thing. Actually, they talked about it for several days and nights.

---

1 The case is known as *Duwamish et al.* v. *United States*. F275. Washington, D.C.: U.S. Court of Claims, 1927.

My brother was the secretary of the Snohomish Tribe, and all the Tulalip soldiers were in that group—something like six or eight. They were all anxious to see if they could get land. So, as I said, the Snohomish organization grew. My brother died suddenly in April 1930.[2] When he died, the group that was together at that time included reservation and nonreservation Indians. After two meetings, they voted me into my brother's place. My father was the president. Later, when they were more established, the bigger group voted to make Thomas G. Bishop their president, and the name of the organization was changed to the Northwest Federation of American Indians.

Thomas Bishop never lived on the Tulalip Reservation. He lived near Port Townsend, on a farm he inherited from his father. He was quite well known, and that is why the Tribe elected him. He was half-Indian. His father was white, which is why he had farmland. He was a senator in the Washington State legislature for a while.

The older Indians had more patience with many of the issues they discussed, but some of them were troubled and they talked about how very blonde and blue-eyed some of the members of the Tribe were. They had very little Snohomish Tribe Indian blood, and there was no requirement on the amount of Snohomish tribal blood they had to have to be a member. The Northwest Federation of Indians became a large organization. Supposedly, there were Indians in the organization from the reservation, but they couldn't tell if they were Indians. None of the off-reservation people were enrolled in the agency here or are on the census roll. They didn't live here. Dozens of people were saying they were Indians. My father usually knew them, but he didn't know all of them personally.

I heard my father and the older ones, such as Ty Stockton, who was my brother, talking about this problem. We had people coming to meetings who were very little Indian. My brother Robert said, "I don't think if it comes to that, the U.S. government Indian office will decide on their roll, and they will only accept the names that are on the agency roll." Then my brother had died and my father was grieving. They felt that they should have what was promised in the treaty, and that was that each Indian would have land. My father talked to the agent about the doctor's refusal to attend the Indians from the reservation.

---

2   He died of a ruptured peritoneal ulcer. See Ryggs (1978) for a detailed description of Robert's death.

Tulalip Tribal Council

They had a council of five members. My father was the president. They did the same things as the Improvement Club: talk about the church, fix the foundation of the church, and fix the roads. It seemed like the roads always had to be fixed. There were some places along this road to Marysville where it seemed no matter how many loads of gravel were piled in there, after a year or less it all disappeared and there was just mud. So gravel in some places along there was being hauled in. They met down at the longhouse, since that was all there was. Sometimes if they had to get together rather fast on something, they sat on the beach in front of the Catholic church. Sebastian Williams and Wilfred Steve were the youngest members, with my father.

They said they sat on the beach to have their meetings because it was simpler and more fun. Otherwise, they had to go all of the way over to the agency. So they called the meeting to order right on the beach. They sat on the logs and talked. My father used to talk about when they organized. There was no money so they put together themselves maybe a dollar, and when they bought envelopes and some typing paper or a notebook they could keep the minutes. Sometimes they met back east of here, where the boarding school was and where the land was being cleared. It is fields and houses now. They sat around. It was all stump land, and sometimes fires were burning in the stumps, but they found places to sit on a rock or log or something. They didn't have money for anything better.

I don't know if there were any minutes from that time. Whatever was written, I think, was maybe lost. I think Wayne found some minutes that Sebastian Williams wrote.

They had several meetings to talk about the Indian Reorganization Act of 1934. I read it. It sounded like a big, terrific change. Indians around here were always a little worried about any big change like that. I think they had several meetings to talk about the Indian Reorganization Act, until they had a meeting and they voted for it. There were more young people who voted. They had a meeting of the tribes and voted for it. There was more voice then, and many more young people were there. I was home in 1934. I came home before Wayne was born in 1928. By 1930 he was two years old, and six years old in 1934 and starting to go to school.

When the Indian Reorganization Act came, my father was older, and he had heart trouble and emphysema. He didn't want to be on the new Board of Directors that was established according to the Indian Reorganization Act. The Tulalip Board of Directors has seven members, and they are elected by the whole reservation. The council of five members was elected by the Tulalip Indians.

We found some of the minutes that Sebastian Williams wrote when they talked about what they would call their new organization in 1934. They knew that in La Conner, the Swinomish Tribe called their new organization the Swinomish Senate. They thought about it and said, "we always had just a five-member council and maybe we could call it something else." The younger people came up with the Tulalip Board of Directors, since if we are going to handle or take care of tribal land, then we are in business; so let's call it a board of directors to take care of the business of the tribes. I never liked the name, but it was reported to the Bureau of Indian Affairs.

Board of Directors

My father was on the Board of Directors at first. He told the people on the Board, "I can stay maybe for one year." He wasn't feeling well. If they met someplace where somebody was smoking, he had a hard time breathing, and so it was a constant worry for us, where he might be. He stayed on a year or two. Then, later, he went to some of the meetings because they asked him to come. They said, "We'd like you to listen and just tell us what you think." They had elected a group of seven members; they were younger. They were all my brother's age. By that time, they were speaking nothing but English at their meetings, and minutes were kept of every meeting. My father just couldn't take it. There was always somebody smoking cigarettes. While he liked the smell, it still used to start him coughing.

Some people said my father was not a chief; he was just a police officer, a police chief. He was the chief of police for five reservations—Tulalip, La Conner, Mukilteo, Suquamish, and Lummi—from 1921 to 1928. Once in a while he would be up at Nooksack. Pressure was on the Indians against drinking liquor, and that was strictly enforced. I never saw any Indians drunk all of the time I was growing up. It certainly became very common by the time I was thirty or forty years old.

In 1934 or 1935, I don't think there were any Indian police any longer; that is when the Indians accepted the Reorganization Act. Some reservations had to enforce their own system of law and order. We had a part-time police force, but they didn't patrol the reservation like the Indian police did when I was little.[3]

The first Board of Directors chairman was Bill Steve, then Ezra "Art" Hatch, Carl Jones, Hubert Coy, and my father. They met the first time down at Mission Beach. Coy had a small store where he sold candy, pop, cigarettes, and cigars. They also sat on the beach. It must have been a nice evening, or later afternoon, because they sat on the logs and had their meetings.

Bill Steve used to talk about it. "When we started, we didn't have a penny to our name." They collected the money among the directors. They had a notebook, so they could write down the minutes and keep track of when they met and when they collected money. The second time they met in front of the Catholic church, inside of Tulalip Bay, and they sat on the beach again. Then the third time, about two or four weeks later, they met on the baseball field. Now it is a residential area. But they met there—sitting on the bench for people who are watching the baseball game. They met in different places because they still had no official place to meet. Later, they were allowed to meet in the agency office. The agent stayed until they were all there, and then he left and they started their meeting.

Life Changes

My father never said anything when I got married. When he was sick and dying in the hospital, I went to see him and that was when he told me, "You get a divorce, do you hear me, and stay at our home. Your son is going to grow up and be a good man, and he should be a leader." He said, "Don't forget our Indian ways. Don't ever put it away from you—not our language and not our ways. You have to dress like the white people. You have to speak their language."

I think my father would have welcomed me home because I was the youngest in the family, and I was the only one they had by then. My older brother was married and then gone, so I was the only one left in the family.

One of the things my father told me on one of his last days was, "Don't leave your mother. Don't leave our people. Don't move to big cities and live a different kind of life. You stay with our people." My mother talked to him

---

3   There is more to this issue that happened in later years because of local police having jurisdiction on the reservation. See Public Law 280. Today, the Tulalip Tribes employs their own police force.

about seeing a priest. I was there. I didn't say anything. I was going to tell my mother, "Just leave him alone." He didn't answer. He never saw the priest, but he always lived up to what his parents and grandparents taught him

Francis and I broke up, and I told him to get out of my house and stay out. I was surprised I got up enough "steam" and packed all of his clothes. He came home one day, and I said, "Here are your things. Your things are all packed." I had his other suit and overcoat. "Take these things and get out of my house." He was quite astounded because he stood there, and he said, "All right. All right. You just remember I am going to pay you back for this." I said, "All you have to do is walk out of the same door you walked in. Don't ever speak to me again." He did call up. I told him, "I am not asking for money or anything. Don't speak to me." It was a big shock for me because in February 1938 my father died, and then I broke up my marriage. It was breaking up anyway.

I thought about it and I finally did come home. We had Wayne. It didn't make any difference to Wayne. My father was the man Wayne knew. I think that is why Wayne is a different kind of person. Quite a lot of the young people and boys who were his age grew up with no father. Until he was ten years old, my father was a big influence on him. Wayne is a good public speaker. He seemed to learn a lot from my father, but William, my younger son, never knew my father. I think William is a nice person too.

About every two weeks we (Wayne and I) came up here to visit my folks. It was a long drive—by then he was asleep. He was just a little boy going to school. Then when we were home, he saw my father every day. Having my older boy seemed to complete my marriage; how I felt about it, anyway, but I still was not happy even though my father was an understanding person. Wayne stayed with my folks so much it didn't upset him for us to divorce. He was already with my folks quite a bit every weekend, since he came home with them on Friday evening. My parents—both of them—were there to pick him up coming out of school at Mukilteo, where Wayne went. On Monday morning, they brought him to school. He had a lot of attention.

I finally got a divorce during the war years, World War II. He got married again. He married a white woman he was already living with. Ten or eleven years after I was divorced, I met George Dover.

So after my father died I had one son, and I came home to stay with my mother. There was no income. In the hospital when my father was sick, he said he was sorry to leave my mother without anything. I remember my mother took his hand and said, "Don't be sorry about anything and don't worry."

My father was an Indian, and he was not able to buy life insurance, although he tried to buy some several times. He tried in his early thirties. He went to Seattle to talk to an attorney about getting a life insurance policy. He was always turned down because he was an Indian. They wouldn't insure an Indian. So when my father was dying, that was one of the things he worried about.

I keep saying I am going to write to Haskell Indian Institute where Henry Roe Cloud was the superintendent, because he took some of my father's letters with him after he was here to talk with him. I thought I would write to the agency and just ask if they knew where those letters are. Those letters were probably burnt up a long time ago, but I could ask on the slim chance that Henry Roe Cloud might have left them at the agency. All I do is talk about it. Henry Roe Cloud got sick and died suddenly. We got a message from the agency that Mr. Roe Cloud had died after my father died. I used to be over there every other day. That's where the post office was, and so I would walk over there. Everybody did. Our newspaper came by mail and we would pick up our newspapers even though they were already a day or two old. So I would be at the agency office and talk with different ones and then walk home again. That's where I heard that Mr. Roe Cloud had died.

On the Board of Directors

I was on the Board after my father died. Bill Steve and some others said I ought to try and get on the Board. I thought, I don't know who would vote for me. I don't know if I would vote for myself. Anyway, I got on. Quite a lot of Indians voted for me. There were two other candidates who got more votes than I did. One was Lawrence Williams. All of the Indians thought the world of him. He is Herman's father. We had one woman before, in 1936 or 1937—Edith Parks. She told me several years after that the Board members were not quite rude, but they didn't really listen to her. I didn't say much of anything because I liked Edith. Whatever I said, the members of the Board listened courteously to me. They followed through on whatever few thoughts I had on something.

I was on the Board of Directors from 1938 until I resigned in 1942. Then I was back on in 1944, 1945, and 1946, and got off for good in 1950 or 1951.

We met at least once a month. The constitution said the Board should meet on Saturday afternoon or Saturday morning. We met on Saturday afternoon, and we were through with our business by 5 or 6 o'clock. Now the

Board meets at 9 A.M. and they talk, talk, talk. They break for noon lunch and talk some more through to about 5 o'clock, if they are lucky, since they can still be talking at 7 o'clock in the evening—tribal business and problems got bigger and bigger each year.

When I was on the Board in 1939, quite a number of white people were already living along the beach, such as Mission Beach. Of course, the tribe had it surveyed into lots. I don't know how big those lots were. Then they surveyed the inner bay here, Tulalip Bay. I think somewhere else they had lots, but those especially at Mission Beach were of interest to us. In 1939 those people along Mission Beach were right on the beach, with their houses; some of them just started as a summer home with only three rooms: a big living room, a big front veranda, and maybe a couple of bedrooms and a small kitchen. We never said anything about the amount they paid for their annual leases. We talked about it once in a while, but for somebody like me, it was a totally new topic. For people like Bill Steve and some other people, they already knew quite a bit about it, because those white people had lived there for several years. I don't know where they paid unless they paid into the agency.

Another topic we discussed was the Priest Point beach. A lot of people were living on the beach. The Tribe talked about it briefly, because we had other big problems, too. But, according to what we always understood, Indians owned the beach land on this reservation. Those people, the white people, brought in fill, and the houses are built on the fill. Several of us went out to look, and you could see where it is filled in; it is a beach, a point. The Tribes should get revenue from the beach area, but it never did. When that allotment was sold—it belonged to Charles Hillaire—a real-estate dealer in Marysville bought it. He is affiliated with Duryee, a real estate company in Everett. He bought the allotment; then he got the beach and just went ahead and sold the beach land. I was going to go out to the courthouse and check the county map. It shows every square foot of land and who it belongs to, but we just never went ahead with Priest Point. I imagine it would be a big lawsuit, and we probably wouldn't win. I don't know. Priest Point was one problem.

The area we call "the agency school land" is three hundred acres along Tulalip Bay. Tulalip Mission School—the Catholic Mission School—and Tulalip Indian School, across the Bay, were located there. It was where the Indians wanted the school to be built when it was established in 1857. When I was on the Board in 1940, we asked about the land, since the school was no longer there. It was just vacant buildings.[4] The Tribes thought that they could survey it into lots and lease it out and have some tribal income. At that time, we had a big fight with the agent. He said, "It doesn't belong to you." He came from Portland; they called him the "area director." We talked about a number of things. I remember he got up from the tables and slammed out the door. The last thing he said before he slammed the door was, "It isn't yours. It never was, and it never will be."[5]

Well, the three hundred acres was just sitting there. Finally, it came to the Tribes without any warning. Nobody said anything. We got the notice that the land was ours. Before that, while the land was just sitting there, the Boys, Girls, and the Club Buildings—those two- or three-story buildings—were torn down by some white people. I think some of the cottages on Tulalip Bay, on Mission beach, were built from the lumber. It was good lumber. It was what they called "old growth." I don't know if any of the Indians got any of the lumber, there might have been one or two, to build a house when the Board got it. It cost the Board quite a bit to have the land surveyed into lots. I think there are fifty lots.

Tribal Enrollment

In 1951 I was secretary of the Board of Directors. I was chief tribal judge of the Tulalip Court of Tribal Offences, Tulalip Indian Court, and then I got sick and I was in the Cushman Indian Hospital in Tacoma. When I got out, we worked on our tribal roll. We didn't have an actual tribal roll; we only had what the agency called a census roll. So we had the Board of Directors and people who came to our March annual meeting appointed a committee of fifteen people to go over the census roll. There were over five hundred names listed of people who were supposed to be Tulalip Indians, but quite a number of those—two or three hundred—were not. They just happened to come to the boarding school, and I guess whoever the clerk was thought, "Oh well, just put Tulalip Tribe."[6] Some of them came from Suquamish, and some of them came from Blaine.

---

4 The boarding school was closed in 1938, and the Indian children attended public school in Marysville.

5 It is trust land and is therefore owned by the federal government.

6 This is especially egregious since there was no Tulalip Tribes organization then or a tribal organization of any kind.

We took about two hundred names off the list, and then we sent the roll to Washington, D.C. It came right back. They said, "You have to give reasons why you took off the names." A woman came from Washington, D.C., and two or three people from the Portland office, and we had several meetings.

The roll goes family by family. Sebastian Williams and I worked on the roll. Williams is a common name around here for a lot of Indians, but there were not many Williamses on the roll. There were a number of Andersons, Sokalofskys, Skoogs. Guess who that is? My niece. She was my brother Robert's little girl. She lives in Minneapolis, and she married a Skoog. We have the names of her four children on our roll. Sub (Sebastian Williams) said, "Skoog?" Then, he didn't say anything for a few minutes, and said, "What is happening to our tribe anyway? Skoog? We have Duplisises, Skoogs." He named some others.

Of course, he knew I was thinking about it, and we talked about it. Sebastian was quite a leader here. But that is what is happening to our tribe. They have all kinds of names. Someday we are going to have to get the tribe to vote what degree of Indian blood we recognize for our tribe, our tribal roll. There is no requirement for the amount of Snohomish tribal blood someone had to have in order to enroll. Some tribes say what blood quantum members should have: any person who is less than one-quarter Indian is not Indian if they are one-quarter Indian and three-quarters white. But if it is less than that, say, they are one-eighth Indian and are nearly all white, they are not Indian. I think Wayne and some of the others are going to talk about it. We are going to have a big "upset" if we ever come to that and specifically say anybody less than one-quarter Indian is not Indian. We have some people on our roll who are one-eighth Indian, and they know that is not Indian.

I told Wayne, some months ago, "It is too bad I can't drive anymore. I would like to see that settled, and have it in our tribal constitution—that anybody who is less than one-quarter Tulalip Indian is not Indian. Of course, some of the Indians will want to start a big, big fight. Some of the younger Indians aren't going to accept it. One of the attorneys asked in Judge Boldt's court if Tulalip had a tribal roll. We really don't. Our list has lots of names on it of people who just happen to work here at the agency or the school, or who lived here for a while but were not born here, aren't members. I know, of course, it will be a big knock-down, drag-out fight. My niece in Minneapolis, Robert's daughter, has grandchildren now. She said she knows her great-grandchildren could be eligible for enrollment, but, certainly, they are not going to be Indian.

Indian Health

We talked about Indian health often, but we never got anyplace. When Franklin Roosevelt was elected president in 1932, there was a big change. I will always remember him. There was some money then for Indian health, but the hunger and sickness went on through the thirties and forties.

Before the Roosevelt Administration, if anything happened to any Indians—you were a student in school, boarding school—they told you to stay home, because the doctor at the agency could tell you were going to die. They sent boys and girls home, and the next year you wouldn't see them again. If they came from Lummi at Bellingham, Swinomish at La Conner, we asked about different girls we were friendly with who had gone home, and the girls from there said, "She died." The boys and girls who went home didn't live more than two or three months. They were already dying in the school.

Indian parents went to the agent to complain and said, "Our children are dying, and we want them to have a doctor's care." Usually there was a doctor at any agency, but sometimes he refused to look at Indians. He took care of the white employees: the superintendent, an assistant superintendent, a chief clerk, and other clerks. In about 1940 or 1950, our agency was small. There was an agent, a chief clerk, a farmer, and a forester. The agent had an assistant and a road supervisor who had a couple of assistants.

As I say, since President Franklin Roosevelt there has been better hospitalization and medical care for Indian people. The only people who had medical care were the boys and girls who went to the Indian boarding schools. The doctor didn't go out on the reservation. Once in a while, the doctor went out on horseback and looked at somebody who got hurt in a logging camp. They broke an arm or a leg. Indian health always bothers me because of my sister dying of tuberculosis in 1917.

Some of our Indian people were taken to Cushman Indian Hospital, now Cascade Vascular Diagnostic Center, in Tacoma. Years ago the buildings there were wooden frame buildings. Now Cushman is a modern brick building. It is no longer a hospital. It was abolished in the 1950s when the Republicans elected Dwight Eisenhower. A number of Indian hospitals all over the United States were closed. Indians were sent home, or in Seattle they were put in the Public Health Hospital.

Health care and hospitalization for Indians was just nonexistent. The Indians just stayed home and had no medical care. I was talking one day about the lack of medical care and hospitalization to a group of about twenty-five women from a church in Everett. On several occasions, I met with women from churches in Marysville and Everett. They came here to discuss problems of Indian people and, in many cases, impressions. One of the women in the group said her sister died of tuberculosis, and there was no care for her either. She didn't think I had any reason to be complaining about it.

I told her, "I have no doubt a lot of white people died of tuberculosis way back then, but the white people had one very important thing that the Indians never had and that was freedom of choice. The white people could go anywhere in the United States that they wished to go. All they needed was enough money to get there. People could move from the East Coast and all of the way to California or Washington. They had freedom of choice and the Indians did not."

Right now we have Indian Health programs within the BIA, and people like me have Medicare. I often wonder how the doctor's bookkeepers keep track of us. I would like to see complete medical care and hospitalization for American Indians. I think we should have it. Most of the years of my life we didn't have complete medical care.

Alcoholism has been the curse of the Indians. A group of women used to come to my house to see me every month from a church in Marysville to see our Indian collection. One of the things they talked about was drunk Indians. One of them said, "They're always drunk and falling around the streets in Marysville." Drinking has been our problem for a long time. It is for many people, but it seems it is worse for Indians because, I think, it is more noticeable for us. If Indians are under the influence of alcohol and drunk somewhere, they are very noticeable. A few times I have seen Indians really far out on alcohol in some of the big cities. I am always sorry, because I know they have had to meet a lot of prejudice.

I told her, "Sometime, even if it's hard, look at one of those young men you see on the street. He is a young man. He is staggering around in that part of town. He can hardly walk, he is so drunk. If you try to talk to him, he will look at you, and it will be a while before he will see who you are." I used to try and talk to one of these men sometimes. I tried to share a couple of dollars with him. I told him, "Will you take this?" He is an Indian, although he doesn't look like much of an Indian.

Let me tell you about that one. Jack. Absolutely so drunk he couldn't stand up. He was drafted in World War II and went overseas. He was in the U.S. Army—the first and earliest army units to land in North Africa. They fought the Germans when they retreated with General Erwin Rommel, who was one of the famous German generals. He was in North Africa, where his army surrendered, and that is where Jack was. They moved their outfit, or what was left of it, from North Africa because so many of them were killed. He landed in Sicily with the U.S. Army because they were going to Italy, into France, and on into Germany. They were just "slogging" along and fighting all of the way because the Germans were in Sicily and Italy too. They landed there, and a number of them got too far ahead because they were all moving ahead, carrying guns and loaded with shells so that they could hardly walk. They had something to eat, not much, what they could carry, what soldiers carry. But, anyway, he was captured by the Germans.

After about two months, his letters stopped coming. Then the Department of the Army in Washington, D.C., notified his parents here that he was missing, and they thought that he was a prisoner of war. Every day the mail came in, and every day his mother and father came to the post office. They thought there would be a letter from their boy. I was postmaster here—or postmistress, some people would call it.[7] A letter finally came from the War Department. His mother just kind of "folded up." She wasn't well, and she died a short time later. He had a younger sister—a pretty girl. After losing her mother and her brother, not knowing where he was, caused her to "fold up," and she died too. So that left only his father. Jack was a prisoner of war in Germany for two or three years. Long after he came back, he talked about it. He never really stopped crying. He would land in a tavern and say, "I kept writing to my mother. I didn't know she was dead."

They allowed one letter from the prisoners of war about once a month or once every two months. The letters used to come. They were special letters. They were folded over so that they could be opened and read. But long after the peace was signed in 1945, and he came home, Jack said, "I can hardly wait to get home so I can see my mother." Nobody had the nerve to tell him she was dead. When he got home, he went running up to where the house was. They lived back here, and their house had burned down. Mind you, he got there and it was just ashes. He looked around. It was late in the afternoon. He saw the chicken house, and there was smoke from a stove fire in there. His father came out. He asked, "Where's Mom?" So they told him. "Well, where's sister?" She is dead, too. He never sobered up after that. Never. I think he had quite a time getting a pension from the army. He was wounded, but not badly—just a flesh wound through his upper arm—but when he tried to

---

7   She was postmaster at the post office in Tulalip Bay from 1938 to 1953.

get his pension, they bluffed him down. They got after him and said, "What are you doing? Are you looking for work? Why not? Where have you been looking?" You know, just put him over. Anyway, he never sobered up. I don't know how long he lived. For two, three, four, five years he was dead drunk and stumbled around in Marysville.

The other one you saw around there was another young man. He was in the army in the Korean War. He and his brother volunteered. They were poor, and I guess he thought that way they could get regular meals. Way back then, I don't know what the rules are now, but they almost never allowed brothers to be together. They landed in Korea when the Chinese joined the North Koreans, and they spilled over that whole countryside and chased the Americans back. They stopped to dig trenches—to try and stop the thousands that spilled into that small area.

They were in a reservoir north of Korea, in trenches, and they were trying to hold the area. They were holding the North Koreans and the Chinese back, and there was an exchange of gunfire. His brother was shot through the head. He was right beside him.

When he came home, he talked about it. He got very drunk and he was drunk every day. I saw him in town. He cried and cried in the tavern. He said he called to his brother. He saw him when he hit the dirt wall of the trench. He fell right down and then he looked at him. Most of his face was gone and the entire top of his head. He said he dropped his gun. He called his brother's name, put his arms around him and hugged him and called him. He said, "You will be all right. Don't leave me. I'm not leaving you. I'll take you home." He was right there, and he saw his brother killed. The top of his head and his face were gone. He was still warm, and he was hugging and holding him. Well, he never was sober either. I notice he is pretty good now. I mean he will drink, but he is not that bad. But then he could hardly walk. Every day, every day, every day.[8]

----

8   When asked how he stopped drinking, he replied that his mother and grand-
    mother took him to the Shakers because drinking was a waste of his time. As
    a Shaker patient, he was "worked on"—with a set of ritual and counseling pro-
    cedures that divested him of the desire to drink—and then he was told to help
    the Səywən, or Smokehouse religion, members. Tribal elders had conferred
    spitiual and historical knowledge upon him, so the Shakers and his family
    wanted him to be devoted to sharing those gifts with others. He is revered by
    Tulalip tribal members.

All of them that you see around there have very bad problems and they drink. Somehow, you feel that if you drink that much it will numb your brain. There are others, girls, who were married to soldiers who were killed in France or Korea. They're drunk too. Eventually, after two, three years they will get married again and finally sober up a little bit.

The Indians had problems, insurmountable problems, for years. White people had a psychiatrist who can talk to people with problems, but then people like that have to be paid. A lot of people, perhaps, have problems. There is nobody to talk to except their own family, and they are all wrapped up in grief, too. Well, so much for alcoholism.

Why do we drink? I remember telling a white woman. I said, "There is only one thing that will make us better. It's not that much." She said, "Well, there ought to be something." I said, "That is for the white man to go back where he came from. All of you go back to Europe where you came from." She said, "That can't be done." I said, "Yes, but that is the only thing that will help the Indians. Everywhere we go there you are, white man, and you are nothing but trouble to us." I did enjoy her. She always had something to say about us, and I tried to answer her. But you can't answer about things that concern people. You can't send white people back to Europe. They would be strangers there, too. Indians here said to one another years ago, "If there was an old country for me to go back to, I would go back to it." Of course, for the Indians there is no old country.

Alcoholism is still our problem. Now we have very young people still in school, and they are drinking. But you would have to be an Indian to understand.

Hospitalization

After World War II, one of our Indian veterans had a drinking problem, and he had a heart attack. The local hospital would not take him. They brought him into the hallway, and a nurse came in and said, "You can't bring him in here. There isn't any room." Some of the Indians tried to tell her that he needed immediate emergency care, but they had to carry him back out and put him in their old car. They brought him home, where he died. I don't think he regained consciousness. We talked about it. As I said, health care and hospitalization on this reservation have been nonexistent. I think we should have complete medical care.

In 1951 I was in the Cushman Indian Hospital in Tacoma for eight or nine weeks. I was surprised I got in. I had something wrong with my liver and kidneys. I had been working then as a tribal judge. An Indian from the agency took me to Cushman. I got there in the evening about ten or eleven o'clock. A doctor came to the emergency room. He said, "You can't expect to come down here at this time of the night and be taken care of. There isn't any room here." I got mad. I started talking loudly. I sat up—even though I had a hard time sitting up. I was really sick, and I sat up on the examining table and put my feet over, and I said—I swore—"Now, you listen to me. I am going to crawl out those front steps and call up the reporters from the *Seattle P.I.*, the *Seattle Times*, and the *Tacoma Times*, *Tacoma Ledger*, or whatever. I want them to come here and take a picture of where you threw me out of this hospital." He was astounded. He went out the door, where he told me I had a lot of nerve to come there. He came back and said, "Don't stand up," trying to take my shoulder, and he got really shook up. I was surprised. He was almost nonchalant when he said, "One can't expect to come down here in the middle of the night." It was impossible to go somewhere else. I got immediate care. The nurse from the upper floor came down. They treated me as if I was almost human.

I shrieked at the nurses on that floor in the hall again three or four weeks later. They said, "You have to go without supper and breakfast before surgery." Well, I went through all of that, but that time I had to go without supper and take some kind of medication and not have breakfast and then have an X-ray. I was hungry. The doctors who came from Seattle and Tacoma said I could have anything I wanted to eat. I said, "Could I have bacon and eggs?" They said, "Sure." So when I went back to my room, I told the nurses I wanted to have bacon and eggs and coffee with cream, please." The nurse went out. I was in bed waiting for my coffee, and after a while, I heard some loud talking in the hall. I was in the surgical ward, and very sick people were getting out of bed. I got mad. I guess I waited about forty minutes. I got up out of bed and, hanging onto the beds, got outside of the door to the hall, and I shrieked at them. The nurses were down the hall, talking. I called out in a loud voice. I said, "If you don't bring me my food, I am going to throw this!" It was a cart. It had cotton, thermometers, and medications on it. "I am going to tip this thing over, and you get it here." They stopped and looked. I was pushing the cart, and I said, "I am going to smash everything that is on here. Now, you move!" I went back to bed. Fifteen or twenty minutes later they came with the grandest breakfast.

During the Seattle World's Fair in 1962, they had an Indian exhibit. I had our Indian artifacts on display there. They had Indians from all over. I hurt my foot; it was painful, and I thought maybe I hurt my ankle. The car that belonged to the Fair Association was a big car, and someone drove me to Harborview Hospital. They put me in a wheelchair. I couldn't stand up anymore. I could just hop on one foot. One of the Indian women stayed with me. I got there about 5 P.M., and I was still there at about 7 or 8 P.M. and didn't see anybody. I could see an entrance to the hospital, a circular rotunda, and stretchers coming in. They were mostly black people, and it looked like we were the only Indians there. There were some white people.

I especially remember a very drunk white man. He was one of those people who was dressed as if he came from somewhere important. He had on a suit and a white shirt, and his tie was hanging loosely. He was awful drunk. The nurses asked him his name. I was close to where people were being admitted. He would say his name, and the nurse would say, "Spell it." It was a simple name like William, for instance. He would spell W-i and then ask her what comes after that. "All right, W-i . . ." He would say "i," stop, think about it, and finally say, "Yeah, that sounds like it." He started over again. "W-i," stop and almost fall down. He was hanging onto the counter, and he said, "What comes after that?" She stayed with him for about an hour and a half to get his name. I thought, why can't she get him to drag out a wallet and see what he had in there? But she was laughing and talking with him, and my foot was swelling up.

I had on moccasins, and they got so tight it hurt worse. By about 8 or 8:30 P.M. the head nurse finally got to me. She had a clipboard and got my name, and then she said, "Oh, you are in the wrong place. You should go down to the Public Health Hospital. That is where the Indians go." I said, "Why didn't someone tell me three or four hours ago? I have been here ever since." "Well, I'm sorry." I said, "Call me a taxi, please." She called a taxi. I asked them to please have a wheelchair out there for me. She said, "I already did that." In just a little while the taxi came, and I got into it. The lady who went with me was able to go down to the Public Health Hospital and stay a few minutes, and then she had to leave. She had family somewhere in town.

So there I was in another big hallway, sitting in a wheelchair, and some doctors in white coats and nurses were going up and down the hall. About eleven o'clock I got mad. I was shrieking as the doctor was leaving the counter and going down the hall. I hollered at him, and I said, "You get back here." I guess he was sort of astounded, too. I told him how long I had been there. He said, "All right. Our emergency room has been full." Right then, he had a sailor who had been stabbed fighting downtown somewhere. So I was brought into the same room, a very big room, where they were working on the sailor. There was a big doorway, and another sailor was with him. They looked so young. They said he was very badly hurt.

So after all of my yelping and getting mad, they x-rayed my foot. Then they wrapped it up with an elastic bandage, and I drove myself home. I don't know how I did it. I don't think we had a phone, or otherwise I would have called George. Here I drove all of the way home at one o'clock in the morning with my foot swollen. I don't think I had any money, or otherwise I would have stayed somewhere.

It seemed like everywhere Indians go, they are kicked out. I don't know if it is any better now. Maybe it is. They talk about the new people—the Vietnamese—and their problems. They don't have any income, and some of them are on welfare. I was thinking about when I couldn't get a job way back in 1940, 1941. The people at the welfare office just blasted me for not getting a job. Anything I could get was housework and that only paid seventy-five cents a day.

Income

When I lived in Seattle, I worked at Boeing and the Twin Teepees restaurant. There were many times when all I had was a dime to eat on all day. So then I drank coffee. I brought my slice of toast to work. I ate that all day. I ate part of it in the morning and part of it in the afternoon. By afternoon, if you haven't eaten anything, then your knees begin to shake, and it is hard for you to walk and stand up and talk because you get so hungry and tired.

When my father died, he didn't have any insurance because Indians couldn't buy insurance. He left my mother with about sixty dollars. We sent my mother's name in to the county welfare department. The caseworker who came to see my mother was a man. I didn't say much of anything because my mother answered his questions. They wouldn't put her on. He said, "You have a lot of resources. You have to sell all of your land that you own—that you are not living on. You will have to sell all of these baskets you have. The canoes out there will bring you enough money to live on." I said, "I own half of those things. I am half-owner of these baskets and canoes, and I am not willing to sell. I think it is important to keep them and to save them."

It was hungry, hungry times for us because I was home. My marriage had broken up, and I didn't have any income either. I walked over to Mission

Beach, to white people's houses, to do housework for seventy-five cents a day, which was a lot of money then.

Later, another caseworker came. I wasn't there. I was doing housework. When I came home in the evening, my mother was very upset. She said the caseworker told her my son and I had to move. We couldn't live with her. My mother spoke up. She said, "My daughter is not leaving this house. Half of this house is hers. My grandson, Wayne, is not going to be wandering around with no roof over his head." He was about ten years old and going to school in Marysville. My mother finally got on welfare. Mrs. Martha Mukey came and put my mother right on, but the supervisor said, "Well, she has resources, and she will have to sell those." So they gave us fourteen dollars a month. We lived "high on the hog" on that. But we didn't sell anything. We just went hungry.

Looking for Work

One time a woman was visiting here from one of the churches in Marysville or Everett. She didn't see why the Indians didn't go out and look for work like she did. She said, "I work!" I am quite sure people would say, "Well, why don't you go off the reservation? Why don't you find work?" We tried. Believe me, I know all about trying to find work.

I worked in Seattle. I worked at Boeing, and I was a hostess at the Twin Teepees restaurant on Aurora Avenue. When I came home, as I said; I found housework with people who lived at Mission Beach. They were some of the earliest families who lived there. I was paid seventy-five cents a day to one dollar a day, and that was considered really working. I had to stand up on stepladders and wash the ceilings. I had to wash windows. It was constant hard work. The houses were not clean. I had to clean things that hadn't been done in years. Women like that want you to scrub the kitchen ceiling, and all of the cupboards, inside and out, and then crawl around on your hands and knees and scrub the kitchen floor. Then, scrape along the corners and along the splashboard with a knife, where the carpet or linoleum meets the wall. They would stand there and say, "Now, you clean that up good!" Working there always reminded me of Tulalip Indian School: orders, commands, commands.

Then you had to contend with someone in her family. Some man wants to push you in somewhere. I think nearly every girl who went to work ran into what they call sexual harassment in the newspaper today. When I was young, it depended upon who the personnel director was. If it was a man, he usually had a proposition. He wanted you to go to bed with him somewhere. "Your place or my place?" Some of these men had a hotel—not a really good hotel—where they would tell you to come and meet them. I think that happens to some of the girls even if they work in an office, but not all of them. I don't know; it all depends on what kind of a job it is. In a way, I thought it was only because I was an Indian, and they thought I was stupid and didn't know anything—so much for income and so much for being hungry. But I do think it is worse for Indian girls. Even if we walked along the street in Seattle, some man would make a remark when we stopped for traffic lights or to cross the street, and tell us how much he will give us. I said once, "I know how to swear."

I knew better than to look for work in Marysville, although I did look for work there, such as dishwashing in a restaurant. The supervisors I talked to in Marysville were quite astounded when I appeared and asked for work twenty years ago. They would say, "We have a long list of people who have applied, and there is no vacancy. It is already filled." Employers in Everett were the same. So even if they talked to you, there were no vacancies. I couldn't even get a dishwashing job. When people say, "Why don't they go out and work?" They wouldn't give Indians any work. The only work that was available, to some extent, was seasonal farm work and working in a lumber mill. But the mills take just so many Indian workers, and they would not take any more.

When Wayne, my son, came back here to work as business manager, he had a conference on employment. One of the counselors in Marysville High School said he used to go and talk to employers in the mills and places where they thought they could hire Indians, but they all said the same thing to him: "They're good workers. They are the best; they are reliable—but when it comes to fishing season, they tell us they have to go fishing, so then they lose their jobs." When they come back some months later, there is no job. He couldn't understand why the Indians would give up a job and go fishing. For people anywhere to drop a job and go fishing sounds like they are doing that for recreation. Well, it isn't recreation with the Indians; it is making a living. They are trying to make money.

In the early 1950s, I looked for work in Everett. I went to every store in Everett and to the hospital. Some of the girls who graduated with me from Everett High School were working in dime stores. One of the big department stores was called Rumbaugh's—where the Bon Marché is now. I tried to find work in the mall. When I got to the first dime store (I don't know whether it was Krafts or Woolworths), I tried to talk to the personnel director, who was a woman. She looked as if she was in her early thirties—a young woman. The girl I knew told me the personnel director's office was way, way back in the store. It was not very big, glassed in, but apparently she saw me coming. She got up and left her desk and walked out. So I met her in the hallway. I called her name and told her my name. I said I was just going to tell her I have come there to apply for work. I told her that I talked with Twila, who worked there. I don't remember her married name. You know, that woman walked right past me. She never said one word.

I looked for work as a dishwasher. I met a woman I knew. She worked as one of the dishwashers at the Everett Yacht Club. Way back then, they didn't have automatic dishwashers. They had to do it all by hand. She told me the other dishwasher had quit, so they were going to hire another lady. I hurried down there. There is a new Everett Yacht Club now; this is the old one. I was just starting up the steps; it was a nice sunny day, and the commodore of the Yacht Club was there. The screen door was open. As soon as he saw me—I had just put my foot on the bottom step of the porch—he came out and said, "What do you want?" I said, "Mrs. So-and-so, who works in the kitchen, said you are going to hire a dishwasher." He said, "You go around to the back." He gestured—like that—with his hands. "Don't come in here." I said thank you, and I started to walk around the building. I just got around to the back, and he came out the back door. He told me, "There are no openings here. Just go away and don't come back. We don't have any openings here." Well, that cut me quite a bit because I knew there was an opening, and I knew the woman they hired. She was also from Everett.

It was pretty hard for Indians to get a job. I have been to every store in Everett. We have been to hospitals. Of course, that was in the 1950s. Now there are some Indians working in the housework division at Everett General. I went to their office, too. As I stood in the doorway, I told the personnel officer, "I've come to apply for work in the house division. I'll mop floors. I'll do everything or anything." She said, "Come in. Are you an Indian?" I said, "Yes, I am." She said, "We come from Texas." She did talk with an accent. But I didn't get the job. She said, "Oh, my lands. Do you see this? She had a big pile of papers. I guess they were applications. She said, "I've got hundreds of applications. I'm going to take the whole thing and throw it in the wastebasket. Oh, you can go ahead and apply, but I'm just throwing them away." So, I don't know. That was rough. Real rough. Just tell you, "Don't come back. Just get away from here. Don't come back." So much for me trying to find work.

Some of the Indian women did housework cleaning cabins north of Marysville. One of our Indian women worked there every day. The beds had to be made, sheets changed and the floors and bathrooms mopped.

I tried to get work at Scott Paper Company after I married George Dover. Sometimes I like to think that maybe they thought I could not do it. There were some women working there. One personnel man said, "Oh, no, there are no openings" and shut the door. When I walked in, a man said, "How tall are you, Mrs. Dover?" When I said five feet two inches, he said, "Without your shoes?" I said five feet. He said, "I am sorry Mrs. Dover. We never take any women who are shorter than five feet three inches without their shoes, and I will tell you why. The machinery in the mill here is geared up and made for people who are five feet three inches or more. In fact, they ought to be five feet five inches or more." Anyway, I stayed there and talked with him. He was nice. He was the only one in the whole wide world, it seemed, who ever turned me down for work and made me feel better that he turned me down for something else besides being an Indian. I couldn't tell him much different—that I was five feet five inches tall.

I belonged to the Everett Business and Professional Women's Organization. I got into it because I was the postmaster of our small post office. I was also asked to join the Zonta Club. It is an affiliate of the Kiwanis Club. I was on the panel for the Washington State Federation of Women's Clubs. It was held at the Monte Cristo Hotel in the Mirror Room. There were huge mirrors all around.

I had quite a time, because the women there were beautifully educated. I talked about Indian problems. There was a beautiful Japanese lady there. She was a living doll. Then a young black lady, and she was a doll also. I will always remember she was very much like Lena Horne. She wore a small flowered hat with a big rose on it. Afterwards, I was talking with the president of the Zonta Club, and I said, "That is really something to put me with all of those accomplished women." Of course, she said, "Oh my, Harriette. You are just as good as they are. You were just perfect."

I was the only Indian there. I remember I thought, I haven't got a penny to my name, so I worried like heck about what I was going to wear. I had a two-piece black dress. It had a jabot, a high lace collar with pleats in the front. But I had the collar for several years, and I thought it didn't look white anymore. So I dyed it rose pink with Tintex. Surprisingly, it came out pretty good. Sometimes Tintex in that color can be pretty poisonous, but it turned out nice. I had a veil from the dime store. I put it around my head and put some dark rose pink flowers on top, and I thought, now that looks like a hat. Anyway, I was a "killer" in that old black dress. I remember thinking how the old skirt that went with it looked like a sad rag because I wore it for several years. Women notice what you are wearing.

The Japanese woman talked about the problems of the Japanese Americans—that was before Pearl Harbor. The beautiful black lady talked about black problems. She came from Seattle. There was a white teacher. She taught in Seattle in the poorer sections. She talked about the poor and the blacks. We could only talk about the problems. There isn't much you can do, but people think, you know. We had ten or fifteen minutes for people in the audience to contribute something to what each one said. Of course, the audience was all interested women, and they were courteous to the beautiful black lady and the Japanese girl who had on a nice sea green suit. It looked beautiful on her.

I talked about welfare. I outlined how hard it was for a lot of Indians to get on welfare. Indians would come into the post office and ask me if I'd take them to Everett. They didn't have a car, so I took them into town. Sometimes I didn't get time to eat. I carried half a sandwich with me, but I would get hungry because I had to wait and wait. I would get them over there by 2:30 P.M. for their appointment, and often we were still there at 4:30. Finally, I went in with one young Indian man. He was married and had a baby, but he was trying to get on welfare. I went in with him because it seemed to me he was too quiet. I didn't intend to help him. I just went along to listen. The woman who interviewed him said, "Have you been looking for work?" He said, "Yes." She asked, "Where have you been? What kind of work? Where? What dates?" She had a pencil, and she was writing down everything he said. I said, "He can't answer that fast." She asked him again, "Have you been looking for work during the last week?" He said, "No. I have to walk several miles from the reservation to Marysville, and then hitchhike to Everett." Then she said, "Well, why not?" So I interrupted her, and I said, "He already told you that he has looked for work for two or three months, and he can't find work. There are a lot of people out of work." She turned to me and said, "I wasn't talking to you." I thought if we stayed there for another hour or two, we were not going to get anyplace. I said, "He has told you already two or three times. He has to walk miles and miles to look for work. It is a waste of time. If he is lucky to get work in a saw mill, he would have to leave at three o'clock in the morning in order to get to work at 8 A.M. or earlier, and perhaps walk through rain and cold." She didn't say anything. Just slammed down her pencil.

I brought him back home. I saw him later. They came in and asked me to take them to town. I asked him, "Did you ever hear from welfare?" "Oh, yes. We get a check every month." I said, "Oh, that's really nice." But it seems like they just chewed up the Indians.

So much for income. There was no chance to find work, to go to work, and to have regular work. Most people would not hire an Indian. But in the 1970s my younger boy worked at Safeway. He went in there one day and asked for work. He had one year at Western Washington University in Bellingham. Then he decided to quit college and join the Air Force.

When I worked in Seattle, a lot of people happened to ask me if I was Chinese. I asked, "Do I look Chinese?" This woman said, "Well, I don't know. I am asking you." I said, "No, I am an American Indian." She said, "Oh." I said, "Tell me who you are." "Well, I'm an American. I came from Texas. And let me tell you, Texas is the greatest place in the world." She walked away. She said she just wanted to know. She said she is an American. I said, "Well, so am I—a real American." She was walking away. I said, "Do you know how Texas was settled?" She turned around and stopped because there was a break in the work hour. She said, "It was settled by all kinds of people." I said, "I'll tell you how Texas was settled. It was settled by murderers and horse thieves from every state in the Union. They escaped to Texas." Some of the women who were standing around were astonished. She said, "Well, as far as that goes, you can say that about any state in the Union," and she started to go away. I said, "I'm glad you said that because that is exactly what the Indians say." In the Carolinas and in New England there were wealthy people, but they were landless people who came from Europe. Of course, my mother would say, "You can't make a mixed-up statement like that one." However, that woman wasn't the only person who thought I was Chinese. I wonder what the Chinese would think.

My niece and her husband had an experience like that, about who is an American, just before World War II, when we were looking for apartments to live in. They were in Seattle, up on First Hill on Bellevue or Belmont Place where there were a lot of smaller apartment houses. They would have a for rent sign in the window. We would knock at the door, and they would look at us and say, ""That apartment has been taken." One woman opened the door and she looked at us. We said, "Your sign in the window says you have an apartment for rent." She said, "Oh, I am sorry. We rent only to Americans." I started to say, "We are Americans," but she slammed the door. I was thinking how that hurts. That used to cut me up: "We rent only to Americans."

Indian women look so astounded when things like that happen, such as signs that say "Americans Only." I hope the people in Seattle who at that time said "We take Americans only" are satisfied with all of the people who have come in recently. I think six thousand Vietnamese people have moved into Seattle. They will have to be assimilated or helped along. I think they are helping them. I think some of them were cut off, because I saw an article in the newspaper saying they had planted opium poppies in their gardens. I hope you are satisfied, White Man. At least the Indians didn't have opium poppies out here way back then.

Some people said I sounded like a racist. Oh, not really. Some of those people got better care and a more courteous response than I ever did, and I feel that I am an American. People in Everett, Marysville, or Seattle, where I went to look for work, they'd have a sign in the window and they'd take one look and sometimes they would ask, "Are you an Indian?" When I would say yes, they would say, "We have already filled that position. We don't have any vacancies."

I understand some of the Vietnamese can't speak English, but their children are going to school. They must be using two languages, and that is what I did. When you are six or seven years old, you are also learning your own language. I spoke Indian all together because my grandma never understood English. Quite a lot of her generation didn't speak English. So I was talking Indian two-thirds of the time. In high school in the English classes we had to parse sentences. I felt like pulling out my hair. I was saying, "Who cares whether the clauses are adverbial clauses? Who cares!" I remember my father told me the white man has a language, that's English. "You learn it. You learn it good. Use their good words because they have some bad words. Learn all of their good words." Well, dear father and grandmother, I have struggled and struggled trying to learn good words.

Second Marriage

George Dover, my second husband, was not an Indian. He was white, and he worked in the logging operations out here. I never saw him before. He lived with his mother and stepfather. They were buying some land, and George worked somewhere else for a while. He came home in between. He came into the little post office where I worked. He and I used to talk about it after we were married. He asked for his stepfather's mail by the name of Campbell. I gave it to him. His mother always got a lot of magazines. I had their mail ready, and I gave it to him.

I said, "Do you know anyone by the name of George Dover?"

Nothing. Just quiet. He had picked up his mail. He looked at me and he said, "You are talking to him."

I said, "Oh! There are three or four letters here for George Dover."

I will always remember how I met him. His mother and I talked about George before. She said, "You ought to meet George." I didn't know who George was. When he came into my little post office, I didn't know him. All I thought was that he was nice looking—large blue-gray eyes and long eyelashes. Of course, he had light hair—almost blonde.

When I was engaged to George and he asked me to marry him, I thought about it for several months. My grandmother told me, toward the end of her life, never to marry a white man. Of course, my father said that, too. When I was fourteen years old, he said, "Remember one thing—never, never marry a white man. Never." My father had died years before, but my mother was still living, and she was very shook up. She reminded me again.

George came several times to take me to dinner, and I thought about it. It bothered me to think that one of the last things my father said was to take care of your mother and go home with your boy if you want a home for Wayne. I think my father felt, somehow, that my marriage was a shaky one for a long time.

I did come home, and for years I was all alone when Wayne was growing up and we were home with my mother. I had William. He was about four years old, and he was missing his own father. I thought William should have a father and a mother. If they are living with their grandparents, then it should be the two of them, just as long as they have a balanced home life.

One of my cousins came to visit from Quileute. She once went to school with me, and I hadn't seen her for several years. She married out there, but she came all of that way to our house. She said, "Harriette, we heard you are going to marry a white man. I am telling you—don't. Don't marry him, because, you know, your father always said all of us must never, never marry a white man." We thanked her for coming. That was a long way to come to tell me what to do.

Levi Lamont was one of my father's cousins, too. He came in the post office. He was one of those people who talked loud and clear. He said, "Sister, if you are thinking of marrying a white man—don't. Do you understand? You are not to marry a white man. Do you understand?" He went out of the post office and he was mad.

Somebody else came in and said they heard I was going to marry a white man. He said, "Don't. You are supposed to keep our blood pure Indian." By that time, I thought, why should I listen to people? I've heard "don't" all of my life. So, I married George.

In the last twenty-five years, the young people on this reservation haven't had any conflicts like that one. Quite a lot of our Indian girls have married white men. We older people talk about it now and then. We say, "This tribe is changing—the girls are marrying white men."

The Indian Shaker Church around the mid 1900s.

Harriette and her son Wayne.

Harriette married George Dover in 1950. From left: Tommy Gobin, Adam Williams, Charlie Sneatlum, (name unknown), George Dover, Harriette Shelton Dover, Ruth Coy, Wayne Williams, Blanche James, Margie James.

Celebration of Marysville Tyee Days, Summer 1947.

Planning Committee of Tulalip Tribes. Front row, from left: Harriette Shelton Dover, Supt. Raymond Bitney, Bill Steve (chair), Charles James. Back row: Arthur Hatch (water superintendent), Sebastian Williams, Lawrence Williams. *Everett Herald* photograph.

Representatives to a Bureau of Indian Affairs conference in Chemawa, Oregon. Harriette is in the first row, far left.

Harriette playing her drum, c. 1982. Photograph by Loran Olsen.

10 / Legacy

I N 1959, after Wayne came back here to be business manager, this tribe sponsored a meeting of the Northwest Intertribal Organization. They met in Everett. Indians came from Spokane, Colville, Okanogan, Yakama, Wenatchee, Fort Collins, and Cowlitz. There were delegates from all over the United States.

I was on a panel that met in the morning from 9 A.M. to 12:30 P.M. I wasn't supposed to be on—Sebastian Williams was. I thought, seven o'clock in the morning at my house is midnight for me. He asked me if I would be the chairman. The conference was being held at the Monte Cristo Hotel, when it was new. When he asked me if I would be the chairman for this panel, of course, I said, "Are you crazy? I don't know anything!" He said, "We have to have somebody on there, and I want you to do it."

I was the only woman on a panel of seven Indians. I had three men on one side and three men on the other, in front of about five hundred or six hundred Indians, in a room that was just standing room only. It took me a long time to get over it, because sitting right next to me was a handsome young Indian man—well, not that young—who came from Yakama. His name was Tony Skahan, and he knew one thing: he was the answer to every woman's prayer. He was very good looking.

Each person on the panel had a subject they were going to talk about. There were two or three of them. There would be an Indian person speak and then a white person, and the white person, I think, came from Washington, D.C. The subject that morning was fractionated Indian lands. I thought I was a "super good chairman." I talked loudly and clearly. I thought nobody is going to back me off of the map. I wore a blue suit and a white blouse. (The suit was a real pretty shade of blue. It wasn't navy blue. It was a bright Belgian blue. Well, it was lighter than that. And anyway I thought I looked like a "killer.") After each one spoke for half and hour, then we opened it up to questions from the people in the audience. One person stood up and said,

"Miss Chairman." I said, "I recognize you," and when they asked a question, I looked to the man I hoped would answer it, and then I said, "Do you have an answer?" The young man sitting next to me, Tony Skahan, said, "You are supposed to repeat the question. You are *supposed* to repeat it *out loud*. The audience way in back didn't hear the question." It took me a while, and I think I did pretty well, even with the criticism, and he said several things all through the three hours.

When I came down from the podium, which was a stage clear across the room, a lot of people came up to me, people I knew from the reservations. Of course, I didn't know many of the people. I will always remember a young attractive lady from Cowlitz in a big crowd. She grabbed my arm and said, "Oh, I want to thank you. You did so wonderfully well! You just showed the men what women can do, and they are always trying to keep the women back. I'm so proud of you." I'm always sorry I didn't get her name. Others said I did pretty well, even wonderfully well, even with the "crumb bum" sitting there giving me "Hail Columbia" every time!

The man whose place I took had gotten sick with an upset stomach, and of course some people said he just had too much to drink. They were having parties the night before. I said, "Well, good." So I had a chance to go on, but I will always remember him. I thought maybe he would come and speak to me afterwards. Three hours is a long time for me to appear before a group. He was in the audience. He did look upset or sick. I would have thanked somebody who took my place, but I guess I was just a crumb to them.

I saw Sub later, and I grabbed his arm and said, "I want to kill you, Sub, and the man sitting next to me. I want to kill him, too!" Sub said, "What's the matter? You did fine! I am helping to build you up." I lost him in the crowd, but I was able to eat. We had lunch in one of those rooms in the hotel.

Indian Education

When Wayne was going to school in Marysville, the Indian children were supposed to be getting lunches. We learned they were given a sandwich of dark bread with lettuce and some kind of dressing on it. Most of the Indian children hated it. Lettuce and bread is fine for people who are on a reducing diet, but Indian children are already thin. They were half hungry for years. I didn't have the nerve then to say anything about it.

Years later I did go to the superintendent of schools about the children's school lunches. I found out the Marysville School District receives a sum of money—I think it was 12,000 dollars a year—to pay for lunches for the Indian children and white children living out here on the reservation who qualify. Money like that kept coming in bigger amounts, because I had another upset with the Marysville School Board sometime later.

I thought I would never forget it. I was talking about school lunches, and I said, "Those children are entitled to hot lunches, such as soup and a sandwich." They were still getting lettuce sandwiches. I wrote to Warren Magnuson. He said the year before he and Henry Jackson had seen to it that Marysville received $225,000 to help pay for a school building that was built three miles north of Marysville and is called Cascade. Along about that time, my youngest boy was going to the second grade. They took children six miles to Marysville, then another three miles to Cascade, north of Marysville, to that school—when there was an elementary school right in town. I went to see the school board.

In Seattle, about ten years ago, quite a number of Indian parents from Lummi and La Conner, and I from Tulalip, called a conference. The parents from Nisqually were talking about the lunches provided by the federal government. Hot meals were supposed to be provided. Nobody told them their children were supposed to receive free hot lunches. Most of them could not afford the twenty-five cents a day for the children's lunch. Some of the Indian children went all day long without anything to eat. The mothers and fathers were just talking. We were seated at a table. They said they did not know that lunches were provided. Their children didn't go to eat lunch, and here the lunches went for all of the white children. Quite a number of the Indian children didn't even have breakfast, and no lunch. The Indian children were supposed to receive free lunches, those who had incomes at a certain level or below. So then the children all went to lunch and had hot lunches.

Two or three of the mothers told us their children, who were first, second, third graders, came home so pleased and excited about their hot lunches. You know how children will come running into a house; they are already talking out loud, telling you what happened. So some of the children came home and said, "Momma, I didn't know I had a rich uncle!" Their moms were preparing evening meals and would say, "What do you mean?" We would say, "Well, we got lunch at school—a nice lunch." They were all lined up. As they went through the door into the cafeteria, the teacher pushed on their shoulders or back, pushed them hard, and said, "You ought to be thankful you have a rich uncle who is giving you free food, free lunches." We said, "I didn't know I had a rich uncle! Teacher said I was lucky; I had a rich uncle who could give me free food." The mothers said, "Now, what did they say? What did the teachers really say?" "That's what they said. You are lucky you have a rich uncle—Uncle Sam, and he is giving you all this nice food." Several children said, "Well, where is Uncle Sam? Why doesn't he come and see us?" So then the mothers had to stop what they were doing and try and explain who Uncle Sam is!

When I was a teacher's aide in Marysville schools, with the third and fourth graders, two other ladies made them go around the room, and we tried to teach them how to do a double step like the Plains Indians do. I noticed some of the teachers couldn't do it; they had a hard time. They had to think about it. You go sideways, straight ahead, like a War Dance. A Grass Dance is one, two, double-step, two. We had a lot of fun teaching them how to dance. First of all, you tell them to make two taps with each foot—and don't take long steps, just tap afterwards. You can learn the toe and heel things. We went around in a big circle in the gym. We beat the drum. Those children loved it. They would ask, "Are we going to dance today? Why don't we dance?"

One of the girls who was in one of those third-grade classes just graduated from high school. She is a waitress in Marysville. She came over and said hello to me. I wondered who she was. She was little in the third grade when I came there. She said, "I learned how to dance, Mrs. Dover." I used to tell them, "All you have to do is just keep time with the music, and you can use this same step to band music or an orchestra, and you can dance."

A young man came here to look at my car two or three years ago for the mechanic I go to in Marysville. Carol Harkins went out to talk with him. The young man said, "Is this the Mrs. Dover who used to teach at the school?" Carol told him, yes, it was. He said, "Those were just the grandest school days of my life. I will remember that as long as I live. Those were so enjoyable." You are astounded to hear somebody liked something! The waitress said, "Mrs. Dover, I just wanted to tell you how much I enjoyed having you come to our classroom. I learned so much about the Indians."

One of the teachers in the fourth or fifth grade in Marysville was angry when I came there to talk and teach about Indian culture, especially the Northwest. She said, "We teach Indian history in the third grade, and that is absolutely enough." When we went to her class, she would flounce out of the room. Maybe someone talked to her, because later she stayed, but I used to get so scared. All of the other teachers appreciated us. They enjoyed it too. Once in a while, the teachers said, "I'm going to go for coffee, if you don't mind." I said, "Oh, no, just go ahead. You can leave the room when I come." But they stayed unless they were dying for coffee.

One of the mothers said, "Mrs. Dover, you made a big difference in my son." He was from Marysville and I guess already getting into trouble. He had already been picked up and was in juvenile court. We picked him out; I don't know why. I guess one of the teachers said, "I wish you would take him." Anyway, he was the tallest one in the classroom. We were going to take him anyway. We would name chiefs. We would say to them, "All right now, classroom, you elect a chief." Then we just picked them out and said, "We'll have him and him," or maybe four chiefs or so in a class. Girls were the princesses. They were so pleased, because they were little. His mother came to tell me that we made a big difference in the boy. He did change. He had a stepfather, and sometimes he went to school and sometimes he played hooky.

If you read something in a book, it goes in one eye and out the other. For example, you can read that the Indians wore covering on their feet, not shoes. They wore moccasins. If you bring moccasins into the classroom, they are really surprised, and they want to look at them and touch them. Even boys. They ask, "How do you get the beads on?" Show them almost anything about Indians' clothing or what they did. Then if you explain it a little more, it makes it more like a living thing to them.

In the Tulalip tribal paper, the *Syacəb*, recently there were two or three references to trouble our young people are having in schools, and some of them are dropping out. They are just not finishing. I think that is what Moira Moses was talking about a little while ago. Is there something I can say to the young people? Why is education important? I don't know whether they will listen to me, or remember what I said.

When our Indian people experience racism, I have had white people say to me that you don't have to pay attention to what people say—just don't pay attention. I said, "Well, it is easy for you to say." But when you are walk-ing into a classroom, just going to your desk, and somebody says, "Indian, Indian, dirty Indian," if you hear that every day, it is pretty hard for you to study. Some of our young people get to the eighth, ninth grade and say, "I don't have to put up with it, the white children calling me names. I'm not going to school anymore. They can't make me."

Two grandparents I know were talking to me one day about their grand-son. I think he is fourteen years old, and he quit school. He said, "I'm not going back. You can beat me up; you can kill me, or put me in jail. I'm not going back—not to Marysville." And so he quit. I guess somebody said, "What are you going to do to make a living?" He said, "I'm going to go fishing." Fishing is a big gamble. But he doesn't know that it is a big gamble. Some of our young people do graduate from high school.

The pressure to be civilized was not that bad until the late 1920s and 1930s. It seemed to me when I was going to the boarding school, and later, that being Christianized and being civilized were a terrific jolt. The pressure was on the Indians, especially on the children.

I remember when I had a meeting of all of the Indian workers. They were teachers' aides in Mount Vernon in the early 1970s. My very best friend, Hazel, Mrs. Gaudet, and I were walking through the hall where the meeting was scheduled. I was saying, "I don't want to be Christianized. I don't want to be civilized. I don't want anybody to tell me that I have to be this way or that way." Hazel had a frown on her face, and she was looking at the numbers on the rooms, and suddenly she said—she was kind of talking to herself— "Now, let's see. . . ." Then she said, "Oh, I am sorry, Harriette. What did you say?" "Oh, Hazel, here I was so inspired and thought about all of those big words, and you never even heard me."

If anybody is confused, it is the American Indian children. It is just as hard for American Indian young people to learn—perhaps harder, because they go from a different community, shall we say American community, where people are in homes, and they go to public schools and their adjustment to that kind of community is just as hard, just as confusing.

When I went to school, we had arithmetic—or today it is referred to as mathematics. The Indian boarding school was terrifying for me. Right now I can recall our third- or fourth-grade class; we had to do long division. It took me almost a month to try and understand what was happening in that process, in long division. I went up to the teacher's desk and told her I didn't quite understand long division. Teachers usually say, "What is it you don't understand?" That kind of question always used to leave me flat. I didn't understand any part of it! Anyway, I was frightened. I couldn't tell the teacher what I didn't understand. The teacher went to the blackboard after school or during recess, took one of the problems out of the book, and she did it.

I kept saying, "Where did this number come from?" She explained that this is the dividend and that is the divisor. In my little mind, I really didn't know yet which is the dividend and which is the divisor. It always did frighten me. I took one of those numbers, to see how many times it would go into the bigger number. Maybe it was a smaller number. It took me almost a month. Night times I cried over it. I was so frightened I used to wonder what they were going to do with me, since I couldn't get it through my head. It was as terrifying as when we sang the song "Marching to Victory," and I thought we were going to Victoria and I would never see my mother again! It terrified me, and I guess it terrified the other children, too.

William, my young son, was in school in the sixties. He graduated in 1967 from high school in Marysville. He started first grade at Liberty School in Marysville. I took him to school the first day, and I told him, "Now you are going to stay there, and I'll come back and pick you up." When we got there—it was a noisy place—we found out where his room was. I walked in the room and stopped at the door. I had his hand. He said, "I don't want to stay here." The teacher was at her desk, and I came in the door. I said, "Good morning." I had found out her name at the office. I told her my name. I started to walk toward her, but she didn't look up. She picked up some papers and was looking at them and shuffling them. So I stopped. Then two young women came in. They were attractive white ladies, and they had the cutest little girls. Both were blonde little girls with wavy hair and little red dresses, red socks, and black patent-leather slippers, and little red bows in their hair. They were dolls. The teacher walked toward them and said, "Oh, good morning" with a big smile, and she said, "And who is this?" She was talking to the little girl, and here I am standing there with my boy. My boy looks like an Indian. He's dark, darker than me. He is a beautiful young person.

She said, "Just find a desk to fit him," and she stayed talking to them. So I took him over and tried some desks. He was winding up to cry. He said, "I don't want to stay here." I told him, "I'll come back. I'll take you home." I saw the tears coming down. Well, it broke me up. It bothered me that she ignored me. She didn't want to talk to me, and she smiled beautifully and talked to those other white young women, and so I went back about a week later.

I came in the door before class in the morning. She was at her desk again looking at some papers, and I said, "Good morning." I told her who I was. She never looked up—again. I said, "I came to see and talk about my little boy." She kept looking at those papers. So I walked up to that desk, and I hit it and made the loudest noise I could make. I said, "What is the matter with you? You don't like Indians?" She said, "Oh, I'm sorry. I was reading." I took those papers out of her hands and threw them on the floor, and I said, "Don't you ever treat me like that again. Do you understand? Is that because I am an Indian?" Of course, I was yelling. I pounded the desk again, and I turned around and walked out. My little boy had already walked out to play.

William came home one day with a note. She said she was sorry if she had hurt my feelings. But even so, she treated William terribly, and I didn't know it. I would ask him, "How is school?" Well, he didn't know how school was. I finally met a couple of the white women who live out here. Their boys were in the same grade as William, and they said, "The teacher is mean to William." The two mothers of William's classmates told me that the teacher would call the class up to the front of the room, row by row. They were learning how to write from one to ten and part of the alphabet. William knew the alphabet and he could write. He was left-handed, but he could also write with his right hand. When he went up to the blackboard, he wrote his 2 and 3 backwards. She left him standing there for two hours while the rest of the class sat down. William stood there. He stood there all day. He never even went to eat.

I didn't hear about it until the following year, but I did go and see the principal, a woman, and I told her what had happened. She said, "Mrs. Dover, she didn't start teaching until she was in her thirties. She was from a poverty-stricken family, so you will just have to be understanding." And have my boy humiliated by her? I kept telling myself, don't get mad. I was liable to get thrown out of the building or get arrested. The principal said she was not cut out to be a teacher. I thought, there is only one thing I want to do to her and that is—kill her. I would gladly slit the woman's throat. It clouded all of his school years, her belittling him and making fun of him.

When Wayne started school, we looked all around Whidbey Island, where I lived. Wayne went across on the ferryboat to the school in Mukilteo. He was awfully small when he was six years old. It seemed it was easier to get to on the ferryboat because otherwise he would have had to walk half a mile along the road on the island to where the school bus would pick him up. Then he would have to go five, six miles to Langley. So every morning he went on the ferryboat to school in Mukilteo and every afternoon he came home on the ferryboat. Some years Mukilteo had marvelous teachers. He had Doris Gibbs at the Rosehill School. She was just wonderful. I stayed there when I brought him. She had a big area, with twenty-six or twenty-seven children. She played a beanbag game with them. She threw the beanbag and talked to each one. When they came up to her desk, she put her arm around their little shoulders and said, "Tell me your name," and she wrote down their names and pinned it on their clothes. They went in a big circle, and she would call out their names and throw the beanbag to them and say, "You are Wayne," or "Kevin" or "Kera." She learned their names, and she had them take off those names and put them on their desk. Then they would play another game or do something else. She would have them in a circle again, and she would throw the beanbag and call their names. Some of them would laugh and say, "That is not my name!"

She was such a grand teacher. Wayne went along swimmingly. He learned easily. But William struggled through, even though he had a good teacher after that first dumbbell. In later grades, the teachers said at the end of the year, "William is very kind. He is always taking care of somebody who needs help or sympathy."

William played linebacker on the Marysville High School football team. He could really run for short distances such as thirty or forty yards, and he was strong. We watched him play on the regular team. When he turned out for the team, they put him on as a running back. I was surprised he could run so fast. At home he moved like molasses in January, but he was really moving when he played football. He played three quarters. At one of the games I heard people just behind us talking about number 43. They said, "My, he looks small, but he's good." They were looking on the program to see who he was. So here we were, sitting there thinking, "Oh, that's my baby." But you don't say anything.

William never played the following weeks. He lined up and kicked off; then they took him out. He never played again. I am sorry I didn't say something to the principal or the coach. I knew a mother who lived in the area. She's not Indian. She went right up to the coach out on the field. She said, "I want my boy to play!" She even went to the superintendent, and her boy used to play. Afterwards, I thought, "Why didn't I go make a fuss too?" William noticed and it also bothered him. A lot of Indian boys turn out for sports, and they never get to play.

He told me three or four years ago he met two classmates in a café in Marysville. They told him, "We've always been sorry that we participated in putting you off from playing football. We had a meeting in the coach's office, and two or three of the white boys said, "We don't want him to play—absolutely not." I guess the coach said, "All right, I don't want him to play, either." And so William used to turn out; they would let him suit up. If you get to suit up, you are sort of progressing. I think that was absolutely a bit of racism.

I was telling myself, I'm going to go up there someday and I'm going to talk to the superintendent of schools; the principal is still there who allowed that to happen. Of course, now the superintendent is somebody different. I would certainly let him know that I am not upset about him, but I am upset about those that went before, and I know they will say, "Why didn't you say something?" Why didn't I say something? I guess I didn't think it would do any good.

I think hardly any of the Indian boys turn out for football, and I think a lot of them like football and basketball. I heard some of the Indian parents talking about it three years ago. They said that the Indians absolutely don't have a chance. I imagine in some places they might let the Indian boys and girls participate.

Employment Programs

Lyndon Johnson, a Democratic president, made medical aid and hospitalization available for Indians on the reservations, then when Reagan, a Republican, got in, those funds were cut. We had young people—fifteen, sixteen, up to maybe twenty-three years old—who had no jobs, and they were not in school. The Democrats under Lyndon Johnson had programs for that age group for a while. They built up my little porches.

I didn't have porches on my house. I just had boxes that you could fall down on. Some of the girls washed the windows and cooked meals for the elderly people who were helpless, crippled, and blind. They worked for months and months, and they earned their money. The government took part of the money and put it in a bank under the child's name, so, when the programs ended, they had a couple of hundred dollars.

The Democratic programs went on for months. The Indian families were able to get food, things like shoes for children and the whole family; and for Indians in western Washington, they could get high rubber boots that fishermen use or can be used in rain or water, because they are an important part of the clothing and gear that Indians in western Washington need. When Reagan and the Republicans got in, all of those programs were cut off, and a lot of the young Indians who had been working had no income. After a month or so they were all up in Everett applying at the welfare office. It really breaks me up when things like that happen. I really ought to be thankful though because I am going to get glasses that are supplied by Indian Health or Public Health. I don't know if that is strictly all for Indians or because I am in my late seventies and now I finally get something. Bless Uncle Sam's heart; I am going to have glasses that I can read with, because I can't really see with these. I have to use a magnifying glass if I want to read the newspaper.

I have a growth under my arm. I have had them before when I was in the Indian boarding school, and I was saying the Indian children died from that. I think I heard on the radio from Public Health that some doctors were saying there is a surprising number of cases of people who have cancer of the lymphatic system. I talked to Neti today, the nurse at the doctor's office, and I already talked to Dr. Hammond, and he said, "Oh, that is nothing but fat." Well, the nurse said she could see the swelling and it isn't excess fat or growth of fatty tissue. She was looking for the doctor to refer me to in Everett. He would probably call up Dr. Hammond and he will say, "Oh, she is just a crazy old woman." I am going to go down to the Seattle P.I. building and look for Hilda Bryant. I met her somewhere. I want a big write up. If you are going to write about the Vietnamese, those poor people, then I want equal space. I am being kicked around, and I am an American citizen. Really, I am an American citizen.

Before we became American citizens in 1928, we were worse than being an outsider. A lot of people were really fine and kind and then there were others who wanted the Indians sent somewhere.

Now I am running up a dead-end street, you might say. I was wondering if I would I ever get down there, do you think? I am sure of what I need, well, what I had way back all of those years when I had a large swelling on my neck. It was a doctor in Everett who used some kind of light; it was really strong, but it didn't have any heat, but they covered my head and my shoulders with a thick piece of rubber. My father took me there every week for a year and a half. It finally went away. Whatever it was because when I came home I had kind of a fever, what they called a low-grade fever. I didn't feel like eating. If I went down to the public health hospital they will probably tell me I have to have a referral and papers from a certain doctor.

The Republicans under Eisenhower had a different training program that was called "Relocation," which was supposed to be helping the Indians. They took the young people from here, especially the young marrieds, all of the way down to California, to San Diego and San Francisco. I asked the agent one time, "Why do they have to take them so far away?[1] Can't they get training in Seattle? I said, "There are some Indians working at Boeing." And I think another steel company in Seattle employs Indians. There were a few other places where they could work. But they took the young Indians who signed up for the Relocation Program all of the way down there, and then for some reason the young people got stranded.

Clyde Hatch, for example, signed up for the Relocation Program. He and

---

1   The Relocation Program required that Indians be dispersed from their reservations to distant cities for job training and later employment. The program lasted from 1952 to 1972 when it was cancelled by Richard Nixon.

his wife and their baby had their way paid to San Francisco for job training. They were furnished with an apartment. They bought food with money his parents gave them. Bu they couldn't sleep at night because the place was full of cockroaches. They didn't know what they were, since they had never seen such bugs before. The cockroaches came out at night, out of the walls, even crawled on their bed and blankets. So they would stand up all night on the bed, holding their baby.

Every morning Clyde went to an office, where he was told by his supervisor to be before eight o'clock. He sat there all day. There was a girl typing, but she never told him anything. They had told him to be sure and be there. He was there about a month. They were hungry, and their rent was going, so they sent a telegram to their folks. I just happened to be visiting them. They were worried about their children. They cabled them some money to come home.

What happened at that time was that Clyde was there at the office every morning, and the girl was typing through the day. He asked her about so-and-so. "He is not in." Later, they found out that he went on a thirty-day vacation to Hawaii, and here were these Indians who were hungry, worried, and lost. This was supposed to be a project to help Indians. In nearly all cases, the Indians came back home, and their parents paid their way back. There wasn't any more money to pay for their rent, and they got hungry and worried—so back they came.

From long ago, in fact, some of us Indians, such as Wayne and I, talk about the pressures that were put on the Indians. The last time it was pretty bad; it was President Eisenhower, a Republican administration. The pressures came down to us, and it was really just like I remember when I was very small. The Indians were pressured from all sides. The Indian agent had a lot of power, shall I say, and it seems as though the priest when he came had a lot of power. It was just pressures all around. Save your soul. Confess your sins. Go to school. You have to be in the Indian boarding school—every boy and girl. Learn to read and write. Learn the English language. Learn to live like the white man. Those things I remember from when I was real small, because I would hear my parents talking about them with other Indians coming to our house every Sunday. My mother would cook big meals on Sunday. And those Indians would stay, and they would talk just about all afternoon with my father, and they would tell about things that were happening to them. The Indians were separated onto their allotments by several miles and roads were practically nonexistent, and so the Indians walked over those muddy trails or narrow muddy roads, or some who had horses would go on horseback.

Some had wagons, like a farm wagon, but to go on a farm wagon was really something because the roads were in bad condition. They would have to go over stumps and logs.

It seemed during all of my growing up life there was pressure all around. The Indians were a hungry, hungry group. They really didn't have money. Their incomes came from, as I said, picking hops—they were migratory field workers and that was not a living—or they worked in the logging camps. It was second nature to them to chop down or saw down trees. In the old days, Indians didn't cut down trees like that. They might cut down one tree to make a canoe or some of the smaller canoes that we called *st(d)əxʷił*. (It isn't really a canoe; it doesn't have a head on it like a canoe.)

I think, generally speaking, the average white people are also busy trying to establish themselves, since they came here from other states. They have their own problems. I hope people notice I am being big hearted in noticing that the white people also had problems. I always disliked white people ever since I could remember. I have never really changed my mind about that except there are many white people who are just absolutely marvelous friends. They would help anybody. There are some Indians who would help, too.

The beginning of the sixties was the end of Eisenhower as president. They were Republicans, and the lot of American Indians was not good. Republicans couldn't care less about Indians. If you have business—big business or any business—they are sure the country moves along and everyone can work. John Kennedy was elected—a very Democratic president—and, of course, I feel he was certainly an outstanding leader. He had, I think, above all things, charm, although a lot of people say he was a spoiled rich young man. I read his speeches before Congress. I am positive he had a very deep feeling for all people—Black, Indian, Chicano.

I don't think the Chicanos received that much attention in the years past. I think white people tended to feel Chicanos or Mexicans were foreigners. They are not foreigners any more than white Americans are. They are mixed with Indian and Spanish. They were not all immigrants into the United States; their families in some cases had been there for hundreds of years in California, Arizona, New Mexico, and Texas. Those states once belonged to Mexico, and the United States moved in and took them over. Living in all of these states were these Mexican Americans and Mexicans. I think they were treated cruelly by the white people, and Indians and blacks have been shot and cheated too.

Martin Luther King Jr. became very well known through his efforts in the 1960s as a speaker for the black people's troubles and problems — their rights. I always admired him. I saw him on the news when they walked several hundred miles in the Freedom Walk. I remember seeing him on the news, speaking in Washington, D.C., and what he said: "I have a dream. I have a dream, and I see the shining mountain." I thought — well, perhaps he has found his dream and probably has found the shining mountain, but it will be a long time before the people have complete freedom.

As I mentioned before, when I was looking for work, a woman personnel officer said, "We hire only Americans." She said, "I mean real Americans." But, I thought, that is the way a lot of white Americans feel: they are Americans, and the rest of us are something else on the face of the earth that they would rather not see. People in Marysville, and places like the town of Marysville, tend to be prejudiced because they have seen Indians drunk much of the time.

As I was saying, the sixties were a real change. It was a change for the better, because Kennedy initiated a lot of programs: the Job Corps, which was a kind of carryover from President Roosevelt, and the Peace Corps, where young people were trained to go overseas to different nations and people. The new Republican administration will phase that out too.

There are going to be thousands of people without a penny of income again. Teenagers here in the CETA [Comprehensive Employment Training Act] program used to go in the months of June and July and cut the tall grass around my house. Of course, the girls and boys would argue. I used to watch them. I would stand it for so long, and then I'd say, "You are just standing around." Some nice looking boy would say, "Who? Me? You are talking to me?" A girl was talking to him. She has a grass cutter or something, and she was trying to give it to him. He was saying, "I can't hold anything!" They would be hollering all day long. I used to open up the door and tell them to come in if they want to have a 7-Up. Most of them never ever took the 7-Up, but they did drink a lot of water. They were fun.

I haven't seen young people since William has been gone, for three or four years. I miss all that yelling over nothing. Arguments used to go on and on, and they never settled anything. But the youngsters who worked for CETA had spending money. The supervisor gave them 20 dollars a week, and the other 20 dollars were put in the bank. It was pretty good money. The bigger boys put the roof on my house.

One morning I was reading in bed. It was eight or nine o'clock and pretty soon I heard hammering. I thought, who could that be here so early in the morning? A lot of Indians say, "Don't call Harriette before two o'clock or she'll be mad." Here it was 9:30 A.M. I got up and took a shower and got dressed. I could hear voices, and so I finally walked outside and here was someone working around in my driveway. I looked up and they said, "We are fixing your roof." I had a car then, so I drove to town, had breakfast in town, and then I went to visit somebody. So I was gone most of the day. When I came back, it was about four o'clock. They were leaving. They worked fast, and they were fun.

Young people used to argue like that when I was young. We had big dinners. Indians are always having big dinners. Young people did the dishes and cleaned the tables, wiped the dishes. Way back then, there were no paper plates. We got into arguments about who was going to wash the dishes. There was always one boy who would do the dishes, and so we would wipe the dishes. Sometimes we started by putting the dish towels or the wet rag on each other's shoulders, saying, "Now you do the dishes." They would try to put it back on us. Just arguments. Sometimes one of our aunts or an older lady would say, "Oh, stop it now and get to work." And then we'd say, "See now? She said for you to go to work." I think the young people still do that today.

Fishing Rights and the Boldt Decision

The United States government attorneys talked with the Indians, and the Indians' lawyers appeared in Judge Boldt's court with the Indians in the lawsuit *United States v. the State of Washington* in 1973. The Indians' case was made stronger with the government attorneys working with the Indians and their attorneys. Judge Boldt heard the case day after day for weeks and months. When the Indians and the white people had presented their statements, then Judge Boldt took them under advisement. He read the transcripts all over again. Now they are typed; the court reporter takes down every word. Judge Boldt studied the whole thing and then that is when he came up with what is called the Boldt Decision. He ruled that the Indians have a right to 50 percent of the total catch of the salmon in this state.

Well, that really broke up the white commercial fishermen and the Steelheader's Association. On Channel 4 news, I saw sometimes eight or ten women who were going by airplane from Seattle to Washington, D.C., to see Senator Magnuson and Senator Jackson and the Washington State delegation. They talked about how hard it was to make a living—for their husbands to make a living. Their husbands had fishing boats and nets that they had to pay for.

It was pitiful. We were sitting here, and I was saying to some of our cousins, "Look what you did to those poor white people." They said, "Yeah, I know."

Before the Boldt Decision in 1974, the Indian fishermen were taking 5 percent, and that isn't exactly 100 percent of the total catch.[2] Now, the other 95 percent was caught by somebody—by the white fishermen. In all of those years, the white fishermen caught over 90 percent of the catch.

In a program at Everett Community College, they had a panel for the students. It included a representative of Washington State Fisheries, and Indian fishermen from Lummi in Bellingham, and Tulalip and Nisqually. I went to other information meetings where people who were interested came. At those meetings, you always hear how steelhead are supposed to be for the sportsmen and the steelheaders.

At the local Fisheries meetings, no matter who the speaker was—an Indian speaker or the director of Fisheries—the same five or six men were always there, adding rough remarks. They were what you might call trouble-makers. They took turns standing up and complaining about what the Indians had been doing to the salmon runs. They said the Indians were destroying the salmon runs because they were taking all of the salmon. So, at one of those places, I called the chairman. I said, "Do you know exactly how much the Indians have taken?" This was in 1976. By that time, the Indians were taking over 19 percent. A year later it was around 22 percent.

The Indians were able to get bigger boats because the fish buyers and the different canneries would loan money to the Indians. Before the Boldt Decision, the Indians didn't have any money. They couldn't buy boats. During all of the years that I was growing up, the Indians made their own fishing boats, and they were small, very poor looking. But that was the best they had. Now they have been able to go up to the San Juan Islands, which is a better fishing ground; better than anything around here. So some of them have been able to make a living.

Quite a lot of the senators in the Congress, I think, are going to wonder, what is the matter with these people who are shrieking about fishing? Why don't they go out and fish? It goes on and on. If anybody should have complained about it, it should have been the Indians. For a hundred years, we were denied fishing for a living, even though Indians tried to change it through the courts.

---

2   Washington State Fisheries gives the same figure for the pre-1974 tribal catches of salmon.

Now Washington State has a federal buy-back program. They are going to buy back some of the fishing boats and gear of the fishermen here in Washington State because they said they can't make anything if the Indians have to have 50 percent of the catch; there is no use going on with fishing. Quite a lot of them are selling their old fishing gear to the government. I have a clipping from the newspaper. It is a long write-up with pictures of some of the fishing boats the fishermen are selling. One young man from Seattle was very pleased with himself because he sold his fishing boat to the government. He had gone fishing the year before, and he figured that he could make money. He went to Alaska. He bought a fishing boat, a gillnetter, for $15,000, and it was big enough for Bristol Bay. Some of the gillnetters around here and in Puget Sound were not big enough for the far north. He didn't say how he got it. But he fished up there for four or five months; then the fishing fleet came down here. He got a chance to sell his boat. He sold it to the government for $31,000. In less than one year, he earned more than the $15,000 he paid for the boat. A lot of canneries or fish buyers would let a man have a fishing boat and gear, and he would sell his fish to them until most of the balance was paid in. Quite a number of fishermen sold their old fishing boats for much more than they ever paid for them.

Congress appropriated 5 million dollars to Washington State to buy back the fishing boats of the white fishermen. But there ought to be an investigation to find out which of these white fishermen are full-time fishermen. Some of them expect to make their entire living from fishing, but hundreds and thousands are teachers, professors, and businessmen. They go gillnetting at night. Some of them have vacations in the summer; they fish from purse-seine boats or are reef-netters. Great numbers of them are not that hard up. Fishing is just a sideline. Some of them make thousands of dollars. Some of them don't do quite that well.

I remember we were talking to a group of men my husband used to work with in Everett. I was with him. We were just visiting. Five men had just come back from Alaska in the fall, but each one made $55,000. It was a good year. Sometimes they don't make that much. It is a gamble. But there ought to be more equality and truth for men who are full-time fishermen. Then, I think, they should be helped if they have lost money. Men who make $25,000 to $30,000 a year in their jobs should not get another $50,000 for a boat they just bought. Now they are willing to sell them because that is fast money. Nobody ever stops to ask them. There was an article in the *Seattle*

Post-Intelligencer about them. Nearly all of them are part-time fishermen. There is no other job than fishing for many Indians.

Indian unemployment is high. Here at Tulalip, it is 43 percent, and some of that is part-time employment. In the Puget Sound area four or five years ago, the figure was 80 percent for Indians. You know when the unemployed general American public gets around 7 percent how much people worry. Five percent seemed workable for years; it will let the economy of the country improve more slowly.

I haven't had any dried salmon for three or four years. We have a smokehouse across the road, where my father and mother lived. The highway goes by it, and the smokehouse turned out to be close to the road—about fifty or sixty feet. I had fourteen salmon hanging up. My husband or I went down at 11 P.M. to keep a small fire burning with green alder wood, so that it produced more smoke than fire. Then, by 5 A.M., I would get up and run down there and fix the fire again. It is out, and it is cold. Then one morning, I went down there and all fourteen salmon were gone. Wayne and his family live where my parents lived. Last year or the year before, they fixed some salmon to dry. I think they only had four or five, and they disappeared in a hurry too.

Nobody in my family goes fishing. My older boy was the business manager of the Tribes for almost twenty years, and he never went fishing for a living. My younger boy is thirty years old. I asked him if he would go fishing here, some years ago. He thought about it for a few minutes, and he said, "No. I'd rather not go fishing. I know we need fish. We have to buy it in town from the market. I have a regular job, and some of these guys don't have any work at all. All they have is fishing."

In the *Seattle P-I* the other day, there was an article: a fisherman's wife was showing how to prepare devilfish.[3] My mother and her relatives thought it was the grandest delicacy, and so did my mother-in-law, Wayne's grandmother; she lived in Sequim. They slice devilfish legs and really relish it. I remember eating it, but it didn't make any impression on me; it seemed kind of bland. I remember my mother cooking it. You know, I don't know how to cook it. I thought she boiled it first and then sliced it and fried it, or she breaded it. I remember my father and us eating it. That must have been the first time I really had it. I barely remember. But I remember getting to the table, and my father eating it. He said, "You aren't supposed to make any remarks about food—just eat it." I don't think I noticed what it was. I just gobbled it down

---

3   Octopus.

because I was hungry. They ate devilfish from here, but not that often. Wayne ate some at a dinner at Lummi, where I was invited to sing my song. Well, we all ate it. It was put on the table along with everything, but I didn't see it; it was way past Wayne. Sam Cagey brought it and handed it to me. Oh, my, I had not seen that for sixty years or more.

I was talking to one of the Indians from Montana or Dakota, and he wondered what fish heads tasted like. What could you get out of it? Of course, our Indians say, "How could you eat raw buffalo liver or drink the warm blood of the buffalo?" He said he had buffalo liver when he was small; they slice it very thin and it is good. "You feel about raw liver like I do about fish heads." Just put the fish head in the oven. A fish head looks like one solid thing, but it isn't. It has all kinds of bones in it, and you can chew the bones because they are kind of spongy; they have their own flavor.

Slade Gorton, the new senator who took Magnuson's place, and the Washington delegation are putting together a bill to present in Congress to change the status of steelhead salmon and make it into a game fish.[4] A game fish can't be caught by any Indian fisherman. It isn't to sell; you catch it for your own use. Catching steelhead and then not selling it isn't going to help a hungry Indian family that much. It will help the white sportsman—the Steelheaders Association—who want the steelhead for themselves. They don't want the Indians catching it in a net and selling it. It's going to be an interesting issue for the Washington State delegation. Oregon and Idaho might join in. Commercial fishermen, sportsmen, and steelheaders have a lot of power; they have money, and they can put the pressure on the Washington State delegations.

I've been wondering, how will those senators and representatives in Congress from other places like Illinois, Alabama, or Maine who don't have steelhead—all of those states and millions of people—how would they feel about making a salmon, like steelhead, into a game fish by an act of Congress? I can't think of anybody more selfish than steelheaders and other sports fishermen. I can see why they love to go out fishing, whether it is along the streams or rivers or out in the ocean, but I don't think, even if I were situated like they are, I would have the "scavvy" nerve to say, "I want it. It's mine. I don't want anybody to have this steelhead salmon but me. It's going to be caught only with hook and line, not net." There are hungry Indians. Well, there are hungry white people. But they want that only for their pleasure.

---

4   The Native culture and the science of biology classify steelhead as salmon, not trout.

Of course, Slade Gorton and members of the Washington delegation are talking very strongly about their bill. They are going to present it in Congress and want it passed. There are over five hundred men and women in the House of Representatives. How many of them are going to feel that this issue is important when it affects only so many people in Washington, maybe Oregon and Idaho, and maybe part of California? It seems so selfish and petty to me. But maybe the congressmen will think that is the greatest thing—better pass it. Judge Boldt's decision does not exclude the steelhead. Wayne, my son, and I were talking about this, and I said, "Don't tell me we would have another long-drawn, drag-out court fight again like the one that resulted in the Boldt Decision."

Indications from the few fishing boats that have gone out are that there are very few salmon. They don't seem to be coming back in numbers like they always have. The runs might start a little later. It always intrigues me that all along this Pacific Coast, from Alaska all the way south to South America, the Russian fishing fleet is out there: Yugoslavia, Poland—you name it—all of the world's fishing fleets are out there. They used to be just twelve miles from this coast. Magnuson introduced a bill, and they changed the limit to two hundred miles by international law. The Russians were pretty upset. They thought we were the rottenest people there were. Here all of these years, they have actually been fishing inside. Indians at Neah Bay said if you go out there fishing six, seven miles like they do, you will see Russian fishing fleets—the biggest fishing fleets in the world.

Russians have nets that are made with steel cables. American fishermen nets are weighted with lead sinkers every so many feet. Russians have cannery ships that process the catches. The nets have a small mesh: only an inch or an inch and a half. It goes down a mile or more into the sea, and when the machinery on the ships haul it in, it brings in everything: immature and mature salmon. The fish out there will be moving into the Sound in a couple of months, and by that time, they will be bigger. Immature salmon are picked up as well as herring and pilchards. They are canned and sent to Russia. It seems to me that sometime in the future there is going to be a big war, because people are starving.

Washington State Fisheries said there aren't many fish out there—not much salmon. There are sportsmen out there at Port Angeles and out at Neah Bay. They can pick up two or three big salmon. I read two weeks ago there are not many salmon coming in; there ought to be more. I know exactly what the steelheaders and the commercial fishermen all along here are going to say: the Indians cleaned up, you know, they took it all last year, so now there aren't any coming back. No spawn. We've killed it off. We took it all. Actually, Washington State licensed too many fishermen, even before the Boldt Decision. They issued something like five hundred licenses for gillnetting, which is done at night. Already there are over two thousand, and more than that were licensed over the years. If they were all in one place, that is practically wall-to-wall fishing. How are the salmon ever going to get through all those nets and get up to the rivers to spawn?

Last month I saw on the news and in the newspapers that commercial fishermen all around Seattle, Tacoma, and Olympia are very worried. They don't see how they are going to make a living because the Indians get half of the whole thing. After the Boldt Decision there was so much trouble. There were lots of write-ups about white fishermen, how they are starving, they have lost their houses and their lots, and one man on television said, "I've lost my wife." He said, "She left me. I lost my house and my lot on account of this; I can't fish. Everything is going to the Indians." I remember I was telling Wayne, and some of them, such as Stan Jones, "Do you see what you folks have done? Indian fishermen, you folks, have ruined the white man's lives. That man's wife has left him." Of course, some of them said, "What man? What wife? Let me see her." Well, the Indians haven't been able to catch half of anything. All of those years, if people took the time to look at the years from 1890 or 1900 to the 1950s, 1960s, just before the Boldt Decision, they would find Indians took 5 percent of the catch or less.

Every year the Washington State director of Fisheries makes a report to the governor and to the people of the state. He tells how many salmon were caught, because every fisherman is supposed to tell when he sells his fish to the fish buyers. If he sold one thousand pounds, the fish buyer writes it down because he is going to pay him. I am just making that up, obviously. The figure is more like five thousand pounds. He gets paid for that amount. The fish buyer brings the catches to the cannery. He is going to get more pay from the cannery for bringing in five thousand pounds. The cannery and the fish buyer and the fisherman—they all make money from the catch.

The Washington State report tells run by run what the numbers of fish are: the spring run is silvers and Chinooks or king salmon; late summer runs are silvers and chum salmon. Every two years "humpies" come in late summer or fall. Washington State has a pretty good count of all of the catches by gillnetters, who fish at night, from the Straits, from Puget Sound, from Point Roberts, and on the ocean coast. The nets on the purse seiners, the largest of the fishing boats, are ninety feet or more. Their nets have a smaller mesh, so they catch everything, and, of course, they have good machinery that pulls it in. The mesh on a gill net is six or seven inches across. You can go gillnetting at night and have only a fifteen-foot boat. You can haul in your net by hand, because that is what the Indians do. By midnight your hands are freezing up. By the time you get home in the morning, the young Indian girls' and wives' and their young husbands' hands are swollen. They are working in cold saltwater and hauling in a wet net.

I was talking with one of the young Indian men here. His hands and arms were aching because he had been fishing. He just happened to mention it. He said he couldn't close his fingers because they were swollen, which happens when your hands are in water for hours, especially saltwater. Now I think most of them have enough money so they can buy rubber gloves.

Before the Boldt Decision, not many Indians had fishing boats or the gear. They were too poor to have good fishing nets. But after the Boldt Decision, there were some companies that would allow an Indian fisherman to have a net and maybe a boat on credit, and then just pay through the years from his catch. In 1974 and 1975, after the decision, the official records from the Washington State Department of Fisheries show the Indians' catch did go up. They caught, as I said before, 19 percent of the salmon; that is, 19 percent of the entire year's catch.[5] They didn't catch many kings or Chinooks because there aren't that many anymore.

But the white fishermen were screaming. They still scream about how the Indians are taking all of the salmon, all of the fish. Even the largest share of 19 percent is a long way from being 50 percent. The white fishermen never look at statistics or records. They just know one thing (it comes from God himself): the Indians are taking all of the salmon. It seems to go on and on. The trouble with fishing in this state didn't end with the Boldt Decision. The Indians have said that the Boldt Decision just opened another big trouble. The white people, the white commercial fishermen, and, especially, the white sportsmen are crying to high heaven: they can't catch any salmon, no fish.

I think I mentioned that I can't imagine a more selfish group than the white commercial fishermen and the steelheaders—the way they are complaining about their steelhead, their salmon, their heritage, "my money," "my heritage." Your heritage, white man, is in Europe. You never ever heard an Indian who appeared on any of the panels or the news who ever said, "My

---

5   The tribes reached 50 percent in 1981.

steelhead," "my salmon," "my heritage." Never. If anybody should have been able to say "my heritage," it should have been the Indians, but none of them did. I remember we were saying we still behaved as though we were high class; as though we came from Indian royalty. It is low class in our Indian culture to yap around: "That's my money. I did this. I did that." If you did something, do it and let it go.

On the television news the other evening, they were talking about the Indians again. A high school in Kirkland cleared out a salmon stream around Lake Washington. One of the young high school boys was saying the Indians are taking all of the sockeye spawn. I was just thinking, it will go on and on. Wayne said the other day, "The Boldt Decision wasn't the final thing. It will go on and on."

Mission Beach

After my son Wayne was working here as business manager for several months, the Board decided to raise the leases for the lots along Mission Beach and Tulalip Bay. Wayne had been working at Boeing in Seattle as a draftsman in the engineering department. Usually, no matter where Indians live, they eventually want to come home to the reservation. Sebastian Williams retired, so then Wayne became business manager. They raised the leases for the lots along Mission Beach and Tulalip Bay, from twenty-five dollars a year for people with homes right on the beach to fifty dollars and then to about one hundred and twenty-five dollars, which was an increase of several times over.

I remember an article in the *Seattle P.-I.* I couldn't afford to buy a paper then, but that one time there was a picture of some of the lessees. They were going to sue the Tribes since that is totally uncalled for to more than quadruple—quintuple, really—their leases. They had several meetings and were just raving. I saw Wayne on television at 6 P.M. They asked him what the Tribes were doing. He said, "Well, it is our land, and we make the plans for how much we will lease it." I remember he emphasized that it is our land. He went on to say that the Tribes have written to people who operated beach resorts all over Puget Sound, and the rates the Tribes were charging were too low, and that the increases are more comparable to the surrounding rates for leasing beach property. Afterward, I met people who told me how awful the Indians were behaving. Poor people. Some of them had beautiful homes in Everett or Seattle and other places, and they had very nice homes on the beaches, too.

Our Tribe is having meetings—this is 1982—and Wayne goes to them. One of the attorneys for one of the lessee groups is Lloyd Meeds. I like Lloyd. I met him a long time ago, when he was a prosecuting attorney, and I helped put him in Congress. He was a good man. Wayne said he met Lloyd in Washington, D.C., and now he is on the opposite side from us. I'm not sure how the meetings about the lease increases are going.

Before the recent Board meeting, two or three white lessees were there in the meeting room. One man was almost speechless, he was so "rowing mad" at these Indians. He was trying to tell them, "You can't do such a thing!" The leases have an escalating clause in five-year installments. So if it goes up, they figured that in fifty years they would be paying an amount that was out of this world. It isn't settled yet. They might go to court. At least, the lessees are threatening to take the Tribe to court.

Wayne was in court from the start when he returned here. Scott Paper Company had bought two allotments in the middle of this reservation and was going to log it. They cut off part of a stream. They had a lake on their allotment, which they bought, and the stream flows into the Tribe's water works that goes for several miles. Wayne wrote them a letter and said they can't change the watercourse. Scott Paper thought nobody could tell them what to do. The tribal attorney took the case to the Circuit Court of Appeals in San Francisco, and the Tribes won that one. Other reservations have had problems like that, too.

Being business manager is a big responsibility. I would see Wayne once in a while and say, "How is business, or how is the Tribe?" I remember the first time I saw him there. He said, "Well, I am father, mother, and football for Indians and for white people—mad Indians and mad white people." He said, "I have to roll over and make them think I am dead."

I knew the people who lived at Mission Beach. For example, in one area there were two adjoining lots. One man—a white man—put in a waterline to the Tribes' waterline. The Tribe had a waterline that went all along the Marysville road and then around to the end of the Point. The lessees had put in their own waterlines from the roadway, and then from the Tribes' line to their houses. Then his neighbor tapped into his line, but he didn't go all of the way to the road. He dug a ditch while this man was gone and put a hole in his line, and that way he didn't have many feet to go to his house. They had quite a quarrel because the man who installed the long line got mad at the other man and got mad at the Tribe for allowing it, and, of course, the Tribe didn't know which man tapped into the waterline. Things like that came up—misunderstandings here and there. Indians, and a few white people, came in to talk or visit. Many of them have lived here for quite a while.

Mission Beach is nothing but houses now, and a lot of white people live there, but it is tribal land. The Tribes lease all of that land, lot by lot. Years ago, fifty or more years ago, that is where the Tribe's money came from, mainly, the leasing of those lots. The land can't be sold, since it is tribal land, but the houses are owned by the people who built them. If, some day, they want to leave, they would have to demolish the house or remove it. They are supposed to leave the land the way they found it.

Last year one of the young people on our reservation, Leslie Parks, asked me if there had always been white people living out here on our reservation. I said no. When I was little—that was a long time ago—the only white people were those who worked at the agency. All of the rest was the entire Indian reservation. The eastern boundary line is on the freeway or I-5, right on the outskirts of Marysville, and then north it is the Fire Trail Road. He just wondered. But it intrigued me that some of the young Indians are wondering why we have white people living here. Now there is hardly any Indian land where only Indians live.

About fifteen years ago, I was talking to some people. They always had such interesting ideas about Indian people. They never saw Indians, just heard about or studied them in high school or college. When I tell them things, they come and look at our Indian artifacts. I remember several women said, "You know, Mrs. Dover, we didn't know the Indians had beliefs or religion. We were told the Indians were ignorant, half-naked savages." Nobody has the time to find out what Indians are.

Thinking of the Bible. We have some legends that tell about the baby who was born; sometimes it was called the Sky or Star Child, but our legends are a little different for the different tribes. In our legend, he became a good hunter, and he had a little fur vest, a little coat made of many colors of feathers. When I was talking to these white people, about fifteen or twenty of them, I said this is a story that is similar to Joseph in the Bible and his coat of many colors. Those white people said, "Well, Mrs. Dover, you can't compare an Indian legend to the Bible. The Bible is an inspired book, inspired by the word of God." I said, "How do you know it is inspired by God?" It was written by several men, and I think the Bible is certainly a marvelous, wonderful book. I haven't read it; I have just read parts of it. But sometimes when I read parts of it, I think, that's what the Indians used to say—what's in the Bible—sometimes. Not all of it. But that legend is in my father's booklet, "Legends of the Totem Pole"; he calls it "The Little Man with the Coat of Many Colors." But when that party of white people said I couldn't compare a legend to the Bible, I said I could compare it, I do compare it, and I said the Bible isn't any more inspired than this is. These legends are old, old. They come from what my parents said, my father used to say, was a time in our history of hundreds of years ago, a time that is like a curtain of fog or mist that covers our past. It is just like in the morning if you look over toward the mountains or over the water, there is a mist that drifts. It takes maybe an hour or so before the sun can shine through. The Indians used to say that is the way of time, our time, when we were on this earth, when we were here. It is like a time that was behind a curtain, a fog, a mist. But we have been here for a long, long time. We have always been here.

When I went to Everett Community College, I had an excellent history teacher—David McCourt. We studied the colonization of America and also South and Central America. All of my life I have hated white people, but now I have seen and read about the things that have happened to them that were never in my high school books: about the treatment of people who came from Europe. They were supposed to be new citizens entitled to rights that were spelled out in the Constitution and the amendments of the Constitution.

I don't think Mr. McCourt understood that what I learned in school before was somewhat distorted. When I was little, in school, they said the people found in this world were naked savages. I told my class at Everett Community College, talking about naked savages, "naked" is a bikini bathing suit. The history books say Indians were naked savages. I think everybody who sees that is thinking "naked" means they had nothing on; whereas they had on a breechcloth, but the white people had never seen anyone with a breechcloth before so the Indians were considered naked.

I heard a fisherman and a reporter talking at a dock in Seattle, and the white man said, "The Indians are nothing but an ignorant bunch of people. They shouldn't have all of the salmon they are getting. They are getting everything. They don't know anything. They don't even have a language." I was sitting here, and I said, "Oh dear, there it all goes again." Nobody thinks we had a language of our own. They feel we are a bunch of loafers and drunks on the reservation.

11 / Seeing the World

M y father and his parents and their group used to talk about the Salmon Ceremony. I talked about it to Wayne fifteen or twenty years ago. He said we ought to do it. He said, "Think about it. Present it to the Board." Then I would forget about it. I sort of thought I might not be well enough to do any of it.

We had our first gathering to talk about the Salmon Ceremony at Bernie Gobin's house in 1970. Morris Dan and Bertha Dan came from La Conner. Others who helped plan the ceremony were Stan and Joann Jones, Gloria St. Germaine, Molly Hatch, Mariah Moses, Fillmore (Big Shot) Amos, and Bob and Celia Jones. I said what I remembered my parents and grandparents said about it. Morris said what he remembered, what he saw when he was very small. We talked until midnight. Some of them had to work, so we all went home, and we decided to meet again a week later.

We talked for several hours, and little by little Morris remembered, or I usually remembered first, and so it began to come back to me what my father said or what he saw and what he participated in. We met again the following week. By the third time, we were putting details on what we remembered, and I was writing it down, jotting things down. We met the fourth week, and by that time I had written down pretty much the way we talked about it.

When our people used to do the ceremony, it took hours and hours, and days and days. We felt we couldn't do it that way; we had to sort of telescope it together. So I wrote what I thought, and we made a good outline: the introduction or the first opening song, the blessing of the longhouse. Then we met again to beat the drums, and Morris sang and we sang what we remembered.

A week later I went to a Board of Directors meeting. They said they would appropriate the money — several hundred dollars — for the dinner. When the Board said they would appropriate the money, then we were really committed to it. We met again and decided it would have to be sometime in June, when it was high tide, that we could hold the ceremony, because we were going to use the canoes and come in with the sun. That is when we had our Salmon Ceremony when we were living in the longhouse. We went down a week before and sort of stood in there and said, "Where do we start?"

When we presented it the first time, we sat on the right-hand side of the longhouse. We were all sitting there and someone said, "Is this where we are supposed to be?" I said, "This is where we sat down."

When we first had the Salmon Ceremony, we were wondering if we were going to be able to get some salmon. Celia Jones said, "I don't think you folks live right." Molly Hatch was standing there. I think our fishermen just came in with some nice silvers or Chinooks. It wasn't enough salmon to serve several hundred people. Then this Tribe had to go to La Conner, and La Conner said they didn't want to sell them; they would donate the fish. Quite a lot of people came from La Conner. Several people said, "Don't put it in the paper, or we'll have a lot of people we don't want coming around—you know, looking around."

Our Salmon Ceremony this year, 1982, had a very small attendance because Lummi had their Stommish Celebration and Marysville had the Strawberry Festival, and some other cities had festivals at the same time.

Two or three months before my mother died she said, "Don't forget to go into the longhouse. Be sure and be there for June or for Treaty Time, and do that every year. Don't let the longhouse stand empty and forlorn or forgotten."

We enjoyed working on the Salmon Ceremony. Some of us the same age, the elderly people, put the ceremony together. We decided we would have an opening song, which was the blessing of the longhouse, because that is what our people used to do. They had certain songs, of certain people, who were what we call *sqəlalitut*, the guardian spirit, and so we put them together. I go around and sing my song. Then we do the opening song. We have the whole tribe go around the longhouse, to every corner, as we remembered my father and mother, and some of the others who remembered their parents and grandparents, said, "This is what we did." It seems as though we remembered how to do it; it didn't come all at once.[1] Our grandparents and parents didn't remember the entire thing from the beginning to the end. They just remember. They would say, "I remember the time when I was in such a place and we sang the opening song—the blessing of the longhouse." That's my song; it's mine. So when we sang the opening song, our tribe went round

---

1   The Salmon Ceremony, like all traditional activities, was forbidden by the federal government.

the longhouse and stopped at every corner, and the drumbeats stopped at every corner and we began again.

Nobody would know, but the melody in the song is the same, only with different words, all of the way through the entire hour. The first opening is when we are standing in the longhouse. It is sung as *sqələbčəxʷ*. "Hear us; we are Indians." *ƛ̓əlabutčixʷ ʔačiƚtalbixʷ*. Those words are repeated, time after time, and we sing it aloud four times. That is what our folks said—all of them. You have to sing it more than that, because we don't get around all of the way through the longhouse, but that is the first opening. "Hear us, *sqələbčəxʷ*. *kʷt* is almost like saying "Hear us!" We are appealing to an almighty creature, but we don't name him. We just say, "Hear us. We are your people. Hear the people, and there were no other people but us. We are the people." That is where the first opening says *sqələbčəxʷ ʔačiƚtalbixʷ*. After we get around the longhouse, and the verse is repeated several times, then we continue on. We sing the other songs. Actually, we sing the same song through, except the words change. It is the same melody, but the words are different.

The next song refers to a visitor who is coming, because in our songs we mention *yùbəčtiya*, which means the King Salmon. *yùbəčtiya*. This is the King Salmon, and we sing that as we go out of the longhouse and down to the beach.[2]

Then when we get back to the longhouse we have speeches. Our people always had speeches. We had Morris Dan from La Conner and Stan Jones, our tribal board chairman. They explain what the ceremony would be. It is a thanksgiving or the giving of thanks of a tribe. Thanksgiving dinner is an American Indian tradition. So these Indians also have what we call giving thanks.

I used to hear my parents and grandparents talking every year about the salmon coming back. Indians used to do ceremonies every year with the first salmon runs. They had their big gatherings. It is more like a tribal thing. The song is for everybody: small children, older people, the whole tribe—everybody. Now that I think about it, I was the one who brought the Salmon Ceremony back to our people. The ceremony was something for the Indians to look forward to and to go to, because the salmon runs came back every year in the spring and summer runs: Chinook, silver, dog salmon.

---

2   Everyone goes down to the beach to welcome the canoe and the young men, who bring in a king salmon that is then carried into the longhouse resting on cedar boughs and on a small platform with handles.

Indians were thankful for all of the runs of salmon. I remember my father saying, "Just supposing some day they never come back? There wouldn't be much to eat."

The Indians used to smoke-dry the salmon by the basketsful. My mother had a smoke house to smoke-dry salmon by the great big basketsful. They were prepared the same way. They were filleted open and kept open by little sticks of cedar and hung up. I remember my mother, she would be working. We would have something like 500 or 600 salmon all dried and that would last us all through the winter and spring. My mother would have baskets of them to give to a number of elderly people because they can't do that anymore. They can't fillet a whole lot of salmon anymore. We used to dry the salmon eggs too. I remember eating salmon eggs and they stick to your teeth. I remember my father saying, "Just chew it real good."

My Song: The Song of the Mountain Woman

I sing my song at the Salmon Ceremony, as I said, in the longhouse and on other occasions. I remember my mother telling me when she was sick (the last time she was sick), a day or so before she died, "Don't ever let a year go by without singing that song. Sing it at least once in the longhouse or in some celebration in La Conner."

The song I sing—should I say, my song—is the song of the Mountain Woman. It is the vision of a woman coming from the mountains, who first appeared to one of my great-grandparents, the one my father named me after [Hialth]. But I never saw her. I never ever heard the song until I heard it when I was sick.

I was very sick. I caught a cold when I went to Seattle to see Wayne's father. It was bitterly cold, and the boat he worked on came in from Port Townsend, Port Angeles, and Victoria, B.C. I got there in the afternoon and I went walking down a bitterly cold street to the Colman dock. I was already feeling sick. I came home and I could not get up the next day, and I had a high fever. So a bad cold turned into pneumonia and pleurisy, and that was when I heard this song.

I was very sick, but I could hear Wayne say something. He was a year and a half old, and I could hear him, sometimes, crying a couple of times, and my mother taking care of him. Dr. Howard came all of the way from Everett. He was a good friend of my father. They met each other in 1890 when they were about the same age. The road between here and Marysville was miles longer than it is now—a winding road full of ruts—but he came in the evenings to see me. Wayne's father told me afterwards that Dr. Howard told my folks he didn't know whether or not I was going to get well. "She is very sick." Wayne's father said that every morning my father and mother walked out to the woods (because this road wasn't there), where they would weep and cry because they thought I was going to die.

All I remember about those awful days was trying to breathe, with that pneumonia and pleurisy. It didn't dawn on me until sometime afterwards that it was the hardest time of my life. It was so hard to breathe in such shallow breaths. My fever was high. The doctor was an outstanding physician and surgeon. Dr. Howard gave me medicine every few hours; it cleared up the fluids that were in my lungs. Pneumonia was a killer all those years ago because they didn't have the medicines, such as antibiotics, that they have today. I went through days and days of high fever. The doctor came, but the days went by, and it didn't seem as though I could see anything—everything looked grayish. I could vaguely see my mother come in and give me some soup or broth, eggnog or something.

One morning, early, everybody was asleep, but somebody would always sit by my bed and stay with me all night. That time it was my father. I had a dream. I was in my dream, but it just seemed so real. I was standing just about in the middle of a bay somewhat similar to Tulalip Bay, but not really like it exactly. It was a bigger bay, although it looked like my home—a bay in Puget Sound with islands and green trees—but it all looked farther away. I was standing in the middle of this strange bay, and the wind started to blow, and it just as rapidly built up into a raging storm. The waves began to come into the beach where I was standing, and the water began to look really black, and it had whitecaps—rolling waves that were white up on top—and the sky was very dark and black. Dark, dark clouds were rolling across the bay. I was looking around the whole bay, and I found out I was alone. I looked in back of me, I turned around and looked all around this whole place where I was all alone. I could see myself. I looked small and, hanging on the back of my shoulders, I had my shawl, the one my father bought me, a pretty plaid shawl.

As I watched, these big black waves came in, and they turned into what looked like alligators or crocodiles: very big lizards with their mouths wide, wide open. Their teeth were what was white on the waves, and they were rolling right in almost at my feet. As I say, I looked all over. The wind was shrieking and whistling. I was very frightened. After I had looked all over and I didn't see anybody, I thought, maybe this is where I die. Those awful animals are going to crawl out of the water, and they are going to kill me. As I was looking all around, then I heard the drum beat. It seemed to come from up in the sky. I could hear it so plainly. Then I heard this song, and I started to sing it and I started to dance up and down the beach. I said to myself, "Nothing is going to frighten me. If this is where I die, I will meet it like my grandparents always said: 'Whatever happens, you meet death with bravery and dignity.'" So, I thought, this is what I have—bravery and dignity.

But I started to dance because of the drum. It got louder. I was dancing like I always dance. I had my arms out, because it seemed as though I was also to pacify these awful, awful animals that were rolling in on these waves. As far as I could see, the whole bay, all of Puget Sound, was covered with those black animals: huge things with white teeth and their mouths wide open. I started to dance, and as I was going up and down the beach, I felt as though I was as light as a feather. I was dancing, and I stopped and looked across the bay, and I looked at my feet. Those awful animals had turned into leaves and wild flowers that were scattered along the shore. At the time, I didn't say "Oh, wild flowers," because I didn't realize then. No. I looked and I thought, "It's not something that is dangerous." I could keep on dancing, and I could hear the song. The drums were getting louder, but I was still all alone, and the drums were still beating, and I was feeling better as I was dancing. Then, I woke up.

My father was sitting beside my bed. He was holding my hand and he was watching me. He had both of his hands on my one hand. He was holding me quite firmly. As soon as I woke up, he said (of course, he was talking in our own language), "You're awake now?" *Kʼlowtʼču*. It was halfway like a question: "You're awake now?" I said, "Yes, I'm awake. I had a dream. I was dancing on a beach all alone. The drums were beating, and they were coming from somewhere, it seems like from the sky, but I couldn't really sing the song that I heard. I was gasping. I kind of remembered the melody, and I started to sing it, gasping along, but I didn't finish it. My father picked it up. He started to sing it the way he heard it. He was still holding my hand. He said, "Oh, you are going to get well. That's going to be your *sqəlalitut*. Now you'll remember. That is going to give you the courage to live for a long, long time." Live right. They always used the word "right." Live right for a long time.

A year or two later, I sang that song in La Conner in the longhouse—the old, old longhouse. I think their longhouse is older than ours, I mean at Tulalip. My father said he used to hear that song when he was small. He hadn't thought about it for years and years until I tried to sing it. Then he remembered that he had heard it when he was very, very small. But he couldn't remember where he heard it. It must have been in the longhouse in Skykomish, because he used to be there quite a bit. Anyway, I sang that song in La Conner. Way back then, I could get around. I always went around the room. I remember my folks saying, "You stop at every corner of the longhouse." The song stops; then you start your song again. My mother and my father said that that was what he heard when he was so little. My father said the Indians from way up the Skykomish River would come down here and sing.[3] The first song they sang was my great-grandmother's song. Then the whole longhouse of Indians would sing her song. My father called it a blessing on the entire longhouse. So, that is my song.

My song is going around quite a bit. I've met some Indians, men and women, from Spaulding, Idaho, who said they heard that song in the Miss American Indian program in Sheridan, Wyoming—a big Indian gathering that is very well known among Indians. Tribes come there from all over, even from Mexico. They said, "If you ever want to see the most beautiful costumes, it is the Mexican Indians." I think those people, Mexicans, came to Albuquerque for an Indian gathering. They didn't get there very often. These people from Sheridan said they knew my song. They said, "We heard your song." The girls from Yakama went around a meeting at the longhouse. Then I heard my song; it was sung by a Yakama woman in Seattle and her two girls. I said, "Oh my!" It was pretty much my song! They are not supposed to do that—sing a person's song without their permission—but the Yakama do. It isn't nice to say, but you hear a lot about it.

I sang my song quite a bit at Treaty Day time. I sing that song every time I go into the longhouse, or wherever the Indians are, they ask me to sing it. I sing it at the Salmon Ceremony and on Treaty Day, shall we say, for the Indians who are putting it on, managing it; they ask me to sing. Of course, all of these Indians here on this reservation know that song. My mother and the others said that it is the song of the Mountain Woman because it came from way up the Skykomish River, from my father's father's people. I think that is kind of interesting. Their longhouse was the farthest one up. Its name had something to do with ferns, like a fern glade or a hillside or something to do with ferns, and it must have been a certain kind of fern because we

---

3   According to Elizabeth Shelton, Harriette Dover's aunt, the Skykomish were high-class Snohomish Indians who moved from Hiboɫb, their village at Legion Park in Everett, to the mountains in the Skykomish River area (Tweddell 1953).

have a couple of varieties of ferns. My mother said, "Don't let the year go by without singing that song. You be sure and sing it."

The Skykomish, Snoqualmie, Nisqually, Swinomish, and Snohomish languages are all pretty much the same. There are differences, but I could always understand them when I was little. They still say I'm from a different tribe of people. My people came from way up the Skykomish River—or part of them did. My grandmother, my father's mother, her people came from ibʷ;b and also dʼəʷadx̌, or Possession Point. They are divided up according to the way they are married. I remember when Indians came to visit, and they stayed with us a year or more. They would help with things. The women washed dishes, cooked, mended, sewed, and scrubbed floors. The men went out to hunt or sawed wood, just for the family.

Once in my life I've been way up on the Skykomish River. It is beautiful country. I remember my mother saying the most beautiful songs came from those people—the Skykomish people from up that river. They had majestic scenery. My father's father's guardian spirit songs came from there, and once in a while I have seen pictures of their mountain places. Of course, they might also call them mountain hunters. Hunting in the mountains, my father said, was different from hunting on Whidbey Island, where our people used to go. The Snohomish Tribe used to go with the Skykomish, too—way up into the mountains for mountain sheep. My mother always called them mountain sheep. Of course, I never really knew there were also mountain goats. They looked the same to me until I saw them on television. Where would I see them? I wouldn't be hunting up in the mountains! The Skykomish River is really beautiful.

Ezra Meeker, in his book *Pioneer Reminiscences,* talked about hearing canoeloads of Indians singing in different parts of the Puget Sound. You could hear them from far away—a couple of miles or more. They came over the water at sunset or any time during the day. Indians kept time singing as they went paddling along during reasonably happy times. Then they didn't sing anymore. By that time, they were moving onto reservations, where they were supposed to be learning the white man's ways and being Christianized.

I guess you might say people of all places—even working people—have pressures on them. Also, from the time you are little, from your church or whatever, you have to learn the precepts of your church, and then you have to struggle through school. My father said that was one of the reasons Indians of Puget Sound and western Washington had young people search for a guardian spirit all through the teenage years. It gives the young people a goal and an ideal to work toward. I don't know how the young Indians of today are.

I remember my parents talking about how scattered we are. Our tribe is no longer living in one place together. We are miles and miles apart. Living miles apart you don't feel that you are neighbors. We all know how troubled we are. I used to hear the Indians the few times they had meetings. They would talk, one speaker after another, and would always encourage each other. They knew we are all cousins and together. I think the young people don't feel that way today. We no longer have our Indian language to unite us.

Now our people don't know our children. I never see who the children are who live near Quilceda Creek, for instance. They wouldn't know me from anybody else. I am just unknown. We don't have the loving interest, loving care for one another, that we used to have. It is all gone. All forgotten. Some of our Indian boys and girls who are in junior high school are quite discouraged, almost mixed up. They don't want to go to school because the white children call them names, and they don't like it. They would rather drop out of school than to keep going. When they drop out in the eighth or ninth grade, then they aren't prepared for any kind of work except laboring or work in the fields.

Wayne was telling me to write something to encourage the young people, and we could put it in our tribal paper. I think about it, then I don't do it. I remember my parents and everybody would talk about how scattered we are. We live miles apart from one another. We don't feel we are members. Although we feel we are tribal members. When I was little we would have tribal meetings, one speaker after another, and we would encourage one another. They would emphasize that we are all cousins. We are together. But I think the young people of today don't feel it that much. We no longer have our Indian language to unite us. That's what I was going to do. I wanted to tape record Book 1 or Book 2 of Professors Hess and Vi Hilbert's book. It is the Skagit language, but it is like this language; although some of the words are different. I thought of reading them page by page. I think Vi did do that, but Wayne said he couldn't understand her. One of our young people at the tribal office was trying to read that book—the book of Indian language—and he is rather far off since he is listening to Vi and her pronunciation is not understandable here.

Indian Healing

One of my father's uncles was an Indian doctor.[4] My father's father's people were born in Skykomish in a longhouse, the one that is farthest up the Skykomish River. We used to know the name of it. The name had something to do with ferns—like a fern glade. It must have been a certain kind of fern because we have a couple of varieties of ferns.

In all of American history, shall we say, or even local state history, Indian doctors did not have a good image. When I was a little girl in an Indian boarding school, I used to get frightened because some of the girls talked about Indian doctors. They said, "You have to be sure you walk properly in front of them, or they will look at you in a certain way and you are going to get sick and you are going to die. They can do that to you." Well, that used to frighten me.

My father told me when I was fourteen years old, "Don't be frightened of him, an Indian doctor. If you are frightened, you will weaken yourself; so always remember you are brave and strong." Even in the last fifteen years, I have heard people talking about Indian doctors: "Oh, you better not be doing anything wrong when you are around them." Those people would really terrify you, but it is mostly talk. Gossip is really all it is. It gets talked out.

I don't know whether to talk about them. As I say, the Indian doctors had a bad image. My mother was the last one I know of who said my father's uncle was a very good Indian doctor. If he was asked to heal, he could. My father remembered a boy his uncle healed. An Indian boy about four or five years old ate wild blackberries where his family was camped in the Puyallup Valley to pick hops in the summer. They used to tell us when we were little, "Don't gulp the berries down. Look at the berry when you pick it off. It might have some grass seeds, and there are certain kinds of grass seeds that, if you swallow them, will get stuck in your throat. It won't go down, and you can't get it back up." So we always looked at them very carefully to see that everything was off of the blackberry. I guess this little Indian boy ate the blackberry without looking. His mother and others tried to get it out with their fingers. Somebody tried to help him. The boy cried and cried and was frightened. The people said, "We better get a real doctor, a white man doctor." They said there was one somewhere in the valley. So somebody went on horseback, and the doctor finally got there. He looked at the little boy,

---

4   Shaman.

looked in his throat. That little boy was just so tired; the doctor tried to use something to get it out, and he started to bleed. So then the little boy was crying and crying. Then the people were sick with worry. There they were in a hop field, and the doctor left and the little boy was in a bad way.

Somebody there knew my great-uncle was an Indian doctor, and they came to ask him if he would come and see what he could do to help the little boy. He talked first. He said, "I will try, but I want you to know that if the white doctor has already looked at him and said there is nothing he could do, I don't know what I could do. But I will try." He got ready and went to the camp of migratory workers. A lot of people were standing around the boy. He was very, very sick—so weak. He had cried so much, and the mother also cried. My great-uncle had some of his people with him, and, of course, they had seen him before and heard of him, but at times like this, the women always left. The women left the place; just the men remained, and the drums beat. The doctor, first of all, began his work by concentrating. My great-uncle reached over and took the little boy and put his mouth to this little boy's mouth and sucked very hard. In our language that is called *utuʔtt*. The grass came right out of his throat. So my great-uncle took it (they had a basin of water) and put it in there. Of course, they sang some more to help the little boy and to kind of soothe his head and chest and arms. My great-uncle said to let him gargle with some Indian herbs. There was nothing wrong with the little boy the next day. He was running around.

The Indian doctor just thought about it and certainly did something no white doctor would do. My great-uncle said they get paid a lot, but he wasn't expecting anything because he was not the first doctor they called. He probably got one or two horses. It took them a long time to get those horses over here. You have to come through a little narrow trail over Snoqualmie Pass.

Way back then, Indian doctors could do several things besides just posing. Of course, my mother thought I was talking about things nobody talks about. Nobody really knows about this; this is just, shall we say, family history. When my father and mother were living during the 1890s, they were sort of newly married in a way. That is a funny way to put it! They were young. My mother already had a son; he was twelve or thirteen years old. He was in the Mission School. His name is Hubert Coy. (My mother liked the name Hubert. Nobody else liked it. He hated the name. He had everybody call him Herb.) But he was in the schoolroom and he got sick. Then the whole Mission School had an epidemic. My mother and father called it "remittent fever." I don't know what it was, but it was a real killer.

Hardly anyone lived. The Indian boys and girls in the school who got it died day by day. They did two funerals a day. When he got sick, they notified my mother, and some others went to see him. He was in the sickroom in the old mission. There was another boy dying, because they had screens around him. My mother and father went to see him and he was very sick, because the next day the screens were around him, too. They told my mother and father he wasn't going to live; he was just too sick. My mother stayed there, of course. She said the rosary; that is what she leaned on. She knelt by his bed, and the Sister Superior stayed with her. My father told her, "I'm going to go down to Spibida and get my uncle and see what he can do." My mother said for him to go and to please try. My father paddled his canoe as fast as he could go down to Spibida and found his uncle and told him his stepson was dying.

He had another uncle. My father and some other cousins, several families—quite a lot of Indian people, in fact—were living there. They all got together in a little Indian home, and the uncle prepared his drums and the song that goes along, his guardian spirit song. Then he stops drumming and singing, and he concentrates. He is thinking. I have seen them. Their eyes close. They are thinking. Then he started to talk, and he said my brother must have been playing where there are graves. Nobody knew there were graves there, but the children had been jumping and running all over.

My mother said she was kneeling by the bed and looking at Hubert. He was covered with perspiration, and he wasn't talking anymore. He had stopped talking the day before. He hardly knew when the sisters came in to wipe his face with cool water. My mother was saying the rosary on her knees with Sister Superior with her, and she said Hubert opened his eyes, and he looked around the room. He saw her, and he said, "I want some dried salmon. I'm hungry." She was praying. My father said he was way down there in Spibida with the uncle who was concentrating and kneeling on his knees.

They always sat in a certain way. The Indian doctors had a way of sitting. He started to talk, and that was what he said, "The Indian children were running around over some old graves way out of the school grounds." In fact, they probably just ran away. He said, "I will do what I can." They do that, you know. It is as if they are gathering up the spirits or the feelings of the person who is sick. Because sickness is sort of spread around like that, and that was what the uncle did, and my father stayed there with him. The uncle said, "He will be all right."

My father had been gone for three or four hours, and by the time he got back, Hubert was awful weak. After those first few words, he didn't say much more—only that he wanted some dried salmon. He remembered that, too. He was talking about it when he was almost eighty years old. He just loved dried salmon. We all did. He was talking about being sick in the Catholic school and dispensary and asking for dried salmon. Of course, it was a nice clean dispensary, but he would just eat it with his hands. Of course, he didn't get it. I think they just gave him some broth.

Indian Shaker Healing

I always believed in Indian Shakers for healing, such as Mr. and Mrs. Lamont—those two people. We had them when my grandson was very sick. I remember my mother said Martha was the last one, and my father said that, too. They had such good "helps,"[5] when they were all praying, and they were singing and keeping time with the bells—what they called "working on you," "working on a patient," working on someone who has come to the Shaker Church and asked for help. Quite a lot of them will concentrate on one or two people. I always had a good feeling about Martha and Levi. They came to our house, and all of us were loaded with grief over the sickness of my grandchild. But when they pray and sing and ring the bells, it gives you a feeling that you are really being helped. They had what we referred to as "spiritual power" when they touched me or touched Wayne.

I had the same kind of feeling with what we always called an Indian doctor. They sing, they concentrate, and they sing their guardian spirit song, or *sqəlalitut*, and the drums beat, and they lay their hands on the head or shoulders or arms of a person they have come to see.

When our cousins, Martha and Levi, helped me the first time, they said that some *sqəlalitut*, guardian spirits, follow Wayne and me around. They are around me and around William. William was in high school at the time. He didn't know much about that kind of thing, because he said "Eeee!" He wondered if he could see them. If he could just feel it. It should give you confidence if you know there are guardian spirits that stay with you and take care of you, keep you from injury.

I remember the time Martha and Levi were "helping" Wayne. When they first began, they stood close by. Martha was standing close to where Wayne was sitting. The song and the concentration go on for some time. Then Martha moved in, touching him, and it turned her halfway around.

---

5   Spiritual ability or power.

It was interesting. Nobody would believe it. Just as she was going to touch Wayne—she went just like that—and it hurled her around. She was an older woman, and she had arthritis so she never moved around that much. She knew that the guardian spirits were around Wayne, but as she moved in close to help, then she remembered and she saw them.

I remember Wayne afterwards said, "That was a nice feeling to know there are friendly guardian spirits around you that are always helping you." Of course, a psychologist would say that is one way of giving a person confidence. Very few families in this tribe, it seemed, had a guardian spirit song that was owned by one family and was called a family totem. My father and the others talked and said they knew about it, but nobody talked about it during all of those years. When they were reminiscing and telling about it, they never thought about it either; just that they had known that this guardian spirit went around sometimes. My father said that that spirit would be far away; it seems to travel around the world. I used to know the spirit song for that animal. I can't remember it now. I think Wayne has a recording of it. I was remembering some of the songs that went with it, different ones of our people, I mean, of my family. It seems to me Wayne was asking me several months ago, and I couldn't remember it. He has it on a tape somewhere. He can't remember where it is. Maybe he knows. He probably does.

It seems to me one of the last times I beat the drum I remember singing it all by myself. I don't know if you would call it a song exactly. It was what we call songs; perhaps they are more like chants. Maybe someone who studied music would have something to say about it. It seems to me I remembered and Professor Olsen[6] took a tape of it, and, like I always say, one person singing out an Indian song is not something a lot of people would want to listen to. If there are several Indians—a hundred Indians—singing the same song, then it is really impressive.

I always feel as though it is only two or three years since our cousins Levi and Martha passed away. I miss them. I was telling Wayne I really need them, because I didn't realize how much their ceremonials in our house made me feel better. I don't think I would have that much confidence in anyone else.

Some of the Catholics were very devout, and they looked upon the Shakers as not Christian. They had been "brainwashed" to think that anything Indian was sinful. The Shakers established themselves and went ahead, espe-

---

6   Loran Olsen, a music professor (now emeritus) at Washington State University.

cially in walking around the room together in a circle[7]—that was not done in the Catholic Church I ever saw. But the Shakers seemed to have put together some of the old Indian ways or culture and something from the white man's Christian religion into the Shaker Church. When I was little, the Shakers did some remarkable healing. My father said, "What do you think can help you a lot? What you think about yourself? If you get sick, you could almost pull yourself through just by telling yourself how strong you are and that 'I've got to get over this. I've got to live.'" Of course, that is from his Indian teaching: what you have in your mind, you pretty much believe it will help you.

There are songs in the Shaker Church that we would call Indian guardian spirit songs. But when the Shakers talked to my father, they said, "No, they are not." Some of those songs—the words that were given to them—are different and apply to the church. The Shaker teachings are to give you strength. They do what they called "the work." When they are all gathering in the church, they know what to say to each other, that there is "work" to do tonight. Somebody is "joining" the church, or somebody has been sick or is sick. They put two, three, or four chairs out in the middle, facing toward their altar, for the sick people to sit on.[8] I saw another Shaker Church at La Conner with an altar like that. It had a big cross placed up on the wall. Smaller crosses were placed along the walls around the room where they had a lot of candles.

They sing Indian songs, but they never used the drums. They used bells—quite large silver or brass ones about five inches in diameter or so. Some of them are bigger; some are smaller. Bells, with the handles, were all laid on the altar at the beginning of the service. These bells keep time to the music like a whole lot of drums. Then there are certain ones who ring the bells, one in each hand. On Sunday nearly all of them would wear long white robes[9] that are quite loose; almost what you might think angels would wear, with big loose sleeves. The women were what I noticed.

You could identify the Shakers by their songs, but not individually. All of those I heard were pretty much like those we heard in the longhouse. I heard them in La Conner. I heard them in Lummi. I didn't think there were that many in Lummi, but there are. I used to listen to Martha and Levi Lamont.

---

7   Counterclockwise.

8   The altar is called a "prayer table" and is always placed on the east wall of the room or the church.

9   The garment also has a medium blue appliqué of a cross stitched on the chest area.

Those two people were with the Shaker Church right from the beginning, and did all of the things the Church members did, such as carrying a candle in the service. Quite a lot of the Shakers carried candles through the night in certain parts of the ceremony, and they went around the whole room with it. Levi said the flame of the candle had symbolic significance to all of them.

I've seen Shakers doing remarkable work in helping alcoholics and very sick people. Some of our people right here who never were sober joined the church, and they stopped drinking. Others were not feeling well or were getting over being sick, and that is what the Shakers called "the work." While the song went on, bells rang; they put their hands on your head and they stamp their feet on the floor, producing a heavy drumlike sound, and it just goes all throughout the church, the walls, the floor. You could feel it even in your heartbeat. People went up to the front and sat in the chairs for healing, for help and prayer. When they "worked on" somebody, quite a number of them, one, two, three, four, would put their hands on the head, forehead, shoulders, arms of whoever wants to be helped. They "brush" the whole body, all of the way down—a very gentle touch—to your lap, clear to the ends the fingers and clear to the end of your feet to take away the sorrow, the pain, the sickness. It is a vibration that I think is quite healing. Then the Shakers put their hands on them, on the sides of their heads, and they make a sweeping motion across the chest and down the arms, and clear to the ends of the fingers and to the end of their feet to take away the sorrow, the pain. Some one or two of them did that to me. I often thought that kind of very soft touch, which is so gentle you can hardly feel it, really has a calming effect. I think the vibrations are quite healing. It makes you feel calm, and you feel like somebody is praying over you, and they are helping you. It gives you a good feeling. It gives you courage.

Some of them carry white handkerchiefs; and when they go around the church room, all of them line up and go around the whole church in a big circle keeping time with their feet. Of course, everybody sings the songs. The bells ring on and on, like a lot of drumbeats. They went around the room in a certain direction, to the right of the door, following one another; going to the right and around the room has something to do with how the sun goes around the earth. It is like a slow march except they are keeping time with the beat of the bells. The floor is vibrating, and people stand up all over the church. The Shakers go by, and they touch your hand to greet you, to let you know that they have a close feeling of brotherhood or sisterhood with you, and you are welcome. You are one of them. I remember we used to go and stand up and hold up our hands, and they came by, each one of them, and touched our hands. You hold up your right hand. They go by in a march or a dance—keeping time—a slow dance, not moving very fast, but around the whole room, and they touch everybody's hand with their right hand, anyone who is standing up with their hand out. They do that at the very beginning and at the end, too, as a farewell to everyone.

They did some remarkable work with alcoholics. Way back then, there weren't any who "backslid." Today, the Shaker Church members are all very young people. I have not been there recently. Quite a number of young people have joined the Shaker faith. Of course, they are not supposed to drink alcohol of any kind.

They all seemed to be so friendly toward each other and visitors who came. I used to go too, and we like to go to the Catholic Church because that is where my mother went. The Catholic Church seemed so quiet and stately. The Shakers were friendlier, shaking everybody's hand, and they used to have big dinners.

I wonder how far they have spread. It is mostly in the Pacific Northwest, and it has spread quite a ways, I think. I don't know how far, but I think there were Shakers in northern California and over east of the mountains and in parts of Oregon. I haven't seen the whole complete thing perhaps. I have been to their church so many times with my father and mother, because they used to invite my father to come. They were mostly along here in Washington, partly along the Oregon coast and northern California.[10] I remember the Indians from here used to go to California for the convention. It is interesting how it spread. Some people in Neah Bay are Shakers. They didn't go to powwows. I think the last several years on the reservation they came to the longhouse. It seems to me I used to hear that they wouldn't go into a longhouse because they believed it was a place of devils.

In the longhouse they walked to the right of the door and all the way around, shaking hands with everybody, and that is what the Shakers did. Only with them, they sang their certain songs and kept time, not with drums, but with their bells.[11] All of the way around, and all of the people stand up, even if they are visitors, members, whatever. You get a feeling of close brotherhood and sisterhood.

---

10 They also have churches in British Columbia, eastern Washington, and eastern Oregon.

11 And by stamping their feet.

Sq̓ʷədiličʼ are the spirit boards. About ten years ago or more, they had *sq̓ʷədiličʼ* down here at the longhouse. It was the first time I had seen *sq̓ʷədiličʼ* for, I don't know, years and years.

Years ago, when I was in high school, we used to go to the longhouse in La Conner. As soon as we got off our cars, they were all together, my father and those people started beating the drums, and they all sang the same song. We would be outside the door, quite a few steps away. There were always people outside, too, shaking hands to the time of the drum. When the longhouse singers hear our drums and hear our song, they know who we are. They say, "Here come the Snohomish."

I just happened to be sick one time when they had the gatherings in the longhouse, because that time I was there and I was talking with somebody, and I said I didn't know he—Kenny Moses—had a guardian spirit of *sq̓ʷədiličʼ*. *sq̓ʷədiličʼ* are used in the longhouse; they are spirit boards. Tommy Bob in La Conner used to have the *sq̓ʷədiličʼ* boards—the two medicine boards. After my father died in 1938, Tommy sang my father's and my uncle's guardian spirit songs. I hadn't seen *sq̓ʷədiličʼ* for years. The *sq̓ʷədiličʼ* went to some man or woman across the hall from me. They came to me, and I thought, "Oh, dear!" I had just said I didn't know that he had *sq̓ʷədiličʼ*. It sounded so good and was really so nice to see and hear again. It stopped right in front of me and moved in very slowly, right straight at me, about three feet away. Of course, there are several hundred Indian people sitting there. I got so scared. One of the young men helping to carry it looked at me, and I could see in his eyes that they don't see anything. They are not looking at any individual Indian.

The *sq̓ʷədiličʼ* moved in; it touched my face very gently. I was just getting over a cold and I had severe headaches. It seemed as though my sinus trouble was worse. Then, the *sq̓ʷədiličʼ*—the other one—also came, stopped, moved around in small circles, moved into someone, and then they touched me very carefully, softly on my arm.[12] One of the young men carrying the *sq̓ʷədiličʼ* said, "Stand up." Of course, the drums were beating and you could hardly hear people talking. So I stood up, and the one who owned the *sq̓ʷədiličʼ* power came walking over in my general direction, and he said, "Move out." So, I moved out about six feet. The *sq̓ʷədiličʼ* moved around my face, both sides of my head, and touched me very lightly so that I could barely feel it. Then

---

12 The boards are "run" in pairs. For more on the medicine boards, see Haeberlin and Gunther 1930; Wike 1951.

it moved over my shoulders and down to the end of my arms very slowly; and as Levi and Martha were saying, it was just helping me.

My mother had died about three or four months before. I used to hold my mother, sit her up, to take medication.[13] Levi and Martha said, "It is helping you so that you don't break down about your mother." People get weak, physically weaker, if they are crying all of the time or mourning somebody's death.

Levi and Martha came and helped me, just us alone, of course, at our home. They say the obvious things, such as, "Your mother would have liked to take you along with her." You have to have something like a sweeping motion to wipe away the feeling, the remembrance of my mother, whatever you are mourning for. I thought that is nice. I remember my father said there is a time for mourning, for weeping for the people who have died, but you must not allow yourself to be absolutely broken down. Once in a while, if people have other children or a close relative die, they almost abandon their children or their family just thinking about their own grief. Of course, my father said, "Don't do that. Don't. There is a time for grief."

Way back in our old days, there were several days in our tribe where it was time for mourning. Of course, it includes taking the cold baths and long walks along the beaches. The cold baths in the morning are the time to weep and cry, because if you cry and cry through the day, then the members of your family will be affected, and their grief is worse. What if somebody else gets sick? I think this is a very nice psychology. One person can upset a whole household with their grief. My father said that was part of their teachings—the Indians—part of my father and mother's teachings. There is a time for grief. There were several things they used to say, and they would repeat them again another time: you shouldn't eat too much; you shouldn't drink too much; you shouldn't sleep too much; and you shouldn't grieve too much. Of course, if you eat too much you will be in trouble because you will put on too much weight!

I had the same kind of feeling as the Shakers when we called an Indian doctor. When they sing, they concentrate and sing their guardian spirit song. The drums beat, and they lay their hands on the head or shoulders or arms of the person they came to see. After my mother died, I had my cousin

---

13 In class Mrs. Dover told us that her mother was hospitalized and had several intravenous lines; she removed them and took her mother home to die. After her mother died, she bathed her in water that contained flower petals.

Morris come to this house.[14] I remember the evening after they did their healing ceremony, Isadore Tom walked in.[15] He was walking slowly, and he stopped here and there and looked at the baskets. Morris just happened to be talking, and Isadore said, "It seems like this lady has lost something." He went around very slowly and stopped. I don't think I ever told him that I had turned things: see how all of these papers and things piled on the table are filed away scientifically?

I had been looking for a small tintype picture of my father's uncle. He was a very important uncle to my father. His English name was Tyee William. His Indian name was Stišayɫ. He was also called Steshail or Stishayl. I have never been able to find that picture. I start out looking on that table and I get so far, then I'm all tired out. I've moved piles of papers and things, and then I would forget what I was looking for and find something else, and I'd get too tired. But I've never ever located that tintype again. He came to see me in 1904 on the day I was supposed to be born, but I came the next day. He was at the treaty signing in Mukilteo in January 1855. My father and his generation said that is the only picture that was taken of that generation of Indians when they were at the treaty signing.

My father talked to Stišayɫ about what he thought about the photo. Nearly all of the Indians refused to have their picture taken. They weren't sure what the camera was. A camera always looks black, and the camera man was covered up when he took the pictures. A cameraman like that always goes through so many motions; he will tell the subject how to stay or stand or sit. "Please stay there and be very still." The Indians had never seen things like that. But Stišayɫ must have gone into a studio in Everett or maybe Seattle. I can't remember. It couldn't have been Everett. Oh, I guess it could have been. I think Everett was incorporated as a township or a city in 1890 or 1891, and our uncle was still living then. He was still living when I was born in 1904, but I don't remember him. Sometime I will look around again. I think it would be something if we had a picture of even just one person who was there.

I went up on the hill of the Tulalip cemetery, where my great-uncle Stišayɫ

---

14 Morris Dan, Swinomish Tribe in La Conner.
15 A renowned healer and spiritualist from the Lummi Tribe who is now deceased.

was buried. All he had was a big wooden cross with his name carved on it. Sometime after that, the cross decayed and fell apart, because now I am not too sure where my great-uncle is buried. As I said, we had a tintype, a picture of him. He was a very devout Catholic, and he had a black velvet ribbon around his neck, with a large cross that hung on his chest. The cross was given to him by Father Chirouse. My father had a picture enlarged of his uncle, from the tintype.

Just before my father died in 1938, Mrs. Hardwick did a painting of him, and when she finished it, she said she would make another one and give it to us. She did that long after my father died. She took the picture of my father's uncle. I thought about the picture, and when my father died I said something to her. She wrote and said she had it, and I knew she did. But she got sick and died suddenly, and her husband didn't know where my great-uncle's picture was. He said a lot of her paintings and things were put into a warehouse with her other furniture. He said he would go through them, but he couldn't tell what kind of a picture it was. I tried to tell him.

I think Stišayɫ was a very disappointed man when he saw how the reservation was and how the Indian people were living, and how the laws and regulations had become more strict. I remember my mother and father talking about how for years and years the Indian agents used to be very strict about Indians leaving the reservation. They had to go to the agency and tell the agent where they were going and how long they would be gone. During the Chief Joseph War in 1876, 1877, my folks said they had to stay on the reservation. Nobody was to go off because some of these Indians would go off on their canoes to Whidbey Island to hunt or to dig clams. The reservation here was too small for their hunting and fishing. There wasn't much to eat and definitely no fish. A revenue cutter, a U.S. launch (by that time they had steel engines), would stop the Indians and the captain would say you have to go back. You can't go any place. My mother remembered that, she was older than my father; they were ordered to go back to Guemes Island. So that was another time of great worry for the Indians. My father was growing up on Whidbey Island. He was born there.

So, these Indians used to leave the reservation at night. I heard my father and his generation talk about how well suited our canoes are. They could go right up in the shallow water and move along with people paddling them. Those canoes moved with paddle power. A canoe could move along for miles without making a sound because the paddlers didn't take their paddles out of the water. You could just turn your paddle and move your canoe ahead and keep moving without taking the paddles out of the water. I was thirteen or fourteen years old when I said, "Let's do that. I want to hear it." Well, you can't hear anything. They move along very quietly.

Two of my father's canoes are in our yard at home. We used the smaller one when I was growing up. Now that I think about it, every weekend, spring, summer, and fall, there were several canoe loads of us who went to the islands. It must have been a very nice feeling for my parents and grandparents to go someplace in the canoes again.

We dug clams at certain times of the year—in later summer. My mother and the women dried the big horse clams. They must have another name than horse clams. They were real delicious to eat. I asked some white people from Whidbey Island if there were still those large horse clams around Langley, but not right at Langley. We used to have so much fun, my sister and some of us children. We located some of those clams, and you have to be real fast because they are in the sand. They can move fast and go straight down into three feet of sand. We used to have so much fun. We would try to grab them as we were tiptoeing around, and we thought they couldn't hear or feel anything. Those things can go down so fast, and they are very strong. My father would come (he had a shovel) and shovel them out. How about that? I thought that was real fun. That was one time we could laugh out loud. We would be calling for my father to come and help us. The people near Langley said the horse clams had pretty much disappeared, because of water pollution, I guess.

I have never seen those things they call geoducks, great big clams. It was the white man who started calling them "gooey ducks." These Indians used to go to Hood Canal, where the Skokomish live, for them. "Gooey duck" in our language is almost the same; the same as the white man has spelled "gooey," but in our language it is *gʷidəq*. It must have had that name long ago, *gʷidəq*. In our language, *gʷidəq* means "to call out to somebody, to many people." In our language, we would just say *gʷidəq* and maybe they would say, *səqtiya gʷidəq*, "call your grandmother." The *dəq* refers to many people, not to just one person. I never had an opportunity to see where those things come from. I guess I was in school when they went. If I were years younger, I would get in a car and run around there and talk to people and see where they are.

Pressure of Religion

Once in a while, my son and us Indians talk about not having a choice in our religion. The priest was here, and so we became Catholic. I think the Catholic religion is beautiful. Their Mass was a beautiful thing, because we had to learn the Mass. The priest talked in Latin, but we had prayer books that told on the opposite page what he was saying. In some ways, we could guess what he said. Several times through the Mass he faced the people. He put his hands together and he said "*Dominus Vobiscum*." Finally, after I could read, we learned what he was saying. I remember I was in the fourth grade, and then it dawned on me that it said, "Peace be with you." "God be with you." "Dominus" is God. "*Dominus Vobiscum*." It was like all foreign languages: This is "God" and "in you," and then at the end is "with God," or "God is with you."

I think the Catholic religion has changed in the last ten years. When I got out of Tulalip Indian School in 1922, I vowed and swore I was never going to go to a church again. I was in church all the time. Pray, pray, pray for my miserable soul. I stayed away. I told my mother, "Please don't ask me. I will go on Christmas and Easter." She never said anything. She was kind of broken up, because she went every Sunday. But it wasn't only the Catholics; it was the Protestants also. If you read about the Puritans, about the Mennonites, some groups, or all of them, were just like that one hundred and fifty and two hundred years ago. In all Christian religions you went to church on Sunday, and you pretty much stayed there all day. You sat on hard benches, and you listened to a preacher for a couple of hours telling you how you should live. My mother and I went round and round about it and got no place.

When I think about the pressure of religion on us, it makes me mad. The pressure of religion on us was bad enough, because when you are little, like we were, you were terrified of hell. You know you are going to die, and you are going to go to hell, and you are going to burn forever. I used to be afraid to fall asleep when I was eight or ten years old. All Christian religions were like that: the pressure was really on the Indians. Those poor misguided people. They were bound and determined to save all of our miserable souls.

Thinking of the Bible. We have some legends that tell of the baby who was born. Sometimes it was called the Sky or Star Child. Our legends are a little different for the different tribes. In our legend he became a good hunter. He had a little fur vest, a little coat, and the vest was made of many colors of feathers. I was talking to some white people and I said that is a story that is similar to Joseph and his coat of many colors. But all of those white people said, "Well Mrs. Dover, you can't compare an Indian legend to the Bible. The Bible is an inspired book; it was inspired by the word of God." About fifteen years ago I said to a group of them, "How do you know it was inspired by God. It was written by several men. I think the Bible is certainly a marvelous book. I haven't read it. I have just read parts of it. But sometimes when I read it, I think that is what the Indians used to say but not all of it. In the legend in my father's booklet *Legends of the Totem Pole* he calls it the Legend of the Little Man with the Coat of Many Colors. When that party of white people said I couldn't compare it to the Bible, I said I could compare it, I do compare it. The Bible isn't any more inspired than this is. These legends are old, old, old. They come from what my parents said, my father used to say, was a time in our history of hundreds of years ago, of a time that is like a curtain of fog or mist that covers our past. It is just like in the morning if you look out toward the mountains or over the water there is a mist that drifts; it takes maybe an hour or so before the sun can shine through, and that is what those Indians used to say is the way of the time, our time, when we were on this earth, when we were here; it is like a time that is behind a curtain, a fog, a mist. We have been here a long, long time. We have always been here.

People who proselytize used to come here. There were some here last summer. They knock at the door, and they give you little pamphlets. They were Jehovah's Witnesses. One time, twelve to fifteen years ago, I was still living across the road at my parent's home. Somebody knocked at the door, and there stood a young man and a young lady. They were attractive looking young people. The young man said, "Madam, is your soul saved? Are you a Christian?" I don't know who I was expecting, but I wasn't expecting them. I said to my mother, "There is a young, quiet couple here, and they want to save our souls." She said, "Why don't you ask them to come in?" Of course, she was talking in Indian, in our Snohomish language. I told them, "I don't give a damn about my soul. I want something to eat." I slammed the door. I told my mother. Sometimes I didn't tell her what I said, but I made a mistake and told her that time. She was speechless. She went back to the kitchen, and I went in, too, because I was drinking coffee with her. She never said anything for several minutes. I knew I had made a miserable mistake. I shouldn't have told her. For several years—I think three or four years—nobody came to our house. I guess they gave up. But you can't save people that way. Of course, it jars them up if you don't believe it.

Some Jehovah's Witnesses came up and knocked on my door recently. I just happened to be in the kitchen. I saw them coming. I thought, who could that be? When they knocked, I opened the door. They had their pamphlets with them. I said, "Oh, thank you. You can't do anything with me. I don't believe in it." Everybody knows there is a God, and you do have to confess your sins. Of course, my father always said, "I don't have to confess my sins to anybody. God is my friend." But that isn't what we call him. Dukʷibəł is our Creator, and he is a friend, although he can get mad, too.

Treaty Day

I didn't go to Treaty Day last year. I can't drive anymore. I couldn't think of anybody to ride with, so I just stayed home. Francey or Herman came to see me.[16] They wanted to know if I would come down and sing my song. I didn't feel equal to anything. A day or so before my mother died she told me, "Don't ever let a year go by without singing your song. Sing it at least once in the longhouse or at a celebration at La Conner or somewhere."

My song is the song of the Mountain Woman. It is a vision, as I said, of a woman coming from the mountains that first appeared to one of my great grandmothers. She is the woman my father named me after. Of course, I never saw her. I never ever heard the song until I heard it when I was sick.

On January 22, 1855, the Indians signed the treaty in Mukilteo. I remember some younger Indians, years ago, saying, "What are we celebrating that for?" I was saying, "It is a celebration," but my father emphasized that it is a commemoration of a time that was very troubled for the Indians. A very troubled time. There were troubles for individual white people and individual Indians, trouble for the Indian agent and listening to all his rules and regulations. Listening to all of the rules and regulations of the Church. There was just a lot of pressure all around. We were talking about it just the other day, Wayne and I, about troubles such as fishing and the commercial fishing—the Indians and the commercial fishermen, the steelhead fishermen. They call their organization the Steelheaders Association.

I haven't heard, not one thing, about Treaty Day this year. I don't think Tulalip is going to have a Treaty Day gathering this year. La Conner and some of the Lummis were talking about how far it is for them to drive down here. The

---

16 Francey Sheldon and Herman Williams.

event goes on all day and all night, and they have to go home in the night. They would like to have the gathering of the Indians on their reservation. We always had Treaty Day. Usually, there is a committee that is already planning a dinner and a supper or a lunch for hundreds of people at Treaty Day time. William, my younger boy, was here, I think it was Sunday evening, and he was saying to me, "If you hear anything about a Treaty Day celebration, let me know and we'll all go." Well, I can't hear very well and I can't see that well either, but I was just thinking, yes, I'd go.

In the spring some of the Indians would come from Seattle. Seattle has a lot of Indians from all over the Middle West, and they have ceremonies. I used to go down there to hear about it. They had one last spring, but I didn't go. I guess I didn't feel well enough to go. William's wife, Marlys, likes those things. Several hundred Indians come from the Middle West, and they do their kind of dancing. I equally enjoy them with these Indians on the coast.

They also have Smokehouse in the longhouse here during the winter.[17] Tulalip didn't have spirit dancers until 1960. They still wear the same outfit. The first, beginning dancer wears a wool or cedar bark headdress, or some of them are made of dyed alder bark. They colored the cedar bark differently. Every year there have been several new dancers. Often they are sixteen years old—quite young. They are kept in a bedroom with some of the older medicine men and women who stay with them to teach them their song. They don't eat, but they are allowed to drink water.

Church of God

We have several different kinds of churches—religions—on this reservation. As a matter of fact, I helped the Church of God get established. I was on the board of directors then. The first preacher was Reverend Shaw. He came from Everett, and he used to come over here every Thursday evening and have prayer meetings. They didn't have any place to meet, and then Adam Williams came. I didn't know he was a preacher. They had barbecued salmon down here at the county Chamber of Commerce. I was one of the speakers.

The Roland Walsby family are wealthy people in Everett. They had money in one of the paper mills, and they owned the casket company. He never worked at all. I think he went up to the University of Washington, and he went back east. He had a beautiful singing voice. He studied music and voice.

---

17 Also referred to now as the Səyəwən religion.

He was kind. He used to come to our house once in a while. He came with Miss Johnston from a Baptist church in Everett: a nice young lady who was a buyer for one of the first paper mills here. She was a very knowledgeable woman. She was born in Canada. She came over when she was young, but she was big in the paper mill business, and she was also gentle, pretty, and kind. She was very religious. They didn't have anyplace to meet. My mother told Mrs. Walsby they could come to our house, and they came every week because there was a piano at our house. She played the piano. Some people came from Everett, too, from that church, and we sang for a couple of hours. We talked and read the Bible. I never, ever really understood the Bible, even though I could read it and it does have very interesting language.

Anyway, the preacher came from that church. He came out here, and he got all worked up. He thought we needed saving, you know. So he established the beginning of a church. They met in the old potlatch hall, the longhouse, and every Sunday they had a service. On Thursday they had a prayer meeting. As I said, they met at our house because we had a piano. So they got started and then they bought land where the church is now and started building a small church. My mother said I should go because Adam had come here with his wife.

We had a big dinner down here, and I was an important speaker, shall we say. Walsby was there and some of the people from the church. Walsby came to me—here were a lot of people in the longhouse. It was in the evening, then or later. He said, "Introduce Adam." I was just through speaking and I was feeling big and important. I said, "Adam who?" He said, "Adam Williams." And so I looked around. A lot of people were around, and I saw him with his beautiful black hair. He came over to shake hands. He was always kind and friendly. His wife was talking with someone. In fact, I didn't know he was married. So I said, "This is Adam Williams from the Swinomish Reservation"—and here he had just graduated from a Bible college in Portland. He was a reverend, but nobody told me. I hadn't seen him in years! I said, "This is Adam Williams." So he spoke a few words, and people clapped, and then Walsby came up to me and said, "Introduce his wife, too." I said, "Oh, where is she?" And so I said, "Oh, dear people. This is Mrs. Adam Williams." She raised her hand and people clapped. You know, I could have killed that Walsby! That was a lame-brain introduction for the pastor who just arrived here!

My mother said I should go every Sunday and help Adam. She was related to Adam's father; they were cousins. She said, "Be there every Sunday and help your cousin." So there I was—very religious, you know—every Sunday.

The status of the church came before the board of directors. We were having a meeting. Hubert Coy, my brother, talked about it at a Board or Directors meeting, and, of course, I was a member. He said the church ought to be stopped. They should be told they can't meet here: this reservation was established as a Catholic reservation from the beginning; that is why the priest is here. We don't want anything like that established here. Some of the other board members said they had not established a congregation and something ought to be done. They should be stopped.

Then I spoke up. "We can't do that." I was proud of myself. I said, "We can't do that." I couldn't say "you" can't. I said "we" can't stop them. Our Constitution (or by laws) specifically states those rights which are guaranteed to the people: freedom of speech, freedom of religion, freedom to peacefully gather wherever they wished. I said, "We can't stop any religion from meeting. They already have a church building. We can't pass a law here for this board and for this reservation that says 'There will be no Church of God, Presbyterian or Methodist.' We can't do it."

They were quiet. They started talking, and they said, "That's right. Freedom of religion is guaranteed by our by-laws." Hubert said, "Yes, but that's outlandish! It ought to be stopped!"

So they almost received a letter from the board saying that they couldn't establish or build a church. To think they would have gone ahead with it if I hadn't reminded them that it specifically says in our Constitution and by laws that "freedom of religion is guaranteed"! So I say that I helped them get established. It would have been established anyway.

I knew Adam Williams before he came here because he was in Tulalip Indian School. He was several years younger than me, and he was from La Conner. He lived in British Columbia, where his mother came from. So we didn't see him much. They had a difficult time getting established anyway, because the congregation didn't have enough money, and the piece of land where the church is was donated to them. Quite a lot of the lumber was donated by somebody from Everett. Anyway, it got built.

Wayne was talking one evening about Adam, and what a marvelous person he was. Adam got sick and died recently, but the tribe adopted all of his children; they are members of this tribe. They never lived in La Conner. People there don't know them at all. Adam was six feet two inches tall, and I was always supposed to listen to what he had to say.

He used to get so worn out. I saw them at least every Thursday and Sunday.

Mrs. Adam would talk about where he had been the night before. Sometimes he would be way around by Tacoma or Edmonds, driving around to pick up people who call him. Someone was stuck someplace with no money. He would get up in the night and go and look for them and bring them home. Busy, busy, busy. Every time there was any kind of trouble—a death in a family—they would go after Adam, and he would drive them around. They would have to go down to the undertaker and pick out caskets, things like that. Adam would just take care of everything. Sometimes he was in juvenile court or some other court hour after hour, helping somebody. Nobody had such loving patience as he. I used to sit by and be so thankful he came. I loved him.

I drove around like that at night, too. Somebody would call me, maybe, from Edmonds. They wanted me to come after them. They left here, and they were going somewhere, Port Gamble or somewhere, and they didn't have enough money, and they couldn't come back. They couldn't go across on the ferry. So I would drive over there and find them and bring them back home. I did that quite a bit. Sometimes they found me in town and wanted me to bring them back home. Then I would bring them home, and there would be some kind of an upset. Maybe their daughter or somebody is gone, and maybe they didn't come home from school. So then they have to go out again and look for them. Maybe the children who are in the eighth or ninth grade are just walking around town. Just . . . I don't know what you would call it—just little family upsets.

When Adam came, I didn't have to go out anymore after anyone. Then Adam got overloaded, and Wayne began getting calls. He would be called to "please come and get us. We are stuck in Seattle or way up here in Mount Vernon." Both of them were driving around in the middle of the night.

An organization asked me to put on Indian dancing. I had Wayne and Herman Williams. They were pretty much the same size as Bernie Gobin's boys and Herman's boys—there were about six or eight or ten of them. They did the spear dance. Then Wayne and Herman were grown up and married and they couldn't do that anymore. Way back then, I had Earnest, a real good Indian dancer. He was always willing and happy to go. I told him what I was always saying to people, "Now, remember, I love you deeply and devotedly. I would do anything in the world for you, so now will you do such-and-such for me?" Of course, they all laughed. One time I said that to a young couple here, and about two or three months later I met them in Marysville on the street, and the first thing they said to me was, "Harriette, you remember you said you loved us deeply and devotedly, and you would do anything in the world for us? Could you give us ten dollars?" I was thinking, I had better not say that to anyone again, because I got into places where they ask not only for money but they wanted me to go way over the mountains to take them to Warm Springs or on long trips, using my car and me paying for the transportation. Sometimes I would say that to some people, and they would say, "I know, I know. Just skip that part and tell me what you want."

The Church of God built up quite a large congregation because a lot of people, white people, came from Everett and Marysville. They would come a long ways to hear Adam preach. It seems to me it has started to fade away. Very few are here, but maybe it is building up again. I don't think the Catholic Church has very many people, either. Churches are not filled. If people work on Saturday, they all go shopping, and on Sunday they are resting. They would rather stay home. If the mother works, then they are doing laundry and all of the housework.

They Looked at Their World

When I was growing up, we came home in the summertime from the boarding school. Every Sunday we walked with my father and mother, way back, about two or three miles into the woods, and, of course, in the summer we picked wildflowers and other things. One of those times, my father had us sit down by a small stream in the woods. Small forest streams always have a lot of ferns and wild flowers, shrubbery that grows on the edges. We were sitting on ferns and things right close to the stream, and my father told us, "Listen to the water talk." I didn't recall hearing something like that, and so we sat still, and we listened to the water. After a while, it sounds like there are a lot of people talking. Some of the bubbles are kind of high and some are kind of low sounding, but it is gurgling along. We just sat there. It seemed like a long while; maybe it was half an hour. It seemed so cool and damp there because it was a hot, hot summer day. My mother was sitting a little higher above. She heard what he said, so she came part of the way down. We were right next to the stream. We listened, and we heard the water talk. Sometimes we could imagine a lot of people talking; it sounds like notes in a song or somebody's voice.

My father did that quite often. We would sit by a stream. Every time we went by, we sat and drank water. It is nice and pure and *cold*. My father always used skunk cabbage leaves for cups. I was just thinking, nobody would ever use them today. Skunk cabbage has large leaves and an attractive yellow flower. My father used to say, "I wonder why the white man called it skunk cabbage." He said that is terrible because it is actually a pretty flower. "It doesn't smell like a wild rose, but it is a pretty smell." Anyway, he would take the cabbage leaves and turn them in a certain way, and they would form what we called cups. We dipped them into the stream and drank out of the leaf. We drank so much cold water, I could feel it in my stomach; it was just loaded with water. It was so much fun drinking out of those leaves. If anybody did that now, I think, maybe you would get sick, because so many places are polluted. But way back then, there was no such thing as pollution in the water or any part of the wilderness. It was all clean and fresh. But I remember sitting there among those ferns and listening to the little stream gurgling along.

After that experience, if I am someplace and there is moving water I usually listen. But sometimes you can't hear it if there are a lot of cars going by or lots of people talking together. We've lost all of that quietness and appreciation of the wilderness places. Our young people never ever heard of it, although I used to tell my own two boys. They know all about it. Maybe a lot of people would think it is the silliest thing to think that the water talks.

My mother and father liked walking through the wilderness trails in the late afternoon. If there was a strong breeze, they would stop and my father would say, "Listen to the wind in the trees." Sometimes my mother would say it. She would stop and say, "Listen to the wind in the trees." Then you listen to the different kinds of leaves and trees; they make slightly different sounds. Sometimes it sounds like they are just sighing. Certain kinds of leaves flicker; they almost turn completely around in their sockets. So they make a silk swishing sound. That was something because then we would listen. You can be alone in a wilderness place and stand still and listen to the wind in the trees. Whenever I said that to Marie Sneatlum, the girl who used to sing (she wrote from Boston, where she was going to a conservatory of music school), she said, "I get so lonely for Tulalip, the sound of the tides and the wind in the trees." I think the majority of white people never realize the Indians looked at those things. They looked at their world: they noticed every kind of animal, all of the changes in the sky. I think that was one of the first things I noticed too: how the world looked; I mean, my little world.

I used to walk with my grandmother up to what is now Mission Beach. She was getting blind, but she knew where Everett was and she knew the islands—Whidbey Island and Hat Island—and she knew where Mukilteo was, because I told her. She asked me, "What color is the sky?" I would tell her, "It is real blue," and I would tell her, "The clouds are very puffy." They are way over or around, or they are not up above. She asked me if we could see Everett, and if Everett had smoke mist above it, or if we could see Mount Rainier, and she wanted to know where the mist is on the mountain. Sometimes it is on the right and sometimes up above, and sometimes it is streaked all over. So I told her where the clouds were. I noticed then if the clouds were dark, if they were moving across the sky.

There were so many things my mother and grandmother asked about. Sometimes I got to my grandmother's house when it was dark. By the time I was fourteen years old, I would run down there and maybe bring her something. She always came out of the door and tried to look around at the night sky. Maybe it was a clear summer night and the stars are sparkling, and she has an idea where the dipper might be. Although, the Indians had a different legend for what is called the Big Dipper. They called it the Four Elk. The dipper part is four stars, and the handle part is three stars. The stars in the bowl of the dipper are elk, and the stars on the handle are the elk hunters. My father and grandfather said the middle star on the handle is the tiniest little star, and that is the hunter's dog; that dog's name is TImə̓lIš.[18]

One of our cousins, Martha Lamont, had a dog named TImə̓lIš. Dozens of people knew he was almost like people. I don't think he knew he was a dog. Martha used to give him a bath, put a child's coat on him; and there he would be, sitting outside in the sun with this coat on, and it looked kind of funny. Sometimes she put a small straw hat on him that just fit his head. He sat there with a funny-looking coat on him and a straw hat and still put up with it. I would say, "Oh, my! You look so nice." Sometimes he looked a little embarrassed, but he put up with it because he loved his mistress. He was a smart dog. He didn't look like much of anything. He was black and white with short hair. A whole lot of people knew TImə̓lIš. If they saw TImə̓lIš walking down the road, they would say, "Where are you going? Go home." He would wag his tail. He might run home and run back again.

In that way, I came to notice everything. Anyway, my mother and father noticed everything. Once in a while, in summer or even in winter my folks would stand outside in the cold, frosty night and look up at the sky. The dipper was far away, in a different direction. It was turned differently, and my father and mother would talk about how bright the stars looked—a cold, glittering night sky in winter.

---

18 The hunter is Changer or Duk^wibəł.

My father and mother loved to be outdoors—to be camping on the beach, camping anywhere, walking through a wilderness trail. We used to go to Whidbey Island. I don't quite remember where, but there was a cranberry bog of native wild cranberries. We used to go there—a whole lot of Indians did—to pick cranberries. I think it was late summer or maybe early fall, because I used to just love it. You could crawl all over in the cranberry bog and never, ever get scratched like you do when you are picking raspberries and blackberries. I fell into all kinds of holes and got nettles, got scratched up. You could crawl on the moss for hours and pick gallons of native cranberries. They all did, but I picked most of the day too. It's easy. I asked somebody who lives on Whidbey Island if there is still a cranberry bog somewhere over there. They said, "Oh, yes. They are somewhere on south Whidbey."

We used to go out there and pick huckleberries. They are the small lowland huckleberries. Whidbey Island had acres and acres of them that were easy to pick: no thorns. We went every fall. We camped on the beach, and my mother and another woman had big baskets, and they picked them full of wild huckleberries. The basket was covered with green ferns to keep the berries cool. Much later, we covered the berries with a piece of wax paper, but then the berries just sort of wilted and were mashed on the bottom. The green ferns kept them whole and fresh.

We were outdoors whenever possible. My father had a canoe with an engine on it. He called it his "gray motor." He was very proud of it. I didn't see anything to it: to me it was just a big hunk of something that moved the canoe around and made noise. The canoe could go through the water just like an arrow. It was forty feet long. If we left Tulalip Bay, we could be in Everett within fifteen minutes; it could really travel. My father rarely let it go so fast, but it went through the water like an arrow.

All of the years I was growing up, I rode in a canoe. My mother rode in the stern of the canoe. She was the captain. The women were the captains. They used the big, wide paddles for the rudder. They looked bigger than the paddles the men had. But we sat close to our mother. It seemed like I was always hungry. She had bread and butter and water. By the time we got over to the island, my father could make a fire in seconds, and it would be burning good, then the coffee or tea could boil. We drank quite a bit of marsh tea, or it is also called Labrador tea. It is a very pretty bright color. I haven't had any for three or four years.

Wayne and I were just talking about how to make sand bread. Anywhere we would go, such as Hat Island, Whidbey, so many places where we would go, we would make bread in the sand under the hot ashes of a campfire. My mother and them would turn it up like this and give it a sharp crack on the sides against the table and the sand falls off, and then they take a butcher knife and scrape it. Annie Fredericks used to live near us. She would bake the bread in our yard, where my father and mother had hauled in several bucketsful of sand. Then they would barbeque salmon, and my mother would have wild blackberries, already canned, from an earlier season, and then we would have sand bread.

I was thinking about the first time we saw some people who said they were Hungarian (I don't think they were). They were fishermen. There used to be quite a few of them—and Yugoslavians—in Everett. We would see them; they were all over the island, on Whidbey, and wherever the Indians went, that is where they went. I think they discovered where we camped was a good place to be and a good place to fish. We would see them camping along the beaches. They were dark-haired and somewhat darker than the white people we had always seen.

The first time we saw them, my father walked up the beach and talked to whoever came in. He was talking with them, and I was standing by the canoe. I was watching, and they never said a word. Maybe they didn't know any English, or maybe they were frightened of my father. I think one of them finally started to talk, and later we found out that they came from Yugoslavia. They were fishermen way over there, too, in the old country. Those people never ever stopped fishing. They were fishing day and night, wherever they went. Way back then, Washington State did not have any fishing regulations—it didn't seem like it. Those people had rowboats. Later, they had quite big motorboats. They became wealthy with their fishing.

We often went to Mount Rainier on trips. We didn't go to Mount Baker. We went up into Mount Rainier National Park, up a trail called Indian Henry's Trail, way back then when I was in high school. We walked for miles, going up a winding trail. It was beautiful—far, far from nowhere. There were acres and acres of mountain blueberries. People called them huckleberries, too, but they are different from the lowland huckleberries. You know when a lot of people move into a place like that those wilderness things die off. Whidbey Island huckleberries are smaller; they look a little darker, and their skins are a little tougher. Mountain blueberries are bigger: as big as my thumbnail. Their taste is similar. The Indians had another name for it: *swedʔx̌*.

The mountain blueberries are very good to eat. If you are ever sick with the flu and have a sore throat, eat some and you will feel better. They are a real good medicine for your throat. My mother canned them. She gave me a dishful, and because I believed it would make me feel better, it did. It seemed to help my throat.

I would like to try and go back there to that Indian trail and see what is up there. We had to walk for miles. My father's cousins went with us. They had two horses, and we took turns riding up the trail on those horses, carrying all of the pots and pans, and tents and things. We were up there for three or four days. My father was talking about how clear the air was, and I noticed it anyway, how clear that air was. Just clear sparkling mornings. You wake up early at five or six o'clock in the morning.

One day I was sitting in a natural mountain meadow. It was covered with all kinds of wildflowers. I used to try and step between them when I walked, but you really couldn't do it. My father said, "Well, it's no use." You will just get slowed down so just keep walking. There were so many varieties of wildflowers. The meadow where I was sitting sloped a little and right across and down was what looked like a big canyon. Right across were big stony cliffs. They were reddish brown and yellow, and just very steep rock. Rocky cliffs. My father came to sit beside me. I was sitting there and looking across, and there was not a thing moving. I guess I looked lonely there, because my father said, "You look so all alone." He was looking around, and he finally said, "There are mountain goats across there." I said, "Where?" He showed me on the cliff, and I looked and looked, but I couldn't see them. It seemed as if there was something moving. So he went back to our camp and got a pair of binoculars. He brought them to me and said fix them so that you can see. I said, "Oh! I can see the mountain goats." My lands! They can jump on that steep cliff, and you wonder what they are standing on. They're down in the valley, where there are trees. I said, "Could we walk over there? How long would it take us to walk?" He smiled, and he said, "Well, if we walked all day, it would probably take us about three or four days." I said, "Oh, that far? That is quite a ways." That is quite a forest down there too. It's so far away. It looked like I could walk there in fifteen minutes.

I don't know why I remembered that. He could see they were mountain goats not mountain sheep. It seems to me it was kind of deceiving, because I never saw the world like they did—like my mother and father did.

Stan Jones leading the Salmon Ceremony.

Harriette speaking at the Salmon Ceremony. Photograph by Loran Olsen.

Harriette Dover and Molly Hatch at the Salmon Ceremony. Mrs. Hatch is holding a Shelton family heirloom: a rattle carved in 1792 to commemorate the passing of their village at Possession Point by Captain Vancouver.

Two of William Shelton's canoes, stored at the Shelton house.
Photograph by Harvey Davis.

Canoes on the way to Hat Island.

Appendix

The daily program of the school [as written by Dr. Buchanan]:

The school bell will be rung and the school whistle will be blown at the periods indicated below. The whistle will not be blown on Sundays.

The kitchen clock will indicate standard school time for all herein designated periods. The engineer will see that said kitchen clock is properly regulated and kept so daily.

The following shall be the daily program, unless directed otherwise, for each Monday, Tuesday, Wednesday, Thursday and Friday:

4:30 A.M.   Night watchman makes kitchen fires and fills wood boxes at kitchen of mess, hospital and school.

5:00 A.M.   Kitchen detail reports at kitchen for duty.

5:30 A.M.   Rising bell. Reveille.

6:00 A.M.   Military drill and getting-up exercises.

6:25 A.M.   Morning roll call; line-up; line inspection by matron and disciplinarian. Absentees reported to office.

6:30 A.M.   Breakfast bell. Breakfast. Mess dining room opens.

7:00 A.M.   Care of rooms, etc.

7:15 A.M.   Sick call. Bugle. All sick report for treatment. Warning whistle: two blasts.

7:30 A.M.   Work whistle. Work begins. Mess dining room closes.

7:30 A.M. to 8:00 A.M. Free play.

8:15 A.M.   First school bell.

8:30 A.M.   School begins. No work other than regular school work in school during school hours.

9:45 A.M. to 10:00 A.M. Calisthenics and breathing exercises; outdoors in good weather; indoors with open windows in bad weather.

11:30 A.M.	Warning whistle: two blasts.
11:35 A.M.	Whistle: one blast. School dismissed. Work details dismissed.
11:40 A.M.	Police grounds for five minutes, all pupils assist.
11:55 A.M.	Mid-day roll call; line-up; line inspection by matrons and disciplinarian. Report absentees.
12:00 P.M.	Dinner bell. Mess dining room opens.
12:45 P.M.	Warning whistle: two blasts.
1:00 P.M.	Whistle: one blast. School begins. Work begins. Mess dining room closed.
2:45 P.M. to 3:00 P.M.	Calisthenics and breathing exercises; outdoors in good weather; indoors with open windows in bad weather.
4:00 P.M.	Afternoon session of school closes. School dismissed.
5:00 P.M.	Warning whistle: two blasts.
5:05 P.M.	Whistle: one blast. Work ceases.
5:25 P.M.	Roll call; line-up; line inspection.
5:30 P.M.	Supper. Supper bell. Mess dining room opens.
6:30 p.m	Mess dining room closes.
6:30 P.M. to 7:00 P.M.	Group Athletics.
7:30 P.M.	Free play.
7:30 P.M.	Evening hour begins (see Evening Hour Program). Evening line-up and roll call. Small pupils retire.
8:30 P.M.	Evening Hour ends. Retreat.
8:45 P.M.	Tattoo. Large pupils retire. Roll call in dormitories.
9:00 P.M.	Taps. Lights out. Good night. Silence.

Saturdays

4:30 A.M. to 7:30 A.M.	Same as on other days. Whistle, bell and bugles as usual.
7:30 A.M. to 11:35 A.M.	Whistle, bells and bugles as usual. Janitors on duty at school house, to otherwise work on double details. Ground and entire plant thoroughly policed and cleaned
11:35 A.M. to 1:30 P.M.	As usual. Inspection, after which half-holiday for pupils.
4:30 P.M. to 7:00 P.M.	As usual.
7:30 P.M. to 10: P.M.	(1) Social. (2) School City. (3) Literary Society. (4) Community Meeting. (5) Open.

Sundays

4:30 A.M. to 7:30 A.M. As usual. Bells and bugles as usual.

7:30 A.M. to 10:00 A.M. Domestic duties, etc., followed by preparation for church.

11:15 A.M.   Mass. Military drill in foot movements in open (weather permitting), under disciplinarian, for boys and girls when there is no Mass. Laundress and disciplinarian conduct pupils to and from church, remaining as monitor in the interim.

11:15 A.M. to 1:00 P.M. As usual. Band concert, conditions permitting.

2:00 P.M.   Sunday assembly. On Sundays when there is mass, one matron conducts to pupils to and from Assembly Hall, remaining as monitor in the interim.

4:30 P.M.   Dress Parade, conditions permitting.

5:30 P.M. to 7:00 P.M. As usual.

7:20 P.M.   General school assembly for large pupils and all employees. Plans for the week or future announcements, assignments, general notices, etc., promulgated at this meeting.

Bells

5:30 A.M.   Rising bell.
6:30 A.M.   Breakfast bell.
8:15 A.M.   First school bell.
8:30 A.M.   Second school bell.
12:00 P.M.   Dinner bell.
12:45 P.M.   First school bell.
1:00 P.M.   Second school bell.
4:00 P.M.   School dismissal.
5:30 P.M.   Supper bell.
9:00 P.M.   Silence bell.

The night watchman will ring the rising bell at 5:30 A.M. and the silence bell at 9 P.M. The school cook will ring all other bells. The chief matron will see that all bells are promptly and properly rung as scheduled above and that all notices indicated or directed by such said signals are observed with exactitude and promptitude.

Whistles

7:15 A.M.	Warning whistle: two blasts.
7:30 A.M.	Work whistle (work begins): one blast.
11:30 A.M.	Warning whistle: two blasts.
11:35 A.M.	Work whistle (work ceases): one blast.
12:45 A.M.	Warning whistle: two blasts.
1:00 P.M.	Work whistle: one blast.
5:00 P.M.	Warning whistle: two blasts.
5:05 P.M.	Work whistle (work ceases): one blast.

The engineer will see that the above whistle signals are given as scheduled, the time being indicated by the kitchen clock. He will see that there is no trifling with such signals and that they are properly, promptly and practically given as scheduled.

Bugle Calls

Blow each call twice:

5:30 A.M.	Reveille.
6:00 A.M.	Drill.
6:20 A.M.	Recall.
6:25 A.M.	First call.
6:26 A.M.	Assembly. Roll call.
6:27 A.M.	Mess call.
7:15 A.M.	Sick call.
11:55 A.M.	First call
11:56 A.M.	Assembly. Roll call.
11:57 A.M.	Mess call.
5:25 P.M.	First call.
5:26 P.M.	Assembly. Roll call.
5:27 P.M.	Mess call.
7:15 P.M.	First call for Evening Hour, Social, Chapel, etc.
7:20 P.M.	Assembly for Evening Hour, Social, Chapel, etc.
8:30 P.M.	Retreat.
8:45 P.M.	Tattoo.
9:00 P.M.	Taps.

The disciplinarian will see that the above bugle calls are given as scheduled; that there will be no promiscuous use of bugle; that legitimate bugle practice be carried on with muted bugle.

The disciplinarian and [?] will train and instruct two battalion buglers in all the calls, etc., on the bugle and assign the various calls among them and see that all such calls are properly, promptly and correctly blown at the periods designated above. Embellishments and oddities are not permissible in established bugle calls. All calls must be blown precisely on time and each call shall be blown twice, the second following the first after a brief interval of a few seconds' length. Calls are to be blown in the manner and at the time specified. Promiscuous calls should be prohibited and legitimate bugle practice should be with muted instrument.

LINE-UP, LINE INSPECTION, AND ROLL CALL

Frequent roll calls, at opportune times, have a salutary morale effect. Those required and scheduled herein, therefore, should be observed as scheduled and detailed. At the periods indicated and designated in the heading of this paragraph, the pupils shall be lined up in their respective playrooms for line-up, line inspection and roll call by the company officers under the direct personal supervision of the matrons and disciplinarians. Admit no untidy, unkept or unclean child to the dining room or classroom. Report all unaccounted-for absentees from roll call to the office at once. A complete written record.

1915

Monday	Sept. 23	Arrival and examination of Port Madison and Tulalip pupils. See general instructions.
Tuesday	Sept. 28	Ditto. Swinomish and Skagit pupils.
Wednesday	Sept. 29	Ditto. Lummi and Nooksack pupils.
Thursday	Sept. 30	Ditto. Lummi and Nooksack pupils.
Friday	Oct. 1	Opening of Industrial Departments. Teachers make first quarterly visitation to neighboring city schools, each teacher handing in a detailed written report (for filing) on each visitation. Physical examinations of pupils continue.

Saturday	Oct. 2	Physical examinations of pupils continue.
Sunday	Oct. 3	Chapel exercises, first of the year.
Monday	Oct. 4	Academic Departments open.
Saturday	Oct. 9	First session of Tulalip School City.
Tuesday	Oct. 12	Columbus Day.
Saturday	Oct. 18	First session of the Literary Society.
Saturday	Oct. 30	The eve of Hallowe'en. Annual Masquerade.
Thursday	Nov. 25	Thanksgiving Day.
Saturday	Dec. 25	Christmas Day.

1916

Saturday	Jan. 1	New Year's Day.
Monday	Jan. 3	Teacher's Visitation.
Saturday	Jan. 22	Treaty Day.
Tuesday	Feb. 6	Franchise Day.
	Apr.	Arbor Day.
Sunday	Apr. 23	Easter Sunday.
Tuesday	May 30	Memorial Day.
Thursday	June 1	Annual picnic for the girls.
Wednesday	June 14	Flag Day.
Tuesday	June 20	Final Examinations.
Wednesday	June 21	Final Examinations.
Thursday	June 22	Final Examinations.
Friday	June 23	Academic Departments close.
Saturday	June 24	Aquatic sports.
		Returned Student's Day.
		Closing Entertainment.
Sunday	June 25	Departure of Tulalip and Fort Madison pupils.
Monday	June 26	Departure of Swinomish and Skagit pupils.
Tuesday	June 27	Departure of Lummi and Nooksack pupils.
Wednesday	June 28	Departure of Lummi and Nooksack pupils.

Lecture and entertainment courses are arranged all through the year as opportunity occurs. The course of the year was especially rich, interesting and instructive. A course of ten lectures on First Aid to the injured, illustrated with demonstrations and with lenter slides, will be given in the last quarter of the school year.

Bibliography

Bancroft, H. H. *Native Races of the Pacific States.* San Francisco: A. L. Bancroft and
    Company, 1882.
———. *The Northwest Coast.* San Francisco: A. L. Bancroft and Company, 1884.
Clark, Norman. *Milltown.* Seattle: University of Washington Press, 1970.
Dover, Harriette. "Memories of a Tulalip Girlhood." In *Vibrations.* Everett, WA:
    Everett Community College, 1970.
Drucker, Philip. *Indian Cultures of the Northwest Coast.* Menlo Park, CA: Chan-
    dler Publishing Company, 1960.
Josephy, Alvin K. *Indian Heritage of America.* New York: Knopf, 1968.
Meeker, Ezra. *Pioneer Reminiscences of Puget Sound.* Seattle: Historical Society of
    Seattle, 1980; reprint of 1905 edition.

Index

Health, 209
Hibołb, 4
Hilbert, Vi, xxvi
Hillaire, Joe, 122
Housing, 38

I

Indian doctors (shaman), 265–67, 272
Indian drinking, 210
Indian Fairs, 167
Indian Reorganization Act, 201
Indian Shaker Church, 175, 268–72
Infant mortality, 132
Interpreter, the, 25. *See also* Taylor, John

J

James, Elson, 159, 160
Jones, Bob and Celia, 256
Jones, Joann, 256, 258
Jones, Stan, xxi
Joseph, Chief, 36

K

Klallam, 5, 57
Krupat, xxi

L

Lamont, Leon, 224, 268, 274
Lamont, Martha, 268, 287
Legends, 3
Lətsxkanəm, 4, 5
Logging, 54, 163, 178
Lushootseed, xiv

M

Magdeline, 9
Manners, 119
McCourt, David, 255
Meeker, Ezra, 53, 263

Mission Beach, 102
Mission School, 7, 256
Montessori School, 7, 35, 96
Moses, Mariah, 256
Mukilteo, xii, 18

N

Native healing. *See* Shamanism
Native plants, 89, 102
Northwest Intertribal Organization, 230

O

O'Donnell, Father, 113
Olsen, Loran, 269

P

Point Elliott Treaty, 6
Prophecy, the, 5

Q

Quilceda Business Park, xvi

R

Religious activity (traditional): belief and
    training, 86–92, 142, 193–94, 278;
    Boarding School, 112; conflicts, 189–93;
    freedom of, 175; pressure, 278
Relocation, 240
Roe Cloud, Henry, 205
Ryggs, Lawrence, xviii, xxii

S

Salmon Ceremony, xxi, 256
Seattle, Chief, 63
Sehome, xii, 37, 55
Shamanism, 265–72
Shelton, Clarence, 157
Shelton, Club, 22, 29